ISRAELI AND PALESTINIAN
NARRATIVES OF CONFLICT

IN SYSTEM

INDIANA SERIES IN MIDDLE EAST STUDIES

MARK TESSLER

GENERAL EDITOR

ISRAELI AND PALESTINIAN NARRATIVES OF CONFLICT

HISTORY'S DOUBLE HELIX

EDITED BY

ROBERT I. ROTBERG

INDIANA UNIVERSITY PRESS

BLOOMINGTON AND INDIANAPOLIS

This book is a publication of

Indiana University Press
601 North Morton Street
Bloomington, IN 47404-3797 USA

http://iupress.indiana.edu

Telephone orders 800-842-6796
Fax orders 812-855-7931
Orders by e-mail iuporder@indiana.edu

The paper used in this publication meets the minimum
requirements of American National Standard for Information
Sciences—Permanence of Paper for Printed Library Materials,
ANSI Z39.48-1984.

Manufactured in the United States of America

Library of Congress Cataloging-in-Publication Data

Israeli and Palestinian narratives of conflict : history's double helix / edited by
Robert I. Rotberg.
p. cm. — (Indiana series in Middle East studies)
Includes index.
ISBN-13: 978-0-253-34767-1 (cloth : alk. paper)
ISBN-13: 978-0-253-21857-5 (pbk. : alk. paper)
1. Arab-Israeli conflict—Historiography—Congresses. 2. Zionism—History—Congresses.
3. Palestinian Arabs—Ethnic identity—Congresses. 4. Textbook bias—Israel—Congresses.
I. Rotberg, Robert I. II. Series.
DS119.7.I82689 2006
956.04—dc22
2006005244

1 2 3 4 5 11 10 09 08 07 06

CONTENTS

❖ Contents ❖

PREFACE

Every conflict is justified by a narrative of grievance, accusation, and indignity. Conflicts depend on narratives, and in some senses cannot exist without a detailed explanation of how and why the battles began, and why one side, and only one side, is in the right. Narratives also create conflict, or at least lead directly into clashes. Stories are stitched together into an all-encompassing narrative that becomes available when and if, for other reasons, hostilities loom between opposing camps, polities, and nations. The texture of the narrative partly determines the contours of a conflict. Thus, conflicts cannot easily start, be consummated, or be resolved without an awareness and attention to the narratives of both sides to conflicts.

The Israeli–Palestinian conflict for primacy, power, and control encompasses two bitterly contested, competing narratives. Both need to be understood, reckoned with, and analyzed side by side in order to help abate violence and possibly propel both protagonists toward peace. This is an immensely tall order. But the first step is to know the narratives, the second to reconcile them to the extent that they can really be reconciled or bridged, and the third to help each side to accept, and conceivably to respect, the validity of the competing narrative.

This book attempts to achieve these goals by creating a dialogue among Palestinian and Israeli authors about such questions by examining the nature and components of the narrative in the context of contemporary Israel–Palestine, and by comparing the versions of narrative fervently held by representatives of the contesting parties.

Israeli and Palestinian Narratives of Conflict originated in a series of discussions about the all-consuming conflict itself, and about the myths on which it and all conflicts feed. Those preliminary talks resulted in two intense seminars in 2003, at the Kennedy School of Government, Harvard University. Many of the individuals who participated in the seminars are contributors to this volume. The talks also led to a report by Deborah L. West, *Myth and Narrative in the Israeli–Palestinian Conflict* (Cambridge, MA, 2003). Along the way the notion of narrative eclipsed the more pejorative examination of myths that had been the initial focus of the discussions. Many of the participants morphed into contributors to this volume. Others were unable to prepare chapters.

This book grew out of strong arguments between the two national camps, and between the two sides and their respective writers. Much of the disputation of the wider conflict was duplicated, vehemently, within the confines of our meetings. *Israeli and Palestinian Narratives of Conflict* hence represents not a consensus but a continuation of an ongoing dialogue between two hotly held and well-expressed sets of views. Within the Israeli camp, moreover, there were and are vigorous disagreements between those who adhere to the tenets of liberal historiography and those who profess extreme versions of revisionism. This book captures the sense and sensibility of both sets of those cross-cutting disputations without indulging in unnecessary rancor.

I am deeply indebted to Kenneth Oye and Philip Khoury, who startled the hare of this narrative, and to Herbert J. Kelman, Stephen Van Evera, and Mary Wilson for greatly assisting in the shaping of our meetings as well as our own narrative. The contributors to this volume have all endured combative sessions with their adversaries, and many rounds of heated editorial revisions. Deborah West, who contributed magnificently to the detailed editing of the chapters, and I greatly welcomed the patience and cooperative instincts of each of the authors. Erin Hartshorn provided much appreciated indexing assistance. The Trustees of the World Peace Foundation, once again, supported this project wholeheartedly, and we are grateful. The initial project, and this book, would have been diminished without the equally important backing of Graham Allison and the Belfer Center for Science and International Affairs, Kennedy School of Government, Harvard University.

Robert I. Rotberg
Cambridge, Mass.
November 2005

ISRAELI AND PALESTINIAN
NARRATIVES OF CONFLICT

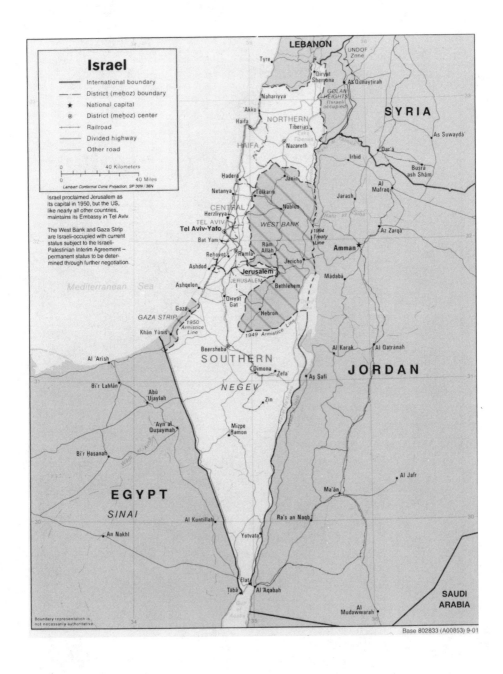

Israel

- ———— International boundary
- ---·--- District (meḥoz) boundary
- ★ National capital
- ⊙ District (meḥoz) center
- +++++ Railroad
- ———— Divided highway
- ———— Other road

0 ⊢———┤ 40 Kilometers
0 ⊢———┤ 40 Miles

Lambert Conformal Conic Projection, SP 30N / 36N

Israel proclaimed Jerusalem as
its capital in 1950, but the US,
like nearly all other countries,
maintains its Embassy in Tel Aviv.

The West Bank and Gaza Strip
are Israeli-occupied with current
status subject to the Israeli-
Palestinian Interim Agreement —
permanent status to be determined through further negotiation.

LEBANON

UNDOF Zone

Tyre

Qiryat Shemona

Al Qunaytirah

Nahariyya

GOLAN HEIGHTS (Israeli-occupied)

'Akko

NORTHERN

SYRIA

Haifa

Tiberias

As Suwaydā'

HAIFA

Lake Tiberias

Nazareth

Irbid

Dar'ā

Hadera

Janin

Busra ash Shām

Netanya

Tülkarm

Jarash

Al Mafraq

CENTRAL

Nablus

Herzliyya

WEST BANK

TEL AVIV

Tel Aviv-Yafo

1994 Treaty Line

Az Zarqa

Bat Yam

Rām Allāh

Amman

Rehovot

Ramla

Mediterranean Sea

Ashdod

Jericho

Jerusalem

Mādabā

JERUSALEM

Bethlehem

Ashqelon

Qiryat Gat

Gaza

GAZA STRIP

1950 Armistice Line

Hebron

Khān Yūnis

1949 Armistice Line

Al Karak

Al Qatrānah

Beersheba

Al 'Arish

SOUTHERN

Dimona

Zefa'

Aş Şafi

JORDAN

Bi'r Laḥfān

NEGEV

Zin

Abū 'Ujaylah

'Ayn al Quşaymah

Mizpe Ramon

Bi'r Hasanah

Al Jafr

EGYPT

Ma'ān

SINAI

Al Kuntillah

Ra's an Naqb

An Nakhl

Yotvata

Elat

SAUDI ARABIA

Tābā

Al 'Aqabah

Al Mudawwarah

Base 802833 (A00853) 9-01

BUILDING LEGITIMACY THROUGH NARRATIVE

ROBERT I. ROTBERG

WARS ARE FOUGHT over tangible resources: rights to, and control over, land, water, and minerals. Wars are also fueled by other palpable grievances: forced removals; episodes of ethnic cleansing; fears of being overwhelmed; objective or imagined security concerns; actual or invented slights; ethnic, religious, or linguistic discriminations; a refusal to respect traditions or claims; and a host of other complaints. Old sores are rubbed raw, and revive antagonisms. New disparities recall earlier subordinations and attacks. One generation's integrated harmony is overtaken by contemporary contentions and bitter rivalry. The urges of nationalism and self-determination arise out of the stony ground of travail, arousals of teachers and preachers, an envy of presumed usurpers, and a gradual rejection of a reconfigured helotry. All of these antecedents to combat, however politicized, emerge out of, or draw upon, a profound historical consciousness.

History is the reservoir of resentment, the fount of blame. History legitimizes; history thus sanctifies. Harking back to foul or fair deeds in an ancient time demonstrates the justness of today's cause and the perfidy of today's opponent. Without an acceptable recourse to the past, gaining legitimacy for rebellion and hostility, plus terror, is impossible. No contemporary cause, however implausible, achieves widespread following without such legitimation—without an evocation of a hoary entitlement or a resurrected accusation of hurt.

All of these truisms, and more, come together in Palestine/Israel, where conflict is endemic and intractable, peace elusive, and each side unfurls an interminable litany of charges and countercharges, claims, and demands. Each proffers credible concerns for security. Each fears the other in enumerated and innumerable ways. Each can point to many instances of perfidy—to abundant reasons for mistrust. Both sides justify this inability to trust by analogy, by reciting a dirge of recent or distant traumas perpetrated by the other. Who did what to whom, and when and why, are the very fodder of contemporary attack and counterattack, and the essence of the difficult security dilemma for both sides under any currently imaginable set of territorial realignments, income readjustments, external security guarantees, political empowerments, and so on.

That one party is conventionally stronger, and one conventionally weaker, hardly helps. Nor is a resolution assisted by demographic disparities, differential fertility rates, the sympathies and tensions of the neighborhood, the postures of the big powers, guilt in Europe and America, a new civil war in Islam, or an upwelling of conservative Islamism.

The gulf of history separates the contenders. Both reach back deeply into the past to legitimize their territorial claims to the lands of the Book. Both reinterpret in their own interests the peopling of these lands or this land. Both draw on and speak authoritatively of attachment to the territory, of rights to all of it or to this or that portion of it. There are few overlapping areas of agreement, for to grant X without receiving Y would vitiate an essential right to Z, and risk losing a bargaining step on the bitter snakes and ladders of ultimate adjustment.

History's Double Helix is an apt metaphor for the Palestinian–Israeli conflict, and for the way that their intertwined reckonings of the past provide fodder and direction for the tit-for-tat battles of the *intifada* and its inevitable response. Palestinians and Israelis are locked together in struggle, tightly entangled, and enveloped by a historical cocoon of growing complexity, fundamental disagreement, and overriding misperception of motives. Despite decades of Israeli revisionist historical reconstruction, and revisions of the revisionism, plus important Palestinian research, much of the fundamental explaining and legitimating of today's conflict remains as hotly contested as it was in 1948 or 1967.

A greater appreciation of the separate truths that drive Palestinians and Israelis could plausibly contribute to conflict reduction. Setting out the two justifying/rationalizing narratives helps us to understand the roots of the conflict and the differentially distorted prisms that fuel it. The two narratives butt up against each other. They view similar events from different angles. They dispute the relative importance of the events themselves and the selection of particularly chosen turning points. They approach legitimacy with different versions of the same story and with varied stories. The two narratives speak strongly about this grievance or that slight, but from perspectives that are placed orthogonally to each other, or juxtaposed in an unexpected manner. Understanding the two narratives is critical to an appreciation of why the

Israeli–Palestinian conflict seems so intractable, even after the death of Yasser Arafat, and why revolutionary mayhem and repressive responses, plus terror and anti-terror, seem so defensible, authoritative, and supported by a reading of their national histories.[1]

This book hardly aspires to resolve such fundamental differences. It does explicate them, however, and does seek to present the Palestinian and Israeli narratives of the past honestly and effectively. Even so, there is no single narrative for either side. This book is comprised of full, authoritative, deeply felt, and consummately researched narratives by experienced Palestinians and Israelis. The book also contains commentaries on those narratives and on the received narratives of the conflict more generally. Furthermore, there are contrasting examinations of the textbook production process on both sides. The chapters on that subject show how young Israelis and Palestinians receive their histories—how they are acculturated to versions of the past.

This book cannot propose a method of fusing the two narratives, or even of reconciling disputed portions of each. That must be a task undertaken in a time of peace by teams of committed experts. One important chapter does offer, however, a way to bridge the narratives, and equally compelling chapters show how difficult that bridging exercise has been and is in practice. The conflict has its own contemporary energy and logic. The architects of antagonism on both sides, and there are many responsible, draw on their own embroidering of the deep past and the middle past, plus the "facts" of the 1948 and subsequent wars. The chapters that follow attempt to narrow, not eliminate, the chasm that separates one strongly affirmed reality from another.

The first of these especially commissioned chapters, by Daniel Bar-Tal and Gavriel Salomon, two psychologists, explains narratives as people's symbolically constructed shared identity. The Palestinian and Israeli narratives, intertwined as they necessarily are, exist as extended conflict stories. Indeed, because both narratives were fired in the crucible of difficult conflict over eighty years, and both are constructed around a contest for the identical territory, they share the same bitter characteristics. Each is consumed by the struggle for national identity. Each posits that any acceptance of the other's identity negates its own. Each is premised on zero-sum views of reality; shared or multiple identities, jointly inhabited territory, or anything that confers mutuality of existential being is consequently antithetical to the nature of the conflict-honed narrative. The narrative exists, furthermore, as a coping mechanism in a situation of interminable conflict. Both the legitimacy of the cause and the nature of the sacrifices that support coping under stress are encapsulated in the narrative.

At the heart of narratives of struggle and response is collective memory. Such memory need not reflect truth; instead, it portrays a truth that is functional for a group's ongoing existence. It should be expected that most collective memories are tendentious, biased, selective, and appropriately distorted. The social reality of the present explains the past. Indeed, a particular past may be invented (as in Serbia and Kosovo, or in Northern Ireland) to suit contemporary needs. It should come as no surprise, therefore, that the Palestinian and Israeli narratives examine past events from strikingly different perspectives and that the same occurrence bears different post hoc determinations. Each is "true" in terms of the requirements of collective memory. At base, the function of the narrative, refined and reconfigured from time to time, is to legitimate the just values of each people (and to delegitimize the other), or to rationalize failures, weaknesses, and excesses. Each side's textbooks (examined in chapters 10 and 11 by Nathan J. Brown and Eyal Naveh, respectively) encapsulate the relevant facets of collective memory, thus socializing future generations to accept the least nuanced explanations of hostilities. As Bar-Tal and Salomon explain, the Israeli textbook story of the 1948 war glosses over the complicated origins of the war, the possibility that Palestinians were moved forcibly from their homes and farms, and examples of Israeli-perpetrated atrocities.

Rightly or wrongly, Israel (and, before Israel, Zionism in Eretz Israel [Land of Israel]) always believed itself beleaguered. Placing a high value on security thus made perfect sense. A defense against Arabs and Palestinians became the highest priority, as did a strong military and a perpetual readiness for war. Heroic deeds were glorified, and the image of David slaying Goliath became the starting point of the national narrative.

Fundamental to the Israeli sense of self, as portrayed in Israel's narrative and in popular belief, is the pursuit of peace. Israelis, and before them Zionists, depicted themselves as peace-loving persons compelled by circumstances beyond their control to engage in violent conflict. Counter to Nadim N. Rouhana's assertions in his chapter in this book, other authors contend that Israelis only reluctantly used violence against Palestinians. Unlike Arabs, the Israelis, these authors believe, continue always to be ready to negotiate a peaceful solution. Narrative assumptions, in other words, are always self-fulfilling; justifications, that is, for suspecting or rejecting an opponent's bona fide intentions. These in-built assumptions also buttress stereotypes of weakness or superiority, justify taking up arms against opponents, and condone all manner of violence to achieve ends sanctified by collective memory.

Narratives are motivational tools. Without the legitimacy conferred by collective memory, mobilizing followers would be impossible. Both Palestinians and Israelis are urged on by the nature of their collective memories to act in the group interest. Likewise, narratives form and strengthen societal identity. They provide its core. As Bar-Tal and Salomon show in chapter 2, "Israeli–Jewish Narratives of the Israeli–Palestinian Conflict: Evolution, Contents, Functions, and Consequences," narratives support a "self-categorization process in which individuals group themselves cognitively as the same, in contrast to other classes of collectives" (33). Uniformity and coordination of group behavior emerge from this process.

More significant, Bar-Tal and Salomon indicate that narratives which develop during intractable conflict have severe mental consequences. Incoming information is selectively received, encoded, and interpreted according to the schemata of the narrative. Doing so limits the extent to which received notions can be altered by new perceptions. Indeed, inculcated by their narrative, group members anticipate the worst from their adversary, and react accordingly. In turn, such a reaction instigates further rounds of hostility and animosity, and on and on. Peace-oriented gestures are thus often rejected as political maneuvers rather than genuine efforts. Overall, the narrative of lengthy conflict helps to close minds, and to prolong the actual conflict. As a result, conflict resolution and eventual reconciliation depend on changes in the collective narratives. One part of that process is learning about a rival group's collective memories. "Acknowledgment of the past," claim Bar-Tal and Salomon, "implies at least a recognition that there are two (legitimate) narratives of the conflict" (39). That statement is what this book is about, and what the remaining chapters attempt to explicate in their diverse ways.

The third chapter, "Forging Zionist Identity Prior to 1948—Against Which Counter Identity?" by Dina Porat, analyzes how Israelis' collective memory was developed and the intellectual history of that memory. Porat asserts that Zionist identity in Ottoman and Mandatory Palestine was forged not against or in antagonism to local Arabs but rather in opposition to diasporic Jewry. After reviewing research findings and a number of memoirs on relations between Arabs and Jews in Palestine from the 1880s, Porat contends that the Zionist movement did not take fully into account the Arabs dwelling around them and in their midst. In the early years the Zionists ignored the "Arab question" entirely, minimizing the possibility that two parallel nationalist movements would grow side by side, and eventually seek similar territorial and national outcomes.

The early reports reveal no particular brotherly love between the new settlers from the pogroms of Europe and the indigenous inhabitants of the land. Similarly, contemporary thinkers like Herzl and others, while foreseeing a vibrant place for individual Arabs (not Arabs as a group) within the utopia that would be created in Israel, envisaged a future for Arabs as a nationality outside of Palestine, in Egypt and Syria.

In the early 1920s, Mandatory Palestine contained 71,000 Christians, 84,000 Jews, and 589,000 Muslims. Some of the Jewish observers of the period dismissed the relevance of the "Arab question." But they were often cut off from Arab sentiment, for few of the immigrants then or later bothered to learn Arabic. Reintroducing modern Hebrew seemed a more important endeavor. Only a rare handful of the new settlers were conscious of local sensibilities, some even adopting Arab attire and keeping special hospitality rooms in their homes for Arab visitors. But they were the exceptions. The Arab rejection of a joint legislative council with Jews, under the Mandate, signaled a new awareness of the political goals of Arabs. The riots of Arabs against Jews in 1929 reinforced that message.

Romantic and ill-founded notions about Palestinian Arabs, according to Porat, were replaced in the 1930s by a newly charged awareness among settlers of how their Zionist project would be challenged by local demands. More Jews were arriving from Europe as well, and Zionist textbooks—the instruments of Jewish nationalism—were teaching schoolchildren little about Arab culture or Islam. Alienation from local Arab life was both physical and mental. Ignorance of the other was profound. A British commission in 1937 found a cavernous gulf between Arabs and Jews, between highly organized democratic modernity and an old-fashioned world. In Porat's quotation from a British report, Arabs entered the picture primarily when they "force[d] an entry with violence and bloodshed" (57). The notion of cultural assimilation in Palestine was a fantasy.

Many of the Zionist thinkers of the time accepted that conclusion, indeed felt that assimilation was almost beside the point. Their project was a Jewish homeland, not a polity that would represent a new departure in the Middle East. The founding fathers and mothers were looking backward to avoid the perils and problems of European ghettos. They believed that the miseries of the shtetl could only be avoided by denigrating diasporic weaknesses and building anew—ever surrounded by but not integrated with Arabs. So they battled against the emergence of a Yiddish or a universalistic culture among the settled Jews. Separating their own society from Arabs strengthened that approach.

Zionism in Israel was not built against the Orient; it believed that its battle was with the diaspora, and about Europe, especially after the Holocaust. Even committed socialists from Eastern Europe felt, naively, that a new Jewish society could be created alongside the existing Arab one. Indeed, as Porat concludes, Zionism always saw its place in a globalized democratic mainstream. Simultaneously, it welcomed the progress of Arab peoples and nations—but not within Eretz Israel.

Saleh Abdel Jawad, the author of chapter 4, "The Arab and Palestinian Narratives of the 1948 War," understands the nature of many of these assertions, and does not refuse to grapple with their reality for Israelis. He accepts, but does not excuse, the Zionist foundational story's exclusion of Palestinians from the history of the land. He also describes Arab tolerance of the early Zionists in their midst, and mentions many instances of effective comity. (Mordechai Bar-On's chapter echoes Jawad in this respect.) Multiethnic coexistence was common, even in the early 1930s, and in Jerusalem. Jawad sets out a vibrant Palestinian framing of the mutual past and mines the pre-1948 terrain, largely shading and correcting the clear Zionist vision of the 1930s. But Jawad also concedes that the Arab revolt of 1936–1939, largely against the British, soured relations between Jews and Arabs. Nationalism became the dominant sentiment among militants in both societies. The battle for Palestine and Israel began in that era, not later.

The focus of Jawad's chapter, however, is the 1948 war, and after. Where many Israeli historians ascribe to Arabs the responsibility for initiating the war, Jawad relates the pre-partition atmosphere of 1947 to show how Arabs had not prepared for war, and how hostilities were far from their collective mind. (Mordechai Bar-On goes farther back and agrees that the seeds of war were planted in the nineteenth century, when Jews from Europe "invaded.") A bigger possible battle was between disunited Israeli factions.

Jawad cites British reports partial to the Arab view that Israeli repression, rather than Arab agitation, precipitated the first major clashes before November 30, 1947. The Jewish Agency and Haganah, the agency's military force, were the main culprits. Jawad argues that the battles from November 30 to December 11 were mere skirmishes, and that the war proper did not begin until after the young Israeli state launched terror attacks on the main Arab cities. The attacks from December 11 to December 13 were decisive: they created, in Jawad's view, a "point of no return" (83) and led inevitably to war.

In chapter 6, "Conflicting Narratives or Narratives of a Conflict: Can the Zionist and Palestinian Narratives of the 1948 War Be Bridged?" Mordechai Bar-On accepts some of Jawad's arguments, but also asserts that the Palestinians ignited the conflict. They were provoked, and Israelis should empathize with and understand the "rational and moral indignation that motivated the Palestinians" (154). Bar-On agrees that the Haganah undertook retaliatory raids, intended as they were to deter further Palestinian violence. But they naturally accomplished the opposite, and the war erupted. Bar-On is at pains to accept that the war emerged both out of Palestinian strategy and the Jewish response.

Expulsions were the point of the war. Although some Palestinians fled, Jawad describes a pattern of explicit, not accidental, ethnic cleansing. He traces much of the impetus for wholesale ethnic cleansing to David Ben-Gurion personally, as well as to the Haganah, the Stern gang, and the Irgun, each having participated years before in the displacement of Arab villagers. With the announcement of Partition, they redoubled their efforts to clear villages in Eretz Israel of Arabs.

Nor were Arabs passive victims, a central Israeli assertion. They did not flee their homes nor were they bid to do so by local leaders, or by Jordanians, a claim advanced by some Jewish revisionist historians. (Jawad criticizes Egyptian, Syrian, and other Arab commentaries that effectively endorse and unwittingly espouse the pre-revisionist, standard, Israeli accounts.) Arab historiography glorifies its own freedom fighters within their specific national contexts while denigrating Palestinians as weak and unprepared. Jawad emphasizes the successful efforts of Palestinian resistance but acknowledges Israel's better organization and support from the then major world powers.

Thus a second narrative is intertwined with the first. Jawad is forceful in examining Israeli pronouncements about the facts of the past, and offering a Palestinian reinterpretation, backed by his own research, or the memories and research of others. A next stage, too late for this book, would be for Jawad, Porat, Bar-On, and others to spend the necessary hours together attempting to reconcile the discordant narratives, or at least delineating the precise contours of disagreement. The events of December 11–13, 1947, have been examined in microscopic detail, but a reexamination now needs to be undertaken collaboratively and painstakingly. So, too, is there a need to reexamine the nature of expulsions and ethnic cleansing. Israeli historians need carefully to review Jawad's evidence and not simply to dismiss it out of hand.

Jawad accepts criticism of the tentative and unformed quality of the Palestinian narrative. Fully half of his chapter is devoted to an explanation of why the historiography of the Palestinian struggle is so protean, so lacking the robust revisionism of the comparable Israeli model. An absence of democracy and democratic values throughout the Arab world, and especially in Palestine, contributes to this deficiency. So does censorship on both sides, the loss in war of troves of relevant archives and materials in general and their confiscation in some cases by Israel, the closure of and difficult conditions of Palestinian universities and intellectual life, and a fundamental lack of resources. Archives in Israel are often inaccessible to Palestinians. The 1948 war had a direct impact, Jawad asserts, on the inability of Palestinians to prepare their own accounts of those years, or to reexamine the quality and texture of the Israeli narrative. The war buried the cultural history of Palestinian cities and intellectual centers. The Israeli army took much of it; the Jordanian army seized critical military archives. According to Jawad, "the totality of a written cultural heritage disappeared" (91).

Jawad's chapter contains a clarion call for serious research by Palestinians on various aspects of both their pre- and post-1948 narrative. He commends the collection and use of oral history. But regardless of the implicit call for collaboration between Israelis and Palestinians, Jawad is no advocate of the cross-cultural pursuit of a common "truth" about the 1948 war or any other decisive watershed. Like many of the other contributors to this book, he is skeptical about the efficacy of the bridging narrative idea advanced by Ilan Pappe in his chapter.

So is Mordechai Bar-On. He asks: "Can we really expect Israeli Jews to forsake their common designation of the 1948 war as their 'War of Independence'?" (143). Likewise, he acknowledges that Jawad and Palestinians are bound to refer to the same war as "*al Nakba*," the catastrophe. No sophisticated historiographical effort, Bar-On asserts, can eradicate or somehow merge those different meanings. One side won the war, the other lost, and such realities must be faced. Their narratives are necessarily opposed. Indeed, since each constitutes the central building block of the opposing identities, the two narratives are exclusionary. They deny the accuracy of the other's story, and, in Bar-On's words, "negate the very existence of the foe as a collectivity" (145). Hence, bridging the narrative gap, or any attempted construction of a unified narrative, is futile. Trying to do so avoids grappling with the underlying substantial meanings of the opposed narratives.

Bar-On, who is critical of much of the standard, triumphant Israeli narrative of settlement and victory in 1948, equally asserts that Arabs in Palestine before 1948 had not constituted a unique nation with collective claims. In that sense only, much of Palestine was "empty" and therefore Zionists were not compelled to realize their dreams through force. Moreover, by 1947, more than half a million Jews, most survivors or escapees from the Holocaust, already lived in Palestine and had nowhere to go. The UN vote to partition Palestine was a logical response both to the tragedy in Europe and to the partially formed homeland in Israel. Bar-On acknowledges the Palestinians' inability to accept Partition, but he also asks Palestinians to understand that the nascent Israelis had no choice but to use military means to create the state that the UN had legitimated. Bar-On, who participated in the 1948 war, defends the necessity of his actions on behalf of the Zionist project and his own personal destiny.

Because of the distinct differences in approach between the usual Palestinian narrative (even Jawad's more nuanced and sophisticated version) and the amended Israeli one, Bar-On recommends historical self-examination, not attacks on the other narrative. For him, this strategy would lead to self-critical revisions exposing a prevailing narrative's nationalistic ideology, transcend simplistic generalizations, and attempt to understand the rationale of the other's behavior and narrative. Nations, after all, are prisoners of their own pasts.

In this context Bar-On concludes a lengthy analysis of the work of Israel's revisionist historians by suggesting that the lesson for Palestinians is not that they should be self-satisfied in their own narratives but that they should learn, instead, to be self-critical. Jawad, even as he advances a critical perspective, argues that Palestine is not free, not mature enough nationally, to engage in the luxury of intense self-criticism, whereas Israel can afford the candor of revisionism. As much as Bar-On agrees, he urges Palestinians to be open, to refuse to accept received myths and narratives at face value. They should be scrutinized from every angle, and with every assumption questioned. Out of that self-critical reexamination will emerge a result far more useful and beneficial than a merged or homogenized narrative.

Although Bar-On and Porat are attuned in their writings for this book to Jawad's careful, yet critical, essay, both take exception to the contribution of another Palestinian scholar, Nadim N. Rouhana. Indeed, Bar-On devotes a section in his chapter to rebutting Rouhana's message in chapter 5, "Zionism's Encounter with the Palestinians: The Dynamics of Force, Fear, and Extremism."

The encounter between Zionism and the Palestinians, Rouhana asserts, was more formative for the modern conflict than the Holocaust; it shaped Israel's forceful and violent approach to Palestinians. Rouhana rejects the Zionist foundational ideas of Jewish nationhood, of the legitimacy of Jewish self-determination, of Palestine as the just home of Jews, and of the exclusiveness of that homeland. The Israelis were invaders. For Rouhana and many others—

in contrast to Porat, Bar-On, and mainstream Israeli ideology—Palestine already (before and during the immigration of Jews from Europe) was the homeland of a distinct Arab group. At the very least, during the Mandate, Arabs lived in organized communities, as a people. Rouhana defines the resulting confrontation as one between a people living on their own lands and a people guided by ideology to claim those same lands as their own.

Given two claims to the same territory, conflict was inevitable. Indeed, writes Rouhana, the use of force against Palestinians was embedded in Zionism, a view Bar-On strongly contests. It was and is naïve to believe, Rouhana continues, that the Israeli state could have been established without extreme violence against Palestinians. Here Rouhana uses the term "violence" to embrace the full range of psychological as well as physical duress. In fact, the protracted use of force is fundamental, he believes, to Israel's relations with Palestinians; Israel's worldview of Palestine and Palestinians is "determined" by domination. It follows that Palestinian resistance, not passive acquiescence, was the natural response.

Resistance is fundamental to the new Palestinian narrative. Indeed, for Rouhana, preserving the memory of loss and discrimination is a central constituent of that narrative. Equally, Rouhana advocates a process of reconciliation that would compel Israel to take genuine responsibility for a long list of injustices to Palestinians, including the illegitimate nature of the Zionist enterprise. Since that result is not likely, the major political restructuring that would be required to realize equality within the contested territory is also unlikely. Painful self-discoveries by the ruling party would entail concessions to the Palestinians that are too raw. The continuing reality, says Rouhana, is power asymmetry, the heavy hand of naked force, and existential and actual climates of fear throughout Israel.

Intransigence is another key concept in parsing the tangle of Palestinian resistance and legitimacy. Bar-On and others ask critics to acknowledge an undeniable grouping of Jews in Israel before Partition, the UN authorizing vote, and, subsequently, the creation of a hard-won national state that could not be ignored or wished away. In chapter 7, "Narratives and Myths about Arab Intransigence toward Israel," Mark Tessler tussles with the Arabs' refusal to recognize that de facto reality in Khartoum, at the 1967 Arab summit, and afterward. He qualifies that instance of intransigence by specifying its largely political component and the natural desire of the Arab heads of state in Khartoum to remove Israel from Arab territory. Withdrawal from the then recently conquered lands of Jordan, Syria, and Egypt had to precede recognition. Thus, Tessler asserts, there was no "unshakeable" commitment by Arab nations to the annihilation of Israel, then or later.

Arab nations were not opposed to forging an accommodation with Israel in the years that followed. Lebanon, Morocco, and Tunisia were all willing to entertain peace with Israel. Egypt pursued a peace initiative in 1977, leading to a treaty between both nations. Had Israel's Likud-led government not refused to make additional territorial concessions, Tessler believes that treaties with other Arab nations could have been concluded. In 1981, Saudi Arabia sought peace through Israeli withdrawals from the West Bank and Gaza, with the creation of a Palestinian state with its capital in East Jerusalem. The Israelis refused.

For Tessler, then, continued Arab hostility toward Israel after 1967 was largely perpetuated by Palestinian statelessness. Arab nations were insisting less on the destruction of the Israeli state than on equal opportunity for Palestine, effectively the two-state solution. After the signing of the Oslo Accords in 1993, Arabs largely accepted Israel's existence. Premised on the establishment of a Palestinian state, they joined the Palestine Liberation Organization in favoring peace with Israel. But the halcyon atmosphere of cooperation was diminished by the failure of the accords to lead to decisive progress for Palestinians. Arab attitudes toward Israel are indeed contextual; Arabs now seek territorial compromise, not the end of the Israeli state.

These conclusions add texture to both narratives and, if accepted, are capable of modifying the overwhelming Israeli belief in deeply rooted Arab as well as Palestinian enmity and intransigence to Israel and the very existence of the Zionist creation. Likewise, if supported by further research, the case for Palestinian open-mindedness can be strengthened. Indeed, according to Tessler, surveys of opinion within the West Bank and Gaza demonstrate that attitudes toward Israel among inhabitants, shaped by "contextual factors and instrumental considerations," are not uniformly hostile (188).

Whereas Bar-Tal and Salomon seek reconciliation through the acknowledgment of the validity of two narratives, no matter how those narratives oppose each other's fundamental truths, Pappe, the author of chapter 8, "The Bridging Narrative Concept," wants to narrow those differences. For him, unlike for Bar-On, Jawad, and others, the construction of a bridge was initiated by historians "who belong to the stronger party and are willing to recognize the other side's narrative and at the same time adopt a more critical approach toward their own." (195). Pappe sees the new revisionist and post-Zionist historians of Israel as the vanguard of the bridging movement. They delegitimized many of the standard Israeli claims about the 1948 war and after, and legitimized Palestinian arguments about the same events, together reducing the gap between the respective group narratives.

Pappe advocates joint historiographical reconstruction involving individuals from both sides who absolve themselves of their national and positional identities. Israeli historians, from this perspective, must learn the Palestinian narrative and be willing to work collaboratively on joint research about the history of conflict, thus dissecting both narratives and thus "bridging" them. If this effort is to succeed, the stronger party, says Pappe, must relinquish its dominant power over knowledge and the weaker party forego its commitment to a particular ideological persuasion. Moreover, bridging these narratives— and in doing so writing a new one—must go beyond elitist and nationalistic history. The process must embrace both social and cultural history, and be interdisciplinary. One successful example of this genre, cited by Pappe, was the recovery of the life of nonpolitical Palestinians in pre-Zionist times. Mandatory Palestine was more a unitary integrated society and system, and less two separated segregated realities. Accepting Jawad's strictures, Pappe also advocates using oral historical testimony to enhance an understanding of the civilian dimension of the 1948 war, and to reinforce Jawad's characterization of forced removals as ethnic cleansing.

Dan Bar-On and Sami Adwan, two psychologists, in chapter 9, "The Psychology of Better Dialogue between Two Separate but Interdependent Narratives," flatly state, counter to Pappe's argument, that bridging narratives will be impossible in the foreseeable future. In their view, the narratives are intertwined but distinct and should so be acknowledged. Bar-On and Adwan are themselves long-time collaborators across the Green Line; they reject the bridging possibility not from theory but from practice. Together, they have been working successfully with mixed groups of teachers to develop an innovative school booklet containing two parallel but separate narratives.

Their model emerged out of an analysis of Palestinian and Israeli textbooks for history and civic education. The texts on both sides reflect "a culture of enmity." What is considered positive on one side (immigrants as "pioneers") is negative on the other (immigrants as "terrorists"). Most maps in Israeli texts eliminate Palestinian cities and towns, although these are intricately enmeshed in the landscape. Likewise, the Palestinian texts eradicate Israeli towns and cities. Some of the texts even disagree on basic demographic facts, citing conflicting numbers for refugees and remaining populations. The texts, according to Bar-On and Adwan, delegitimize the rights, history, and culture of the other.

Neither side's textbooks recognize the suffering of the other, not even with regard to the magnitude of the Holocaust or al Nakba.

Teachers are agents of change. Bar-On and Adwan hypothesize that experienced Israeli and Palestinian teachers, working together, once they come to terms with each other and the other's narrative, can shift gradually from their own hateful collective memories toward the development of two more neutral narratives. The participants can become sensitive to the other side's painful issues and then be able to create new narratives that are a little more interdependent and bridged. The objective of the exercise was for the teachers themselves to collaborate and develop shared history texts and then use them to teach their separate ninth- and tenth-grade classes.

Bar-On and Adwan led the group through a painful process of sharing their interpersonal stories amid the external violence of the ongoing second intifada and the response to it. The teachers then reviewed lists of seminal events in the joint history of Palestine/Israel. Initially they chose three—the Balfour Declaration, the 1948 war, and the first intifada of 1987—about which to construct new parallel narratives, translated into both local languages. The actual creation of the narratives proceeded iteratively and without difficulties. When the new narratives were presented to students in 2003, however, the Palestinians studying under the harsh conditions of the occupation found it hard to listen to the Israeli narrative. They were suspicious and antagonistic, of both the narratives and their teachers. Israeli students were somewhat more receptive, but they, too, regarded the Palestinian narrative as propaganda and were critical of their teachers as well.

Together the teachers realized that they had not presented the parallel narratives in a sufficiently full context. To do so they had to rewrite the booklet to include a generous explanation of what they themselves had discovered during their several years of collaboration. They also understood that they had to negotiate more effectively in order to produce narratives that were more interdependent—more accommodating to the opposing narrative—and more responsive to their antagonists' views. In other words, they discovered that they could only build the foundations of a bridge across a gulf of collective memory, but not the central span itself. Or, as Bar-On and Adwan conclude, two societies cannot create a single narrative. Thus the two narratives must remain until the two societies go their own ways or merge as one.

Schools are the means by which one generation socializes another and transmits the essence of its collective memory to a succeeding generation. The more dynamic element in that transmission process are the teachers, but the actual texts are formative as well. From the 1950s, Palestinians used Jordanian and Egyptian texts in the West Bank and Gaza, respectively. After the 1967 occupation of these territories, the same texts were employed, but in censored versions. In 1994, the Palestinian National Authority began preparing its own texts, a process that Nathan J. Brown explores in chapter 10, "Contesting National Identity in Palestinian Education." Meanwhile, in Israel, the state adapted earlier textbooks and continued to modify them as the state grew more mature. In chapter 11, "The Dynamics of Identity Construction in Israel through Education in History," Eyal Naveh explains that Israeli teachers and students have always had greater choice, since the Ministry of Education provides lists of acceptable options, and local school districts had some freedom to choose among the alternatives.

Through the lengthy process of commissioning, writing, producing, and introducing textbooks for Palestinian schools from 1993 to 2004, the Palestinian National Authority sought to define the nature of the Palestinian nation well before the fundamental issues of nationhood and nationality had been resolved, a process that continues. Thus the curriculum project was the first and most significant exercise of national responsibility by and for Palestinians. The first committee actively to construct a curriculum wanted to break dramatically with the stale, authoritarian, and rote texts of the past. But this proposal was too radical for the emerging state, and the Palestinian educators and leaders who have been producing texts since 2000, two every year for different grades from primary school through high school, are engaged in a massive pedagogical compromise. They must also provide answers in each text to critical questions: What is Palestine? Who are the Palestinians? Who is a citizen of Palestine?

The Palestine that has emerged in the texts, Brown reports, is timeless: first Muslim under caliphs, then British under the Mandate, and finally divided into Jordan, Egypt, and Israel. The maps in the texts do not clearly demarcate or label Israel, nor do they provide borders for the new Palestine. Past and present geography is blurred, the Oslo Accords go unmentioned, and unpleasant de facto geographical realities are not spelled out.

Palestinians are defined explicitly by order of the Palestinian Ministry of Education in terms of their religion, family and family values, nation, and homeland. Obedience and loyalty to the family and the state are emphasized. Nationalism and national identity are everywhere. Schools fly the national flag, and blackboards exhibit nationalist slogans. An earlier attempt to secularize education and educational definitions was rejected. Qur'anic verses support lessons on proper behavior and hygiene, and are even employed to strengthen the teaching of sixth-grade science. The defense of the homeland becomes a religious duty, particularly since Palestinian, Arab, and Muslim identities overlap and reinforce one another. Islam and the Arabic language unify the homeland. The textbooks also insist on national unity and on tolerance—for Christians and Muslims within the Palestinian polity. There is almost no discussion of Palestine's relationship with Israel, Zionism, or Jews.

The Palestinian curriculum process focused not on what body of knowledge should be taught but, rather, on what kind of citizen should emerge. The Ministry of Education rejected the original committee's notion that critical thought should be emphasized. Instead, the final curriculum stresses the transmission of traditional values and customary ways of understanding those values. Individuals are meant to serve society as a whole, and therefore education must enable individuals to perform their duties successfully. Overall, however, the Palestinian textbooks, Brown says, are remarkable for the controversies that they avoid and the subjects, such as Israel, with which they refuse to deal. They do not purport to lay the foundations for peace. Yet, with all of their evasions and silences, they do not teach hate.

Nor do the Israelis, through their own texts. But, as Naveh explains, the old Zionist project of Jewish renewal through the creation of a new state and a new identity is largely moribund. The nation building of the 1920s through the 1940s, and well into the creation of the new state, has accomplished its purpose so well that young Israelis are less conscious than ever of their special roots. The schools are no longer able to transmit a strong sense of collective memory to a skeptical, globalized generation.

As Porat suggests in the early part of this book, Israeli education was originally focused on a denigration of the Jewish diaspora. The reclaiming of sovereignty after returning from a lengthy exile was fundamental. In 1954, elementary school history classes were intended to instill love for the state of Israel. Their purpose was to transmit knowledge of the Jews' great past and to foster an appropriate national awareness. The standard Zionist narrative was at its core. The culture and accomplishments of European Jewry were important, whereas an understanding of human civilization and world history was relegated to the margins of instruction. As Naveh asserts in his chapter, the history core curriculum was "trapped in ethnocentricity" (253). It also emphasized (as the Palestinians did in this century) that individuals were meant to serve their nations. No personal fulfillment was as true or as important.

In addition to the texts of the young nation, the schools introduced a range of ceremonies, remembrance days, and special holidays to foster patriotism and emotional bonds with the state. Each of these events, as well as the national curriculum and teachers as its expositors, and commemorations of the Holocaust, reinforced and supplemented the national narrative. But the state began to retreat from its educational role after the 1967 war; pluralism became relatively more salient in Israel, and the unified curriculum of the 1950s gave way to a broad search for pedagogy that looked more to the future. The emphasis on national history was somewhat reduced in the mid-1970s, and world history entered more fully into the curriculum. The history of the Sephardim was embraced as well. Most radical, however, was the inclusion in the 1975 history curriculum of material on Arabs and the Palestinian–Israeli conflict, but not on the Palestinian narrative.

A new core history curriculum was issued in 1995 that sought to expose students to new historical research (the revisionists and the post-Zionists, for example) and to develop critical skills of analysis. It sought to deter dogmatism and emphasized tolerance. Radically, it emphasized the unity of history, eschewing the traditional textual divisions between world history and Jewish history. Self-consciously, the 1995 curriculum reduced the usual emphasis on ethnocentric and national identity issues. Yet, Arabs in Israel (and outside), and their histories, were still ignored or marginalized, as was Russia, supplier of 1 million Israelis. Reflecting the maturity of the Israeli state, the new curriculum exposed a fundamental tension between liberal democracy and the affirming of a collective, traditional, national identity. Should the educational system glorify and serve the older Zionist imperative? Or should it, can it, move on despite the real challenges facing a twenty-first-century Israel? Clearly, amid the unresolved political and social future of the state, schools and texts cannot answer these questions alone. Nor can they be expected, without broad political support, to de-emphasize the central themes of the old narrative in favor of a bridging paradigm.

Until each side recognizes the validity of the other's narrative—until conditions exist that permit a mutual, cross-national examination of the opposing narratives—conditions conducive to a reduction of conflict, or to delegitimizing the whole quality of the existing conflict, will not emerge. The lessons of this book are that the gulf between the narratives remains vast, that no simplified efforts at softening the edges of each narrative will work, and that the fundamental task of the present is to expose each side to the narratives of the other in order, gradually, to foster an understanding, if not an acceptance, of their deeply felt importance to each side. The contents of the narratives impede conflict resolution, and the schools on both sides are doing too little to reduce the impact of traditional narratives, but those are unavoidable concerns in a time of bitter, still not fully resolved conflict.

NOTE

1. For recent discussions of similar phenomena, see Edy Kaufman, Walid Salem, and Juliette Verhoeven (eds.), *Bridging the Divide: Peace-Building in the Israeli-Palestinian Conflict* (Boulder, 2005); Paul Scham, Walid Salim, and Benjamin Pogrund, *Shared Histories: A Palestinian-Israeli Dialogue* (Jerusalem, 2005); Peter Rodgers, *Herzl's Nightmare: One Land, Two Peoples* (London, 2005); Virginia Q. Tilley, *The One-State Solution: A Breakthrough Plan for Peace in the Israeli-Palestinian Deadlock* (Ann Arbor, 2005); and Bernard Wasserstein, *Israelis and Palestinians: Why Do They Fight? Can They Stop?* (New Haven, 2003).

2

ISRAELI–JEWISH NARRATIVES OF THE ISRAELI–PALESTINIAN CONFLICT
Evolution, Contents, Functions, and Consequences

DANIEL BAR-TAL AND GAVRIEL SALOMON

HUMAN BEINGS HAVE a basic epistemic need to live in an environment that is meaningful, comprehensible, organized, and predictable.[1] They strive to perceive their world in a meaningful way in which events, people, and things or symbols are not understood as isolated stimuli but are comprehended in an organized way, one that provides meaning to the new information.[2] This sense of understanding is essential for one to feel that the world is predictable and controllable.[3] When this factor is absent, human beings experience stress and often act abnormally. This rule applies to individuals as well as collectives. That is, individuals strive not only to order and understand their individual world but also their collective world. A meaningful life for many people often derives from their membership in a particular group, and ultimately one's individual life is inextricably interwoven within collective structures, events, and processes. That an individual's experiences are often determined by their membership in the collective is vividly illustrated by the Israelis and the Palestinians.[4]

People construct their world in a way that is functional for their needs, shunning uncertainty on both the individual and collective levels. Our focus in this chapter is on the collective level as we set out to show that society members construct shared "societal beliefs," defined as enduring beliefs on issues of special concern for a particular society and which contribute to a sense of uniqueness among its members.[5] Societal beliefs, organized around thematic clusters, refer to characteristics, structure, and processes of a society and cover the various domains of societal life. Generally they concern societal goals, self-images, conflicts, aspirations, conditions, norms, values, societal structures, images of out-groups, institutions, obstacles, problems, and so on. Essentially, they constitute a shared view of a society's perceived reality and, as such, provide the collective narrative of that society.

Following Bruner, we conceive of collective narratives as social constructions that coherently interrelate a sequence of historical and current events; they are accounts of a community's collective experiences, embodied in its belief system and represent the collective's symbolically constructed shared identity.[6] The collective narrative of a society provides a basis for common understanding, good communication, interdependence, and the coordination of social activities, all of which are necessary for social systems to function. The beliefs comprising the collective narrative are often featured on the public agenda, are discussed by society members, serve as relevant references for decisions that leaders make, and influence choices and courses of action. Societal institutions actively impart these beliefs to society members and encourage their acquisition.

This chapter analyzes narratives that are constructed in times of conflict, focusing particularly on the Israeli–Jewish narrative of the Israeli–Palestinian conflict. We elaborate on the intractable nature of the conflict, which serves as a context for the evolvement of the particular narrative. We describe the ethos of conflict and collective memory, which constitutes the essence of the narratives of societies involved in intractable conflict. We describe the main functions of this narrative and their consequences. Finally, we discuss implications for reconciliation and peace education interventions.

The Context of Intractable Conflict

Intractable conflicts are defined as those that are protracted, irreconcilable, violent, of zero-sum nature, total, and central; parties involved invest their major resources in such conflicts.[7] This chapter describes the context of intractable conflict as the major experience responsible for the evolution of its narrative. Specifically, it concentrates on the Israeli–Arab conflict or, more accurately, on the Israeli–Palestinian conflict, analyzing the Jewish side.

The Israeli–Palestinian conflict is centered on the contested territory known as Palestine, an area that two national movements claim as their homeland. For more than ninety years Palestinian nationalism and Zionism, the Jewish national movement, have clashed recurrently over the right for self-determination, statehood, and justice. Moreover, for many years the conflict was perceived as one of national identity. Palestinians and Jews each believed that acceptance of the other's identity would negate both their own case and their own identity.

Each side believed that if it were to be considered a nation, the other could not be considered as one. Acknowledging the other's nationhood was seen as accepting that group's right to establish a national state in the contested land, which in turn was believed to weaken one's own claim for the same land. Thus the issue of the territorial claims touches on the very fundamental issue of national survival.[8]

The Israeli–Palestinian conflict started as a communal confrontation between the Jews and Palestinians living in British-ruled Palestine and evolved into a full-blown interstate conflict between Israel and Arab states during the war of 1948. Since the 1967 war, with the occupation of the West Bank and Gaza Strip, the conflict continues on both interstate and communal levels.[9] According to Sandler, each new phase involved intensive violence, was followed by the introduction of new parties to the conflict, and led to the development of new patterns of hostile interaction.

For a long time the conflict seemed irreconcilable and total. The dispute concerned elementary issues involving the basic existential needs of each side, and so finding an agreeable solution for both parties was impossible. In various attempts to resolve the conflict peacefully, Israel's minimum requirements exceeded the Arabs' maximum concessions, and vice versa. Therefore, it is not surprising that the sides involved perceived the conflict as being of zero-sum nature, and mobilized all possible efforts and backing within the group and the international community in order to win it.

The Israeli–Palestinian conflict has been violent almost from the start. At first, economic boycotts, demonstrations, strikes, and occasional violence erupted, reaching a climax in the Palestinian rebellion of 1936–1939. Following the UN decision in 1947 to divide the land between the Jews and the Palestinians, a full-scale war broke out which claimed many thousands of lives, including civilians. Also, and of great significance, hundreds of thousands of Palestinians became refugees. Through the years at least four additional wars were fought—in 1956, 1967, 1973, and 1982—and, between them, violent activities erupted continuously. They included military engagements, infiltration of hostile forces, terrorist attacks, bombardments, air raids, and so on. Between 1987 and 1991 Palestinians in the areas occupied by Israel in 1967 waged an uprising (*intifada*); in 2000 the Palestinians began their second intifada, called the Al-Aqsa intifada.

It should be noted that even though some intractable features are still present, the nature of the Israeli–Palestinian conflict changed after Egyptian president Anwar Sadat's visit to Jerusalem in 1977. The peace treaty with Egypt in

1979, the Madrid conference in 1991, the agreements with the Palestinians in 1993 and 1994, and the peace treaty with Jordan in 1994 are watershed events in the peace process, and have greatly affected Arab–Jewish relations. The eruption in 2000 of violent confrontations between Israeli Jews and Palestinians was a major setback to the peace process and has had an important influence on the quality of intergroup relations between Jews and Arabs in the Middle East.

The conflict has continuously been on both sides' public agenda. The involved parties learned to live with a harsh and violent reality. Until the death of President Yasser Arafat, it was almost impossible to imagine an alternative to the conflict. Coping with it became a way of life for both the Israelis and Palestinians.

In extreme cases, the seven characteristics of intractable conflicts described earlier are explicit and salient, inflicting threat, stress, pain, exhaustion, and cost in human and material terms. Those affected must adapt in both their individual and social lives. From a psychological perspective, this adaptation requires the meeting of two basic challenges.

First, basic needs must be fulfilled, such as the needs for mastery, safety, and positive identity, which are all diminished during an intractable conflict. Of special importance is the satisfaction of the need to understand the conflict in a way that can provide a coherent and predictable picture of the situation. As noted, individuals try fully to comprehend the situation so as to reduce uncertainty and ambiguity.[10]

Second, psychological adaptations are necessary to cope successfully with the ordeals posed by intense conflict, and with all of the concomitant adjustments and challenges that such coping entails on both the personal and societal levels. Among the many challenges posed by such conflict is to ensure that the survival of group members. Parties to the conflict must prepare themselves for a long struggle, and this effort requires the recruitment of human and material resources. Thus, adapting psychologically strengthens coping strategies such as loyalty to society and country, and engenders high motivations to contribute, persistence, withstanding physical and psychological stress, readiness for personal sacrifice, unity, solidarity, maintenance of a society's objectives, determination, courage, and endurance.

To meet these basic needs and be able to cope, society members construct an appropriate psychological repertoire, which includes shared beliefs, attitudes, emotions, and capacities. Of special importance in this psychological repertoire are narratives that pertain to collective memory and to the ethos of conflict. The narrative of collective memory focuses on the society's remembered past. In contrast, the ethos of conflict narrative, denoting the configuration of central societal beliefs, deals mainly with a society's current goals, capacity, and experiences. The next two sections discuss these narratives.

Collective Memory

The collective memory narrative has a number of characteristics. First, it does not necessarily tell a true history but rather describes a past that is useful for the group to function and even exist. It is a story that is biased, selective, and distorted, that omits certain facts, adds others that did not take place, changes the sequence of events, and purposely reinterprets events that did take place. In short, it is a narrative constructed to fit the current needs of the group.[11] As Wright stated, with regard to Great Britain: "Far from being somehow 'behind' the present, the past exists as an accomplished presence in public understanding, In this sense it is written into present social reality, not just implicitly as History, National Heritage and Tradition," but restores the "essential and grander identity of the 'Imaginary Briton.'"[12] The narrative of past events, moreover, not only undergoes major revisions to suit present day needs but is often invented years after the events have actually taken place. Thus, for example, Walker claims that the memories of the 1690 Battle of the Boyne in Northern Ireland were invented for political purposes in the nineteenth century.[13] A second characteristic of the collective memory narrative is that it is shared by group members and is treated by many as truthful accounts of the past and a valid history of the group. Third, the body of a collective historical narrative appears to entail both memories of past events (for example, the conquests of William of Orange, the siege of Masada, and the battle of the Alamo), as well as memories of more recent, conflict-related events. These more recent memories, some of them personal memories that intertwine with the collective memory pool, turn into historical memories the longer a conflict lasts. They exert a powerful force in shaping present-day attitudes, perceptions, and behaviors.

It follows that opposing groups in a conflict will often entertain contradictory and selective historical narratives of the same events. Also, whereas one group might emphasize certain events, the other may not even include them in its set of collective memories. By including or omitting certain historical events and processes from the collective memory, a group characterizes itself and its historical experiences in unique and exclusive ways.[14] Thus, the narrative of collective memory is perceived by group members as self-characterization. It tells the particular story of a group's past and outlines the boundaries for a group's description and characterization. In short, the narrative of collective memories relating to an intractable conflict provides a black-and-white picture, and enables parsimonious, fast, unequivocal, and simple understandings of the history of the conflict.

In terms of contents, the narrative of collective memory touches on at least four important themes that influence the perception of the conflict and its management. First, it justifies the outbreak of the conflict and the course of its development. It outlines the reasons for the supreme and existential importance of the conflicting goals, stressing that failure to achieve them may threaten the very existence of the group. It also disregards the goals of the other side, describing them as unjustified and unreasonable.

Second, the narrative of collective memory of intractable conflict presents a positive image of one's own group. The contents of the narrative can pertain to a variety of positive acts, traits, values, or skills that characterize a society. It reflects the general tendency toward ethnocentrism documented in different groups, but in times of intractable conflict it gains special significance.[15] Groups involved in such conflicts engage in intense self-justification, self-glorification, and self-praise.

Third, the collective memory narrative delegitimizes the opponent. Since societies involved in intractable conflicts view their own goals as justified and perceive themselves in a positive light, they attribute all responsibility for the outbreak and continuation of the conflict to the opponent.[16] The narrative focuses on the violence, atrocities, cruelty, lack of concern for human life, and viciousness of the other side. It describes the adversary's inhuman and immoral behavior, and presents it as intransigent, irrational, far-reaching, and irreconcilable. The adversary's character precludes any possible peaceful solution, and therefore the conflict cannot be resolved. All of these beliefs show the opponent to be an existential threat to the group's survival.

Fourth, this particular narrative presents one's own group as a victim. This view develops over a long period of violence as a result of a society's sufferings and losses.[17] Its formation is based on beliefs about the justness of the goals of one's group and on one's positive self-image, while emphasizing the wickedness of the opponent's goals and delegitimizing the opponent's characteristics.[18] In other words, focusing on injustice, harm, evil, and the atrocities of the adversary while emphasizing one's own society as just, moral, and human leads society members to see themselves as victims. Believing one is the victim implies that the conflict was imposed by an adversary who fights not only unjustly but immorally.

Thus, for example, Jewish–Israeli collective memories as presented in school textbooks describe the waves of Jewish immigration as an expression of national aspiration to build a state for Jewish people in their ancient homeland. The immigrants bought land from Arab landowners to build Jewish settlements with the will to live peacefully beside Arabs. The collective narrative focuses on Arab violence aimed at Jews and portrays it as vicious riots and massacres. According to the accepted narrative, Arabs rejected any compromise to settle the conflict, and in 1947 even rejected the UN decision to divide the country into two states—Jewish and Palestinian; instead, they initiated a war against the Jewish minority which drew in seven additional Arab states that invaded the newly established state of Israel. On the other hand, the schoolbooks have not mentioned, until recently, the massive, often "encouraged" departure of Palestinians-turned-refugees during the 1948 war or the atrocities carried out by the Israeli army, for example, in Qibya or Kfar Qassem. Nor are initial attempts by Arabs to sense Israel's willingness to negotiate a peaceful settlement ever mentioned in school textbooks. All the major wars are described as defensive—wars in which Israel successfully repelled Arab aggression.[19]

Ethos of Conflict

In addition to the narrative of collective memory, societies also evolve a narrative about the present that we call an ethos. "Ethos," defined as the configuration of central societal shared beliefs that provide a particular dominant orientation to a society, gives meaning to the life of a particular society.[20] The ethos narrative provides the epistemic basis for the present direction of a society, its major aspirations, goals, means, concerns, and images. The narrative indicates to society members that their behavior is not just random, but represents a coherent and systematic pattern of knowledge. This narrative implies that the decisions of society's leaders, the coordinated behavior of the members of society, and the structure and functioning of the society are all based on coherent and comprehensive beliefs that justify and motivate members of society to accept the system and to act in a coordinated manner.

The evolution of the ethos narrative is influenced by the conditions in which the society lives over a long period of time and the collective experiences that shape the society during this period. We suggest that under prolonged conditions of intractable conflict societies develop a particular ethos of conflict that provides a clear picture of the conflict, its goals, conditions, and requirements, as well as an image of one's own group, and of the rival group. This narrative is supported by the collective memory narrative, and the same themes appear in both. At the peak of intractable conflict, the beliefs are often shared by the majority of society members, but the extent of sharing may increase or lessen with a change in the nature of the conflict. The extent of sharing also depends on various societal and political factors. In general, societies may differ in the degree to which members share societal beliefs about a conflict.

In view of the intractable nature of the Arab–Israeli conflict, the Israeli Jews evolved an ethos during the late 1940s, 1950s, 1960s, and early 1970s that was functional for the demanding, stressful, costly, and prolonged situation of that time. This narrative enabled the Israelis to adapt and successfully cope with the conflict's painful consequences. That ethos of conflict narrative, it has been suggested, consisted of eight themes of societal belief, which are discussed in the following sections.[21]

The Justness of the Israeli Goals

This theme concerns the rationale behind the goals that led to the conflict and particularly the justification of those goals in terms of their importance. The Jews' return to Eretz Israel (Land of Israel), with the aim of establishing their own state after 2000 years of exile, was inspired by the nationalist ideology of Zionism. This ideology provided Jews with goals and a justification for them.[22] These goals centered first on the establishment of a Jewish state in the ancient homeland of Eretz Israel. Historical, theological, national, existential, political, societal, and cultural arguments were used to justify those goals. They included arguments such as the following: that the Jewish nation was founded in Eretz Israel, the ancient Land of Israel; that during many years of ancient Jewish history Eretz Israel remained the Jews' homeland; that during their exile Jews maintained close spiritual and physical ties with Eretz Israel, continuously aspiring to return to it; that the continuity of Jewish life never ceased in that ancient land; and that the persistent experience of anti-Semitism in the diaspora, resulting ultimately in the Holocaust, highlighted the need of the Jewish people for a secure existence in their old homeland. The conquest of the Sinai, the Gaza Strip, the West Bank, and the Golan Heights in the 1967 war greatly augmented the territorial dimension of the Israeli goals. In the aftermath of the war, many Israeli Jews believed that Israel had the right to retain these territories. Their shared beliefs pertained to the Jewish people's exclusive rights to

Judea, Samaria (i.e., the West Bank), and the Gaza Strip, and to the security importance of the Golan Heights, parts of the West Bank, and the Sinai.

In the context of justifying these Israeli goals, attempts were made over the years to refute Palestinian claims. The contested territory was often described as being sparsely populated by Arabs, who, moreover, had only moved there in recent centuries. The Palestinian national identity was also denied, the claim being made that they were Arabs, part of the Arab nation, and that their national Palestinian identity was a relatively new development. Finally, Palestinians' claims of attachment to the land was questioned by describing the land as desolate, neglected, and desertlike—that is, until the Jews came back to cultivate it. Only then did the Arabs return.

These societal beliefs motivated the members of Israeli–Jewish society to fight for their goals and to endure the stresses, sacrifices, and costs of intractable conflict.

Security

Throughout this enduring conflict the Israeli Jews have always believed that the security of the country and its Jewish citizens was seriously threatened.[23] Therefore, achieving a sense of security, one of the basic Zionist reasons for returning to Israel and establishing a Jewish state, became the central need and value. Security acquired the status of a cultural master-symbol in the Israeli–Jewish ethos.[24] Israeli society became a "nation under arms" or a "nation in uniform," living always, in a "dormant war."[25]

Assigning the highest priority to the value of security, the society did all it could to motivate its members to serve in the armed forces, and to encourage the best qualified to volunteer for the most important institutions and units, for example, the air force, the commando units, the Mossad, or the General Security Services. All channels of communication and agents of socialization paid tribute to the security forces.[26] Service in the Israeli Defense Forces (IDF) was viewed as an entrance ticket to Israeli society, and refusal or evasion of service was socially frowned upon. Those who volunteered to serve in special institutions or units were accorded high prestige. The top-ranking officers were ascribed a special status that allowed them not only to act as authorities on a wide range of issues but also to be accepted into any field upon retirement, including politics, industry, business, the civil service, and even cultural institutions and education.[27] At the same time, a legacy of wars and battles was developed and heroism was glorified. Military heroes received special honors, and society commemorated those who had fallen in military service, gave financial support to their families, and aided those who had been injured in the line of duty.[28]

The fundamental societal beliefs of the ethos delineated the conditions that were assumed to ensure security. First, Israel had to develop military power of the highest quality to deter Arab aggression. Second, Israel had the right and duty to use its armed forces to defend itself against Arab threats and even to initiate military acts, including war, to prevent possible Arab attacks on Israel. Third, Israel should not rely on help from foreign military forces or be dependent on international public opinion or the views of foreign leaders and international organizations—the UN, for example. Fourth, land was regarded as the country's most important national strategic asset.

In sum, these societal beliefs were functional for the violent confrontations of the conflict, since they assigned a high priority to security, provided a rationale for societal decisions and actions, and motivated members of society to participate in the conflict and accept and cope with stressful conditions.

Positive Collective In-group Images

The societal beliefs of positive collective in-group images involve the attribution of positive traits, values, intentions, and behaviors to one's own society. Israeli Jews viewed themselves as a "new people," reborn in the land of Israel.[29] Initial positive stereotypes saw Israeli Jews as tenacious, hard-working, courageous, modern, and intelligent, and then as moral and humane. With respect to the first set of traits, various stories and myths were amassed about the Jews' behavior in times of peace and war, while their morality and humanity referred to their behavior toward Arabs. This positive in-group presentation also invoked the Jewish heritage. Jewish culture, religion, and traditions were regarded as being at the heart of Western civilization and morality. Certain segments in the society regarded Jews as the "chosen people" and a "light unto the nations." These beliefs encouraged moral strength and feelings of self-worth.

One's Own Victimization

Beliefs about one's victimization and unjust Arab aggression offer a positive in-group image and a delegitimization of Arabs. Beginning with early encounters with Arabs, attempts to harm Jews physically, halt their immigration, or prevent them from settling in the homeland were considered by the Israeli Jews as evidence of victimization.[30] Their beliefs that they were victims were greatly reinforced when, following the establishment of the state of Israel, Palestinians and the Arab states tried to annihilate the new state, and continued to attack it. The wars that were fought, the Arab embargo on trade with Israel, and the terrorist attacks on Israeli and non-Israeli Jews all confirmed to the Israeli Jews their status as victims. These contentions also suited the Jewish belief in their own persecution.[31]

During the ongoing conflict, the belief in their own victimization gave the Israeli Jews the moral incentive to fight Arabs, to seek justice, and to turn to the international community for moral, political, and material support.

Delegitimizing the Opponent

Intractable conflict fosters the evolution of negative stereotypes and especially negative societal beliefs that deny the adversary group—in this case, Arabs—its humanity. Indeed, the process of mutual delegitimization has been one of the bitter manifestations of the long years of conflict between Israeli Jews and Arabs.[32] For many decades Israeli Jews referred to Arabs as a general category, without differentiation.[33] From the very beginning the encounters between Jews, mostly from Europe, and Arabs, living in Palestine, fostered negative stereotyping.[34] Arabs were labeled as primitive, uncivilized, savage, and backward. In time, as the conflict deepened and became more violent, they were perceived as murderers, bloodthirsty, treacherous, cowardly, cruel, and wicked. After the establishment of the state of Israel, these delegitimizing beliefs about Arabs still prevailed and were transmitted through institutional channels.[35] Arabs were also blamed for the continuation of the conflict, for the eruption of all of the wars and military clashes, and for intransigently rejecting a peaceful resolution.[36]

Arabs were also characterized as striving to annihilate the state of Israel and to drive the Jewish population into the sea. During the height of the conflict, from the 1940s to the 1970s, all Arabs were perceived as one undifferentiated entity, and all Arab nations were seen to display a uniform attitude toward the state of Israel. Only after the peace treaty with Egypt did the Jews differentiate between Arab nations. This differentiation has continued to develop as Israel has built separate relationships with different Arab nations. But "Arab" continues to be used widely today as a general label, often with derogatory overtones. Palestinians, who were identified as a separate nation only in the late 1970s, were perceived as an enemy of the Jewish people, and many of the delegitimizing terms were also applied to them. In fact, for decades they were referred to as "Arabs." With the Oslo Accords, the delegitimizing views became more differentiated, but the eruption of the second intifada brought back the delegitimizing labels.[37]

Patriotism

During the intractable conflict, Israeli Jews made a special effort to convey beliefs that would instill patriotism.[38] In the context of the conflict, extreme sacrifices were asked of Israeli Jews, including economic hardship and prolonged military service and reserve duty. Patriotic beliefs called for various forms of dedication, such as settling in outlying or desolate areas, volunteering for the security forces, and working for society's welfare. These beliefs even called for the ultimate sacrifice, the readiness to die, as part of the violent confrontation with the Arabs, which included Palestinians. Those who acted as models of patriotism were glorified, while those who left the country (labeled "deserters") or did not fulfill their duties to the state (e.g., by not serving in the army) were stigmatized. Such patriotic beliefs increased cohesiveness and mobilized the members of Israeli society to participate actively in the conflict and to endure hardship and even loss of life.[39]

Unity

Beliefs in unity have helped Israelis to ignore internal disagreements and conflicts so that society is united in the face of external threats. Israeli–Jewish society strove to foster unity and build a sense of belonging and solidarity by emphasizing beliefs about the need for unity. Common tradition and religion were emphasized, and an attempt was made to minimize the ethnic differences within a society whose members came from various parts of the world. Unity was also reinforced by setting specific lines of agreement; those who expressed opinions or exhibited behavior outside the accepted consensus were frowned upon.[40] The consensus pertained particularly to societal beliefs about the Arab–Israeli conflict, and also to the justness of Israel's goals and the means of ensuring security.[41]

Beliefs about unity strengthen society from within, augment a sense of commonality and solidarity, and allow energy to be directed toward coping with the external enemy.

Peace

Societal beliefs about peace center on the society's ultimate goal, namely, peace. During the intractable conflict with the Arabs, Israeli–Jewish society cherished peace as a value, conceived of it as a dream, a prayer, a belief in utopian images. Israeli Jews were thus stereotyped as a peace-loving people forced by circumstances to engage in violent conflict. They were seen as being ready to negotiate and achieve peace, whereas the Arabs, who rejected any peaceful resolution and even refused to have direct contact with Jews, were viewed as the sole obstacle to progress. Such beliefs inspired hope and optimism, strengthened the Israeli Jews' positive self-image, and contributed to an empathic self-image in the outside world.

Societal beliefs of collective memory and ethos of conflict complement each other and together constitute a holistic narrative that society members share. Some themes appear prominently in both narratives, such as just goals in the conflict, a positive self-collective view, a self-image as victim, and delegitimization of the other side. These themes, which constitute the epistemic basis of the conflict, provide the focal points that contribute to the continuation of the conflict.

Functions of the Conflict Narratives

Narratives are not only responses to political events, serving to provide a comprehensible explanatory cognitive schema; they also actively affect the events by assigning them meaning and thus shaping the political process.[42] The reciprocal relationship between political events and a collective narrative takes center stage during a conflict, a time when both the epistemic and political functions of narratives are most needed.[43] Indeed, when one side acts in a conciliatory manner and the other, in light of its narrative-guided perceptions, rejects the move as a public opinion stunt and politically motivated trap, political escalation follows. There are six major functions that narratives of ethos and collective memory accomplish in times of intractable conflict.

First, as noted, collective narratives illuminate the conflict situation. An intractable conflict is extremely threatening, bringing on stress, vulnerability, uncertainty, and fear.[44] Because of the ambiguity and unpredictability of the conflict situation, individuals need fully to comprehend the conflict in order to draw a meaningful and predictable picture of the situation.[45] Narratives fulfill these demands, providing information and explanations about the nature of the conflict, answering vital questions: Why did the conflict erupt? What was its course? Why does it continue, and why can it not be resolved peacefully? What is the enemy's responsibility and contribution? How did the in-group act in the conflict? What are "our" goals in the conflict, and why are they existential? What challenges face society?

Second, narratives justify the acts of the in-group toward the enemy, including violence and destruction, allowing group members to carry out misdeeds, cause intentional harm, and institutionalize aggression toward the enemy. This function of the narrative resolves group members' feelings of dissonance, guilt, and shame. Human beings who behave normally do not usually harm other human beings. Sanctity of life is one of the most sacred values in modern societies. Killing or even hurting other human beings is considered the most serious violation of the moral code.[46] In an intractable conflict, however, groups hurt each other in severe ways, resorting even to atrocities, ethnic cleansing, and genocide. Narratives allow this violence; they enable individuals to attribute their immoral behavior to external factors.

The belief that we are the victims and they are the perpetrators, a self-perception of righteousness and superiority, is justification to harm the other side.[47] Such self-images place one on a higher moral ground, clearing one side of responsibility for acts of violence against the other. In this way one legitimizes one's actions.[48]

Third, narratives create a sense of differentiation and superiority. They sharpen intergroup differences by describing opponents in delegitimizing terms while glorifying one's own group. Since societies involved in intractable conflicts view their own goals as justified and perceive themselves positively, they attribute all responsibility for the outbreak of a conflict and its continuation to the opponent. This narrative focuses on the violence, atrocities, cruelty, lack of concern for human life, and viciousness of the other side. It describes the opponent as inhuman and immoral, and depicts the conflict as irrational, far-reaching, and irreconcilable, thus precluding a peaceful solution.

Fourth, narratives inspire mobilization and action. They justify the goals of the conflict and focus on the delegitimization, intransigence, and violence of the opponent, thus implying the necessity of the group to exert all of its efforts and resources in its struggle against the enemy. Such beliefs arouse patriotism, which leads to a readiness for sacrifice in order to defend the society and the country, and to avenge the enemy's past violence. Narratives also remind group members of violent acts in the past to indicate that these acts could recur. The group should therefore carry out violent acts to prevent possible harm by the enemy and to avert perceived danger and threat.

Fifth, as mentioned above, narratives affect political events by assigning them particular meanings. One group sees its own political concessions and compromises, such as Prime Minister Ehud Barak's conciliatory moves at the Camp David summit in the summer of 2000, as great sacrifices, while the other side, looking through the lenses of its own narrative, dismisses such moves as a smoke screen.[49] Viewing such efforts as insincere, frustration and a sense of betrayal set in and outbursts of violence soon follow. The outbreak of the second intifada soon after the failure of the Camp David summit is a case in point.

Finally, narratives contribute to the formation, maintenance, and strengthening of social identity, which is crucial to any society or group. Individuals must identify themselves as group members for the group to exist, a condition widely accepted by social scientists. A concept of self consists of a collection of self-images that includes both individuating and social categorical characteristics.[50] The former represent personal identity and the latter social identity. Social identity is an identification, to varying degrees of importance, with different groups. It is based on a self-categorization process in which individuals group themselves cognitively as the same, in contrast to other classes of collectives.[51] On this basis, the uniformity and coordination of group behavior emerge.

Clearly self-categorization is fundamental to define oneself as a member of a society, but it is only the initial phase; one must also accept additional beliefs that provide meaning to one's social identity.[52] Individuals, as thinking creatures, cannot be satisfied with mere self-categorization as a way to become a member of society. An elaborate system of beliefs is needed that justifies and explains their belonging to the group, describes their characteristics and concerns as society members, and explains the meaning of their social identity.[53] The narratives of collective memory and of ethos of conflict fulfill this important function. They provide the contextual basis for social identity.[54]

In view of the important functions that narratives fulfill during intractable conflict, attempts are made to institutionalize them, a process characterized by four features:

1. *Extensive sharing.* The beliefs of the narratives are widely held by society members, who acquire and store this repertoire as part of their socialization from an early age.
2. *Wide application.* Institutionalization means that society members not only believe in the narratives but also put them into active use. They surface in daily conversations, are referred to by leaders, and are employed in societal channels of mass communication.

3. *Expression in cultural products.* Institutionalization of the narratives is also expressed in cultural products such as films, TV programs, books, theatrical plays, and so on. They are part of a society's cultural repertoire, relaying societal views and shaping attitudes. Through these channels such beliefs are broadly disseminated, reaching every public sector.

4. *Appearance in educational materials.* Narrative beliefs are included in the textbooks used for school socialization. A significant element of institutionalization for these beliefs are then disseminated to the society's younger generation. Moreover, the perceived authority of school textbooks lends an element of truth to such societal beliefs. Given compulsory school attendance in most societies, new generations are exposed to these beliefs and the narratives become part of the political, social, cultural, and educational context of society.

Institutionalizing the narratives consolidates them and facilitates their perseverance and durability, even in the face of contradictory information. Opposing arguments are rejected, and society uses control mechanisms to ensure that its members do not change the narratives or entertain alternate beliefs. During an intractable conflict these beliefs become part of a rigid repertoire resistant to change.

Consequences of the Narratives

Collective narratives are socially and psychologically shared constructs and therefore have consequences affecting how information is handled, in much the same way as strongly held conceptions and theories influence perceptions, and anticipatory schemata shape the selection and interpretation of information.[55] This influence is particularly apparent during intractable conflicts when uncertainty reigns and events need to be processed and interpreted in light of a wider conceptual framework, namely, the narrative that pertains to the conflict.

The consequences of a narrative have to do with the ways one anticipates incoming information and selectively processes, encodes, interprets, recalls, and acts upon that information. When members of a society strongly adhere to a narrative, which is typical in a time of intractable conflict, they tend to absorb what fits the content of the narrative and dismiss the information that opposes it.

As Rapoport describes, society members often expect that their hypotheses about their adversary will be confirmed.[56] For example, anticipating that a rival group will be negatively disposed to them, they act accordingly. Because they suspect the adversary of negative intentions and behavior, they themselves act toward the rival group in a negative way, instigating hostility and animosity, and thus confirming the initial expectations and creating a vicious circle of resentment.

Narrative-guided expectations are realized in a sequence of steps that begins with paying selective attention to certain information and excluding other information incongruent to the narrative. Sensitivity toward narrative-congruent information is heightened, leading to increased bias against certain other kinds of information—a bias fueled by people's apparent proclivity to confirm rather than deny expectations.[57] This pattern is influenced by hatred of the opposition and the creation of emotionally laden linguistic labels, such as "Arabs."[58]

Acceptable information is encoded in ways that allow it to be assimilated into preexisting schemata.[59] Once encoded, the information is processed more elaborately and rehearsed more frequently than information that does not fit expectations.[60] The information thus becomes more resistant to being disproved, increasing a group's confidence in the truth of the information as selected, encoded, and processed.[61]

The information is also interpreted by more sophisticated theories such as the idea of a collective narrative.[62] Believing that those on the other side are "conservatives," people interpret the opposing views on contentious issues as more extreme than their own, displaying what has been termed "naïve realism."[63] The peace-oriented gestures of both Palestinian and Israeli leaders are another case in point. These gestures are consistently rejected by the other side as no more than political maneuvers, such as the one made by President Bashar Assad of Syria in late 2003 and by Israel's president Ariel Sharon in early 2004. Both offers, interpreted as ill-intended, were dismissed outright as not worthy of serious consideration.

Finally, information that conforms to the narrative is better remembered and more easily recalled. Spread repeatedly through various channels of communication, the narrative is ever present in the minds of society members. Bodenhausen has shown that people can better recall information that is incriminating, rather than exculpatory, regarding a negatively stereotyped group, as a function of the way that the evidence was initially processed.[64] Banaji and Bhaskar's findings support this claim, namely, that new information congruent with prior-held knowledge is better recalled.[65]

Finally, it should be stressed that although the narratives that evolve in a conflict situation enable those involved to adapt better to conditions of intractable conflict, these narratives also maintain and prolong the conflict. They become a prism through which society members construe their reality, collect new information, interpret their experiences, and make decisions about their course of action.[66] Participation in an intractable conflict tends to "close minds" and facilitate a tunnel vision that precludes a consideration of contrasting information and alternative approaches to conflict resolution.[67]

Implications for Reconciliation

Clearly any move by society members toward a peaceful resolution of the conflict and eventual reconciliation requires changing the collective narratives.[68] This in turn requires the adoption of a psychological point of view that serves not only to understand the conflict but also to examine possible avenues for reconciliation and associated dilemmas. These issues are discussed at greater length elsewhere.[69]

Recently Bar-Tal elaborated on the type of psychological changes that he considers necessary for reconciliation.[70] He specified the modification of five narrative themes formed during the conflict, namely, themes surrounding the groups' goals, attitudes toward the rival group, ideas about one's own group, relationship with the opponent, and peace.

The group's goals. An important change for achieving reconciliation concerns the narrative regarding the justness of the goals underlying the outbreak and maintaining the conflict. If not abolishing this narrative altogether, the societal aspirations expressed in the narrative goals that caused the conflict need to be indefinitely postponed. New societal beliefs about goals must be formed—beliefs that propose new goals for the society that are shaped by the conflict resolution agreement and that focus on maintaining peaceful relations with the former enemy. These new beliefs also must rationalize and justify the new goals, including new symbols and myths.

The rival group. Another condition for reconciliation is a change in the perception of the adversary. In times of conflict opponents are delegitimized in order to explain their aberrant behavior, as well as the outbreak and continuation of the conflict, and to justify the negative actions taken against them.[71] Instead, opponents need to be legitimized and personalized: legitimization grants humanity to adversaries and allows them to be viewed as an acceptable group with which to maintain peaceful relations; personalization enables hostile groups to view their rivals as humane, trustworthy, individuals with legitimate needs and goals. The new beliefs also need to embody a balanced stereotype of the adversary that acknowledges both positive and negative characteristics. Finally, this new way of thinking should envision the opponent not only as a perpetrator of the conflict but also as a victim.[72]

One's own group. In a conflict situation each group tends to maintain a one-sided, glorified self-image that ignores and censors any information that may shed a negative light on the group. In the reconciliation process each group must take responsibility for its role in the outbreak of the conflict, its contribution to the violence including its immoral behavior, and its refusal to engage in a peaceful resolution. Simply put, the new societal beliefs need to portray one's own group in a complex multifaceted way. As noted, acknowledging one's own contribution to the conflict is essential for reconciliation.[73]

Relationship with the opponent. Societal beliefs during a conflict support confrontation and animosity.[74] To promote reconciliation, new beliefs need to stress friendship and cooperation, especially equality and mutual sensitivity to the needs, goals, and general well-being of the other. These new beliefs must present past relations within a new framework that revises the collective memory and synchronizes the former rivals.

Peace. Both parties in an intractable conflict yearn for peace but view peace in amorphic and utopian terms without specifying realistic ways to achieve it. New societal beliefs must be formed that recognize the multidimensional nature of peace, outline the true costs and benefits of achieving it, understand what it means to live in peace, and specify the conditions and mechanisms for its achievement—such as negotiating and compromising with the rival. Maintaining peace requires ongoing sensitivity and attention to the needs and goals of the other.

Acknowledging the past, particularly the injustices and harm each side has done to the other, is crucial for reconciliation. Collective memory holds a firm grip on people's shared identities, beliefs, and attitudes toward the other. Such beliefs are not easily shaken, as they facilitate the group's collective sense of purpose. Reconciliation, it is widely agreed, requires the formation of a fresh common outlook of the past, a change in collective memories. Once this common outlook is achieved, both parties move significantly closer to mutually effective peace. As Hayner noted: "Where fundamentally different versions or continued denials about such important and painful events still exist, reconciliation may be only superficial."[75]

Does allowing historical memories to surface facilitate or hinder reconciliation attempts? Devine-Wright argued that highlighting historical memories is *not* helpful as it can easily lead to entrenchment.[76] Maoz has shown, however, that historical memories may be unavoidable.[77] Sometimes, the stronger side in a conflict wants to look toward a bright future, evading the past if at all possible, while the weaker side wants to return to past events to emphasize the harm done to it. When the stronger group does not acknowledge the damage that it has done, reconciliation is jeopardized.[78]

As the Truth and Reconciliation Commission in South Africa and To Reflect and Trust (TRT) workshops suggest, facing personal history that is embedded in collective history may well be a necessary step in attaining reconciliation.[79] In Bar-On's words: "Probably the acknowledgment and working through process of the Holocaust that took place in the original TRT group enabled the Jewish–Israeli members to acknowledge and start to work through their role in relation to the Palestinian–Israeli conflict."[80] Reconciliation implies that both parties not only go over what happened in the past but also truly acknowledge past events.[81] Indeed, recognition and acknowledgment is "given urgency by the supposed link between recognition and identity."[82]

A related issue is the expectation of mutual legitimization of each side's collective narrative. Because a major outcome of collective narratives is the delegitimization of the other side's narrative, a major goal toward peace is to legitimize the narrative of the other group.[83] One may argue that when there are grave inequalities between the two sides, with one side feeling oppressed by the narrative-guided actions of the other, mutual legitimization is unattainable.[84] In some cases, therefore, progress can be achieved in the peace process only when modest goals are set.[85]

Legitimization may not need to pertain to all of the components of the narrative. Different elements of collective narratives, as in all ideologies, have different degrees of significance.[86] The existence or abolition of a Jewish independent state in Israel is central to both the Israeli and Palestinian narratives; it is the precise issue on which the two most sharply disagree. Less important is the belief that members of the other side are inferior. Accepting the humanity of Israelis is clearly a far easier task for Palestinians than legitimizing the basic tenets of the Zionist narrative. Bar-Natan has recently found that developing interpersonal relationships between Jewish and Israeli–Palestinian youth through encounter groups generally makes Jewish participants more willing to have contact with Palestinians and more amenable to accepting the Palestinian perspective on the conflict.[87] Palestinian youth, on the other hand, while generally becoming more agreeable regarding contacts with Jews, do not grow more willing to accept the Israeli–Jewish narrative. Nevertheless, although legitimization was only partially achieved in these encounter groups, such interaction may be sufficient to pave the way for reconciliation.

The literature, however, is equivocal on whether contact between members of rival groups facilitates legitimization.[88] Pettigrew provided a list of necessary conditions, but ones difficult to meet, for successful contact between adversaries.[89] Yet, evidence shows that when at least some of these conditions are met, such as intensive interaction or the development of friendships, perceptions change and an adversary's narratives are seen as more legitimate.[90] More important, it has been found that participation in peace education programs, specifically by Palestinian youth, acts as a *barrier* to perceptions and feelings toward Jews caused by the ongoing intifada.[91]

Reconciliation necessitates changing the narratives of collective memories by learning about the rival group's collective memory and admitting one's own past misdeeds and responsibility for contributing to the conflict. Acknowledgment of the past implies at least a recognition that there are two (legitimate) narratives of the conflict.[92] This recognition is an important factor in reconciliation, since the collective memories of each party about its own past underpin the continuation of the conflict and obstruct peacemaking. Through the process of negotiation, in which one's own past is critically revised and synchronized with that of the other group, new narratives can emerge.[93] Given time, this new historical account of events should substitute each side's dominant narrative of collective memory.

Conclusion

Societies are bound together by a number of factors, functions, and institutions; prominent among them is the collective narrative with its roots in shared historical memories which supports a narrative of the ethos. In times of conflict, the narratives of the collective memory and the ethos of conflict center around beliefs pertaining to one's righteousness, sense of victimization, delegitimization of the adversary, patriotism, one's desire for peace, and the like. These narratives fulfill crucial functions during the period of conflict. They range from the epistemic function of reducing uncertainties caused by the conflict to providing justification for the conflict situation and the actions taken to cope with it; from the motivational function of mobilization to the facilitation of patriotism; and from the provision of a sense of identity and purpose to that of a sense of uniqueness and superiority. Importantly, narratives also affect actual political and social events and processes by providing their particular interpretations—determining, for example, if an action by the rival is serious or not, a threat, or a genuine gesture of good will, thereby affecting the actual response to these acts. In this sense, narratives that arise in response to the conflict partake in sustaining, even escalating it. Thus they play a part in the developed vicious cycle. Narratives evolve in times of conflict, and they also contribute to its continuation, which in turn reinforces their validity and prevents their change.

In this cycle, one of the consequences of collective narratives during conflict is the way that they affect the handling of conflict-related information such that it will be assimilated into narrative-related mental schemata and thus confirm its contents and beliefs. They determine selective attention, to the exclusion of narrative-incongruent information, information processing, interpretation, and memory. In other words, one can speak of narrative-directed informational bias. Another class of consequences is their effect on political and social events, and the prolongation of the conflict. A third consequence is the delegitimization of the other side's narrative, ethos, and current experiences. The focal point for reconciliation attempts becomes the attainment of the legitimization of the other side's narrative, including the acknowledgment of its history.

NOTES

1. Peter Berger, *The Sacred Canopy* (Garden City, NY, 1969); Leonard Berkowitz, "Social Motivation," in Gardner Lindzey and Eliot Aronson (eds.), *The Handbook of Social Psychology* (Reading, MA, 1968, 2nd. ed.), III, 50–135; Clifford Geertz, *The Interpretation of Cultures* (New York, 1973); Daniel Katz, "The Functional Approach to the Study of Attitudes," *Public Opinion Quarterly*, XXIV (1960), 163–204; Janusz Reykowski, "Social Motivation," *Annual Review of Psychology*, XXXIII (1982), 123–154.

2. Salvatore R. Maddi, "The Search for Meaning," in W. J. Arnold, and M. M. Page (eds.), *Nebraska Symposium on Motivation 1970* (Lincoln, 1970), 137–186.

3. Susan T. Fiske and Shelley E. Taylor, *Social Cognition* (New York, 1991, 2nd ed.); Fritz Heider, *The Psychology of Interpersonal Relations* (New York, 1958); G. Kelly, *The Psychology of Personal Constructs* (New York, 1955); Robert W. White, "Motivation Reconsidered: The Concept of Competence," *Psychological Review*, LXVI (1959), 297–333.

4. Richard Jenkins, *Social Identity* (New York, 1996); Henry Tajfel, *Human Groups and Social Categories: Studies in Social Psychology* (Cambridge, 1981).

5. Daniel Bar-Tal, *Shared Beliefs in a Society: Social Psychological Analysis* (Thousand Oaks, CA, 2000).

6. Jerome Bruner, *Acts of Meaning* (Cambridge, MA, 1990).

7. Edward E. Azar, P. Jureidini, and R. McLaurin, "Protracted Social Conflict: Theory and Practice in the Middle East," *Journal of Palestine Studies,* VIII (1978), 41–60; Daniel Bar-Tal, "Societal Beliefs in Times of Intractable Conflict: The Israeli Case," *International Journal of Conflict Management,* IX (1998), 22–50; Gary Goertz and Paul F. Diehl, "Enduring Rivalries; Theoretical Constructs and Empirical Patterns," *International Studies Quarterly,* XXXVII (1993), 147–171; Louis Kriesberg, "Intractable Conflicts," *Peace Review,* V (1993), 417–421.

8. Herbert C. Kelman, "The Interdependence of Israeli and Palestinian National Identities: The Role of the Other in Existential Conflict," *Journal of Social Issues,* LV (1999), 581–600.

9. Shmuel Sandler, "The Protracted Arab-Israeli Conflict: A Temporal-spatial Analysis," *Jerusalem Journal of International Relations,* X (1988), 54–78.

10. Berkowitz, "Social Motivation"; Reykowski, "Social Motivation."

11. Sirka Ahonen, "Remembrance: Cultural Memory," *Zeitschrift fur KulturAustauch* (1999), http://www.ifa.de/z/remember/ezahonef.htm.

12. Patrick Wright, *On Living in an Old Country: The National Past in Contemporary Britain* (London, 1985), 142, 165.

13. B. M. Walker, *Dancing to History's Tune: History, Myth, and Politics in Ireland* (Belfast, 1996).

14. Irena Irwin-Zarecka, *Frames of Remembrance: The Dynamics of Collective Memory* (New Brunswick, NJ, 1994).

15. Richard A. LeVine and Donald T. Campbell, *Ethnocentrism: Theories of Conflict, Ethnic Attitudes and Group Behavior* (New York, 1972).

16. Daniel Bar-Tal, "Causes and Consequences of Delegitimization: Models of Conflict and Ethnocentrism," *Journal of Social Issues,* XLVI (1990), 65–81.

17. Daniel Bar-Tal, "Collective Memory of Physical Violence: Its Contribution to the Culture of Violence," in Ed Cairns and Michael D. Roe (eds.), *The Role of Memory in Ethnic Conflict* (London, 2003), 77–93.

18. Jerome D. Frank, *Sanity and Survival: Psychological Aspects of War and Peace* (New York, 1967).

19. Ruth Firer, *The Agents of Zionist Education* (Tel Aviv, 1985), in Hebrew; Elie Podeh, *The Arab-Israeli Conflict in Israeli History Textbooks, 1948–2000* (Westport, CT, 2002). See also Nathan Brown, "Contesting National Identity in Palestinian Education," and Eyal Naveh, "The Dynamics of Identity Construction in Israel through History Education," chapters 10 and 11 in this volume.

20. Bar-Tal, *Shared Beliefs in a Society.*

21. Bar-Tal, "Societal Beliefs in Times of Intractable Conflict."

22. Shlomo Avineri, *The Making of Modern Zionism: The Intellectual Origins of the Jewish State* (London, 1981); David Vital, *Zionism: The Formative Years* (Oxford, 1982).

23. Asher Arian, *Security Threatened: Surveying Israeli Opinion on Peace and War* (Cambridge, 1995); Janice B. Stein and Michael Brecher, "Image, Advocacy and the Analysis of Conflict: An Israeli Case Study," *Jerusalem Journal of International Relations*, I (1976), 33–58; R. A. Stone, *Social Change in Israel: Attitudes and Events, 1967–1979* (New York, 1982).

24. Dan Horowitz, "Israeli Perception of National Security (1948–1972)," in Benjamin Neuberger (ed.), *Diplomacy and Confrontation; Selected Issues in Israel's Foreign Relations, 1948–1978* (Tel-Aviv, 1984), 104–148, in Hebrew; Charles S. Liebman, Eliezer Don-Yehiya, *Civil Religion in Israel: Traditional Judaism and Political Culture in the Jewish State* (Berkeley, 1983).

25. Dan Horowitz, "The Israeli Concept of National Security," in Avner Yaniv (ed.), *National Security and Democracy in Israel* (Boulder, 1993), 11–53.

26. Moshe Lissak, *Israeli Society and Its Defense Establishment* (London, 1984).

27. Yoram Peri, *Between Battles and Ballots: Israeli Military in Politics* (Cambridge, 1983).

28. Daniel Bar-Tal, Dan Jacobson, and Aharon Klieman (eds.), *Security Concerns: Insights from the Israeli Experience* (Stamford, CT, 1998).

29. John E. Hofman, "The Meaning of Being a Jew in Israel: An Analysis of Ethnic Identity, *Journal of Personality and Social Psychology*, XV (1970), 196–202.

30. Aluf Hareven, "Victimization: Some Comments by an Israeli," *Political Psychology*, IV (1983), 145–155.

31. Daniel Bar-Tal and Dikla Antebi, "Siege Mentality in Israel," *International Journal of Intercultural Relations*, XVI (1992), 251–275; Charles Liebman, "Myth, Tradition and Values in Israeli Society," *Midstream*, XXIV (1978), 44–53.

32. Dan Bar-On, "Cultural Identity and Demonization of the Relevant Other: Lessons from the Palestinian-Israeli Conflict," in Arieh Y. Shalev, Rachel Yehuda, and Alexander C. McFarlane (eds.), *International Handbook of Human Response to Trauma* (New York, 2000), 115–125; Daniel Bar-Tal, "Delegitimizing Relations between Israeli Jews and Palestinians: A Social Psychological Analysis," in John Hofman (ed.), *Arab-Jewish Relations in Israel: A Quest in Human Understanding* (Bristol, IN, 1988), 217–248; Yoram Bilu, "The Image of the Enemy: Cracks in the Wall of Hatred, *Palestine-Israeli Journal*, IV (1994), 24–28; Kelman, "The Interdependence of Israeli and Palestinian National Identities."

33. Daniel Bar-Tal and Yona Teichman, *Stereotypes and Prejudice in Conflict: Representations of Arabs in Israeli Jewish Society* (Cambridge, 2005).

34. Ian Lustick, *Arabs in the Jewish State* (Austin, 1982).

35. E.g., Adir Cohen, *An Ugly Face in the Mirror: National Stereotypes in Hebrew*

Children's Literature (Tel-Aviv, 1985), in Hebrew; Risa Domb, *The Arab in Hebrew Prose* (London, 1982); Tom Segev, *1949: The First Israelis* (Jerusalem, 1984), in Hebrew.

36. David Ben-Gurion, *Israel: Years of Challenge* (Tel Aviv, 1969), in Hebrew; Yehoshafat Harkabi, *Arab Strategies and Israel's Response* (New York, 1977); Jacob J. Landau, *Israel and the Arabs* (Jerusalem, 1971).

37. Daniel Bar-Tal, "The Necessity of Observing Real Life Situations: Palestinian-Israeli Violence as a Laboratory for Learning about Social Behavior," *European Journal of Social Psychology*, XXXIV (2004), 677–701.

38. Avner Ben-Amos and Daniel Bar-Tal (eds.), *Patriotism: Homeland Love* (Tel Aviv, 2004), in Hebrew.

39. Amos Elon, *The Israelis* (London, 1971).

40. Sammy Smooha, *Israel: Pluralism and Conflict* (Berkeley, 1978).

41. Pnina Lahav, "The Press and National Security," in Avner Yaniv (ed.), *National Security and Democracy* (Boulder, 1993), 173–195; Moshe Negbi, *Paper Tiger: The Struggle for a Press Freedom in Israel* (Tel Aviv, 1985), in Hebrew.

42. John W. Burton (ed.), *Conflict: Human Needs Theory* (London, 1990).

43. K. Foster, *Fighting Fictions: War, Narrative and National Identity* (London, 1999).

44. E. J. Lieberman, "Threat and Assurance in the Conduct of Conflict," in Ronald Fisher (ed.), *International Conflict and Behavioral Science* (New York, 1964), 110–122.

45. Burton, *Conflict;* Maddi, "The Search for Meaning."

46. Alan Donagan, *The Theory of Morality* (Chicago, 1979); John Kleinig, *Valuing Life* (Princeton, 1991).

47. Gavriel Salomon, "A Narrative-based View of Coexistence Education," *Journal of Social Issues*, VI (2004), 273–287.

48. Ervin Staub, "The Origins and Prevention of Genocide, Mass Killings and Other Collective Violence," *Peace and Conflict: Journal of Peace Psychology*, V (1999), 303–336.

49. Ifat Maoz, Andrew Ward, Michael Katz, and Lee Ross, "Reactive Devaluation of an 'Israeli' vs. 'Palestinian' Peace Proposal," *Journal of Conflict Resolution*, LXVI (2002), 515–546; Lee Ross and Andrew Ward, "Psychological Barriers to Dispute Resolution," in Mark Zanna (ed.), *Advances in Experimental Social Psychology* (San Diego, 1995), 103–135.

50. Henry Tajfel, *Social Identity and Intergroup Relations* (Cambridge, 1982); Henry Tajfel and John C. Turner, "An Integrative Theory of Intergroup Relations," in Stephen Worchel and William G. Austin (eds.), *Psychology of Intergroup Relations* (Chicago, 1986), 7–24.

51. John C. Turner, Michael A. Hogg, Penelope J. Oakes, Stephen D. Reicher, and Margaret S. Wetherell, *Rediscovering the Social Group: A Self-Categorization Theory* (Oxford, 1987).

52. Daniel Bar-Tal and Neta Oren, *Ethos as an Expression of Identity: Its Changes in Transition from Conflict to Peace in the Israeli Case* (Jerusalem, 2000); John C. Turner, *Social Influence* (Milton Keynes, 1991); John. C. Turner, "Some Current Issues in Research on Social Identity and Self-categorization Theories," in Naomi Ellemers, Russell Spears, and Bertjan Doosje (eds.), *Social Identity* (Malden, MA, 1999).

53. K. Foster, *Fighting Fiction.*

54. Neta Oren, Daniel Bar-Tal, and Ohad David, "Conflict, Identity and Ethos: The Israeli-Palestinian Case," in Yueh-Ting Lee, Clark R. McCauley, Fathali M. Moghaddam, and Stephen Worchel (eds.), *Psychology of Ethnic and Cultural Conflict* (Westport, CT, 2004), 133–154.

55. Richard Nisbett and Lee Ross, *Human Inference: Strategies and Shortcomings of Social Judgment* (Englewood Cliffs, NJ, 1980); Ulric Neisser, *Cognition and Reality: Principles and Implications of Cognitive Psychology* (New York, 1976).

56. Anatol Rapoport, *Fights, Games and Debates* (Ann Arbor, 1960).

57. Mark Snyder, B. H. Campbell, and E. Preston, "Testing Hypotheses about Human Nature: Assessing the Accuracy of Social Stereotypes," *Social Cognition*, I (1982), 256–272.

58. Lee Jussin, Tom E. Nelson, Melvin Manis, and Stan Soffin, "Prejudice, Stereotypes, and Labeling Effects and Sources of Bias in Person Perception," *Journal of Personality and Social Psychology*, LXVIII (1995), 228–246; Ann Maass, A. Milesi, S. Zabbini, and D. Stahlberg, "Linguistic Intergroup Bias: Differential Expectations or In-group Protection?" *Journal of Personality and Social Psychology*, LXVII (1995), 116–126.

59. Mahzarin Rustum Banaji and Roy Bhaskar, "Implicit Stereotypes and Memory: The Bounded Rationality of Social Beliefs," in D. L. Schacter and Elaine Scarry (eds.), *Memory, Brain, and Belief* (Cambridge, MA, 2000).

60. Gary V. Bodenhausen, "Stereotypic Biases in Social Decision Making and Memory: Testing Process Models," *Journal of Personality and Social Psychology*, LV (1988), 726–737.

61. Karl Weick, *The Social Psychology of Organizing* (New York, 1979).

62. Nisbett and Ross, *Human Inference.*

63. Ross and Ward, "Psychological Barriers."

64. Bodenhausen, "Stereotypic Biases."

65. Banaji and Bhaskar, "Implicit Stereotypes and Memory."

66. Marc Ross, *The Management of Conflict* (New Haven, 1993).

67. Rapoport, *Fights, Games and Debates.*

68. Daniel Bar-Tal, "From Intractable Conflict through Conflict Resolution to Reconciliation: Psychological Analysis," *Political Psychology*, XXI (2000), 351–365.

69. E.g. Daniel Bar-Tal, "Nature, Rationale and Effectiveness of Education for Coexistence," *Journal of Social Issues*, LX (2004), 253–271; Daniel Bar-Tal and Gemma

Bennink, "The Nature of Reconciliation as an Outcome and as a Process," in Yaacov Bar-Siman-Tov (ed.), *From Conflict Resolution to Reconciliation* (Oxford, 2004), 11–38;. Bar-Tal and Teichman, *Stereotypes and Prejudice;* Gavriel Salomon, "The Nature of Peace Education: Not All Programs Are Created Equal," in Gavriel Salomon and Baruch Nevo (eds.), *Peace Education: The Concept, Principles and Practices around the World* (Mahwah, NJ, 2002), 3–14; Salomon, "A Narrative-based View."

70. Bar-Tal, "From Intractable Conflict."

71. Bar-Tal and Teichman, *Stereotypes and Prejudice.*

72. Bar-Tal, "From Intractable Conflict"; Herbert C. Kelman, "Transforming the Relationship between Former Enemies: A Social-Psychological Analysis," in Robert. L. Rothstein (ed.), *After the Peace: Resistance and Reconciliation* (Boulder, 1999), 193–205.

73. Salomon, "The Nature of Peace Education."

74. Bar-Tal, "Societal Beliefs in Times of Intractable Conflict."

75. Priscilla B. Hayner, "In Pursuit of Justice and Reconciliation: Contributions of Truth Telling," in Cynthia J. Arnson (ed.), *Comparative Peace Processes in Latin America* (Stanford, 1999), 373.

76. Patrick Devine-Wright, "A Theoretical Overview of Memory and Conflicts," in Ed Cairns and Michael D. Roe (eds.), *The Role of Memory in Ethnic Conflict* (New York, 2003), 9–34.

77. Ifat Maoz, "Multiple Conflicts and Competing Agendas: A Framework for Conceptualizing Structural Encounters Between Groups in Conflict—the Case of a Coexistence Project of Jews and Palestinians in Israel," *Peace and Conflict: Journal of Peace Psychology,* VI (2000), 135–156.

78. Michael D. Roe and Ed Cairns, "Memories in Conflict: Review and a Look to the Future," in Cairns and Roe (eds.), *The Role of Memory in Ethnic Conflict,* 171–180.

79. P. Enslin, "The Truth and Reconciliation Commission as a Model of Peace Education," in Salomon and Nevo (eds.), *Peace Education,* 237–246; Dan Bar-On, "'The Other within Me:' Israel as a Laboratory of Condensed Interactions of Conflicts," paper presented at the Tenth Annual Conference of the International Association for Conflict Management, Koerber Foundation, Hamburg, Germany, June, 1999.

80. Dan Bar-On, "Conciliation through Storytelling: Beyond Victimhood," in Salomon and Nevo (eds.), *Peace Education,* 115.

81. Kader Asmal, Louise Asmal, and Ronald S. Roberts, *Reconciliation through Truth: A Reckoning of Apartheid's Criminal Governance* (Capetown, 1997); Wiseman Chirwa, "Collective Memory and the Process of Reconciliation and Reconstruction," *Development in Practice,* VII (1997), 479–482; Lily Gardner Feldman, "The Principle and Practice of 'Reconciliation' in German Foreign Policy: Relations with France, Israel, Poland and the Czech Republic," *International Affairs,* LXXV (1999), 333–356; Grahame Hayes, "We Suffer Our Memories: Thinking about the Past, Healing, and Reconciliation, *American Image,* LV (1998), 29–50; Hayner, *"In Pursuit of Justice and Reconcilia-*

tion"; John P. Lederach, *"Beyond Violence: Building Sustainable Peace,"* in Eugene Weiner (ed.), *The Handbook of Interethnic Coexistence* (New York, 1998), 236–245; Aletta J. Norval, "Memory, Identity and the (Im)possibility of Reconciliation: The Work of the Truth and Reconciliation Commission in South Africa," *Constellations,* V (1998), 250–265; Aletta J. Norval, "Truth and Reconciliation: The Birth of the Present and the Reworking of History," *Journal of African Studies,* XXV (1999), 499–519.

82. Charles Taylor, "The Politics of Recognition," in Amy Gutmann (ed.), *Multiculturalism: Examining the Politics of Recognition* (Princeton, 1994), 25–74, quote at 25.

83. Bar-Tal, "Societal Beliefs in Times of Intractable Conflict;" Salomon, "The Nature of Peace Education."

84. Salomon, "A Narrative-based View."

85. Marc Ross, " 'Good Enough' Isn't So Bad: Thinking of Success and Failure in Ethnic Conflict Management," *Journal of Peace Psychology,* VI (2000), 27–47.

86. E.g., Jean-Claude Abric, "A Structural Approach to Social Representation," in Kay Deaux and Gina Philogene (eds.), *Representations of the Social* (Oxford, 2001), 42–47.

87. I. Bar-Natan, "Meeting between Adversaries: Does Liking of the Other Individuals Generalize to Their Groups?" unpub. Ph.D. dissertation, Haifa University, 2004.

88. Ed Cairns and Miles Hewstone, "Northern Ireland: The Impact of Peacemaking in Northern Ireland on Intergroup Behavior," in Salomon and Nevo, *Peace Education,* 217–228.

89. Thomas F. Pettigrew, "Intergroup Contact Theory," in Janet T. Spence, John M. Darley, and D. J. Foss (eds.), *Annual Review of Psychology,* XLIX (1998), 65–85.

90. Ifat Maoz, "Is There Contact at All? Intergroup Interactions in Planned Contact Interventions between Jews and Arabs in Israel," *International Journal of Intercultural Relations,* XXVI (2002), 185–197; Bar-Natan, "Meeting Between Adversaries."

91. Yifat Biton, "Israeli and Palestinian's Understanding of 'Peace' as a Function of Their Participation in Peace Education Programs," unpub. Ph.D. dissertation, Haifa University, 2002.

92. Hayner, "In Pursuit of Justice and Reconciliation"; Jeffrey S. Kopstein, "The Politics of National Reconciliation: Memory and Institutions in German-Czech Relations since 1989," *Nationalism and Ethnic Politics,* III (1997), 57–78; Norval, "Truth and Reconciliation."

93. Asmal et al., *Reconciliation through Truth;* Hayes, "We Suffer Our Memories"; Aletta J. Norval, "Memory, Identity and the (Im)possibility of Reconciliation."

3

FORGING ZIONIST IDENTITY PRIOR TO 1948—AGAINST WHICH COUNTER-IDENTITY?

DINA PORAT

THERE IS A growing consensus that the identity of a group, whether a people or a nation, is forged not only from within but in relation to other groups against whom certain basic boundaries are defined. Indeed, part of the current widespread critique of Zionism focuses on its alleged historical failure or refusal to develop its identity vis-á-vis the counter identity of the Palestinian Arabs. While acknowledging the relative absence of this particular "other" in Zionist discourse, this chapter proposes that the real "other" decisive for Zionism were the diasporic Jews and everything they represented.

A 1995 collection of essays, *The Shaping of Israeli Identity—Myth, Memory, and Trauma*, mentions the presence of Arabs on 20 pages out of 238, and does so just en passant.[1] The author of a 1997 research project on *The Sabra—A Profile*, 480 pages long, dedicates 25 of them to the image of the Arab in the pre-1948 Hebrew high school textbooks.[2] The same number of pages mentions Arab nationalism in the classic, *The Making of Modern Zionism*.[3] The 1998 issue of *Israel Affairs*, entitled "In Search of Identity: Jewish Aspects in Israeli Culture," does not mention an Arab impact on the identity dilemma.[4]

In *Story of My Life*, Dayan described the moment that he understood the complexity of the situation: on the one hand he spoke Arabic and as a youngster had close, sometimes even friendly, relations with his Bedouin neighbors (Arab-el-Mazarib) who lived close to Nahalal, the first Hebrew *moshav*—a collective agricultural settlement—in the valley of Jezreel. His father tried to instill in him the belief that Arabs were inferior and robbers and killers, but he "liked their ways of life, appreciated them as workers, tied to the land, engraved in the landscape surrounding me. I had no doubt we could live peacefully with them."[5] When, in the beginning of the 1930s, murders of Jews by the Ez el-Adin el-Kassam underground occurred in the valley, Dayan rode on his horse to the elders of the el-Mazarib. The admiration of the elders for the "Kassamiye" murderers, whom they depicted as idealists and modest, pious individuals, motivated by deep religious and national feelings, made Dayan understand the "national, religious and emotional abyss between the Arabs and Zionists; it divides even when it is hidden from the eye."[6] His daughter said: "My grandparents on my mother's side spoke fluent Arabic, as the family had lived in Jerusalem, and had close relations with Arab lawyers, merchants and certainly with neighbors."[7]

The tone of the former examples ranges from patronizing through dismissive to understanding. Meir Ariel, a famous Israeli singer, added a tone of acknowledgment, defining the impact of Arab presence with the following line: "at the end of each Israeli popular song, there sits an Arab with a narghile [a Middle Eastern smoking pipe]." One should take into consideration that popular songs, especially when sung in groups, are a decades-long characteristic of Israeli culture, perhaps replacing prayers.[8]

It is this chapter's proposition that Zionist identity—from its inception at the end of the nineteenth century to the establishment of the state of Israel in 1948, that is, over three generations—was not forged in opposition to the Arab population residing in Palestine or Palestina (as it was termed under the Ottomans and as Palestina–Eretz Israel, as termed later under the British Mandate). The local population will be referred to as Arabs, since the term "Palestinians" emerged in the post–1948 era. The definition used for "national identity" follows Smith, *The Nation in History*, which offers a solution for the current scholarly debate on the beginnings of nations by acknowledging the impact of early history rather than its continuity—of long historical processes that bring about gradual changes rather than a sudden or artificial birth of a nation. Smith's method acknowledges, especially, the "ethno-symbolic" components, such as myth and collective memory, that connect the present to the past. Smith's theory best fits the Zionist movement as a national phenomenon. Disregarding the history of the Jewish people, he maintains, equals disregard for the basis of the Jewish nation and state: "its name, location, language, its Law of Return, memories, symbols, values, its myths and traditions."[9] Components of national identity such as language, self-perception, and identification with values, past events, and ethnic characteristics should therefore be at the center of discussion.

To substantiate this assumption, one must first examine sources reflecting the ideas and opinions of the forefathers of Zionism regarding the Arab population, and Zionist political and intellectual leaders' quest for the ingredients needed to build a new Jewish person. Then, if indeed the assumption proves valid, and only few traces are found in these sources attesting to the Arab presence as a source for identity, one needs to ask why.

The accumulated source materials and research concerning the relations between Jews and Arabs as of the 1880s, when the modern Jewish settlement in Palestine began, are vast in scope and variety. Regarding primary source material, a recent introduction to a collection of essays concludes that "all the authors refute the widespread contention [that] . . . save for small and marginal groups within it—[the Zionist movement] did not take into account the Arabs dwelling in Eretz Israel and ignored the 'Arab question' altogether" and that therefore "the possibility of mutual understanding between the two nationalist movements was precluded."[10]

Taking into consideration Ettinger and colleagues' counter-contention, it is my second assumption that most of the references in early Zionist writings to the Arab population deal with the conflict between the two parties and mainly with the political–military–geographical aspects of that conflict. From today's point of view, only a surprisingly small part of that material considers the presence of the Arabs as a factor in the internal debate among Zionists about who they were or wished to be, and who they were not and certainly did not wish to be. The underlying reasons that produced so few references are not to be found necessarily in an ill will that the Zionist movement harbored against the Arab local population but in the circumstances of Zionist creation.[11] The diversity and multiplicity of streams and polemics always present in Jewish public life—and Zionism is no exception—are reflected in the differing intensities by which the possible impact of Arabs on Zionist identity was considered.

The First Stage: 1880 to 1918

There were 24,000 Jews in the country in 1880, and 525,000 Arabs, a proportion of 1:22 (compared to a 1:40 proportion in 1800, with 6700 Jews and 268,000 Arabs). In Jerusalem there were 14,000 Jews and 10,000 Arabs. In 1915, there were about 90,000 Jews and 590,000 Arabs, a proportion of 1:6–7, with 46,000 Jews in Jerusalem, 10,000 Muslims, and 16,000 Christians.[12] The country, when looked at from Europe at that time, seemed desolate, wild, sparsely populated, and ruled by a capricious, oriental regime—a risky venture for Jews.

Noteworthy among the pre-1880 Zionist thinkers was Hess, a theorist of socialism and later of the Jewish national movement. He published *Rome and Jerusalem: The Last National Problem* (1862), under the influence of the European national liberation movements. Foreseeing the downfall of the Ottoman Empire, he suggested the establishment of a Jewish commonwealth in Palestine, and "a re-establishment of Arab states in Egypt and Syria."[13] "Thus," says Avineri, "decades before the emergence of an active Arab national movement, Hess's universalistic nationalism leads him to become one of the first to call for both Jewish independence and Arab national self-determination."[14] Hess did not visit the Middle East nor did he comment on Arab culture or identity as related to that of Jews. The other "Foretellers of Zionism" who followed in the 1860s and 1870s, such as Rabbi Yehuda Hai Alkalai, Rabbi Zvi Hirsch Kalischer, Peretz Smolenskin, Moshe Leib Lilienblum, and Yehuda Leib Pinsker, author of *Autoemancipation,* one of the Zionist founding texts, mentioned the Arab population in Palestine in a few sentences or not at all.[15]

Among those who did visit the new Jewish settlements in Palestine and set pen to paper upon returning to Europe in order to share impressions with the Jewish public was Ahad Ha'am, (meaning "One of the People," a pen name of Asher Ginsberg), a brilliant essayist and political philosopher who preached cultural-spiritual Zionism. Following his 1891 visit, he wrote "Truth from the Land of Israel," an often quoted reproach. He admired the achievements of the first settlers, yet at the same time was aware of the existence of an Arab population, and, much like Hess thirty years before him, foresaw a possibility that an Arab-Palestinian national movement would be established. "We tend to believe abroad that Palestina is nowadays almost completely deserted, a non-cultivated wilderness [...] we tend to believe abroad that all Arabs are desert barbarians, an asinine people who does not see or understand what is going on around them. This is a cardinal mistake. The Arab, like all Semites, has a sharp mind and is full of cunning." He warned his readers that the Arab local population would react against the settlers once it felt threatened, and then "will not easily give up its place." Moreover, he scolded settlers who contended that the only language that Arabs understood was that of force. He advocated treating the locals with "love and respect, justly and rightly," because they do indeed respect fortitude but only if coupled with justice. Otherwise, they might, in the long run, prove vengeful.[16]

Ahad Ha'am's essay, published upon his return to Europe, seems to be the first attempt to understand the identity of the local population, its self-esteem and character traits, and compares Arabs to Jews ("like all Semites"). It should be noted that he pinpointed, even during a short visit, the necessity to recognize dignity and honor as central values in Arab culture. As a result, he became the sharpest critic of the cruelty or humiliation perpetrated by some of the settlers toward Arabs, claiming that their behavior deviated from the lessons taught by Jewish history: they should have practiced "love and respect, justly and rightly."

The settlers of the first Aliyah immigrated to Israel beginning in 1882, both as a reaction to the pogroms in southern Russia and as a fulfillment of Zionist aspirations. Upon settling in the country, when they owned a piece of land of their own, and when Arabs worked for them, they were carried away by a new sense of freedom from their former European yoke. During that process, claimed Ahad Ha'am, some of them forgot Jewish and biblical codes of behavior toward "the stranger [or native] at your gates."[17]

It follows that the Arabs should have had, according to this assessment, a role in fortifying the settlers' Jewish identity, by forcing them—by their very presence—to practice, or at least to contemplate, these codes. Ahad Ha'am's moral and personal stature among the first Zionists, especially the groups of "Hovevei Zion" (Lovers of Zion) in Russia, who initiated his trip and from whom some of the first settlers originated, added weight to such warnings.

Ten years later, in 1902, Herzl, founder of political Zionism, published his *Altneuland* (Old new land), a utopian futuristic novel describing life in the "New Society"—an imaginary Jewish cooperative commonwealth prevailing in Palestine in 1923. This society sought to incorporate the best of all worlds. Herzl's utopia was described as clean, well-organized, democratic, open-minded, and modern—much more modern than was 1902 Europe.[18] Herzl, aware of the presence of an Arab local population, offered a utopian solution: Arab individuals would be welcome in the New Society as citizens with equal rights. Indeed, a central protagonist in the novel is Raschid Bey, whose education combined the best of Arab and Muslim traditions and manners with the scientific knowledge and liberal values of Europe. A member of the New Society, he often praised the many benefits Arabs enjoyed thanks to the development of the country by Jewish immigrants.

This thoroughly humanistic and universalistic yet somewhat naïve picture is flawed by two elements: first, clearly it was Raschid Bey who had to modify his culture and identity so as to be admitted into the New Society, the rules of which were formulated by the Jewish majority. "More than premeditating the relations between Jews and Arabs in Palestine, Herzl's mind was set on the relations between these Jews and the countries from which they came," claims Shapira.[19] Second, although Arabs are admitted as individuals whose rights are guaranteed, Herzl's vision does not include them as a group. "The issue of an Arab national movement never crossed his mind," states Avineri, much as the idea had not yet crossed that of the ruling Ottomans, the Western powers, or even the Arabs themselves. It had not yet become an issue.[20] Indeed, Hess wrote about Arab nationalism as fulfilled outside Palestine, in Syria and Egypt, and Ahad Ha'am's essay warned that a national movement might start somewhere in the future as a reaction to Jewish presence. When Herzl wrote his novel, the signs of a national awakening were still too embryonic to be regarded as a primary consideration. More central is that an Arab presence was not mentioned at all in Herzl's "The Jewish State," the 1896 booklet that mobilized Zionism into a political movement, and which is considered its founding text.[21]

"A Hidden Question" is the title of another frequently quoted essay, by Epstein (1907). He advocated the purchase of only unpopulated lands, and the cultivation only of those considered unworthy, so as not to wrong poor *fellahin,* land tenants and field laborers. Epstein disregarded the fact that those responsible for the fellahin's conditions were the *effendis,* the landowners, who lived in Arab capitals off the sweat of their subordinates. Moreover, he reproached his fellow settlers for forgetting that "the people living . . . here has a sensitive heart and a loving soul. The Arab, much as any other person, is strongly attached to his land." But Arabs proved helpless to change their poverty and remove their ignorance. Only Jews could build schools, hospitals, libraries, and cheap kitchens for Arabs. Thus "two ancient Semite nations, gifted and looking for a [better] future," would complement each other.[22]

Epstein was not the only one holding such opinions. Menachem Ussishkin, a prominent Zionist leader originating in Hovevei Zion and later holding central positions in Palestine, followed the same line, wishing to rehabilitate not only Arab bodies but Arab souls as well. This wish was motivated by his feeling that before World War I, when he visited Palestine, thanks to the Zionist enterprise, he could not detect any rapprochement between the two cultures. Therefore he advocated bringing, "our brothers, of the same race, a true culture . . . and bring[ing] back to life their spiritual, not only the[ir] material, life."[23] Leo Motzkin (also a Hovevei Zion leader); settlers of the Petach Tikva (the first *moshav,* a non-collective settlement of farmers); Rabbi Benyamin; Yosef Lurie, a teacher and educator; Nissim Malul, a Sephardic journalist; Haim Margaliyot Kalvaryski; and other activists who spoke and wrote about coming close to Arab culture and language, and even about intermarriage (Benyamin) or complete integration in the Arab culture (Malul, a rare case)—all had contradicting concerns. They were aware of the paternalist, even missionary nature of their suggestions. Their intention was not to convert the Arabs to Judaism but rather to help them find their Arab identity (Epstein) and improve it with modernity and cleanliness. Conversely, most of them were worried that such a closeness would endanger the Jewish culture and values. Yet, all acknowledged the presence of the Arab population, and warned: "We have completely forgotten that there are Arabs here [. . .] as if they did not exist."[24]

The Second Stage: 1917–1929

The first British Mandatory census in 1922 registered 83,790 Jews, 589,177 Muslims, and 71,464 Christians. There were about 34,000 Jews in Jerusalem compared to about 13,400 Muslims and 14,700 Christians. These numbers, slightly lower than before, were a result of expulsions by the Ottoman rulers during World War I. Despite at least three violent Arab attacks that took place in 1920–1921, the Zionist movement entertained cautious hopes that, under a British umbrella, immigration to and development of the country would continue and lower the resistance of the Arab population, who would eventually realize the benefits of Zionism. Indeed, the years after 1921 and before 1929 were relatively calm, and allowed political, and sometimes social, contact between Zionist and Arab leaders.

Goldmann, later president of the Zionist World Organization, visited Palestine and published his impressions in an essay entitled "The Arab Question in the Land of Israel" in 1924, quoting local Jews who asked him: "Who are the Arabs [. . .] who sees or notices them . . . An Arab question does not exist at all. It is some kind of a hoax."[25] He thought that there was still, and would be for many years to come, enough space for the two people, and was concerned about such attitudes of Jews. If violence broke out, it would be because Jews ignored the Arabs, instead of understanding that they, the Jews, as the better-educated party, should wisely build relations with their local neighbors.

Goldmann broached an issue of major importance—the language barrier: almost none of the Zionist leaders, educated in Europe, studied Arabic. (Moshe Shertok, later Sharett and first foreign minister, whose parents decided to live for a few years in an Arab village, was one of the few who did.) But some Jewish settlers knew Arabic and used it to communicate with the Arab workers, as did the Sephardic communities and families living in the mixed holy cities—Jerusalem, Safed, Tiberias, and Hebron—before 1880. Members of Hashomer—the Guard—a group of a few dozen persons, founded in 1909 and dedicated to armed self-defense, adopted local habits and attire, mainly those of the Bedouin and Druze, because they were considered fighters. Because of their efforts to appreciate Arab customs (such as having special rooms for Arab guests, reciprocating hospitality) they were accused of "orientalism."[26] Arabs did not master European languages or the Hebrew spoken by the settlers. The absence of a common language created an abyss that exists today, when most Israelis cannot communicate in Arabic.

Goldmann did not refer to the reasons that led to this situation—reasons connected to culture, identity, and self-perception. He pointed to everyday life, to human relations that simply could not develop without a common language, and to the limitations of the Zionist leadership in explaining itself to the local population. "Why don't we have newspapers in Arabic, that could disseminate our real intentions and plans," asked Goldmann, warning that the educated Christian Arabs, who led the opposition to Zionism, owned the presses, while the poor Muslim majority had none. The lack of such a basic means of communication, concluded Goldmann, could be explained only by the light-headedness and dangerous indifference exercised toward the "Arab question."[27] Although correct, Goldmann overlooked one aspect: the enormous efforts needed in order to revive ancient Hebrew and make it a natural part of modern life in the country, and the struggles within the Yishuv (the Jewish community in Eretz Israel) that amounted to a "cultural war" against Yiddish and German brought from Europe.

An argument often raised by those preaching a moral, humane attitude toward Arabs, such as Ahad Ha'am, Epstein, and others, was a variation of the commandment: "and therefore shall thy camp be holy."[28] In other words, moral and humane behavior are required first for one's own sake, for the purity needed to keep one's camp united and led by common values. "The Arab question is, after all," wrote Goldmann, "a Jewish question," a test case of the morality and humane values within Jewish society.[29] That argument became relevant again in 1928, when the British Mandatory government sought to establish a legislative council common to Jews and Arabs. The latter rejected the idea, as they had rejected all suggestions for a political arrangement during the British Mandate. Nonetheless, it spurred a stormy debate among Zionists. Leibovitch, a Hebrew university scholar, raging prophet, and voice of moral stature reacted: Zionism needed the tools of a nation-state only if they joined its immanent universal and Jewish values. Under certain conditions, he claimed, Zionism could renounce some components of political life and still maintain its essence. Only when acting on a basis of complete parity could Zionism claim its rights with full moral strength.[30]

Scholem, a researcher of the Kabbalah, also took part in the debate, as an individual and as a member of Brith Shalom (a covenant of peace), a small political movement founded by intellectuals in 1925. He suggested that it was a grave mistake to assume that a very long time would elapse before local Arabs reached a high degree of political development and of self-governance. "[We] forget, how quickly analphabets study in Arab Palestine, and how much the Fellah is interested in education for his child [. . .] and in political issues."[31] Two years after he wrote this assessment, the British Mandate census revealed that 940 out of 1,000 Jewish men over the age of 21 were literate compared to 219 Arabs, and 753 Jewish women compared to 18 Arab women.[32] His own impressions sustained his ideas: Zionists invented two scarecrows—the ignorant fellah and the egoist effendi, and neither image held, since the fellahin were gradually changing. Scholem, like Leibovitch, advocated that the Jews in Palestine should pull themselves together, renounce such false images, and return to their original morals, for their own sake.

Such ideas were central to the Brith Shalom, whose slogan called for a binational state based on complete parity and a common Jewish–Arab political platform. The small group of about sixty members and a hundred sympathizers included Zionist activists such as Arthur Rupin, its first leader, scholars such as Martin Buber, and immigrants from Germany. Both Rupin and Buber, although the latter in less emphatic terms, spoke about a new Middle Eastern community created from a merging of Jews, Arabs, and Armenians. The movement's press dealt extensively with similar issues.[33] These ideas were very much opposed by most other Zionist factions. Nonetheless, during the 1920s, many Zionist spokesmen, including opponents of Brith Shalom, described the fine moral and intellectual traits of the Arabs as a basis for cooperation. But these verbal declarations did not contradict the practical notion that Zionism should go its own way, building as much as possible until a solution was found.[34]

The Third Stage: 1930–1948

In 1931, there were 174,000 Jews, 760,000 Muslims, and 88,000 Christians, a proportion of 1:5. About 51,000 Jews lived in Jerusalem compared to about 20,000 Muslims and 19,300 Christians. The proportion changed drastically in 1935, with the escape of Jews from Nazi Germany, to 1:2.6, with 355,000 Jews and 940,000 Arabs, both Muslims and Christians. In 1947 the proportion reached 1:2, about 600,000 Jews and a 1.3 million Arabs. The notion that with the development of the country Arabs were bound eventually to consent to Jewish presence gradually gave way to the recognition that the more the Zionist enterprise grew, the more Arab objections would be fortified.

During the 1930s, with the Jewish population increasing thanks to immigration and to the growing number of sabras (those born in Eretz Israel), the education system crystallized. The increasingly violent means used by the Arab resistance changed the image of Arabs and alienated sabras. Formerly romanticized images, such as the "noble savage," or the brave free Bedouin as an antithesis to the diasporic Jew, had in any case been fostered by few Zionist newcomers even before the 1930s. Such images were replaced by those of an underdeveloped society that refused to benefit from Jewish innovations, and of cruel killers of women and children, especially following the 1929 riots in Hebron and Safed, two mixed cities where Jews and Arabs had been neighbors for centuries.

Hebrew school textbooks included very little material about Arab culture and history or about Islam and its traditions. The Arab language was taught, but with little emphasis. There were no excursions into the country—a beloved must for schools and youth movements—that permitted encounters with local Arab youth, and there was hardly any mention of life together in the same school or settlement. Alienation was physical as much as it was mental. "The textbooks show that the main impact [on the pupil] originated not from what they told him about the Arab and his culture, but rather from what he was not told. More than the Arab was described as negative or positive—he was pushed into a forlorn corner, and sometimes was practically wiped out of consciousness." Even as enemies they were not regarded in concrete terms, wrote Almog in his research on sabras.[35] Sabras, free of their parents' inhibitions, growing up away from Europe, had no room for the Arabs in their world. It was as if Arabs did not exist. Even later, Shapira wrote, before the 1948 war, Arabs played a marginal role in the public eye, "not hated, not loved, not taken into consideration—part of the landscape."[36] Nonetheless, the presence and impact of some of the Dayan/Alon generation of sabra, who later became commanders and fighters in their twenties in 1948, especially in the Palmach elite units, and who knew the locals intimately, should be acknowledged.

In 1937, Lord Peel's Palestine Royal Commission published a 400-page report. As an exemplary work of research and analysis, it spared no one—not Arabs, Jews, or Britons. "We did not expect," admitted the commission members, "to find so wide a gulf between them [Arabs and Jews] or one so difficult to bridge." The Commission explained: "With every year that passes, the contrast between this intensely democratic and highly organized modern community and the old-fashioned Arab world around it grows sharper, and in nothing, perhaps, more markedly than on its cultural side."[37] Here the report showers compliments on the literature, science, university, and music developed by the Jewish newcomers, yet criticizes their educational system for being "an instrument of Jewish nationalism"—one that fastens the child's mind before all else on being proud of the traditions and achievements of the Jewish people, and on rebuilding a Jewish nation in its ancient homeland.[38] Arabs, the report continues, "hardly come into the picture except when they force an entry with violence and bloodshed." The average Jew went about his work and tried to forget about Arabs. In some of the old farmers' settlements, there used to be some sense of kinship and comradeship that came from working side by side with Arabs, but little was left of that feeling by the time the report was written, and it was hardly ever shared by more modern, Western-minded Jews. "It has long been obvious," the commission stated bluntly, "that the notion of a cultural 'assimilation' between Arab and Jew is a fantasy."[39]

A major question stems from the three stages of relations with Arabs. Were those leaders who did discuss or mention a possibility that the Arab presence might affect Zionist identity marginal to the mainstream? Obviously they came from all hues of the political and intellectual spectrum and did not share a common denominator. The many polemics, tendencies, and even one-man factions that characterized Zionism did not allow for an obligatory canonized mainstream. "Zionism is a family name," said Oz, and, as in any family, all kinds of relatives are embraced, including those who are in strong disagreement with each other: Polish-romantic, nationalist, mystified Zionism, Russian–Tolstoyian–Narodnik, middle-class, Marxist, religious-messianic, religious non-messianic, and quasi-fascist—altogether "a federation of dreams."[40] With all due respect to Oz, there was a Zionist consensus shared by a mainstream, whose parts agreed at least on the general outline of the movement: Zionism was characterized by constant criticism and opposition coming even from within the consensus. This dispute, according to Kovner, is "a cornerstone in the culture of the Jewish people."[41]

Although there is no common denominator for all those who advocated accepting or acknowledging an impact of Arab presence on Zionist identity, a number of common lines exist: those who did not regard the establishment of a political Zionist entity as a primary goal were more prone to come closer to the Arab culture. So was Brith Shalom, whose political convictions certainly turned its members into outsiders. Additionally, many of them came from Germany whereas most of the Yishuv came from eastern Europe. Goldmann held a longstanding debate with David Ben-Gurion because he regarded the Jewish diaspora as no less important than a state, and because he tried his hand at

independent peace initiatives. Both issues, and his personal non-socialist conduct in times of general austerity, made him a permanent outsider in the eyes
of the local leadership. At least three (Ussishkin, Motzkin, and Ahad Ha'am)
came from the Hovevei Zion circles, and not all of them were sure about a fully
attributed political entity, certainly not Ahad Ha'am, who always advocated a
spiritual-cultural center in the Land of Israel. Epstein and Lurie were educators, who, much as Leibowitz (always an opponent of Hassidism and a member
of the moral opposition) were concerned about Jewish and universal values.

We should not assume that these men all regarded the rapprochement with
Arabs as a test for public morality. A number of Zionist leaders, whose goal was
a Jewish state, spoke on formal and non-formal occasions—most notably during the Zionist congresses—about integrating into the Semite East, about the
fine traditions and character of Arabs, and on the need to regard them as human beings and as a part of the common local heritage. The Zionist attitude
toward Arabs was not then a matter of disputed consensus, or a challenge to
values, but rather an expression of personal opinion.

The influence that some of these leaders and thinkers still exercise on Israeli
education and public discourse has no correlation either to the number or
length of opinions that they once expressed about Arabs. Ahad Ha'am, representing one extreme, is still very much at the center of teaching and historiography, as is Herzl, at the other end of the spectrum. Goldmann managed to
maintain a central position despite being an enfant terrible. Apparently the
weight and importance of Zionist leaders originated elsewhere. More important is why did Zionists rarely mention Arabs as a cultural and social entity
who could have had a bearing on the evolving Zionist identity? Was it, Laqueur
asked, "a case of real, if astonishing blindness?"[42] Attempts to explain this phenomenon must be rooted in the context of time and place, and not influenced
by current realities.

Gorny, in speaking about the intentional effort to build a separate Jewish national society surrounded by political, social, economic, cultural, and
even military walls, concluded: "these walls seemed a necessary condition for
the growth and strengthening of the Jewish society, due to the feelings of
weakness—not arrogance—that a public feels in its first steps as a national
community."[43] Gorny was referring to the very beginnings of Jewish settlement, when its achievements were still miniscule and its very existence doubtful. Moreover, he emphasized, skirmishes between Jewish and Arab villagers
resembled events in many other distant areas of the Ottoman Empire, where
the inhabitants' safety was not at all guaranteed.[44] The skirmishes, therefore,

could have been considered at the time as not necessarily specific to Arab–Jewish relations or as decisively bearing on the future of those relations.

The fragile structure of the Ottoman Empire in its last stages was another reason why the Zionists paid little heed to the Arabs. Such aspirations were supposed to find their solution in Greater Syria and Egypt. Chaim Weitzman, president of the Zionist World Organization, tried to reach an agreement with the Arab national movement immediately after World War I. He proposed that the Zionists would acknowledge Arab national rule in Syria in exchange for Syria's renunciation of Palestine. That idea remained popular in Eretz Israel, and other such attempts to realize an agreement followed Weizman's.[45] In a recent essay the Jewish–American intellectual Herzberg went one step further. No one, he claimed, regarded the half million inhabitants of Palestine at the end of the nineteenth century as anything but a small and insignificant part of Arab society at large. Their cultural centers were always elsewhere: in Egypt, Syria, and Iraq. That is why Zionists claimed that most Arabs could ignore the Jewish settlement: "The fact that they are not given sovereignty over [this] land does not have an imminent effect on the culture of the Arabs at large and on their self-esteem."[46] Thus Avineri explained Herzl's lack of awareness of Arab national aspirations as occurring "at a time when neither the ruling Ottomans nor the Western powers nor even the Arab population itself were aware of its imminence."[47] When both Pinsker and Herzl were writing their manifestos, they were not as sure as they were later that Palestine was indeed the only place for Jews. They had contemplated other solutions for the Jewish people. This fundamental issue had to be resolved before tending to the "Arab question." Moreover, reestablishing a lost Jewish national dignity, and making European gentiles respect it, was much higher on their immediate agenda.[48]

Shapira maintained that recognizing the presence of a competing national movement meant understanding that an unavoidable collision would occur in the future. "Such a recognition was impossible for a public that constituted [in the early 1920s] some 10 percent of the general population."[49] Weakness made Zionists ignore the signs that an Arab national movement would strengthen in the future, and instead choose a peaceful, humanist, and especially socialist perspective. The further Arab society advanced, the greater likelihood for peace, or so the Zionist leaders thought. The socialists especially believed that the violent Arabs, like the Russian *pogromchik*, needed first to be part of world progress. Judging Arabs, their culture, and desires by a European and mainly East European yardstick was naive. Yet it played "a most important role on the educational level, advocating a human—though paternalist—attitude to the

Arab, avoiding hostility and contempt."[50] Shapira emphasized the socialist ideology brought about by the East European settlers, who wished to avoid exploiting the Arab proletariat by creating a new Jewish society and economy that would exist alongside, rather than replacing, the Arab society and thus avoid clashes between the two.

Together with the political and ideological context of the time were the intentional efforts to circumvent demographic reality. The country, as described by early Zionist historiography, seemed mostly barren. "Emptiness and desolation were connected to the absence of a people," wrote Bartal.[51] It was thought that redemption from the flawed diaspora could be achieved through an organic connection to the land, and to those living on it. Bartal was referring to Ben-Gurion and Ben-Zvi, later, respectively, the first prime minister and the second president of Israel, who subsequently published their research on the historical origins of Arab fellahin at the end of World War I. According to them, fellahin descended from the ancient Hebrews, and their impact was evident in the language, traditions, customs, and place names. Fellahin preferred conversion to exile from the cherished land, and thus maintained a continuity of Jewish presence in the country, especially in the Galilee and Judea, mostly in the Hebron area. The two authors did not ignore the locals, Bartal claimed, but instead turned them into a part of their own Jewish history. European non-Jewish scholars and researchers had already considered the same idea from the nineteenth century, and Hebrew University anthropologists followed in the 1930s.[52] This theory, which gained few followers, was marginalized in later Zionist historiography, and would have had an even smaller impact had its two initiators in Palestine been of lesser fame.

Zionist historiography followed a similar pattern. Local Arabs were an issue for research during the British Mandate, "but as a study of a neighboring society per se, rather than in the context of its relations with the Yishuv society," claimed Gelber. Relations with the Arabs, he continued, were discussed in textbooks and monographs but always as a secondary issue, while the main concern was the political and military struggle for the realization of the Zionist plans. "In that regard," he went on, "the historiography of Zionism reflects the understanding of Zionist policy makers, that London, and later New York and Washington, would decide the fate of the Zionist enterprise, and not Baghdad, Damascus, Cairo, or Nablus. The thrust of the historiographical effort, much [like] the political one, was tied to Britain, and relations with Arabs occupied but a marginal space." Focusing on relations with the British further reduced space for discussing the Arab influence.[53]

The absence of Arabs from school textbooks was based on politics, Almog claimed; talking about a problem enhanced the need to solve it. The textbooks reflected the newcomers' intense focus on their own affairs, even to the point of viewing the Arab presence as accidental, and therefore temporary, merely a peripheral matter.[54] Amnon Raz-Krakotzkin agreed and carried the argument further: "the Arabs were actively cast out of memory . . . their existence was mentioned, but not as part of the historical discourse." The end result matched the goal, he claimed, that of emptying the country, and assessing its original demographic and cultural character as irrelevant. He also reported, interestingly enough, that the first settlers did not regard the country as empty; they simply did not perceive the locals as carriers of consciousness and history.[55]

The origins of Zionist identity are based in the need to draw a clear distinction between Zionism and earlier forms of diasporic existence: Zionist identity was forged and fostered vis-á-vis the Jewish diaspora. The Zionist movement was created as a way to solve the miseries of the Jewish situation in the diaspora by returning to the land of Israel and thus opening a new page in history. This process necessitated severing all ties to the past, denigrating the diasporic Jews and their characteristics, and glorifying the bravery of the new Jews.

Since Zionism began, the "negation of the diaspora" has undergone many changes; most notably it has become more moderate, but it has also become tied to later Israeli attitudes toward other groups within the population.[56] These changes, and the extensive academic and public debate aroused by them, are beyond the scope of this chapter. But the Arab population living in Palestine at the end of the nineteenth century was outside the Zionist effort to disconnect itself from the diaspora, and had no bearing at all on the painful relations between Zionism and diasporic Jews.

Diasporic Jewry was a conglomerate of opinions and factions. Zionism, which was emerging with the development of Hebrew culture in nineteenth-century Europe, had two particular obstacles to deal with. One was the flourishing of Yiddish culture which gave birth to a rich body of literature and poetry, educational systems, research, and a press, all posing serious competition to the parallel reemergence of Hebrew. A second problem was the increasing numbers of Jews of universal rather than national orientation who either left Judaism in general or abandoned their communities in particular to assimilate into the surrounding societies. Among them were rationalist *maskilim* (learned secular Jews), liberal non-Zionist nationalists, socialists, and Marxists. All were no less vehement than Zionism in negating the diaspora and describing Jewish existence as humiliating, insulting, and depressing. First and foremost they turned against the traditional Jewish way of life and its leadership. According to Gorny, when Zionist Jews immigrated to Palestine they brought with them their anxieties about this double danger—the rivaling rich Yiddish culture and the competing lure of a universal solution for humanity at large. "The conclusion was a maximal separation between the resurrecting Hebrew culture and [the] Arab culture" in order to avoid the potential of a third competing society.[57]

The Holocaust enhanced these problematic relations. Until 1948 the self-perception of the Yishuv was one of an avant-garde offering the only possible solution and haven for the Jewish people in general. Therefore it was in charge of rescuing European Jewry. Following the Holocaust, and facing the meager results of its rescue efforts, Zionist leadership had to find ways to maintain their identity as rescuers. They also needed to be in the avant-garde. The first could be achieved by organizing the survivors on their way to Eretz Israel. The second could follow a convenient depiction of European Jewry as if divided into two main categories: the few who fought back, motivated by their Zionist prewar education, and the majority who did not, because they were overwhelmed by Nazi might and could not resist physically under the unprecedented circumstances created during the war. Those who fought back understood that the essence of Zionism was the wish to take one's fate in one's own hands, and therefore could become part and parcel of the Yishuv in spirit. The second group, despite the grief of their plight, could become a collective embodiment of a diasporic Jew, a mirror image of the fate from which Zionism tried to escape. But attitudes in the Yishuv toward the resistance and the survival of European Jews during the Holocaust kept changing.[58] The Holocaust complicated Zionism-diasporic relationships even further.

A second component of Zionist identity was the European origin of most of the Jewish newcomers, and their roots in a continent imbued with culture, traditions, science, and aesthetics to which Jews had abundantly contributed for more than 2000 years. In terms of numbers, three-quarters of the newcomers between 1914 and 1945, and 90 percent in the 1930s, were born and raised in Europe.[59] Jewish immigrants coming from Europe to build a modern homeland perceived that the discrepancy between them and local Arabs, natives of an underdeveloped area, was too deep to make Arabs even their adverse partner for identity, as the Peel Commission had emphatically stated. *Arabers* ("Arabs" in Yiddish and German) was a term pejoratively used by Jews, and especially by well-educated ladies who immigrated from large European cities, to air their frustration when confronted with the heat, flies, sand, and camels ridden by biblically dressed locals. When told that Muslims were relatives of the Jews and therefore could not be the adversary, Ze'ev Zabotinsky, leader of the Zionist revisionist movement retorted: "Ishmael is not our uncle. We belong, thank God, to Europe and during 2000 years we helped create its culture."[60] "We will not become Asians, culturally and anthropologically inferior, much as the Anglo-Saxons did not become Indians in North America, Hottentots in South Africa and members of the Papua tribes in Australia," declared Max Nordau at the Eighth Zionist Congress in 1907. He was trying to refute the claim that the return to Palestine meant the uprooting of Jews from Western culture only to have them sink into the primitive Middle East.[61] Nordau's answer was rooted in the zeitgeist of nineteenth-century Europe, when the superiority of the white man as the source of culture and enlightenment for the world at large was "unquestionable."

"The Orient was almost a European invention," wrote Said in his introduction to *Orientalism*, which he defined as "a way of coming to terms with the Orient that is based on the Orient's special place in European Western experience. The Orient is [. . .] the source of [Europe's] civilizations and languages, its cultural contestant, and one of its deepest and most recurring images of the Other." In another, later introduction, he added that "the existence and development of every culture need the existence of a different and competing alter-ego."[62] Although a very tempting theory, orientalism, according to Said's definition, is not in accordance with Zionist–Arab relations; the other, the different and competing alter ego, was not the Arab, but the diasporic Jew, against whom Zionism was created. The Orient in the Zionist idea was not at all a European invention; it was rather the location of an ancient homeland, a sound historical and geographic reality.

Said could be of great use to post-Zionists in today's debates. They regard Zionism as a variant of European colonialism, and hence treat the Orient and its Arab population from a European standpoint. A recent similar theory claimed that a double consciousness, both Zionist and colonial, marked a two-way attitude toward Sephardic and oriental Jews: Zionists deemed Sephardim as part of the national general effort, whereas the colonialists depicted them as the ethnic "other" in European and hence in Zionist self-definition, much like Arabs. But Zionism did not define itself vis-á-vis Sephardic Jews before 1948, when their numbers in the country were small. Indeed, Shenhav, who advocated this theory, dedicated most of his research to post-1948 developments.[63] Most Israeli historians do not accept the attribution of colonialism to Zionism, and point at the strong Orthodox Jewish—not necessarily Zionist—identity that Sephardic Jews maintained when surrounded by Arab society before 1948 in Palestine and in Muslim countries. The idea of integrating into an Arab society equals heresy for Orthodox Sephardic Jews.[64]

The third strand of Zionist identity is the participation of Jews in revolutionary movements, especially the East European leftist ones in the beginning of the twentieth century, and later the deep admiration for the Soviet Union, fostered in left-socialist circles. Their small number in the Jewish population notwithstanding, some of these persons were leaders in the Yishuv, and the sources of some of the ideals that shaped the identity and consciousness of mainstream Jews. Their self-perception was one of "*metaknei olam,*" those righting the wrongs of society in the world at large—of individuals dedicating their lives to their ideals. A few considered poor Arabs part of the world proletariat who should be educated and organized to become part of the general socialist struggle. But they were few, and the needs of the Jewish newcomers proved stronger. Such struggles, and the collective settlements—kibbutz, kvutza, and moshav—based on the principles of socialism, where women wished to play an equal role and children were not educated within the family, seemed many light years away from local Arab, Muslim, feudal society.

The fourth factor was political anti-Semitism, which started in the 1880s, parallel to the rise of political Zionism. Indeed, the struggle for a Zionist identity was waged on two corresponding fronts: being a Zionist meant being the opposite of what anti-Semites' imagined Jews to be but also the opposite of how Zionists viewed diasporic Jews. In other words, both anti-Semitism and Zionism depicted Jews in a thoroughly negative light, but for opposite reasons. Anti-Semites were in constant fear of the "other" but needed it as an external symbol of evil, whereas Zionists wanted to distance themselves from the "other" and emerge as its counterpart. Thus, Middle Easterners were alien to the relations between Judaism and Christianity, or secular European anti-Semitism, and also to the desire of Zionists and non-Zionists alike to disprove the anti-Semites' defamation of Jews. The Holocaust, with its branding of Jews as "*untermensch,*" or subhuman beings, enhanced this goal. Jews refused to accept that the Nazis and their accomplices had the right, much less any cultural basis, to pass judgment on an ancient civilization.

One last factor shaping Zionist identity was a conviction that the Jews are unique. Just as other national movements boasted ties to the past, Zionism linked itself to the ancient history of the Jews that began in the land of Canaan, claiming to be its continuation and entirely disregarding the diaspora in-between. The Zionist movement called for a return to the places where the

Bible had been written, the revival of Hebrew, a desire for an authentic and natural bond to the land, and a basic feeling, shared by most if not all Jews, that they were the continuation of a civilization that went back many thousands of years, despite its changing forms and characteristics. Jews were imbued with a feeling of cultural and intellectual standing, which stemmed from a religious belief that they were "the chosen people"; from a secular claim that, although small in number, they had contributed culturally and morally to world civilization; and from a personal conviction that they, as a people, had compelling characteristics such as a traditional lack of illiteracy and exceptional self-organization despite a surfeit of internal disputes.

Although the Zionists wanted to be perceived not as the "chosen people" but as "any other nation," still their traditional self-image persisted, even despite their determination that, "as any other nation," a Jewish state would be "or lagoyim"—a moral and humane lighthouse whose beam would spread from Jerusalem to the world. As a result, there could be no meeting of minds between the national entity of Zionism, its internal disputes and multiple factions notwithstanding, and the local population, perceived by Jews as awaiting awakening and development.

Conclusion

Israeli identity after 1948 is characterized by constant change, extreme variety, and a series of tensions. Although the Arab–Israeli conflict continues to intensify, the main factors that have shaped Israeli identity have remained Jewish or Western. Israeli identity has emerged from Israelis drawing closer to Judaism in its various forms, from acknowledging their diasporic roots, from the dissipation of tension between the idealized sabra and the threatened, post-Holocaust Jew, and from a closer sense of ties to Jewish history. The post-war, anti-Semitic, polarized depiction of Jews and Israelis as one entity, miserable and weak yet capable of manipulating and dominating the world, still helps to produce a polarized self-perception that wavers between heights and depths.

The sense of uniqueness has not disappeared. On the contrary, the more the Holocaust is studied and proved to be unique, the more it becomes clear that no other nation has been singled out as an outright antithesis to Nazism. The role played by the Holocaust in Jewish and Israeli identity and public life has not diminished with time, and, in some aspects, has considerably increased. The proportion of survivors in the Jewish population in the 1950s, about 1:4, is still about the same, if their descendents are taken into consideration.[65] The Zionist claim that there would be increasing normalcy between Jews and gentiles once a Jewish state was established has not materialized, and anti-Semitism has been on the rise since the late 1960s. Nonetheless, five Jewish generations have been born in the country, and a strong sense of place, language, and local culture is now part of Israeli identity.

Israel's self-perception is still Western, idealizing democracy, modernity, and innovation. The rise of fundamentalism among Muslims, and the opposition of most Muslim religious leaders to these values, continues to keep Jews and Muslims apart in the Middle East and elsewhere. A struggle also continues within Israel between the secular majority and the religious Zionists, and the growing Orthodox minority. Another bitter debate rages around the small but vociferous group gaining international attention, the post-Zionists, and their claim for a non-Jewish state, one comprised of "all its citizens." Recent research, including some in this volume, reflects these trends, and still allocates too small a space for Arab culture, language, and thought as a potential source of influence or debate.

Had the Zionists acknowledged the Arab presence from the very beginning of Zionism, and had all its factions declared a wish to integrate into the Middle East and to foster at least some aspects of a local identity and culture, would relations between Arabs and Jews have evolved differently? Had Jews been angels of righteousness, would it have indeed mattered? As Ettinger suggested, was the lack of rapprochement on the part of the Zionists the reason why relations deteriorated, or did the circumstances in Europe, the Middle East, and the balance of world power bring about an inevitable conflict? Finally, is it possible that Zionists did not ignore the Arabs so much as their guilty feelings and tendency toward self-criticism made them claim later, so that from today's perspective, with daily tragedies on both sides, it seems a fundamental fault?

The Middle East as it was and remains today is not the culture into which most Zionists wanted to integrate or identify with. The local Arabs and the population of the neighboring countries were never a yardstick for comparison or achievement for Zionists. Jewish ambitions and dreams lay elsewhere. In 1942, the Zionist conference in New York demanded a solution for the homeless Jews in the postwar world, free immigration to Palestine, the reclamation of its desolate lands under the supervision of the Jewish Agency, and that "Palestine be established as a Jewish commonwealth, integrated in the structure of the new democratic world." The conference reiterated the attitude stated in former Zionist congresses welcoming the economic, agricultural, and national development of the Arab nations and states, and expressing a "readiness and desire for full cooperation with its Arab neighbors" but did not specify that some of the Arabs belonged in Eretz Israel.[66] Nor did it mention any cultural development or desire for integration into the Arab world. Zionism has always seen its place in the broader democratic mainstream.

There are two dreams. The first is that of the stranger in Kafka's novel who wished to reach the castle and be warmly welcomed and accepted there. He was the Jew, insulted and rejected, who craved to be an essential part of those who belonged inside the castle. He was the Zionist who wished, as every page of Herzl's *Altneuland* showed, to be accepted as an equal by the other nations whose ideals he shared. The second dream is Laqueur's: "The Zionist leaders simply could not consider the presence of half a million non-Jews as an insurmountable obstacle, formidable enough to make them give up their cherished dreams about the return of the Jewish people to their homeland."[67]

NOTES

I thank my friends and colleagues, Avi Bareli and Shalom Ratzabi, and my dear cousin, Yosef-Haim Yerushalmi, for reading this paper carefully and providing useful comments.

1. Robert Wistrich and David Ohana (eds.), *The Shaping of Israeli Identity: Myth, Memory and Trauma* (London, 1995).

2. Oz Almog, *The Sabra: The Creation of the New Jew* (Berkeley, 2000), 296–317.

3. Shlomo Avineri, *The Making of Modern Zionism: The Intellectual Origins of the Jewish State* (London, 1981).

4. Dan Urian and Efraim Karsh (eds.), *In Search of Identity: Jewish Aspects in Israeli Culture* (London, 1998).

5. Moshe Dayan, *Story of My Life* (Tel Aviv, 1976), 32–33, in Hebrew.

6. Ibid., 33.

7. Yael Dayan, personal conversation with Dina Porat, February 14, 2004.

8. Thanks to Avi Bareli for reminding me.

9. Anthony D. Smith, *The Nation in History* (Cambridge, 2000). For the quote, see the Hebrew version (Jerusalem, 2000), 51–52.

10. Shmuel Almog (ed.), *Zionism and The Arabs: Essays* (Jerusalem, 1983), vii.

11. Avineri, *The Making of Modern Zionism,* 122; League of Nations, "Report of the Palestine Royal Commission" (London, 1937), 123; Anita Shapira, *Visions in Conflict* (Tel

Aviv, 1988), 23–25, in Hebrew; Yosef Gorny, *The Arab Question and the Jewish Problem* (Tel Aviv, 1985), 52, in Hebrew, on "the original sin of the Zionist movement."

12. Most secondary sources take their numbers from the *Statistical Abstract of Palestine,* Office of Statistics (Jerusalem, every year), published by the Mandate Government statistician, (see the 1940 volume, 10), and from the *Statistical Handbook of Jewish Palestine* (Jerusalem, 1947), published by the Department of Statistics of the Jewish Agency. (See 46–47). These sources indicate the numbers for the second and third stages as well.

13. Moses Hess, *Rome and Jerusalem: The Last National Problem* (New York, 1916), 89, 209–210, in Yiddish.

14. Avineri, *The Making of Modern Zionism,* 45.

15. Ibid., chapters 4–7; Walter Laqueur, *A History of Zionism* (London, 1972), 3–84. Yehuda Leib Pinsker, *Autoemancipation!* (Berlin, 1882). Rabbi Yehuda Hai Alkalai came from today's Serbia, Rabbi Zvi Hirsch Kalischer from Germany, and Peretz Smolenskin, Moshe Leib Lilienblum, and Yehuda Leib Pinsker from tsarist Russia.

16. Ahad-Ha'am, "Truth from the Land of Israel," *Hamelitz,* June 19–30 and August 15–17, 1891.

17. Deuteronomy 14:21.

18. The most used Hebrew edition is the Tel Aviv, 1943, twelve-volume selection of Herzl's writings. See III, 120–128.

19. Shapira, *Visions in Conflict,* 23.

20. Ibid., 37; Avineri, *The Making of Modern Zionism,* 100.

21. "The Jewish State" or, more accurately, "The State of the Jews," was first published in 1896 in German, and has since been translated into many languages. New Hebrew printings or editions appear every few years, usually about 70–80 pages long.

22. Yitzhak Epstein first offered his ideas in a closed session during the Seventh Zionist Congress in Basel in 1905, and then published it in *Hashiloah,* one of the first Hebrew newspapers, (1907), 193–206.

23. Gorny, *The Arab Question,* 54–55.

24. For a description of all these opinions, see ibid., 52–64; for Lurie's quote, see ibid., 52. See also Laqueur, *History of Zionism,* 172. For one of the best descriptions of these activists, see Neil Caplan, *Palestine Jewry and the Arab Question, 1917–1925* (London, 1978), 127–142.

25. Nahum Goldmann, *On the Roads of My People* (Jerusalem, 1968), 18, in Hebrew.

26. Almog, *The Sabra,* 301–303, 305–308. On the teaching of Arabic, see Michael Assaf, *The Relations between Arabs and Jews in the Land of Israel, 1860–1948* (Tel Aviv, 1970), 48–56. On Hashomer, and on the Sephardic Jews, see Moshe Sharett, *A Personal Diary* (Tel Aviv, 1978), in Hebrew. On orientalism, see Zvi Rosenstein, *History of the Workers' Movement in the Land of Israel* (Tel Aviv, 1955), 117, in Hebrew.

27. Goldmann, *On the Roads,* 18.

28. Deuteronomy 23:15.

29. Goldmann, *On the Roads,* 18.

30. Yeshayahu Leibovitch, "Basic Assumptions for an Internal Zionist Debate," *Jüdische Rundschau,* October 18, 1929. See also Caplan, "The Constitutional Struggle," in *Palestine Jewry,* 146–165.

31. Gershom Scholem, *Explications and Implications: Writings on Jewish Heritage and Renaissance* (Tel Aviv, 1989), II, 63–67, in Hebrew.

32. *Statistical Abstract,* 1940, 15.

33. For the intellectual origins, see Scholem, *Explications and Implications,* 61–92; and Shalom Ratzabi, *Between Zionism and Judaism: The Radical Circle in Brith Shalom, 1925–1933* (Leiden, 2002). For the political impact, see Shmuel Dothan, *The Struggle for Eretz-Israel* (Tel Aviv, 1981), 56–63, in Hebrew.

34. Laqueur, *History of Zionism,* 196; Nahum Sokolov, Chaim Weitzman, and David Ben-Gurion, for instance, spoke in such terms in the Zionist congresses.

35. Almog, *The Sabra,* 300; "Report of the Palestine Royal Commission," 118 and 336.

36. Shapira, *Visions in Conflict,* 68, 70.

37. "Report of the Palestine Royal Commission," 116.

38. Ibid., 335.

39. Ibid., 119–120.

40. Amos Oz, *Under This Blazing Light: Essays* (Tel Aviv, 1979), 92, in Hebrew.

41. Yechiam Weitz (ed.), *From Vision to Revision: A Hundred Years of Historiography of Zionism* (Jerusalem, 1997), 3–29, in Hebrew; Abba Kovner, *Beyond Mourning* (Tel Aviv, 1998), 225–232, in Hebrew.

42. Laqueur, *History of Zionism,* 210.

43. Gorny, *The Arab Question,* 13.

44. Ibid., 23–27; Shapira, *Conflicts in Vision,* 37–38; Yehoshua Porath, *The Emergence of the Palestinian-Arab National Movement, 1918–1929* (Jerusalem, 1976), 14–22, in Hebrew; Assaf, *The Relations between Jews and Arabs,* 309–333.

45. Porath, *The Arab National Movement,* 56–99; Dothan, *The Struggle for Eretz-Israel,* 18–24; Caplan, *Palestine Jewry,* 171–178.

46. Arthur Herzberg, "The Roots of Arab Opposition to the Jews in Eretz-Israel," in *Kivunim Hadashim* (New Directions), IX (2003), 13–22.

47. Avineri, *The Making of Modern Zionism,* 100; Porath, *The Arab National Movement,* 14–22. Apparently Boas Evron, in *Jewish State or Israeli Nation?* (Tel Aviv, 1988), somewhat misinterpreted Porath as claiming that Arab nationalism started in the late nineteenth century.

48. Shapira, *Visions in Conflict*, 27. Nevertheless, Palestinian and Arab scholars have accused Herzl since the 1970s of plotting deliberate maltreatment of the Arabs, and read his 12 of June 1895 diary entry as a proof of his wish to transfer them. But at that time he was not yet sure whether Palestine was indeed the right solution for Jews. See above, note 20, and the full debate in Derek J. Penslar, "Herzl and the Palestinian Arabs: Myth and Counter-Myth," in *Israel*, VI (2004), 149–161, and an exchange between Ran Hacohen and Baruch Kimmerling, ibid., 163–170, and Benny Morris, ibid., 171–173.

49. Ibid., 46.

50. Ibid., 37.

51. Israel Bartal, in Weitz, *From Vision to Revision*, 48.

52. Ibid., 44–46.

53. Yoav Gelber, in Weitz, *From Vision to Revision*, 81–82.

54. Almog, *The Sabra*, 292–293.

55. Amnon Raz-Krakotzkin, in Weitz, *From Vision to Revision*, 121. Raz-Krakotzkin is a historian of medieval times, whereas the others mentioned here deal with modern history.

56. Yossi Yona, in a review on Shapira's "Where Did the Negation of the Diaspora Go," *Alpaim*, XXV (2003), 9–56, published in *Ha'aretz/Sfarim* (December 24, 2003), claimed she did not deal with the impact of the negation of the diaspora on the negation of the Palestinian, Sephardic, and feminist discourse. Regarding the Palestinian discourse, see Amnon Raz-Krakotzkin, "Exile in Sovereignty: To the Criticism of 'The Negation of the Diaspora' in Israeli Culture," *Theory and Criticism*, IV (1993), 33–55. Regarding the Sephardic discourse, see Gabriel Piterberg, "The Nation and Its Tellers; National Historiography and Orientalism," in *Theory and Criticism*, VI (1995), 81–103. Regarding the gender discourse, see Daniel Boyarin, "The Colonial Masquerade Ball: Zionism, Gender, Imitation," *Theory and Criticism*, XI (1997), 123–144. It seems that she does not agree with this triple thesis.

57. Gorny, *The Arab Question*, 13.

58. Dina Porat, *The Blue and Yellow Stars of David: The Zionist Leadership in Palestine and the Holocaust, 1939–1945* (Cambridge, MA, 1990); Roni Stauber, *A Lesson for a Generation, Holocaust and Heroism in the Israeli Public Discourse during the 1950s* (Jerusalem, 2000), in Hebrew; Tom Segev, *The Seventh Million: The Israelis and the Holocaust* (Jerusalem, 1991), in Hebrew.

59. Statistical Abstract 1940, 13; "Report of the Palestine Royal Commission," 122; Porat, *The Blue and the Yellow*, 13–14.

60. Laqueur, *History of Zionism*, 184.

61. Gorny, *The Arab Question*, 38–39.

62. Edward W. Said, *Orientalism* (New York, 1978), 1, and the epilogue to the 1995 Hebrew edition (Tel Aviv, 1995), 289.

63. Yehuda Shenhav, *The Arab-Jews, Nationalism, Religion, and Ethnicity* (Tel Aviv, 2003), 17–19.

64. Yosef Gorny leads an academic and public struggle against the attribution of colonialism to Zionism and against post-Zionism in general. His latest is an answer to Yossi Yona (see note 56, above) in *Ha'aretz/Sfarim* (January 7, 2004).

65. Dina Porat, "Some Effects of the Holocaust on Israeli and Foreign Policy," in Aharon Oppenheimer (ed.), *Sino-Judaica: Jews and Chinese in Historical Dialogue* (Tel Aviv, 1999), 159–163.

66. *From the First Congress to the Partition Division* (Tel Aviv, 1967), 33, in Hebrew.

67. Laqueur, *History of Zionism,* 218.

❖ 4 ❖

THE ARAB AND PALESTINIAN
NARRATIVES OF THE 1948 WAR

SALEH ABDEL JAWAD

THE 1948 ARAB–ISRAELI war was one of the most important events in the contemporary Middle East. Its consequences and impact go beyond the geographical limit of the area and the historical time in which it occurred. Because of the issues left unresolved by the 1948 war and its aftermath—on the Palestinian side, the refugee problem in all its dimensions and the unmaking of a Palestinian state; on the Israeli side, control over the whole of Mandatory Palestine and hegemony over the region—the 1948 war soon became the "mother" of the many wars that followed.[1]

As a corollary to this unresolved struggle, the historiography of the war also became a battlefield for two opposing narratives. In the Arab–Israeli conflict, writing history is a political act that "not only represents the past but also . . . molds the past."[2] To some degree, the struggle between narrative and counternarrative is universal. As Said put it: "The development and maintenance of every culture requires the existence of another, different and competing *alter ego*. The construction of identity . . . involves the construction of opposites and 'others' whose actuality is always subject to the continuous interpretation of their differences from 'us.'"[3]

But in the Palestinian and Israeli cases, the writing of history is especially controversial and contested, as it constitutes one of the main foundations of legitimacy for both parties. The Jewish and Israeli Zionists have produced a comprehensive, coherent story composed of two sets of assertions. The first are the "foundational myths" which are principally a story of origins, going deep into the past. The second relates directly to the 1948 war, its immediate antecedents and consequences. The Palestinians, for their part, also have foundational myths and narratives of the 1948 war. This chapter explores some of the major reasons why the Palestinian narrative, although often containing more accurate insights, nevertheless remains fragmented and not fully comprehensive.[4]

Israeli versus Arab Narrative

On the Israeli side, the foundational myth is composed of heroes (the Jews) and villains (the Arabs). Its main points are that Jews are a nation with 3000 years of history, who have been given the "Promised Land" as a contract between God and his own "chosen people"; Jerusalem is central to Jewish religion and history; the history of the land under Arab Muslim rule was a story of continuous decline; during the period of the Jewish diaspora, the promised land stood empty of people and civilizational achievements—only with the return of Jewish settlers did it bloom; Palestinian nationalism is nonexistent or, in the best case, only a reaction to Jewish claims.[5] This is the common picture of an empty Palestine waiting to be redeemed by the Zionist modernizer.[6] As is evident, the Israeli foundational myth has been formulated in such a way as to exclude Palestinians from the history of "the land."

The second set of legitimating myths concerns the reasons for and conduct of the 1948 war and its aftermath.[7] These myths include those concerning Zionist acceptance and/or Arab rejection of the UN resolution to partition Palestine; that the war was initiated by Arabs who are therefore responsible for all of its consequences including the fate of refugees; that Palestinians voluntarily left their homes on orders from Arab governments and Jews "made strenuous efforts to persuade their Arab neighbors to stay [but] they failed"; that the Arab states had united to destroy the Jewish state that had just been proclaimed; that Israel fought for its survival since Arabs wished to push them into the sea; that the utterly inadequate, poorly clad, and ill-equipped Jewish Defense Force alone met huge Arab armies (a Jewish David facing an Arab Goliath); that the Haganah (the military force of the Jewish Agency) and the Israeli army were "the most ethical in the world" (in this formulation the Deir Yassin massacre becomes an exception perpetrated by "dissidents"); and, finally, that Israel subsequently sought peace but no Arab leader responded.[8]

In the shadow of this massive and partisan Israeli mythology, Palestinians did, in fact, construct their own story, sometimes independent of the Zionist mythology and sometimes in reaction to it, at times mythical and at other times more factual. The Arab mythology is also composed of two sets of stories: one also foundational and a second focused on *al Nakba* (the catastrophe), as the war of 1948 is known in the Arab world. The foundational Arab myths contain many elements, the most important being that Palestinians are a people whose ancient and deeply rooted history in the land of Palestine existed long before Jews appeared on the scene; Palestine has always been a melting pot in which a variety of nations, cultures, and tribes intermingled throughout the centuries; and the Jewish presence in Palestine was marginal even in biblical times and was absent for 2000 years. In the words of Glock, "the outcome [would have to be] a historical picture that [honors] the spatial Islamic continuity and the Jewish absence of 2000 years."[9] To counter the Zionist official narrative which denied Palestinian national identity, a minority of Palestinians went so far as to argue that Palestinians have existed since the dawn of recorded history, while the majority argues—more rationally—that before the appearance of the Zionist movement, a local national identity was in the process of formation.[10] Some assert the centrality of Jerusalem in the lives of the inhabitants of Palestine, both as a religious and as an administrative center, and as a catalyst for the modern Palestinian identity. The Arab narrative continues: Jerusalem is also important for Muslim history and religious practice, and played a crucial role in the early Islamic period; Palestine is part of the Arab world and part of a civilization that had an important influence on human progress; Jews were part of this civilization and, contrary to their persecution in the West, were treated with tolerance. The elements of this foundational story are widely accepted, with some differences between elite and popular culture, throughout the Arab world and within Palestinian society.[11]

When it comes to the Arab story about the 1948 war, however, discord prevails, except about the responsibility of the Israelis and their Western, superpower sponsors. On this point, Arab historiography endorses the following positions: the superpowers, especially Great Britain, are responsible for the creation of the Palestinian problem by virtue of their installing a Jewish state in the heart of the Arab world; the 1948 war was inevitable because of Zionist intentions to build an exclusively Jewish state; and Israel is fully responsible for the refugee problem. The very nature of the events of 1948 is framed in disparate ways by Israeli and Arab historiography ("war" vs. "ethnic cleansing"). There is controversy about the national agendas of particular Arab states. There is no agreement in evaluating the leadership of King Abdullah of Jordan and the Mufti of Palestine. No consensus exists regarding the role of each Arab army or of Arab armies in general, or the relative strengths of military and civilian authorities. Even the military capacity of the Israelis is not assessed in the same way by all Arab commentators.

The discord in Arab narratives is not only a matter of ideology or patriotism. Disputes are common *within* each of these discourses, arising from the fact that these narratives were based more on speculation and abstraction than on empirical research. To a large extent, this state of affairs is responsible for the hegemony of the Israel narrative, at least until the mid-1980s, when a second Israeli "revisionist" narrative emerged. This more recent work by the Israeli "new historians" weakened and sometimes even refuted much of the older Israeli narrative, documenting Israeli aggression against Palestinians. Yet even the new historians (who do not speak with one voice) continue to be divided about the subject of a centralized commitment on the part of the Israelis to massive population transfers, amounting virtually to a master plan of ethnic cleansing.

In the last twenty years Palestinians, including Kamal Abdul Fattah, Issa Khalaf, Beshara Doumani, and Rashid Khalidi, have provided a number of excellent general historical studies.[12] Some of these works, like the writings of Nazzal, Masalha, Kanaana, and especially Walid Khalidi, focus on the war.[13] Even much earlier Palestinian works were translated into Hebrew, apparently for military history research, Israeli intelligence, and propaganda.[14] However, a solid and comprehensive narrative about the 1948 war is still lacking. Nevertheless, an outline of this emerging Palestinian narrative is discernible in the following propositions, widely shared by Arab and Western authors studying the 1948 war: There was a well-organized and intentional ethnic cleansing.[15] Massacres were an intentional instrument of ethnic cleansing. Except for works by 'Aref al-'Aref and Muhammed Nimr Khatib, who document some massacres, other writers have not presented systematic evidence on this subject.[16] Nevertheless, oral histories continue to bring more and more massacres to light, and their occurrence is often confirmed by Israeli army documents.

The Arab narrative categorically rejects Israeli allegations that Arab leaders ordered Palestinians to evacuate their villages, even if, in some cases, residues of this myth remain in the popular discourse, mainly because Palestinian refugees listened to Israeli-sponsored, Arab-language radio, which was used to wage psychological war. Despite pan-Arab rhetoric, Arab armies acted on nationalistic lines. It follows that the Arab narrative will have to explain changes over time in solidarity among Arab nations—varying all the way from Arab countries going to war on behalf of Palestinian rights to these same countries later being abusive and oppressive to Palestinian refugees. Finally, Palestinian writers were also unanimous in their affirmation of a conspiracy among the superpowers, especially Britain and the United States, to favor Israeli interests.

This chapter examines three major reasons for the failure, beyond the lack of serious empirical research, to create a satisfactory and coherent Arab narrative.

1. The fragmentation of the Arab narrative not only along national lines, but also within national stories on class and sectoral lines (i.e., military vs. civilian) and varying with the changing fortunes of various Arab political doctrines and strategies;
2. The inability of Arab historians to disentangle themselves from Israeli formulations even when they have unmasked the more mythical elements of the Israeli narrative; and
3. The lack of access to the kinds of documentary and archival sources from which robust and trustworthy historical scholarship would ordinarily be drawn.

The first two points are already somewhat well known, whereas the difficulties of Arab historiography rooted in the destruction of the written Palestinian heritage and in the problems associated with archival materials are less well understood and therefore more fully discussed later in this chapter. Moreover, the difficulties of writing history are not only a problem of archives, but also implicate Arab sociopolitical systems for the lack of protection that they afford free, empirical, research that brings to light what Weber called "inconvenient facts."[17]

The Fragmentation and Multiplicity of Arab Narratives

The most common view of the current Arab narrative is that it is nationalistic and apologetic. Indeed, each Arab country that participated in the 1948 war has its own story. There is a Palestinian narrative, and Jordanian, Egyptian, Iraqi, and Syrian narratives as well. And although all the Arab leaders claimed to fight for Palestine, each actually fought the war of 1948 strictly on national terms, "guided by their domestic agendas and national interests."[18] Those interests are reflected in their respective national narratives in which "criticism in any given country was . . . often directed against the actions of other Arab states."[19]

This charge, though valid, is simplistic. The Arab narrative is fragmented, as noted above, not only along national lines but within them. For example, most Jordanian historians are military men; they write approvingly of the role of the Jordanian forces and their political leader (King Abdullah) during the war.[20] But a dissident voice comes from a former army colonel, Abdullah Tall, who as early as the late 1950s emphasized Zionist-Transjordanian collusion during the war.[21] Tall could not publish his work in Jordan and instead chose to publish in Cairo, where he lived as a political refugee—an indication of the problems with Arab democracy discussed throughout this chapter.

In each country the narrative is fragmented essentially along class lines. Official, popular, and elite narratives compete for legitimacy. So, for example, among the Palestinians, there is a huge gap between the official narrative represented by the writings of Mufti Haj Amin Husseini, the principal Palestinian leader, or Emile al-Ghoury, his main assistant, on the one hand, and, on the other, the writing of 'Aref al-'Aref, an independent Palestinian chronicler who has produced the best Arab narrative of the war.[22] Al-Aref, along with other Palestinian intellectuals, such as Mussa Alami, Waleed Qamhawi, and Naji Al-lush, did not hesitate to criticize Palestinian leadership, Palestinian organizations, and Palestinian society.[23]

The popular version of the Palestinian narrative is reflected in the testimonies of Palestinian peasants, later refugees, as recorded in the monographs of the *Palestinian Destroyed Villages* series of the Birzeit University Research Center. A nationalist elite version of the same events is revealed in diaries and memoirs such as those of Khalil Sakakini and his daughter Hala, 'Ajaj Nuweihd, Edward Said, Hisham Sharabi, Raja Shehadeh, and Elias Sanbar.[24]

Some Palestinian historians and intellectuals found a partial explanation for the Arab defeat in 1948 in the theoretical framework of explicit social class analysis. In studies written between the middle and the end of the 1960s, writers like Ghassan Kanafani, Naji Allush, and A'bdel Wahab Kayali argued that prominent feudal, semi-feudal, and bourgeois leaders acted in accord with their class interest, which sometimes contradicted the national one.[25] At the very least, Palestinian elites tried to balance their own interests between the popular nationalist movement and the British authorities of the Mandate, who favored the local elites over Palestinian peasants, if not over Jewish settlers. In such works, villagers are presented as the hearts and souls of the nation, an analysis which may derive some of its power from Marxist antagonism toward the bourgeoisie.[26] In the 1970s, Sayigh, who was one of the first pioneers to use oral sources with academic rigor, continued this trend.[27]

Swedenburg, however, provides an additional and even more persuasive argument: the Palestinian peasantry with its ties to the land has become a national signifier. He postulates that the production and circulation of a Palestinian peasant identity and its icons has been fundamental in terms of the

sustained cultural mapping of a Palestinian identity as against "the fragmentation of the Palestinian people and Zionism's refusal to acknowledge the legitimacy of a Palestinian identity."[28] Miller confirms Swedenburg. She shows
that the years of the Mandate mark the formative point in which the Palestinian peasantry became a symbol of the nation. By the 1920s, in struggles over
land sales, nationalist writers "were demanding that the villagers preserve continuity as a symbol of Arab Palestine."[29] Antonius, author of the classic *The
Arab Awakening*, bemoaned the loss of traditional life in light of the Palestinian peasants becoming increasingly proletarian in the first quarter of the twentieth century.[30]

Many of these writers came from Arab nationalist backgrounds. In the context of the 1967 loss, which included not only a military defeat but also the
discrediting of Arab nationalist beliefs, they embraced Marxism to different
degrees. In doing so, they were part of a more general development which, over
time, saw the ideology of Arab nationalism give way to the emergence of
Marxism, Islamism, and Palestinian nationalism (represented by the *Fatah*
movement).

Other criticisms of the Palestinian elite came from historians who were
themselves members of this elite. Al-'Aref noted, "but the rich from the Qatamon neighborhood [West Jerusalem] did not prepare themselves for that [to
defend themselves and their neighborhood] and they could have done so, if
they had wanted to, since many of them were very rich. And I am sorry to say
that this mistake [i.e., the rich and the sons of the elite fleeing], their failure of
duty toward their country, and leaving the battle for the sons of poor and
middle classes most of whom are workers, villagers, and small landlords was
committed in all of the neighborhoods and Palestinian cities and not only in
Jerusalem or Qatamon."[31] At the end of his condemnation, al-'Aref uses a verse
from the Qur'an: "If we want to destroy a town we let the corruption of the
rich flourish."[32]

Not only are popular histories distinguished from official ones, and class
analysis distinguished from elite apologetics, but there is also a consistent difference in the way that Arab historians treat military and civilian leaders. With
few exceptions, Arab historians tend to be silent when it comes to evaluating
the performance of military leaders while being highly critical of civilian political leadership. An undifferentiated view, owing mainly to ignorance of military history, has had critical implications for military-civilian relations in Arab
societies even to the present day. One of the major results of the 1948 war was
the discrediting of the old social and political classes and the legitimization of

the military as redeemers.[33] In this context, Arab historians writing about 1948 contributed considerably to the popularity of this simplistic dichotomy. For example, there is a myth, now completely refuted, that the Egyptian army in Palestine was defeated because it had been equipped with defective arms by corrupt politicians.[34] Similarly, with regard to the Iraqi participation in the 1948 war, the anecdote of "*mako awamer*" (which, in the Iraqi dialect, means no orders were given to the Iraqi units in Palestine to open fire or intervene) is used to discredit Iraqi civilian leaders. Anecdotes such as these helped to delegitimize these regimes and to justify military coups in Egypt, Syria, and Iraq. Arab societies have paid a high price because of this myth of civilian incompetence and military redemption.

The Failure to Contest Israeli Paradigms

Amid this welter of contradictory stories, I argue that although the Arab narrative often is apologetic, biased, and designed to legitimize particular states or movements, these qualities alone do not explain the still unfinished Arab historiography.

Arab historians obviously contest the mythical elements of the Israeli accounts. But these historians nevertheless sometimes remain trapped in Israeli paradigms. For example, they generally accept the characterization of the events of 1948, prior to the entry of Arab armies, as a "war" rather than a project of forced removals conducted by coordinated Zionist militias under the leadership of the Jewish Agency and David Ben-Gurion. Concerning the causality of the war, Zionist historiography uses the plan of Partition as a point of departure. This version of the Israeli narrative is like a history that explains World War I by citing the assassination of the Archduke Francis Ferdinand without mentioning the competition among major European powers for control over colonies. Arab historians try to evoke deeper reasons for the war—that is, the Zionist objective of creating an exclusionary Jewish state with no place for Arabs. In doing so they follow the advice of Thucydides, who reminds us that historians should dig deeply to find the ultimate reasons that cause nations to go to war, and not to be distracted by the triggering event:

> To the question why they [Lacedaemon] broke the treaty, I answer by placing first an account of their grounds of complaint and points of difference, that no one may ever have to ask the immediate cause which plunged the Greeks into a war of such magnitude. The real but unavowed cause I consider to have

been the growth of the power of Athens, and the alarm which is inspired in Lacedaemon; this made war inevitable.[35]

Although the Arab approach to the causes of the war is historically correct, the Arab failure to contest the Israeli version of the actual beginning of the "war" compromises their ability to challenge Zionist allegations that Arabs are responsible for the war and all of its consequences. Too often, they also accept the premise of eternal enmity between Arabs and Jews, and the presentation of Palestinians during the war as nothing more than victims.

Although it is beyond the scope of this chapter to liberate the historiography of Palestine from Israeli colonialist and triumphalist assumptions, I show, for the examples mentioned above, how these paradigms should be challenged.

One of the most critical elements of the Israeli mythology that must be challenged concerns the beginning of the war. Historians of the 1948 war, *including most Arabs,* accept the argument that the war began on November 30, 1947, just hours after the UN General Assembly Partition plan was announced (and rejected by the Arabs) late on the night of November 29. Palestinians are thus responsible for the beginning of the war.

A typical Israeli book begins: "The first organized Arab attack took place on the morning of November 30, on the road to Jerusalem. At 8:12, at the Kfar Sirkin intersection, the Arabs ambushed a bus carrying twenty-one Jewish passengers from Netanya to Jerusalem, killing five. Twenty minutes later, the same gang attacked a bus carrying Jews from Hadera to Jerusalem, killing two passengers."[36] The conventional Israeli narrative adds two events: the burning and looting of Jewish stores in one of the markets in Jerusalem on December 2, 1947, and the appeal of the Arab Higher Committee (AHC) for a three-day general strike beginning on the same day.

But let us look more closely at the events of November 30—the attacks on the buses, the looting of the market, and the AHC call for a general strike. The Israeli narrative presents the perpetrators who opened fire on the two buses as one criminal group. It is therefore extremely telling to notice that the Israelis, who had a network of Arab collaborators during the 1948 war, do not provide any information about the gang supposedly responsible for the start of the war that cost the lives of 6,000 Israelis and tens of thousands of Arabs. Some Israeli sources, including Morris, even hint that this attack could have been unrelated to partition and was, instead, an Arab reprisal against a series of organized Jewish attacks on Palestinians committed before Partition was announced.[37] In one of these Israeli attacks, eleven Palestinians were killed, including seven from a single family, the Abu Laban family.

To understand the then situation in Palestine, it is important to broaden the time frame and to recall that Palestinians were prospering in the years after the 1936–1939 revolt against the British. During World War II, relations between Arabs and Jews were characterized by relative calm. Palestinian, Jewish, and British archival sources converge in indicating that, despite nuances here and there, the Palestinians were not in the mood to wage war.

Shai (the term for Haganah Intelligence Service reports on Arab activities) documents from the Haganah archives suggest that Palestinian society wanted quiet after the disruptive and destructive years of the revolt. Despite reports about some small gangs perhaps "connected to the Mufti" who engaged in political provocation against Jews, the Haganah intelligence service made it clear that this was essentially behavior by a very small number of people who were also conducting criminal activities within Palestinian society. This conclusion echoes the 300 interviews with Palestinian refugees that I conducted with my students between 1996 and 2003. Our interviews are unanimous in showing that the soon-to-be refugees made no military preparations to go to war. In fact, even after weeks of violence, Ben-Gurion himself, in his diaries, mentions that the peasants, who comprised the majority of Palestinians, did not want to participate in the "troubles" unless they were pushed to do so by force.[38] Even one month after the Partition plan, Ben-Gurion noted that "the Arab villages did not intervene [in the war]. Are they going to intervene?"[39] He continued the same day, "The areas are calm. We can suppose that it will remain calm if we minimize the provocation and don't waste our energy on aggression."[40]

In contrast, the situation was very tense on two other fronts: between Zionist forces and the British, and also between Zionist groups. Zionists viewed the British White Paper of 1939 as an act of hostility because it emphasized that the Balfour Declaration did not imply the creation of a Jewish state and limited Jewish immigration to Palestine, and, finally, it restricted the sale of Arab lands to Jews. Although all Jewish organizations opposed the White Paper, they were divided among themselves and even internally within each group as to the best way to deal with it. The strengthening of the right-wing Irgun Zvai Leumi (National Military Organization) and Stern Gang groups led to a dramatic deterioration of British–Zionist relations and even to group-to-group relations within the Yishuv (the pre-state Jewish society and its institutions). The danger of an internal Jewish civil war was real.

After the end of World War II, Ben-Gurion was very anxious because of the possibility of clashes among Jewish factions and because of the "relaxed" situation between Arabs and Israelis. In his 1946 writings he emphasized that the real enemy was the Palestinians, not the British, and that the military option would decide the combat. To that end, Ben-Gurion exploited a number of minor incidents during 1946 and 1947 that had been committed by Arab criminal gangs who victimized both Jews and Arabs.[41] This gave Ben-Gurion an opening to inaugurate a policy of disproportionate reprisal which had huge political and psychological implications and was a departure from the organization's policy of restraint and proportionality (*hafflga*) during the 1930s. The policy of disproportionate response was more aligned to the terror tactics of the right-wing groups who used explosives against Arab civilian targets, a tactic that Ben-Gurion himself had condemned in 1938–1939.

According to 'Abdel Hafith Muhareb, Ben-Gurion's policy shift in 1946–1947 succeeded in heightening tensions between the Arab and Jewish communities.[42] Economic relations, however, and even social coexistence in the mixed Arab–Jewish cities remained relatively untroubled.

Sir Alan Cunningham, the British Commissioner for Palestine, concluded that "the initial Arab outbreaks were spontaneous and unorganized and were more demonstrations of displeasure at the UN decision than a determined attack on Jews. The weapons initially employed were sticks and stones and had it not been for Jewish recourse to firearms, it is not impossible that the excitement would have subsided and little loss of life been caused. This is more probable since there is reliable evidence that the Arab Higher Committee as a whole, and the Mufti in particular, although pleased at the strong response to the strike call, were not in favor of serious outbreaks."[43]

Cunningham believed that Haganah was involved in provoking an escalation of the conflict. On December 15, 1947, the High Commissioner reported that the Jewish Agency was also responsible for the "dissident" Stern Gang and Irgun terrorism. He noted that "the dissident groups are now working so closely together that the Agency's claim that they cannot control the dissidents is inadmissible."[44] Cunningham's assertion that the Arabs were not solely responsible for starting the conflict is confirmed by the text of a meeting of the Zionist leaders in January 1948, where Gad Machnes, an expert on Arab affairs, reported that "the Palestinian Arabs were divided and a majority among them did not want a war."[45]

I argue that all skirmishes and clashes from November 30 to December 11, 1947, were spontaneous actions and that the war proper only began with coordinated, large-scale terror attacks in the heart of Palestinian cities and villages. Between December 11 and December 13, a series of attacks—including an explosion in a civilian gathering near the Damascus Gate, the killing of nearly the whole of two families in the village of Tieret Haifa, and the undercover attack in the villages of Abasieh, Yazur, Balad il-Sheikh, Ramle, and central Jaffa—led to the deaths of some sixty Palestinian civilians in the most horrible way and provoked strong feelings of fear and revenge. Together the events of December 11–13 created the point of no return from which the war began.[46]

Only recently have a few Israeli "new historians" come to the reluctant admission that expulsion played a large role in the events of 1948.[47] Many of them, especially Morris, still consider expulsions to be a by-product of military action. To date, Pappe is the sole Israeli historian to go so far as to challenge the very use of the term "war" when he says: "The little research we already have indicates clearly that, contrary to the description which emerges from the Israeli military archives in many parts of Palestine, in 1948 there was no actual war but rather wide-scale operations of ethnic cleansing. Civilians, not soldiers, are the subject matter, and therefore ethnic cleansing rather than military maneuvers should be the focus of historical research."[48] Palestinian historians have been quicker to adopt the term "ethnic cleansing" and also have understood that war was a tool of ethnic cleansing rather than the reverse. Palestinian historiography needs to go further, however—to write "the social history of military operations rather than military history."[49]

The *Palestinian Destroyed Villages* series, which used oral history extensively, represents the first such work. Its message is particularly urgent in light of Israelis' success in labeling any Palestinian behavior they do not like as a "war." Thus when Israelis call the first and second *intifadas* "wars" they create an image of parity that is wholly spurious, and they focus attention on military actions rather than social conditions. The challenge to the Israeli privilege of naming wars cannot focus solely on the current situation but must go back at least as far as the events of 1948.

The second of many elements that must be challenged is the paradigm which describes Jewish–Arab relations only within the frame of conflict and killing. As with other issues, Arabs and Jews have conflicting versions of their joint history. Zionist historiography holds that Arab–Jewish relations historically were ones of persecution and enmity in which Jews, at best, were accorded the status of a protected (*Dhimmi*) community under Ottoman and other Islamic rules.[50] By integrating the worst episodes from ancient history with the war of 1948, Israeli historiography guarantees the image of a perennial conflict. This element is critical not only because it legitimizes action against the Palestinians; it also goes to the heart of portraying the Orient as similar to the old Christian, anti-Semitic Europe, thereby justifying the raison d'être of Zionism: the necessity for an exclusive Jewish state.

In contrast, Arab historiography is divided between two extremes: a portrait of exaggerated harmony, a golden age of tolerance between Arabs and Jews before the advent of Zionist settlers, and a backlash view of implacable opposition ever since.[51]

These versions are, of course, ahistorical. Muslim–Jewish relations are immensely more complex; they have varied over time, by location within the far-flung Arab Muslim world, and among different subgroups within Jewish and Muslim communities.[52]

On the basis of theology, Muslims considered Islam to be the culmination and perfection of the Jewish and Christian traditions. While Muslims considered Jews and Christians to be "people of the book" (*ahl al-kitab*), worshiping the same God, they nevertheless *did* place themselves (as did Jews and Christians) in a higher position based on their faith. The Muslim conviction of religious superiority, however, did not generally extend into hardened prejudices based on race, ethnicity, or language. Jewish prophets are highly respected, as is Jesus; the Qur'an even considers Jesus, and Solomon and his son David, legendary Jewish kings, God's emissaries. Islam thus is a religion that adopts the central figures of both Judaism and Christianity, coming to recognize them as constitutive of its own identity.[53] In many cases, the rituals and habits of Islam and Judaism (for example, the prohibition against eating pork and the requirement of circumcision) even brought these two faith communities closer to each other than either was to the Christian world. Jews were very active in the Arab–Muslim civilization and shared with Muslims the sad experiences of massacres by the Crusaders and the Spanish inquisition.

Jewish life under Muslim dynasties varied with the quality of individual Muslim rulers. There were rulers who abused Jews, although such rulers were usually abusive across the board, mistreating their Muslim and Christian subjects as well.

During Ottoman rule, one historian explained the life of different communities including Jews in these terms:

> Remarkably, this polyethnic and multireligious society worked. Muslims, Christians and Jews worshipped and studied side by side. The legal traditions and practices of each community, particularly in matters of personal status— death, marriage, and inheritance—were respected and enforced throughout

the empire. . . . Opportunities for advancement and prosperity were open in varying degrees to all the empire's subjects. . . . For all their shortcomings, plural societies did allow diverse groups of peoples to live together with a minimum of bloodshed. In comparison with the nation-states which succeeded them, theirs is a remarkable record.[54]

Within this configuration of multiethnic coexistence, Arabic-speaking Palestinian Jews were defined in diaries and memoirs of the later Ottoman period as *Abna' al Balad* (sons of the country), *yahud awlad Arab* (Jewish sons of Arabs), and compatriots.[55]

My study of Christian–Muslim relations in the twin Palestinians towns of Ramallah (Christian) and el-Bireh (Muslim) also shows excellent relations between Muslims and Christians between 1800 and 1920. Political factionalism was based on affiliation with two sociopolitical parties—the Qays and the Yemeni—and not on confessional affiliation. Muslim clans from el-Bireh allied themselves with Christian clans from Ramallah against other Muslim clans in el-Bireh and other Christian clans in Ramallah. People in the two cities had identical responsibilities and privileges. They even created a legend which shows their brotherhood over the centuries.[56]

Nor are my data exceptional. Scholch also notes that "in the feuds and fighting in the Jerusalem mountains with its mixed Muslim–Christian population, there had never been a confrontation between Christian and Muslim *hamulas* or villages as such. Rather, the formation of factions . . . transcended religious divisions. This [harmony] was viewed with displeasure by the French consul in Jerusalem, who reproachfully remarked with respect to the Catholics of Beit Jala that factional affiliation seemed more important for them than religious affiliation. According to him, for the world to be in order, the socio-political front line should have run between Christians and Muslims."[57]

From the mid-nineteenth century, missionary schools promoted education and modernity in general in Christian Ramallah. At least in the early decades, Muslims chose not to participate in these schools since their declared objective was conversion. This factor of conversion played an important role in gradually distancing the two communities and in promoting Ramallah, educationally and economically, at the expense of el-Bireh. This example shows, on the one hand, the extent to which relations between Muslims and other religious communities were amicable, and, on the other hand, how a differential exposure to "modernization" determined future relations.

This model can also be applied to Arab (native)–Jewish relations in the country. Shared enrollment of Jewish, Muslim, and Christian students in the same schools promoted mutual understanding and "a shared civic identity" for a small elite.[58] Such schools included the Jewish Alliance Israelite schools, established in 1882, the *nizamiyyah*, the Ottoman public schools first established by the Turkish law of 1869, and various Christian schools such as the Anglican girls' schools in Jerusalem and Haifa.[59]

Into this complex but generally peaceful mix at the end of the nineteenth century came an influx of European Ashkenazi Jews, speaking European languages or Yiddish, and seeking to establish a Zionist project claiming sole dominion over a "promised land" to the exclusion of the established communities already in place. The new Jewish immigrants looked different from their neighbors, had a different culture, and regarded the "natives" as inferior. The second wave of Zionist immigration, between 1904 and 1914, further exacerbated the situation because its members embraced the concept of exclusively Jewish labor which they applied on the collective farms, or *kibbutzim*. The kibbutz, however, was not the only form of Jewish landholding. There were independent Jewish farmers and Jewish cooperatives (*moshavim*) that often used Arab labor. Arab workers were "diligent and skillful and their name as good workers precedes them."[60]

In many cases, despite tensions around the land questions, good relations prevailed between Jewish settlements and Arab villages. Benvenisti, a former deputy mayor of Jerusalem and a well-known Israeli intellectual, draws the following picture of relations between a Palestinian village and its kibbutz neighbors. "Generally, good relations prevail between the two settlements. There are hardly any disputes between them. . . . [T]hey often had their work tools and household instruments mended in the kibbutz machine and carpentry shops . . . The people of [Abou Zureiq] enjoyed the benefits of medical assistance from the kibbutz for a small payment. Social relations include[ed] mutual visitations, and distribution of the Arabic language newspaper of the Jewish Workers Federation."[61] In cities and some villages, there were trysts and intermarriage, although not typically.

In addition to changing immigration patterns, the second major change that occurred in Palestine was the transition from Ottoman to British rule between 1917 and 1948. "Broadly speaking we can say that patterns of employment, investment and public spending by the Mandate [i.e., British] authorities created new arenas of integrated social domains. . . . [T]he globalization of the European life style also produced the beginnings of 'mixed' communities in middle class neighbourhoods in Jaffa, Haifa and areas of Jerusalem."[62]

These trends clashed, however, with the increasing diffusion of Zionist ideology among Jewish immigrants, and with the rising tide of Arab nationalist sentiments, which expressed itself in the Arab revolt of 1936–1939, directed against the British, in no small part because of British support for Zionist settlements. During these years relations between Arabs and Jews were poisoned, as even the Arabic-speaking Jews, now a tiny minority of Jews in Palestine, distanced themselves from the Arab nationalist struggle.

In the years following the Arab revolt, multiple Jewish militias including the Haganah, the Irgun, and the Stern Gang began to pursue an active policy of displacing Palestinian villagers. Such practices accelerated dramatically with the announcement in 1947 of the Partition plan. Benvenisti's memoir, which describes an earlier peaceful coexistence, details its unraveling:

> The lovely [Arab] homes . . . attracted the attention of their Jewish neighbors . . . as early as December 1947, Jewish settlers broke into homes in the village of Jamasin, which bordered on Tel Aviv . . . A few villages in the area had established good connections with neighboring Jewish communities, and even expressed willingness to surrender and to continue living under Jewish rule. In spite of this (and even after several villages did surrender and hand over their weapons) their inhabitants were expelled by force of arms and with the help of psychological warfare.[63]

Yet, even in this context, many Palestinian villages entered into nonaggression pacts with the largest Jewish militia, the Haganah. (The Israeli army abrogated these pacts as soon as it had the men and materiel to do so, but, nonetheless, the existence of nonaggression pacts on the very eve of the war mitigates the picture of eternal enmity.)

The human tragedy of the Nakba, which followed immediately upon the creation of the Israeli state, understandably pushed all Arab historiography into an anti-Zionist backlash. Arab writers can be divided into Marxist, nationalist, and Islamist, but none is exempted from the limitations of this backlash.

Neither contemporary Israeli nor contemporary Arab historiography has done much to honor the complexity of Arab–Jewish relations. On the Israeli side, Zionist historiography has little use for a history of centuries-old, Arab-speaking Jewish life under Muslim rule. And on the Palestinian side, acknowledgment of Muslim–Jewish coexistence smacks of collaboration. For example, in 1995 I gave a lecture at Birzeit University at the First International Conference on Palestinian Studies. The paper, entitled "Non-Aggression and Good Neighbor Oral Agreements between Palestinian Villages and Jewish Settlements during the 1948 War," focused on five villages—Sheik Muwanas, Deir

Yassin, Zarnuqa, Abou Zureiq, and Caesaria. All of the villagers had good or excellent relations with neighboring Jewish settlements. In the last case the villagers had worked as faithful guards on Jewish farms for decades. Nevertheless, they were expelled. In three of these five villages, not only were villagers expelled but they were also massacred. I offered these examples to show that relations between Palestinians and Israelis, even during the war, included more than enmity, and that Israelis expelled even friendly Arabs from their villages. Even so, the paper was almost unanimously criticized by the Arab attendees, especially those who came from the villages that I mentioned, because they were afraid of being portrayed as collaborators. The Israeli accounts also omit the history of friendship with Palestinian Arabs, the better to justify the expulsions that they perpetrated.

The third misleading element of the Israeli paradigm is the assertion that Palestinian identity is restricted to the status of being a passive victim or a coward. The old Israeli history portrayed Palestinians as a passive people who fled their homes without cause, thereby revealing the shallowness of their ties to their land. Benvenisti describes this at some length:

> The ultimate proof of the superiority of Zionist love of the homeland was to be found in the panicked flight of hundreds of thousands of Arabs from their homes (in 1948–49). [According to Ben-Gurion] the Arabs left "quite easily, after the first defeat, even though no danger of destruction or massacre awaited them." . . . This competition over who was more attached "to this land" was just a variation on a conventional tenet of Zionist ideology: The Arabs neglected the land . . . and therefore they have no right to the homeland . . . [W]hen it comes right down to it, who cares for that which is not his?[64]

The older Israeli politicians and historians claimed that Palestinians were victimized by their own leaders. The Israeli "new historians" are willing to recognize Israeli expulsions and to portray Palestinians as the victims of both Israeli and Arab leaders. Sadly, Arab writing, while different from the Israeli narrative, still echoes the "Palestinian as victim" theme. Even though Arab historiography glorifies freedom fighters within each separate national narrative (Syrians and Algerians against the French, Libyans against Italians, etc.) it portrays Palestinians during the 1948 war only as victims and rarely as active agents. For decades, Palestine was seen as a weak, unprepared society overwhelmed by a stronger and more organized force while, paradoxically, the strength of the surrounding Arab countries and armies was wildly exaggerated in Israeli writing.

Although this paradigm of Palestinian weakness reflects the very real pain of the ethnic cleansing, expulsion, and destruction suffered by the Palestinians, it is not the whole story because it misses all of the evidence of Palestinian effectiveness and resistance. In the end, Israeli society was indeed stronger and more organized, and had important international support, especially from the old and new superpowers—Britain, the United States, and, during the 1948 war, the Soviet Union.[65]

Despite these realities, however, a deeper understanding of the war shows a Palestinian community awakened by the UN Partition plan and the aggressive behavior of Zionist militias like the Haganah, the right-wing Irgun, and the Stern Gang. Thousands of peasants sold fertile lands and their wives' gold to buy rifles and ammunition.[66] Even when their resistance proved ineffective and they were driven out of their villages, they waited in nearby orchards. Thousands were killed trying to return to their homes. While they were never able to conquer well-fortified Zionist settlements, for months they succeeded in harassing and sometimes paralyzing the movement of Zionist convoys. Sometimes their interdiction of convoys involved them in battles against the Palmach, the elite forces of the Haganah. So, for example, Tabenkin, a well-known Zionist military leader wrote: "the Arabs attacked with a very inferior force that only used light, not automatic arms. I doubt if they had thirty men. This was against the superb Palmach Battalion, fully armed including twenty armored cars. The failure of the convoy was decisive and its defeat led to the Jerusalem road blockade."[67]

The village of Deir Yassin, famed as the site of a massacre, embodies the depiction of Palestinians only as victims. This picture omits the fact that there was a pitched battle at Deir Yassin, in which forty Palestinians held off a much greater Israeli force for eight hours.[68] Even after the massacre at Deir Yassin, and the restructuring and rearming of the Zionist forces into the Israeli army, dozens of villages fought bravely against being dispossessed. Most Palestinian military leaders were also competent in the field. They fought side by side with their men, and, in fact, the three main Palestinian military leaders (Abdel Qadir al-Husseini, Hassan Salameh, and Ibrahim Abou Dayeh) were killed in action in front of their men. The war legitimately can be presented not only as a disaster but also as a saga of heroism revealing deep attachment to the land and a capacity for self-sacrifice to defend it.[69]

This is a point of importance not only to historiographical writing but also to political analysis, since it contradicts the Israeli narrative, which views Palestinians exclusively as a passive people. Only in the rarest cases, and then only because of debates internal to Israeli historiography, is there any Israeli willingness to recognize Palestinian military competence or Israeli cowardice. Thus, for example, Milstein, a right-wing critic of Rabin, recognizes effective Palestinian military bravery against Haganah forces.[70]

These examples will have to suffice to suggest the work that lies ahead for Palestinian historians. Yet simply to call for further research is too facile. In the case of Palestinian historiography, the conventional remedy of returning to the documents and archives of the past is not so easily accomplished.

The Destruction of the Written Palestinian Heritage

The Israeli victory in the 1948 war had a direct impact on the capacity of Palestinians to write their own narrative. As Anderson wrote: "nations accumulate memory through the printed word" and, for Palestinians, most of their printed *world* disappeared with the war.[71] Essentially the 1948 war was a project of ethnic cleansing. It included not only the destruction of 80–85 percent of the Palestinian villages that fell under Israeli control and the expulsion of approximately 60 percent of the Palestinian people, but it was also directed at silencing even the memory—uprooting even the landscape—of the people being dispossessed.[72] Palestinian cities were likewise subjected to massive population transfers and the expropriation of Palestinian property, including their cultural heritage.

Of eleven Palestinian cities that fell to Israeli control, five—Safad, Majdal, Tiberiade, Beisan, and Beer-Saba'—were completely depopulated, reducing their inhabitants to uprooted, homeless, and penniless refugees. The Arab parts of Jerusalem (West Jerusalem), where the core of the Palestinian intelligentsia lived, faced the same fate. Five other cities—Jaffa, Haifa, Lod, Ramle, and Acre —were almost completely depopulated. Only one Palestinian city—Nazareth— remained intact—in deference to the Vatican and public opinion in the Christian world.

Most of the accounts of these events miss the point that these cities represented the intellectual core of the Palestinian society. The effect of the occupation of the Palestinian cities on Palestinian culture was actually more significant than the fall of the villages. The cities were the custodians of a cultural identity that was in the midst of being formulated. Israelis destroyed or confiscated all public libraries, printing presses and publishing houses, the land registry, the archives of municipal councils, hospitals, schools, and cultural centers. Private libraries, family papers, and personal diaries of intellectuals were also taken. *In the areas that fell under Israeli control, which included the main cultural and intellectual centers of Palestinian society, the totality of a written cultural heritage disappeared.*

An example of the loss of libraries and personal papers is that of Moustafa Mourad al-Dabbagh, whose 6,000-page manuscript of the history of Palestine (*Biladuna Filastin*) was thrown overboard by an Arab sailor in Jaffa port in the scramble of refugees fleeing the intensive bombardment of the city. Dabbagh had compiled Palestinian village profiles and, only decades later, was able to re-create this masterwork in an eleven-volume series. The first Palestinian encyclopedia (*al-Mawsu'a al-Falistinyeh*), published in Damascus in 1984, is based on his study and presents data for 391 villages.[73] In a similar vein, Bolus Farah, a Palestinian Communist who always preached Arab–Jewish solidarity and who had many Jewish friends, recounted in his diaries: "The same day, I went to my house in the street of the Prophet (*shari' al-Anbia*). I was expelled, dealt the worst blow, in that the one who usurped my house shouted 'Aravim' (Arab, in Hebrew). I said, 'This is my house, khawaja' but the khawaja (gentleman)'s face turned red, he frothed at the mouth, and almost choked on his anger as he insulted me in Hebrew. If I was very sad it was mainly because of my books and papers and the things with a sentimental and personal value, things very precious to me and meaningless, worthless to him."[74] The family of George Antonius succeeded in sending most of his books abroad but failed to rescue many of his personal papers.[75] Muhammed Batrawi, a famous Palestinian critic, tells the sad story of being unable to retrieve family photographs that he had hidden when, as a member of a work crew sent from an Israeli detention camp, he was accidentally assigned to an Israeli supervised labor force in his own village.[76] Tawfiq abou Su'ud, an educator who later became the head of the Birzeit University Board of Trustees, laments the loss of a library of rare Arab literature that he had spent thirty years collecting.[77] Similarly, Khalil Sakakini, the author of the curriculum used for decades in schools throughout the Arab world, deeply mourned the loss of his library, built up over a lifetime. He wrote:

> Goodbye, my precious, valuable, well-chosen books! I say my books, meaning that I didn't inherit you from parents or grandparents. . . . And I didn't borrow you from other people either; you were brought together by this old man standing in front of you . . . Who would believe that doctors used to borrow medical books from me. . . . [N]o linguistic problem ever arose in one of the

government departments without those concerned consulting me, because they knew my library was the most likely place to find a solution . . . Goodbye, my books! I don't know what became of you after our departure. Have you been looted or burned? Have you been honorably transferred to a public or private library? Or have you been carted over to grocery shops so that your pages could be used for wrapping onions?[78]

Fortunately Sakakini was able to take with him thousands of pages of his personal diaries. They now form one of the principal primary sources about life in Palestinian society at the end of the Ottoman period and throughout the years of the Mandate. Their richness suggests the magnitude of the loss of similar materials from other Palestinian writers.

The personal experience of losing family documents continues to the present day. On April 23, 2004, Israeli journalist Amira Haas wrote in *Ha'aretz:*

The family of Nadia Abdullah, known as Umm Ghassan, learned from its experiences. After losing family pictures from their home in Acre in 1948, they decided in 1982, during the Israeli assault on Beirut, to give all their photographs to Druze friends for safekeeping. In 2000, with the outbreak of the intifada, one of Nadia's children, who had worked for a Jordanian bank in Ramallah but was forced to leave when Israel did not renew the work visa in his Jordanian passport, took all the pictures with him. He figured they would be safest with him, in Amman.[79]

Even more recently, from Rafah, she writes:

Palestinian families who live close to the Egyptian border learned the lesson years ago: They keep small bags filled with important documents, some cash and a few sentimental items always ready. Whenever bulldozers plowed toward them, or whenever tank shells crashed nearby, or whenever helicopters hovered above—as happened as recently as May 12—they grabbed their bags and fled.[80]

Haas's articles also show that newspapers can provide a very important data source for historians. In 1948, Palestinians lost their newspapers as well as the archives of those newspapers. In only two cases—*Falastin* (Palestine) and *a'Difa* (The Defense)—do microfilm records exist. But they are expensive and, to be viewed, require even more expensive machines, so they are not widely available to Arab scholars.

Documents of organizations that resisted Israeli military incursions were particularly the target of confiscation. Only days after its occupation of the West Bank and the Gaza Strip in 1967, Israel seized all political documents of the National Palestinian Movement from 1948 to 1967 that were found in the headquarters of the Jordanian administration and intelligence service in the West Bank and in the Egyptian administration in Gaza Strip. These documents have become part of the Israel State archives, housed in the building of the Israeli Cabinet—a revealing symbol of the Israeli will to appropriate the Palestinian heritage. Israeli historians were able to publish from these sources (for example, Cohen, *Political Parties in the West Bank under Jordanian Regime, 1947–1967*), whereas it is extremely difficult for Palestinian scholars to do so.[81] Although, legally, Palestinians can access documents in Israeli archives, their practical ability to do so is always limited by language barriers, the need for hard-to-get special permits, and so on. Doing so has also been rendered impossible by Israeli measures governing the movement of Palestinians.

The archive of al-Jihad Almuqadas—the only organized Palestinian military force during the 1948 war—was lost in four successive stages. The first part disappeared immediately in 1948, with the fall of the Palestinian cities and villages. The main part, housed in the two villages of Birzeit and 'Ein Sinia (in the West Bank), was confiscated by the Jordanian army, which took control of this area in May 1948. To this day we do not know if the Jordanians have kept this part of the archive or if it was lost or destroyed. A smaller part of the archive was hidden with one of the members of the Husseini family, who burned it in 1967 for fear of the Israeli reprisals that would follow its capture.[82] The last part of the archive was housed in the Arab Studies Institute Archives (within the Orient House collection) under the directorship of Faisal Husseini. In 2001, two days after Husseini's death and three days after a suicide bombing in Tel Aviv, the Israelis confiscated the entire Orient House collection, which included the most extensive collection dedicated to Palestinian history in Jerusalem and the Occupied Territories, and 1.5 million documents, including the remaining al-Jihad Almuqadas materials.

Nor are confiscations confined to the Occupied Territories. During the invasion of Lebanon in 1982, another large collection of Palestinian documents was lost when the Israelis occupied the Palestinian Research Center (PRC) and transported its entire contents to Israel. The PRC was the central archive of the Palestinian people, its heritage and memory. Although Israel was supposed to return documents from the PRC in the context of a prisoner exchange agreement that included prisoners' belongings, no one knows what was lost, what was returned, and what happened during the period of storage.

The foregoing shows that the problem of Palestinian documents is not confined to the 1948 era, nor to the land of the Occupied Territories, for the written political heritage of and about the Palestinians has been, like their land, always subject to confiscation.

Censorship and Control

As Rogan and Shlaim wrote:

> History plays a fundamental role in state formation, in legitimizing the origins of the state and its political system, in the Middle East as elsewhere. Governments in the region enjoy many direct and indirect powers over the writing of history. . . . [S]chool texts in history are the preserve of the state. Most universities in the Middle East are state-run and . . . [funded]. National historical associations and government printing presses serve as filters to weed out . . . unauthorized histories and to disseminate state-sanctioned truths. As promotion within the historical establishment is closely linked to adherence to the official line, historians have had little incentive to engage in critical history writing.[83]

Those who dare to defy pay a certain price, as the cases of Israeli historians and intellectuals like Simha Flapan, Uri Milstein, and Teddy Katz illustrate. The situation in the Arab world is even far more severe. Arab historians have to cope with a different level of control and censorship, which relates to the lack of democracy and free expression. Typically, the government of each Arab state censors and fights historical literature directly or indirectly critical of its own regime. The greatest absolute taboo comes when one criticizes *al-Za'im* (the Leader). Personally, my doctoral dissertation, "Fath Movement and Leadership," was never published because it demystified the leadership of Yasser Arafat. Said's *The End of the Peace Process: Oslo and After*, which was very critical of Arafat, was banned by the Palestinian authorities.[84] In Jordan and Syria, bookstores have no trace of books critical of the Hashemite or Assad dynasties. Even in the National Jordanian Library, books of a critical nature are confined to one room, and access to those works is granted only on a case-by-case basis.

Israel enjoys a robust democracy within its Green Line borders. In severe contrast, military rule in the Occupied Territories exercises a censorship of a different order and magnitude, even compared to the lack of free expression in the Arab world. Not only are publications that directly criticize the occupation censored but also those that speak to Palestinian resistance, and Palestinian identity, culture, and history. Israel controls each book that enters the Occupied

Territories. The effect is so intrusive that even university libraries cannot secure full collections of any review or journal that deals with the Arab–Israel conflict or Palestinian culture. Benvenisti summarizes the aims of Israeli censorship as the desire to eradicate written "expression that could foster Palestinian nationalist feelings, or that suggest that Palestinians are a nation with a national heritage."[85] It must also be noted that Israeli censorship has been institutionalized under military orders, and that it has given rise to an ever expanding list of banned books, focused particularly on Middle Eastern history and Arab authors.

Other Israeli policies in the Occupied Territories also have a direct impact on the capacity of Arab intellectuals to produce scholarly work. Adding to the problem of archives (discussed above and below) and censorship, the chronic problem of university closures, and checkpoints that render travel nearly impossible, take their toll. One example will suffice: my own Birzeit University was closed sixteen times between its founding in 1974 and 2004. One of those closures—which extended to all Palestinian universities—continued for four years, from 1988 to 1992. During this time, scholarly work could be done only out of private collections or abroad.

To be fair, universities in other Arab countries also have failed to produce significant work on the 1948 war. So we need to search for other factors that impede this work. Among them are the lack of research orientation in Arab universities, heavy teaching loads, and the lack of research funds. Each undermines scholarly productivity. And even for those who overcome these barriers, access to the necessary documentary sources can be difficult.

Problems Pertaining to Arab, Israeli, and International Archives

The challenge for historians lies not only in the destruction of documents, and the censorship and control of scholarly materials, but also in the organization of archives in the Arab countries, in Israel, and in the West.

Not a single Arab country that participated in the 1948 war has opened the archive of the relevant time period to the public. Unlike Israel (see below) and Western democracies, Arab countries have developed no rules governing the declassification of political and military documents, nor do they appear likely to do so any time soon. In Jordan, the same dynasty that directed the war forms the current regime. In Egypt, since 1952, political leaders (Presidents Gamal Abdel Nasser, Anwar Sadat, and Hosni Mubarak) are drawn from the military class which was defeated in 1948. Any declassification will reveal failures that have the potential to embarrass current regimes, which are therefore reluctant to open such a Pandora's box.

Recently, exceptions to the rule of censorship have been made at a few archives on a case-by-case basis. For example, some Egyptian generals were allowed to see Egyptian army documents. General Ibrahim Shakeeb, who was for four years the head of the Egyptian army's military history department, was able to complete a doctoral dissertation, later a book, entitled *Palestine War, 1948, the Egyptian Vision.*[86] Similarly, Mohammed Hassanin Haykal, an Egyptian journalist, published two volumes about the 1948 war, with an appendix composed of hundreds of selected documents (e.g., telegraphs) of the Egyptian army.[87] In Jordan, volumes of selected documents about the war which strengthen the legitimacy of the Hashemite dynasty were also released.[88] According to an American researcher, at least one part of the Jordanian National Archive has been opened to the public.[89] However, it is well to remember the caution expressed by Shakeeb, who noticed that many Egyptian army documents were false—dispatches composed by anxious or vainglorious field commanders. Fully knowing the situation of the Arab armies during the 1948 war, Shakeeb's note of caution can be extended to the documents of other Arab armies as well.

More typically, however, Arab archives are closed to independent researchers. Beyond the problem of censorship, there is little sense in the Arab world, either among archivists or ordinary citizens, that archives are national resources that belong to the people. Documents are not systematically collected, and such collections are not in public demand.[90] My associates and I faced this problem while working in the Birzeit University Research Center. My subject was the massacre in the village of Dawayme. I knew from the work of Sami Hidawi of the existence of a list of names of the victims of the massacre.[91] There was a copy of this list in the Hebron police department and another with an officer in the Jordanian Army. However, the Center field researchers were not allowed to access the archives, nor did the archives acknowledge the existence of the list.

In the Israeli case, there are rich and varied archives. In addition to confiscated Palestinian materials, Israeli archives include records from political institutions, especially the Jewish Agency, Zionist military organizations, the army, political parties, the archives of all kibbutzim, and dozens of personal papers and diaries written by many of the political and military leaders who were important at the time of the 1948 war.

The Israelis undoubtedly possess a great treasure of firsthand sources. For example, all of the minutes of the meetings of the Council of Ministers of the Israeli government since the first day of the Council's existence have been recorded verbatim by professional stenographers. Thus, every single sentence and the name of the minister who uttered it are captured for the record. This practice is rare. Most governments produce summary minutes of their official proceedings, which are much less detailed.[92]

When Israeli law codified access to Israeli archives, it decreed that, in the case of political papers, documents be opened to the public thirty years after their creation, and, for military and security documents, fifty years after their creation. But there are three cases when political and military papers can be withheld. Shielded from disclosure are papers that might (1) endanger the security of Israel; (2) damage Israel's image or reputation, especially internationally; and (3) embarrass living Zionist or Israeli leaders.

These exceptions create both trivial and substantial opportunities for censorship. A trivial example is the blacking out from the protocols of Cabinet meetings passages that show Ben-Gurion swearing at Menachim Begin.[93] A critical example involves the censorship of information to be found in the same sources about the "excesses" and "deviant behavior" (i.e. massacres and atrocities against Palestinians) committed by Israeli forces in 1948.[94]

Morris is considered to be one of the new historians who has dealt with these restrictions. More than ten years ago, his request to see the "Shapira Report" (a compilation of "deviant behaviors" by the Israeli army during the 1948 war) was refused. Morris appealed to the High Court of Justice to revoke this restriction on the grounds that the "Shapira Report" was a political document as defined by the Israeli Ministry of Justice and not a military document. When Morris went to the High Court it became clear that a ministerial committee comprised of two ministers decided which files were censored under the justification that they harmed the security of the state.[95]

How is it possible for Morris and others to know about a censored report? Palumbo, who authored one of the most important books about the massacres of the 1948 war, wrote insightfully about the tension between secrecy and disclosure that makes Israeli documents at once frustratingly incomplete and startlingly revealing.[96]

There are some documents from Israeli archives which suggest a general design to expel Palestinians from their new state in 1948. Why were these Israeli documents made available to researchers? Apparently, the Israelis had three choices. They could have kept their material totally closed, unconditionally available, or restricted to scholars. Granting total access to all files from 1948 would have been unthinkable. No nation would allow the unrestricted opening of all its files which dealt with such a sensitive subject as the expulsion of hundreds of thousands of civilians. Total closure of all 1948 files was equally impossible. The Israelis are a people who pride themselves on their western practices. While doing my own research, I was told by an Israeli archivist: "Of course, like all civilized countries, we open our archives under a 30-years rule."

To have kept all the files on 1948 closed would have been not only an admission of guilt but would have been similar to the policy of Third World countries to which Israelis consider themselves superior. Thus, keeping the files of the Office of Advisors on Arab Affairs and many files from the Ministry of Minorities closed, while removing, according to the assistant director of the Israel State Archive, "about two percent" of the material from open files was the only policy possible for Israel. A few embarrassing documents were released. But in general the Israeli Government's policy of limited access has been successful in convincing many people, via the revisionist [historians], that the Jewish state is not responsible for creating the refugee problem that has plagued the Middle East for so many decades.[97]

Palumbo's analysis can be used to account for such information as that reported by Agence France Presse and quoted in *Al Quds*. Yeshua Freundlich, of the Israel State Archives, reported that "95 percent of censored documents [of the Israeli cabinet] concern either crimes perpetrated by Israeli soldiers against the Arab population or practical expulsion procedures. But we did not censor the general political discussion concerning the expulsion of the Palestinians."[98] But note that Segev, an Israeli new historian, partially contradicts Freundlich's assertions. He maintains that some policy discussions were also censored—for example, Ben-Gurion's suggestion to the Cabinet on September 26, 1948, to violate the Israel–Jordan cease-fire, explaining that Israel could benefit from the renewal of the fighting to complete the occupation of Galilee and to expel 100,000 Palestinians. The Cabinet refused his suggestion.[99]

Access is not the only difficulty with Israeli archives. Typically, Israeli documents miss the human dimension of the Palestinian experience of expulsion. To a large extent, the Israelis dehumanized the Palestinians—as did other perpetrators of ethnic cleansing projects in history. Thus the Palestinians are faceless in the Israeli archives, and their fate is captured mainly in numbers. Villages are portrayed only as military targets, never as human communities, and, likewise, their inhabitants are never recognized by name or credited with recognizable human emotion.

Zionist leaders such as Ben-Gurion understood the danger of creating explicit documentation about their plans to "transfer" Palestinians out of their homeland. Consequently, there is no "black box" or "smoking gun" documenting a centrally controlled plan of expulsion.[100] Nevertheless, in the hostile environment that the Zionist movement created against the Palestinians, there was no need to give explicit written orders. The "silent urge" of the Zionist military was, in any case, to "do what can't be said" (i.e., to expel the Palestinians).[101] The best example of this urge is what happened in Lod during the occupation of that city. When Itzhak Rabin, the commander of Operation Dani (which was responsible for the occupation of Lod and Ramle), asked Ben-Gurion what to do with the inhabitants of the two cities, Ben-Gurion refused to give him a written order, or even a verbal one, to transfer the inhabitants. Instead, he waved his hand to indicate what was to be done. The expulsion then proceeded.[102] The position of the Israeli censors who deleted this case from Rabin's diaries in 1978 shows the care that Zionist propaganda has taken to suppress material that would call into question the legitimacy of the founding of Israel. Moreover, any reader of the diaries of Ben-Gurion will find that he imposed severe self-censorship on himself long before the Israeli censors did.

One final problem with Israeli archives is that of forging or falsifying documents. Here, Morris's words are significant. He writes: "In trying to produce or maintain an unblemished record, nations and political movements sometimes rewrite not only their history but also, it appears, the documents upon which that historiography must necessarily be based. The Zionist movement and the State of Israel are no exceptions; indeed, they may be among the more accomplished practitioners of this strange craft."[103] He follows this opening observation with eighteen pages of examples of materials that exemplify the "strange craft" of falsification.

Together, these factors—restricted access, self-censorship, and falsification of documents—make Israeli archives a dangerously incomplete source for writing the history of the 1948 war, especially in the absence of independent Arab archival material.

The problems with archives extend to Western collections. For example, in 1997 and 1998 I visited the headquarters of the International Committee of the Red Cross (ICRC) in Geneva. Its archives had just opened, and I was hoping to find information regarding Israeli massacres during the 1948 war. I expected to find substantial documentation because I knew that, during the 1948 war, the ICRC had been active on the ground, assisting refugees, monitoring conditions, negotiating prisoner exchanges, and delivering humanitarian aid to detention centers. But I found that, in the entire archive, only the well-known massacre in Deir Yassin is mentioned. This omission is particularly suspect in light of the fact that even Zionist archives, as well as UN documents and Arab oral histories, have revealed the existence of dozens of atrocities and massacres. I also went through the entire ICRC photo archives and, to my surprise, found not one set of pictures except those regarding the murder of Count Folke Bernadotte, specifically pictures of his bullet-riddled car and his coffin in the French Consulate. I raised the question of whether the archives had been "cleaned" of documents incriminating to Israel and was assured by officials that no such cleansing had occurred. Thus, the disparity between the known activities of the ICRC and its documentation remains to be explained.

Similarly, the United Nations archives in New York, which I visited in 2004, continue to classify certain documents even fifty-five years after the events that they describe. The question is, who is protected by this discretion? Palumbo argues that the UN limits access to documents that might damage its own reputation, but the implication of this standard for particular research questions is unclear.[104]

All of the above considerations show that the problems of the Arab narrative are not due solely to problems of nationalism, ideology, or apologetics. The practical difficulties of securing the relevant information must also be taken into account, especially since Arab governments do not protect freedom of expression nor respect the kind of empirical research that a complete and persuasive Palestinian narrative requires.

Palestinian Oral History—Necessity, Credibility, and Specificity

If recourse to documents cannot be expected to remedy all of the problems of Palestinian historiography, one source has proven immensely valuable: Palestinian oral narratives. Oral testimonies are well-established data sources in classical and contemporary history outside the Middle East, having proven their value by traditional criteria of academic rigor.

But in the contested case of Palestinian historiography, all Israeli historians, old and new, except Pappe and Katz, at first refused the voice of oral history, which is often the voice of the victim. The old Chinese saying that "one stroke of a quill pen is better than a thousand memories" speaks to this hesitation. Their concerns are not entirely baseless for, despite the importance of oral histories, they are also in many ways inherently troublesome. Memory can be unreliable and the capacity to recall details may fade or be distorted, especially after many years have passed. Interviewers' questions may be biased, clearly seeking one answer over another and thereby distorting the record. When the imperfect process of recall is further embedded in a highly ideological context, the credibility of oral testimonies may be even more problematic. Palestinians themselves were aware of these challenges. In fact, the *Birzeit Research Center Review* was the first to publish a paper on the problems of Palestinian oral history.[105] I must admit that written sources, including Israeli documents, are sometimes more accurate about dates, times, and battle strategies than the information retrieved through oral histories.

In the Palestinian case, however, the difficulties of oral testimony are countered by two considerations. First, oral traditions have always been the main tool of collective memory, deeply embedded in traditional Palestinian society. Until the end of the nineteenth century only a small minority was literate, and history was always a matter for oral narration. Second, because of the destruction, falsification, and restricted access to documents, detailed above, oral histories become, by default, an important strategy for retrieving lost data. In fact, all new works about the 1948 war, including those that make extensive use of Israeli archival material, are validating Palestinian eyewitness accounts.

Whether historians rely on oral or written sources, the real issue is the accuracy and credibility of their material. Palumbo, for example, speaking about Palestinian oral narratives, captures both the hesitation and the affirmation of oral sources.

> Clearly, the testimony of Arab refugees must be used with great care. Initially, I decided not to use the memoirs of Palestinian survivors of 1948, but I soon realized that their testimony was verified by non-Arab sources. For example, there is the case of Amina Musa, an Arab peasant woman from Kabri, a small village in Galilee, who described the devastation of her village on May 21, 1948, during a Zionist attack aimed at apprehending Faris Sirhan, a Palestinian nationalist leader in the area. Within the diary of General McNeil, a retired British officer with large landholdings in Galilee, the entry for May 21 reads: "Every house in Kabri demolished. Faris Sirhan's big new house was the first to go up. He is a member of the Arab Higher Committee in Damascus."[106] On other occasions I found that the refugees' estimates of casualties in Zionist atrocities was lower than those of the U.S. and other neutral observers, who, in some cases, counted the bodies of victims. Of course, not all Palestinian testimony is without error. Taken together with non-Arab verification, however, it can be a useful source for students of this period, particularly since 1948 is not just a historical controversy but also a human tragedy.[107]

Nor was Palumbo's experience idiosyncratic. A number of other researchers who have relied on oral testimonies have been vindicated when other data sources (Israeli archives, foreign memoirs) became available. For example, Nazzal's work on the Palestinian exodus from Galilee, which was based on oral interviews, and which he wrote as a Georgetown University doctoral dissertation in 1974, was confirmed twenty years later by Morris, using declassified Israeli documents.[108] Similarly, the Birzeit Research Center's work on Deir Yassin, published in 1987, estimated the number of victims at 100.[109] This estimate has proven to be more accurate than the documentary sources of the Jewish Agency, the Red Cross, and the British authorities (who maintain the number as 254) and shows not only the validity of oral history but also the disinclination of Palestinians to exaggerate their claims. Efrat ben Ze'ev, an Israeli researcher who studied three Palestinian villages, concluded that there was no contradiction between the testimonies of the villagers and information in the Israeli archives.[110] Illa Hershavi conducted oral history on the village of Dawayme in 1984, and her work, likewise, was later confirmed by the Israeli documents.[111] The Birzeit Research Center published data on two massacres—in Tieret Haifa and Abu Shusha. At the time of publication in 1984, Israeli historians remained silent. In 2004, Morris implicitly confirmed the massacre at Abu Shusha.[112] As for Tieret Haifa, Morris confirms the presence of burned bodies consistent with oral testimonies, although the Israeli army continues to dispute the interpretation of the presence of burned bodies.[113]

But if oral testimonies often converge with documentary evidence, a question arises: What do oral testimonies add to the record? Fraser, the author of a major oral history of the Spanish civil war, says that, "major historical works . . . have charted most of the features of that conflict, and it would be vain to hope to add anything new to the overall map of the period. But . . . one area has remained unarticulated: . . . never more than at a time of extreme social crisis does the atmosphere become a determining factor in the way people respond to events. For however intangible, it is never abstract or distant. It is what people feel. And what people feel lays the ground for their actions."[114]

Finally, Laurens says that, with oral history, "for the first time, the voice of its victims makes itself heard in the Israeli historiography. History becomes embodied with a soul, with flesh and blood, the history of the terror that was suffered has become audible."[115]

In short, despite their initial disclaimers, even Israeli historians have come to acknowledge implicitly the validity and value of Palestinian oral testimonies. In regrouping all these fragmented stories, the Palestinian oral history of

1948 reveals the existence of vast forced removals. Fifty-five years later, Morris came to accept this thesis, even if he also justified the acts which it describes.

Conclusion

This chapter has examined aspects of the Arab and Palestinian historiography of the 1948 war. The Israelis have characterized Arab historiography as apologetic, legitimacy-seeking, and, overall, not credible. While the book edited by Rogan and Shlaim presents a more balanced view, blaming *both* sides for writing "nationalist histories . . . guided more by a 'quest for legitimacy' than by an honest reckoning with the past," it fails to recognize the substantial contributions of recent Arab (mainly Palestinian) scholarship and the growing compilation of Palestinian historiography.[116]

In fact, in the last two decades, because of the quality of recent Palestinian scholarship, Israeli historians have been obliged to respond to Palestinian authors. This response took different forms—from open acceptance to implicit (and grudging) acceptance to rejection. Masalha's work created a chain reaction in Israeli historiography, obliging it to examine more deeply the question of the transfer.[117] Kimmerling now acknowledges Khalidi's work about Plan Dalet as a blueprint of forced removals.[118] The author's concept of sociocide as the theoretical framework for understanding Israeli policies toward Palestinians has been adopted by Israelis under the name of "politicide."[119] Works by Nazzal, Sayigh, and the Birzeit Research Center underlie Benvenisti's and later Morris's characterization of Israeli conduct as "ethnic cleansing."[120]

Nevertheless, weaknesses and biases remain in the Arab narrative of the 1948 war. The fragmentation of the narrative along multiple lines and not only on a national basis, the failure to disentangle it from some Israeli paradigms despite a real effort to dismantle certain Israeli myths, its inability to overcome the destruction of the Palestinian written heritage, and the censorship of Arab archives have all played a role in limiting the power of the Palestinian narrative. Some of these flaws can be easily corrected, for example, by using the voice of the victims and exploiting Western and Israeli archives.

Beyond any technical difficulties, a fatal shortcoming is the absence of an Arab national project to produce a comprehensive work based exclusively on empirical data and concrete historical research, and not on political discourse and ideology. The work I am calling for would need to be much less mythic than its Israeli counterpart but equally effective in informing Palestinians of their history and entering into their everyday discourse and practice. That this

Palestinian narrative will have to be forged in the context of an unfavorable balance of power, in the absence of a Palestinian state, and in the absence of democratic traditions of free inquiry makes the work more difficult but no less urgent.

This chapter is written from the assumption that the Palestinian narrative is important in itself. But not everyone agrees that it is. Israeli politicians, usually so dedicated to remembrance, are even willing to speak Arabic to say, "*Illi Fatt Matt*"—"What's done, is done; forget the past." Given seemingly irreconcilable stories, some academics also have wondered about the wisdom of looking to history in the midst of the enormous practical and political difficulties that Palestinians face. Thucydides, however, that ur-historian, would understand the need for an empowering Palestinian narrative. In his history of an earlier war, he reports a statement by Athenian representatives: "We will not make a long and unconvincing speech, full of fine phrases, to prove that our victory . . . justifies our empire . . . Let . . . us say what we really think and reach a practical agreement. *You know and we know, as practical men, that the question of justice arises only between parties equal in strength,* [for] the strong do what they can and the weak submit."[121]

Thucydides' Athenians spoke from the victor's perspective—well known for its propensity to have the last word in the writing of history. But Burke also reminds us that "history is forgotten by the victors. They can afford to forget, while the losers are unable to accept what happened and are condemned to brood over it, relive it, and reflect how different it might have been."[122] In struggling to write their own history, Palestinians are attesting to the importance of equality, at least in narratives. In this gallant insistence, they are demonstrating another aspect of the resilience celebrated by Beit-Hallahmi when he wrote:

> After 1948 the Zionist dream called for the natives to leave the stage of history and disappear. They were expected to vanish into oblivion. Instead, they became the spoilers. Following a total defeat and disintegration in 1948 they have refused to disappear quietly. . . . They have always been a party to the events in the Middle East . . . From total unknowns they had become an entity about whom the whole world was concerned. . . . The goal of the Palestinian[s] . . . since the 1960s was to put [themselves] back on the stage of history and they have succeeded.[123]

In the end, Palestinians need to write their history in order to heal themselves. But such healing-through-history can arise only if Palestinian history is written in the spirit of "people [whether Arabs or Jews] who will look to memory as an instrument of learning and salvation, rather than of denial and repression."[124]

NOTES

I thank the following institutions and individuals for supporting this work in a variety of ways: Professor Robert Rotberg of the Belfer Center's Program on Intrastate Conflict, Kennedy School of Government, Harvard University, and Deborah West, Program Coordinator of the Program on Intrastate Conflict; the Program for Scholars at Risk, and especially Jacqueline Bhaba; the Department of History, Harvard University, especially Professors John Womack and Janet Hatch; the Middle East Center of Harvard University, especially Professor Roger Owen; and, for their invaluable editorial suggestions, Professor Susan Slyomovic of MIT, Professor Henry Munson of the University of Maine, and Professor Eve Spangler of the Boston College Department of Sociology.

1. In the words of Ze'ev Sternhell: "Israel no longer makes do with the demand that the Arabs recognize it as a sovereign state but also demands acceptance of its hegemony"; quoted in "The Logic of Body Counts," *Ha'aretz* (April 2, 2004).

2. Susan Slyomovic, "The Rape of Qula, a Destroyed Palestinian Village," in Ahmed Sa'di and Lila Abu-Lughod (eds.), *The Claim of Memory: Palestine, 1948* (New York, forthcoming).

3. From Said's new afterword to *Orientalism*, quoted in Rashid Khalidi, *Palestinian Identity: The Construction of Modern National Consciousness* (New York, 1997), 9–10. Israeli historian Uri Ram gives a similar explanation of Jewish identity and history: "Isaac Marcus Jost (1793–1869) did not consider the Jewish people as a cohesive unit, but rather thought that 'external' circumstances conditioned the differing perceptions of Jewish identity, an identity which might, under suitable conditions, fade away" ("Zionist Historiography and the Invention of Modern Jewish Nationhood: The Case of Ben Zion Dinur," *History and Memory: Studies in Representation of the Past;* special issue: *Israeli Historiography Revisited,* VII [1995], 101).

4. While there is a vast literature defining myth and narrative, in this chapter I use these terms in a way that is consistent with the usage at the conference "Myth and Narrative in the Israeli Palestinian Conflict." In reporting on conference proceedings, Deborah West wrote: "Throughout the conference the term 'myth' was generally considered to indicate a story, often about the origins of a group, which was not historically true. The term 'narrative' was used to indicate a person's or group's story of what they perceived to have happened" (*Myth and Narrative in the Israeli-Palestinian Conflict* [Cambridge, MA, 2003], 1).

5. Ilan Pappe, *Israel-Palestine Question: Rewriting Histories* (London, 1999), 3.

6. Maxim Rodinson, "Israel Fait Colonial," *Les Temps Moderns*, CCLIII, (1967), 51; published in English as *Israel: A Colonial-Settler State?* (New York, 1973); Beshara

Doumani, "Al-tarikh wa l'adat al-Tarikh lil-Filastin al-'uthmaniyya wa-l Intidabiyya" (Historical reconsideration of the history of Ottoman and Mandatory Palestine), *Afaq Filistiniyya*, VI (1991), 5–7.

7. For a succinct discussion of these myths, see Rogan and Shlaim's summary of Flapan, in Eugene Rogan and Avi Shlaim (eds.), *The War for Palestine: Rewriting the History of 1948* (Cambridge, 2001), 3.

8. Statement in 1948 by Moshe Shertok Sharett, Foreign Minister of Israel, before the Political Committee, United Nations S-0617/0002/04. "The Jewish Agency received now more details about the occupation of Deir Yassin by groups of dissidents. It expresses shock and disgust at this barbaric action. This operation substantially contradicts the spirit of the Yishuv . . . [and] the regulations of the Geneva Convention which was accepted by the Agency without reservation" (in Yehuda Slotsky, *Safer Toldot Ha Haganah*, [Tel Aviv, 1972], 1548; translated by Ahmad Kalifah as *The Palestine War 1947–1948: An Official Israeli Account* [Beirut, 1986], 442).

9. Albert E. Glock, quoted in Efrat Ben-Ze-ev, "From Oral Traditions to Historiographical Enterprises: Uprooted Palestinians Documenting Their Lost Village," paper presented at the Third Mediterranean Social and Political Research Meetings, March 20–24, 2002, Florence, Italy.

10. Moustafa M. al-Dabbagh, *Biladuna Filastin* (Our Country Palestine), (Kofr Qar', Israel, 1991, 2nd ed.). See, for example, Khalidi, *Palestinian Identity;* and Muhammad Y. Muslih, *The Origins of Palestinian Nationalism* (New York, 1988).

11. For example, the concept of the melting pot is deemphasized in Palestinian popular culture, which prefers the story of descent from a single prestigious tribe of progenitors.

12. Kamal Adul Fattah and Wolf-Dieter Hutteroth, *Historical Geography of Palestine, Transjordan and Southern Syria in the Late Sixteenth Century* (Erlangen, Germany, 1977); Issa Khalaf, *Politicism in Palestine: Arab Factionalism and Social Disintegration, 1939–1948* (Albany, 1991); Beshara Doumani, *Rediscovering Palestine: Merchants and Peasants in Jabal Nablus, 1700–1900* (Berkeley, 1995); Khalidi, *Palestinian Identity.*

13. Nafez Nazzal, *The Palestinian Exodus from Galilee, 1948* (Beirut, 1978); Nur Masalha, *Expulsion of the Palestinians: The Concept of Transfer in Zionist Political Thought, 1882–1948* (Washington DC, 1992); Walid Khalidi (ed.), *All That Remains: The Palestinian Villages Occupied and Depopulated by Israel in 1948* (Washington, DC, 1988); Sharif Kanaana, *Still on Vacation! The Eviction of the Palestinians in 1948* (Jerusalem, 1992).

14. Benny Morris, *The Birth of the Palestinian Refugee Problem, 1947–1949* (New York, 1987, 1st ed.), 307 n. 41, notes that the work translated by Sabag for Israeli use includes the writings of Muhammed Nimr Khatib, *Ahdath al-Nakba* (The events of the Nakba) (Beirut, 1967, 2nd ed.). The first edition was published in Damascus in 1951 as *Min Athar al-Nakba* (In the Wake of the Nakba).

15. Traditionally the term "ethnic cleansing" was not in use on either side until re-

cently. As Slyomovic, "The Rape of Qula" notes: "To describe why Palestinians left in 1948, the terms used by historians imply widely divergent ideological, and hence policy, conclusions: expulsion versus self-expulsion, abandonment, flight, exodus, evacuation, uprooting, displacement, dispersion, exile, depopulation, population transfer, ethnic cleansing, sociocide and politicide." Only rather recently has the term "ethnic cleansing" been used, on the Palestinian side, by the author, and, on the Israeli side, by Pappe, *Israel-Palestine Question*.

16. 'Aref al-'Aref, *Nakbot Filastin walfirdous Maafqud* (Palestinian Nakba and the Lost Paradise) (Beirut, 1956–1958), 6 vols. Page citations in this chapter are taken from a pirated copy (Dar al-Huda publishers, in Kofr Qar', Israel, n.d.) in the author's possession. Khatib, *Ahdath al-Nakba*.

17. Max Weber, "Science as a Vocation," in Hans Gerth and C. Wright Mills (eds.), *From Max Weber* (New York, 1958), 147.

18. Rogan and Shlaim, *The War for Palestine*, 5.

19. Ibid.

20. Suleiman Mussa, *Ayam la Tunsa al-Urdun fi Harb 1948* (Unforgettable Days: Jordan during the 1948 War) (Amman, 1982, 1st ed.); Saleh al-Shar', *Mudthakrat Jundi* (Soldier's Memoirs) (Amman, 1985 and 1989), 2 vols; Sadeq al-Shar', *Harpuna Ma' Israel, 1947–1973* (Our War with Israel, 1947–1973; Lost Battles and Victories) (Amman, 1997).

21. Abdullah Tall, *Karithat Filastin* (The Disaster of Palestine: Memoirs of Abdullah Tall, Leader of the Battle for Jerusalem) (Cairo, 1959, reissued in a pirated edition, 1999).

22. Muhammed Amin Husseini, *Haqaiq 'an qadiyato Filastin* (Facts about the Case of Palestine) (Cairo, 1956, 2nd ed.); Emile al-Ghoury, *15 Ayar 1948* (May 15, 1948: concentrated, scientific political study about the real causes of the Nakba) (Beirut, 1959); al-'Aref, *Nakbot Filastin*.

23. Al-'Aref, *Nakbot Filastin*; Musa Alami's *'Ibrato Filastin* (Lesson of Palestine) appeared in abbreviated form in *Middle East Journal*, III (1949), 372–405; Walid Qamhawi, *The Nakba and the Reconstruction* (Beirut, 1956); Naji Allush, *al-muqawama al-'Arabya fi Filastin* (Arab Resistance in Palestine) (Beirut, 1967).

24. Khalil Sakakini, *Katha Ana Yadnia* (Such Am I, Oh World) (Jerusalem, 1955). See also excerpts from Khalil Sakakini in English in Salma Khadra Jayyusi (ed.), *Anthology of Modern Palestinian Literature* (New York, 1992), 671–684; Hala Sakakini, *Jerusalem and I: A Personal Record* (Jordan, 1990); 'Ajaj Nuweihd (ed. by Bayan al-Hout), *Memoirs of 'Ajaj Nuweihd: 60 Years with the Arab Struggle* (Beirut, n.d.); Edward Said, *Out of Place: A Memoir* (New York, 1999); Hisham Sharabi, *Embers and Ashes: Memoirs of an Arab Intellectual* (Beirut, 1978); Raja Shehadeh, *A Stranger in the House* (New York, 2002); Elias Sanbar, *Le bien des absents* (Paris, 2001).

25. Ghasan Kanafani, *Thawrat 1936–1939 Fi Filastin* (The 1936–1939 Revolt in Palestine) (Beirut, pirated copy); Abdel-Wahab Kayyali, *Tarikh Filastin al-hadith* (Palestine: Modern History) was originally a Ph.D. dissertation entitled "Palestinian Arab Reactions to Zionism and the British Mandate, 1917–1939," submitted to the School of Ori-

ental and African Studies, University of London. First published in 1970, it has been reprinted a number of times, and translated into English and French. Taught in many Arab universities, it is the only book of its kind to be published and distributed by a major Western publisher; Allush, *al-muqawama;* Abdel-Wahab Kayyali, *Palestine, A Modern History* (London, 1978), (Arab version, Beirut, 1972).

26. Hillel Cohen, "Why Do Collaborators Collaborate? The Case of Early Palestinian Collaborators with Zionist Institutions (1917–1935)," unpub. paper.

27. Rosemary Sayigh, *Palestinian from Peasant to Revolutionary* (London, 1979), 58–72.

28. Ted Swedenburg, "The Palestinian Peasant as a National Signifier," *Anthropological Quarterly,* LXIII (1990), 18–30.

29. Ilana Miller, *Government and Society in Rural Palestine, 1920–1948* (Austin, 1985).

30. George Antonius, *The Arab Awakening: The Story of the Arab National Movement* (Philadelphia, 1939).

31. Al-'Aref, *Nakbot Filastin,* I, 290.

32. *Qur'an,* Surat al-Israa, 16, in ibid., 291.

33. Fawaz Gerges, "Egypt and the 1948 War: Internal Conflict and Regional Ambition," in Rogan and Shlaim (eds.), *The War for Palestine,* 151.

34. Ibrahim Shakeeb definitively refutes this myth, in his *Harbu Filastin, 1948: Rau'ya Missriya* (Palestine War, 1948: The Egyptian Vision) (Cairo, 1986), 482–509, 588–589.

35. Thucydides (ed. and trans. Richard Livingstone), *The History of the Peloponnesian War* (New York, 1960), 46.

36. Uri Milstein with Aryeh Amit, *The Rabin File: An Unauthorized Expose* (Jerusalem, 1999), 165.

37. Benny Morris, *Righteous Victims: A History of the Zionist-Arab Conflicts, 1889–1999* (New York, 1999), 189–190.

38. David Ben-Gurion, *Diaries, 1947–1949* (trans. into Arabic by the Institute of Palestinian Studies) (Beirut, 1993), entry for December 11, 1947, 50.

39. Ibid., 83.

40. Ibid., 84.

41. For a detailed account by Israeli sources of these gangs—and their lack of responsiveness to Arab leaders—see Slotsky, *Safer Toldot* (in Hebrew), 1201–1202; (in Arabic), 14–16.

42. 'Abdel Hafith Muhareb, *Haganah, IZL, and Lehi: The Relations among Zionist Military Organizations, 1927–1948* (Beirut, 1981).

43. Cunningham Papers, Middle East Center, cited in Michael Palumbo, "What

Happened to Palestine? The Revisionists Revisited," *The Link,* XXIII (1990), 34, http://student.cs.ucc.ie/cs1064/jabowen/IPSC/php/db.php?aid=818.

44. Ibid.

45. *Ha'aretz* supplement (November 17, 1978), cited in Palumbo, "What Happened to Palestine?" 36.

46. The best account of the killings is taken from oral testimonies that were collected for the first time in the Birzeit series, *The Palestinian Destroyed Villages.* The Birzeit Research Center conducted research from 1993 to 1995, and later, from 1996 to 2003, additional research was done by me with the help of my students. These testimonies can also be confirmed, by Israeli, British, and Palestinian documentary sources. For information on the village of Tieret Haifa, see Adel Rahim Mudawar (ed. Saleh Abdel Jawad), *Tieret Haifa: Palestinian Destroyed Villages* series, 21 (Birzeit, 1995); and the "Register of Patients from Haifa Government Hospital" (copy in author's possession). For the killings in Abasieh, see oral history testimonies from the author's research and the *New York Times* (December 14, 1947). For information on the Damascus Gate (Jerusalem) attack, the killings in Jaffa, Yazur, Balad il-Sheikh, and Ramle, see Masalha, *Expulsion of the Palestinians.* The number of the dead is always a matter of controversy, in part because not all scholars count those who die a few hours or days after the attacks. In the case of Tiriet Haifa, for example, official British documents record twelve fatalities (counted on the spot), but an examination of Haifa Government Hospital records indicates a higher death toll of eighteen.

47. The four Israeli versions of the expulsion, in chronological order are that "Palestinians left because of Arab orders," "Palestinians fled," "Palestinians were transferred," and "there were forced removals."

48. Ilan Pappe, "The Bridging Narrative Concept," chapter 8 of this volume.

49. Ibid.

50. Salim Tamari, author interview, Ramallah, 2002.

51. For example, al-'Aref, *Nakbot Filastin;* Sami Hadawi, *Palestine, Loss of a Heritage* (San Antonio, 1963).

52. Youssef Courbage and Philippe Fargues, *Christians and Jews under Islam* (London, 1997), argue that the phases of rapid decline of the minorities occurred in the wake of confrontation with the Christian West—at the time of the Crusades, after the Spanish *Reconquista,* with the collapse of the Ottoman Empire and as a result of colonialism and World War I, and with the creation of the state of Israel.

53. Tarif Khalidi, *The Muslim Jesus* (Cambridge, MA, 2001) 6, 23.

54. Benjamin Braude and Bernard Lewis, "The Central Lands," *Christians and Jews* (New York, 1982), I, 1, quoted in Charles D. Smith, *Palestine and the Arab Israeli Conflict* (New York, 1988). 11.

55. Autobiographies and diaries of Khalil Sakakini, *Yawmiyyat* (Ramallah, 2003), I; and Wasif Jawhariyyeh, *al Quds al Uthmaniyyah* (Jerusalem, 2003), quoted in Salim

Tamari, "Ishaq al-Shami and the Predicament of the Arab Jew in Palestine," draft of paper for the Institute of Jerusalem Studies, 2003.

56. Saleh Abdel Jawad, "Bireh and Ramallah al-Turath wa-l-mujtam'" (Bireh and Ramallah Clans—an Anthropological Study), *Anthropological and Folklore Quarterly Review of the In'ash al-Usra Society,* XXVIII, (1996), 37-53.

57. Alexander Scholch, "The Emergence of Modern Palestine (1856–1882)," in Hisham Nashabe (ed.), *Studia Palaestina: Studies in Honour of Constantine K. Zurayk* (Beirut, 1988), 81.

58. Tamari, "Ishaq al-Shami"; Ela Greenberg, "Educating Muslim Girls in Mandatory Jerusalem," *International Journal of Middle East Studies,* XXXVI (2004), 2.

59. *A Survey of Palestine Prepared in December 1945 and January 1946 for the Information of the Anglo-American Committee of Inquiry,* II, reprinted in full by the Institute for Palestine Studies (Washington, D.C., 1991), 635; Greenberg, "Educating Muslim Girls," 2.

60. Meron Benvenisti, *Sacred Landscape, the Buried History of the Holy Land since 1948* (Berkeley, 2000), 75.

61. Ibid., 77.

62. Tamari, "Ishaq al-Shami."

63. Benvenisti, *Sacred Landscape,* 137.

64. Ibid., 247.

65. Anwar Nusseibah, in his unpublished memoirs, says: "Two rival great powers, the US and the USSR, who had so far managed to disagree on almost everything else, were somehow persuaded to see an identity of interest over Palestine and to support a common policy towards it. This in itself was a phenomenal success for the Jews. Great Britain had sat on the fence, to all appearance only a spectator, although it was a drama which she herself had created, produced and acted. She had no need to do more. Partition was of her making."

66. Virtually all the oral testimonies collected at the Birzeit Research Center and by the author as part of *The Palestinian Destroyed Villages* series confirm this point.

67. Yosef Tabenkin, quoted in Milstein, *Rabin File,* 12.

68. Walid Khalidi, *Deir Yassin* (Beirut, 1998); Sharif Kanaana and Nihad Zitawi, "Deir Yassin," Birzeit Research Center, *The Palestinian Destroyed Villages* series, 4 (1987).

69. For historiographers, the important point is that there is a growing literature on "weapons of the weak" and multiple literatures that seek to retrieve histories of cultural resistance by Jews to Nazism, by women to sexism, slaves to slavery, and colonial subjects to colonial powers (James Scott, *Weapons of the Weak: Everyday Forms of Peasant Resistance* [New Haven, 1985]). While the search for Palestinian resistance will undoubtedly become part of this literature, it is important to note here that we are speak-

ing of real acts of military opposition and defiance, not only acts of cultural resistance (personal communication to the author from John Womack).

70. Milstein, *Rabin File*, 11–12, 137, 232, 248–251, 253, and passim.

71. Benedict Anderson, *Imagined Community* (London, 1983), 77.

72. Interview with Kamal Abdul Fattah, Birzeit University, 2002.

73. al-Dabbagh, *Biladuna Filastin*, 7–8.

74. Bolus Farah, *Min al-'uthmaneya ila adawlat al-'ibrya* (From Ottomanism to the Hebrew State) (Nazareth, 1985), 197.

75. Antonius, *The Arab Awakening*.

76. Interview by Fatima 'Assi, under the author's direction, May 7, 2000.

77. Tawfiq abou Su'ud, "*Muthakarat 'an alharb fi lid*" (Memories about the War in Lod), in Amin Abou Leil (ed.), *On the first Anniversary of the Death of Tawfiq abou Su'ud* (Cairo, 1982).

78. Sakakini, *Such Am I, Oh World*, 393–394.

79. Amira Haas, "The Wanderings of Umm Ghassan," *Ha'aretz* (April 23, 2004).

80. Amira Hass, "One Step ahead of the Bulldozer," *Ha'aretz* (May 21, 2004).

81. Amnon Cohen, *Political Parties in the West Bank under Jordanian Rule, 1947–1967* (Ithaca, 1982). In the introduction, Cohen cites sources taken from confiscated Jordanian intelligence service documents concerning the Palestinian national movement.

82. Author interview with Faisal Husseini, August 1984.

83. Rogan and Shlaim, *The War for Palestine*, 2.

84. Edward Said, *The End of the Peace Process: Oslo and After* (New York, 2000). The ban was not effective in the case of this book.

85. Meron Benvenisti, *Israeli Censorship of Arab Publications* (New York, 1983), 1.

86. Shakeeb, *Harbu Filastin*, 11.

87. Mohammed Hassanin Haykal, *al-'uroush wal-Juyoush Hakatha indala'at Harb Filastin* (Thrones and Armies: This is How the Struggle in Palestine Exploded, Readings in the Diaries of the War) (Cairo, 1998), 2 vols. See I: 96–458; and II: 211–562.

88. *Wathaiq Hashimeya awraq la-Malik "Abdullah* (Hashemite documents: papers of King Abdullah the first), II (1994); VI (1995); XI (ed. al-Beytt University Publications, Amman, 1998).

89. Robert Satloff, reviewing Benny Morris, in *Middle Eastern Studies*, XXXI (1995), 954, quoted in Efraim Karsh, *Fabricating Israeli History: The New Historians* (London, 1997), 5–7.

90. Personal communication, 2004, to the author from Roger Owen, a prominent Middle East scholar who has worked in archives in many Arab nations. Similarly, in my

own visit to the Egyptian National Archives in 1995, I was informed that the part of the archives housed in the Habdin Palace had been closed for many years, because the space was being used by the Republican Guards and no one had transferred the documents to a more accessible location.

91. Sami Hadawi, *al-Hassad al-Murr* (Hebron, 1979), 146. This book was originally published in English as *Bitter Harvest* (New York, 1967).

92. Personal communication from Benny Morris, interview in the Hebrew University, February 23, 1995.

93. Ibid.

94. *Al-Quds*, February 9, 1995, 6.

95. Interview with Morris, February 23, 1995.

96. Michael Palumbo, *The Palestinian Catastrophe: The 1948 Expulsion of a People from their Homeland* (London, 1987).

97. Palumbo, "What Happened to Palestine?"

98. *Al Quds*, February 9, 1995, 6.

99. Ibid.

100. In personal correspondence to the author, Womack writes: "reading of the missing 'black box' or 'smoking gun,' I thought of Hitler's missing orders for extermination of European Jewry, the lack of which has not yet stopped historians from arguing that the orders we know he did give certainly warrant the argument that he intended to wipe out Jews and others in the way of German rule westward and German demographic expansion eastward—and that his intention in these orders was perfectly clear to his subordinates all the way down to the lowliest German policeman assigned to military duty. Likewise, I think of the current uproar over torture in U.S. prison camps. We [historians] have a pitifully narrow and childish idea of how 'statesmen' proceed, as if we did not want to know. Not even General [Augusto] Pinochet said, 'Kill him,' or 'kill them.' The real political order to kill is always a euphemism. Only in stories and plays do we have to say it, as children say it in their play." The self-same logic—that mass killings can be organized without centralized written orders—applies to other instances of mass killing in the Russian gulag, the Chinese "Great Leap Forward," the killing fields of Cambodia, and the Bosnian and Rwandan genocides.

101. Erskine Childers, "The Wordless Wish: From Citizens to Refugees," in Ibrahim Abu-Lughod (ed.), *The Transformation of Palestine* (Evanston, 1971), 165–202.

102. David K. Shipler, *Arab and Jew: Wounded Spirits in a Promised Land* (New York, 1986), 32–35.

103. Benny Morris, "Falsifying the Record: A Fresh Look at Zionist Documentation of 1948," *Journal of Palestine Studies*, XXIV (1995), 44.

104. Palumbo, "What Happened to Palestine?"

105. Ted Swedenburg, "Problems of Oral History: The 1936 Revolt in Palestine," *Birzeit Research Review*, II (1986/1987).

106. McNeil diary, Middle East Center, St. Anthony's College, Oxford University, cited in Palumbo, *The Link*.

107. Palumbo, "What Happened to Palestine?"

108. Nazzal, *The Palestinian Exodus*.

109. Birzeit University Research Center, *The Palestinian Destroyed Villages* series, 4 (1987, 2nd ed.). Aref al-'Aref also uses the number 110 (al-'Aref, *Nakbot Filastin*, I, 173).

110. Efrat ben Ze-ev, author interview, Hebrew University, 1996.

111. Illa Hershavi, *Hadashoat* (August 24, 1984).

112. Morris put the death toll at about thirty (*The Birth of the Palestinian Refugee Problem Revisited* [New York, 2004], 257). In a *Ha'aretz* interview, "The Survival of the Fittest," with Ari Shavit, on January 9, 2004, Morris gave the number killed as seventy.

113. After the occupation of the village of Tieret Haifa on July 16, 1948, twenty-eight elderly and paralyzed men and women remained. They were taken in a bus, to be evacuated to Arab areas. But instead of being delivered to the Arab lines, they were burned to death in a field where kerosene had been spread on the dry plants and then set alight. The Arab League brought charges concerning this massacre before the UN, but the killings were vigorously denied by the Israelis, who claimed that the "story may have originated in the burning of 25–30 bodies 'in an advanced state of decomposition' found near 'Ein Ghazal. For lack of timber . . . the bodies were only partially consumed." The IDF response to the UN also challenged all the names on the list of victims. Morris, when dealing with this case, paraphrases the IDF denial in the text, but in a footnote he quotes "an enigmatic, partly censored document that indicates that something amiss had indeed occurred." This partially censored army document, whose censorship Morris never questions, refers to an ongoing IDF "trial" concerning "the 28." The Palestinian account of the massacre can be found in the Birzeit Research Center's *Palestinian Destroyed Villages* series, 19: Tieret Haifa (1995) by Abdel Rahim al-Mudor, editor and supervisor: Saleh Abdel Jawad; Efrat ben Ze-ev, interview with the author, Hebrew University, 1996, translated and gave me copies of some of the correspondence between the IDF and the UN. For Morris, see *The Birth of the Palestinian Refugee Problem Revisited*, 440, and nn. 167, 458.

114. Ronald Fraser, *Blood of Spain: An Oral History of the Spanish Civil War* (London, 1979), 29, as quoted by Rosemary Sayigh, "Survivors of the 1948 Expulsion: A Second Call for 'A Race Against Time,'" Birzeit Workshop on Oral History, November 21–22, 2003.

115. Henri Laurens, lecture given at the French Cultural Center, Jerusalem, 1998.

116. Rogan and Shlaim, *The War for Palestine*, 2.

117. Masalha, *Expulsion of the Palestinians*. For example, Morris says that "the other

major innovation here is the addition of a new chapter on Zionist thinking about 'Transfer'" (*The Birth of the Palestinian Refugee Problem Revisited*, 5).

118. Baruch Kimmerling, "Benny Morris's Shocking Interview," January 26, 2004, http://student.cs.ucc.ie/cs1064/jabowen/IPSC/php/db.php?tid=30; Walid Khalidi, "Plan Dalet: the Zionist Blueprint for the Conquest of Palestine 1948," *Middle East Forum*, XXXVII (1961); Walid Khalidi, "Plan Dalet Revisited," *Journal of Palestine Studies*, XVIII (1988), 3–70.

119. "Sociocide" is a concept that denotes policies used by one political entity for the total destruction of another, not only as a political national group but also as a society in all of its economic, social, and cultural dimensions. Its final objective is ethnic cleansing and the complete replacement of one society by another. Israeli policy in Palestine can be usefully understood as an example of sociocide. For further development of the concept as it applies to Palestine, see Saleh Abdel Jawad, "Sociocide: The Zionist Scheme for the Destruction of the Palestinian Society," paper delivered at the "100 Years after Basl" conference and reprinted in three parts in Jerusalem Media Center, *Palestine Report* (1997). The earliest formulation of the concept is found in Jawad, "Genese et Evolution d'un Mouvement de Liberation National: Le Fath," doctoral dissertation in political science, Université de Paris X-Nanterre, 1986; Baruch Kimmerling, *Politicide: Ariel Sharon's War against the Palestinians* (London, 2003).

120. Nazzal, *The Palestinian Exodus;* Sayigh, *Palestinian from Peasant;* Birzeit University Research Center's *Palestinian Destroyed Villages* series; Benvenisti, *Sacred Landscape*, 144–192; Morris, *Ha'aretz* interview, "The Survival of the Fittest," with Ari Shavit (January 9, 2004).

121. Thucydides, *The History of the Peloponnesian War,* 267 (my emphasis).

122. Peter Burke, "History as Social Memory" in Thomas Butler (ed.), *Memory: History, Culture and Mind* (Oxford, 1989), 106.

123. Benjamin Beit-Hallahmi, *Original Sins: Reflections on the History of Zionism and Israel* (New York, 1992), 158–159.

124. Hani Shukrallah, "History's Nightmare," *Al-Ahram Weekly* (March 22–28, 2001).

5

ZIONISM'S ENCOUNTER WITH THE PALESTINIANS

The Dynamics of Force, Fear, and Extremism

NADIM N. ROUHANA

THIS CHAPTER EXAMINES the impact of the Zionist idea and how the implementation of that idea transformed Palestine from an Arab homeland into a Jewish state. This chapter also discusses the collective behavior of the colonizers—those who took over the homeland—vis à vis the colonized, whose homeland was claimed by outsiders and was successfully taken over.[1] This analysis uses the national ideology and experience that guided the pre-state and post-state mainstream Zionists in order to historicize and contextualize the emergence of dynamics within Israeli society and its treatment of and attitudes toward all segments of the Palestinian people—those under occupation, those who are citizens of Israel, and those who are still in forced exile for nearly sixty years. I argue that these dynamics are creating a new Zionist hegemony, at the center of which is a combustive mixture of force, fear, and extremism that is leading Israel—with strong public support—to commit war crimes in the Occupied Territories; to exclude its own Palestinian citizens through various means including "democratic" legislation; to entrench the denial of its responsibility for the forced exile of the majority of Palestinians; and further to resist the right of the refugees ever to return.[2] I suggest that the roots of this mixture can be traced back to the characteristics of Zionism's encounter with Palestinians. I advance arguments about the dynamics that this encounter produced.

The Encounter

The encounter between Zionism and Palestinians is the most significant modern national experience for Palestinians and for Israelis, to the extent that the Jewish historical experience helped to shape Zionist views of and behavior toward

Palestinians. This encounter has a more prominent place than the Holocaust in Zionist–Palestinian relations, even though the Holocaust is undoubtedly the most important experience in Jewish modern history. That the Holocaust had a profound impact on conflict-related behaviors, feelings, and perceptions goes without question, but the essence of Israelis' "national" views of Palestinians has been shaped for more than a century by the asymmetric, forceful, and violent encounter between both groups.

The encounter has been between an indigenous people in a homeland defined by the political unit known as Palestine ever since the 1914 British Mandate was established, and another group of people, the Zionists, who came from outside of Palestine, mainly from Europe, and developed a modern ideology based on three key principles:

1. The Jews are a nation and should establish their own state as an expression of national self-determination. Jews who do not live in that state are in exile, and only the establishment of a Jewish state will return Jews to a condition of "normalcy" as a nation among all nations. By establishing a Jewish state, Jews will end their long exile in a redemptive process of returning and building their homeland. Originally, Herzl did not have a particular country in mind for the Jewish homeland but described "a country where Jews would be able to dwell among themselves and develop their national life as a people."[3]

2. A Jewish state should be established in Palestine. Although Palestine was not the only location considered for establishing the Jewish state, the scale was tipped in favor of Palestine by the obvious historical and religious connections to the land of Palestine as well as by other factors. Theoretically, Zionists could have sought to establish a Jewish state elsewhere—for example, Uganda and Argentina were once considered as possible locations.[4]

3. Once Palestine was targeted as the future location of the Jewish state, Zionists wanted Palestine to become the *exclusive* homeland of the Jewish people and not the land of both the Jewish people and the people of Palestine. Mainstream Zionists, therefore, did not seek partnership with the people who lived in Palestine to build a common homeland but rather to *transform* the country into an exclusively Jewish homeland.

I see no reason why Palestinians should have a problem with the first of these principles. However, the last two—that Palestine is the homeland of the

Jewish people and that it is exclusively their homeland—are detrimental to the national encounter between Arabs and Jews in Palestine. The first idea in and of itself is not of direct concern to Palestinians. Had Zionists chosen to establish their state elsewhere, say in Australia, another location that the Zionists considered, Palestinians would obviously have been spared this encounter.

The Zionists prepared open, deliberate, and detailed strategies for establishing their own state and homeland in Palestine through the massive immigration of Jews to Palestine and for transforming it into a Jewish state. They built Jewish institutions and "liberated" the land from the Palestinians. All along the Zionists used a discourse that stressed the return of the Jewish people to the lands of their fathers. The plan was not clandestine. To the contrary, Zionist goals and their means to achieve them were discussed in a rich body of literature that openly described how they would take over the land from the indigenous Arab population and what they would do with its Arab population.[5] Ideas such as the expulsion of the Arabs, judaization of the country, and population exchange (expelling the Arab citizens of the land in return for taking Jews from Arab countries), were discussed ever since the project was first envisioned in the late nineteenth century. Those discussions continued even after the state was established with regard to Palestinians who became citizens of Israel.[6] Nowhere in mainstream Zionist discourse was it ever seriously considered to share the land with its people—the Palestinians.[7]

Until the Zionist project started, that same land was the indisputable homeland of its own indigenous population under Ottoman rule, as in many other countries of the Arab Middle East at the time. Whether this Zionist project should be considered legitimate, whether Palestine could ever have been considered the homeland of a people who came from Europe and elsewhere who often knew little about Palestine and its people, is usually considered an ideological position, and not a moral judgment.[8] Whether one believes that this project is justified and that Palestine is the homeland of the Jewish people who, according to the Zionist narrative, waited in exile for 2000 years to return, that belief will not change the nature of the encounter but only how the conflict is represented and interpreted. Also irrelevant to the essence of the encounter is whether one argues that the Arab people of Palestine had a distinct national identity (which has not been argued here despite the persuasiveness of the argument) when the Zionist project started or whether this identity emerged later, along with other national identities in the Arab Middle East, or even whether the very encounter with Zionism expedited the formation of a Palestinian national identity.[9]

In order to follow the logic of this chapter, the reader will have to appreciate two basic facts: that Arabs existed in the geographical area known as Mandatory Palestine, which was set up in the aftermath of World War I; and that these Arabs lived in organized communities (cities, towns, and villages) and developed political, economic, and social institutions, including political parties, local governments, a vibrant press, an educational system, cultural institutions and cultural life, active nongovernmental organizations, and so on. Even if the reader does not want to accept that these Arabs had a distinct national identity, they were a people and Palestine was their homeland. Palestine was the homeland of the Palestinian Arabs under the British Mandate in the very same way that Syria and Lebanon were the homelands of Syrian Arabs and Lebanese Arabs, respectively, under the French Mandate (which started and ended at the same time as the British Mandate in Palestine). The essence of the encounter, therefore, took place between a group of people living in their homeland and a group of people who arrived from other parts of the world guided by an ideology that claimed the same homeland as exclusively theirs.

Zionism's Culture of Force

From the moment Zionism was conceived, force has been a central component of its relationship with Palestinians. The seeds of protracted conflict are based in the relationship between colonizer and colonized, and thus are inherent to the dynamics of the encounter between the Zionist movement and Palestinians. It has always been naïve or self-serving to think that a Jewish state could be established in a homeland inhabited by another people except through the use of force. The Jewish state could have been established only through force and violence, because the homeland had to be taken over or "liberated" from the Palestinians. The use of force against Palestinians is embedded in the idea of Zionism itself, with the extent and type of force to be used determined by the extent of the resistance that it encounters.[10] Indeed the use of force against Palestinians and Arabs in general became a cornerstone of Israel's deterrence policy, and so it emphasized force in its relationships with its Arab neighborhood.[11]

Apart from the issue of how the use of force was justified and how taking the indigenous people's homeland was legitimized, the idea of a Jewish state necessitated taking the land, "dunam by dunam," from the indigenous people who "occupied" the same land on which the Zionists wanted to establish their homeland.[12] Indeed, Zionism celebrates most forms of violence that have been applied against the Palestinians, as I will demonstrate below.

The term "violence" can embody a broad range of meanings. It not only indicates physical aggression against another person or group but should be understood in a broader sense that includes social, cultural, legal, and financial *or* symbolic force and pressure, as well as physical methods to coerce people to submit, accept, or acclimate to what they would otherwise consider immoral, wrong, or unacceptable.[13] Galtung's introduction of the term "structural violence" and his ensuing discussion of cultural violence are most useful in this regard.[14] Structural violence refers to the obstruction of human potential by economic and political structures and institutions. Cultural violence is what makes personal and structural violence acceptable through the use of national justification, ideological legitimation, and socially sanctioned public discourse. But when I use the term "structural violence" to argue that it is one of the forms of violence inherent in the Zionist project, I invoke a stricter definition: I limit the term to economic, political, and other structures and institutions that are intentionally, or at least openly, employed to obstruct the human potential of one segment of the Palestinian people.

When violence is used in a political context, as noted by Arendt, it is instrumental by its nature. "Like all means, it always stands in need of guidance and justification through the end it pursues."[15] Thus the violence I discuss below is mostly instrumental—a means to achieve an end.[16] But without this instrumental violence in its various forms the Zionist project could neither have been implemented nor could it continue to exert its main goal, an ethnic Jewish state.

Prior to 1948, many Jews immigrated illegally to Palestine. Justification for such actions aside, Zionists were so proud to have forced these illegal immigrants on the indigenous inhabitants that they named these newcomers *maapilim*, which literally means brave, gutsy, and spirited. They celebrated their success in getting them to participate in building a homeland for the Jewish people in the homeland of another group of people.

Zionists boasted about "liberating" the lands from the Arabs, and they considered the land gained from Arabs, by whatever means, as *"geulat ha'aretz,"* redeeming the land from the enemy.[17] This so-called liberation took various forms. In the pre-state years, Zionists were proud to have purchased the equivalent of about 7 percent of what became Israel. But even these purchases were viewed in the Zionist narrative as innocuous. Zionists bought the land from poor peasants, and from landlords they nicknamed *effendis* (landlords), and then blamed the landlords for abandoning the peasants who were on the land. At the same time they were proud of the kinds of manipulations that they were using. Herzl, for example, proposed sending secret agents to offer landowners high prices for their land, create unemployment, and persuade the people of Palestine to leave their country.[18] When he proposed this "voluntary expropriation" of land, Herzl had no moral qualms whatsoever about employing these violent means for "redeeming the land." Zionist literature never gave a second thought to the fact that this process occurred while the indigenous population was under foreign (Ottoman and later British) rule and lacked a national government to regulate the transfer of land to buyers who secretly worked on behalf of Jewish organizations for the explicit purpose of taking over not only the land but also the *homeland*. On the contrary, the expedience of these measures for "voluntary expropriation" was appreciated.[19]

Zionist armies used the force of guns, terror, and massacres to bring about the expulsion of Palestinians during the 1948 war.[20] Without that expulsion, Israel could not have been established as a state with a great Jewish majority.[21] Once the vast number of Palestinians in the part of Palestine that became Israel was expelled—or left under the duress of war—the Palestinians were prevented from returning to their homeland forever; Israel refused to accept the refugees back. Laws were enacted to expropriate their property and prevent their return. Thousands of refugees who tried to return to their homes and families were shot and killed.[22] Their property—the property of a nation— became spoils of war and were taken by the Jewish state and given to Jewish citizens and Jewish immigrants. Many of these houses still exist in the major Palestinian cities that became Israeli cities, such as Haifa, Acre, Jaffa, Tiberias, and Safad. Even under future possible conditions of peace, Israel will not permit Palestinian refugees to return to their homes because doing so would threaten the "demographic character" of the state.[23] After Israel was established in 1948, it used force and structural violence to take land even from Arabs who remained and became Israeli citizens. Israel placed these Arab citizens under military rule for nearly twenty years and legislated special laws explicitly designed to transfer land from Arab citizens to Jewish citizens. In this way Israel confiscated close to 70 percent of the land owned by Arab citizens.[24] In open acts of structural violence against its own citizens, Israel prevented relatives of those Arabs from returning, closing its immigration gates almost hermetically to Arabs, encouraging economic dependency in the Arab community, and seeking actively to co-opt their elites and encourage further segmentation.[25]

Israel developed a legal system that openly gives preference to Jewish over Arab citizens. It institutionalized discrimination against Arab citizens, per-

petuating their disadvantaged status in Israel.[26] That Arab citizens are exposed
to open, legal, and institutional discrimination is, by and large, no longer disputed in Israel. Various Zionist political parties and groups differ in the justification that they provide for this form of violence—not over whether it exists.
These acts of structural violence were deliberate and inevitable in the sense that
they were required for maintaining Jewish control of an ethnic Jewish state.

In a major project that represents symbolic and cultural violence, Israel re-
named towns, streets, mountains, and the landscape, imposing biblical and
Hebrew names and erasing the original Arabic names in a transparent campaign of denial of the country's history.[27] The Israeli government organized the
official public calendar according to Jewish time, both religious and national,
ignoring its own Arab citizens. It degraded the status and use of the Arab language in multiple ways, including reducing its status within the Arab educational system itself. These are only examples of the means—violent instruments
—for maintaining the ethnic Jewish character and Jewish domination of the
state.

Perhaps one of the most hideous forms of Zionism's symbolic violence is
the open and continued obsession of the state and the Jewish public with Arab
demography in Palestine in general and inside Israel in particular.[28] An increase
in the number of Arab citizens (which is possible only by natural increase as
Israel's gates are virtually closed in the face of Palestinians, or people of Palestinian origin) is considered a demographic threat.[29] Thus Arab citizens live
with the daily reminder that their Jewish compatriots, and what is supposedly
their state, view them and their children, families, and most heinously their
newborns, as a malignant existential threat on par with cancer (an image often
cited by Israeli public figures when referring to Arab demographic growth).
Jewish citizens, many academics and intellectuals, and governmental agencies
and leaders all devote time and resources to figuring out how the perceived
demographic danger can be controlled. Indeed, seeing in Arab citizens a demographic threat is inherent in Zionist ideology itself, as Zionism can only be ac-
tualized, and the self-image of a democratic state maintained, if the Jewish
population remains a majority. The political Zionist elites succeeded in instill-
ing this fear in the Jewish public through the production of a hegemonic political culture imbued with the values of maintaining the Jewish majority and
the Jewish character of the state, as well as Jewish domination over non-Jews.
Fear of non-Jews, particularly Arabs, makes it difficult for Jewish citizens and
groups to resist this hegemony, although some of them do. One legal manifes-
tation of this symbolic violence lies in racist immigration laws. Many Zionist

scholars label the Law of Return as "preferential," not "racist," which is important for Israeli liberals' self-image. But it does not change the violent nature of this law for Arab citizens. This law gives any Jew (including the children or grandchildren of a Jew) from anywhere in the world, regardless of their connection to the land or their ideology (they could be anti-Zionists), the right to become an Israeli citizen (and accordingly a settler in Palestinian territories), while not conferring that same right on a relative of an Arab citizen, even a relative of the first degree, or an Arab who resided in Palestine before Israel was established.

The obsession with demography allowed strong public support for a law enacted in 2003 that prevents Palestinian spouses of Israeli citizens (which in practice means Arab citizens) from living in Israel or even being considered for naturalization. Even Zionist scholars, political leaders, and human rights activists deemed this law racist.[30] The United Nations Committee on Racial Discrimination raised "serious concerns" about the law and reported that it found that the law contravenes "many international human rights instruments."[31]

It is no wonder that Zionism's main relationship with Palestinians is characterized by force, violence, and domination. Only through force could the Palestinian homeland have been taken and transformed. Only through force could Israel have controlled and dominated a Palestinian minority as explicitly unequal citizens.[32] Similarly, the Zionist Jewish identity of the state and its openly discriminatory legal and constitutional expressions could not have been imposed on the indigenous population except through the use of force. The occupation of the West Bank and Gaza in 1967, the ongoing land acquisition and Jewish settlement in the West Bank, and maintenance of the occupation against the will of the occupied were all achieved by using brute force, oppression, and gross violations of human rights, which eventually penetrated Israeli culture itself. The same pattern of taking Arab land by force or by legal and bureaucratic machinations continued in the West Bank and Gaza after the 1967 occupation and continues today in the West Bank after the Israeli withdrawal from Gaza in 2005.[33] Israel has already obtained state and private Jewish control over about 50 percent of the occupied West Bank by using such tactics.

Because the land and the resources of the country had to be taken by force from its Palestinian inhabitants, two main components of Israeli political culture were defined in their relationship to the Palestinians. First, Israel internalized a culture of force and domination when dealing with Arabs. This protracted use of force became part and parcel of many Israelis' relationships with Palestinians and possibly part of their very identity, as their collective existence is defined by power over this most significant other in their national experience. The Israelis' worldview of the Palestinians, and inevitably of themselves, is determined by forceful domination and the resulting distorted justifications.

Second, Israel—official and public—developed an elaborate system of justifications related mainly to the means of violence, and a system of denial related to the very existence of Palestine as a homeland of the Palestinians, and even to the existence of Palestinians themselves. This component of denial is not discussed in this chapter.

The ultimate expressions of this culture of violence are clear today: the brutal force—condoned by a majority of Israelis—that Israel used almost daily in the Occupied Territories for more than four years of the Palestinian uprising; the fact that Israeli soldiers are rarely if ever held accountable for harm done to Arab civilians; the construction of walls and barriers that are designed presumably to protect Jews but in reality destroy the lives of Palestinians; the use of a vast network of administrative controls, such as the new "permanent residency" status for Arabs whose homes happen to fall between Israel's formal border and the new wall; and the popularity of a prime minister who is faced with charges of war crimes. The old adage that "Arabs understand only the language of force" is without doubt a deep part of Israel's political culture and partially underlies its violent domination of Palestine and Palestinians.

The idea of a Jewish state for the Jewish people, the first of the three ideas of Zionism, had no inherent seeds of force or violence until the location for its implementation was chosen. But the idea of a Jewish state *in Palestine* contained the seeds of domination, exclusion, force, and violence, and could be achieved and maintained only by these means. Even inside Israel itself, within its 1967 borders, only through structural, symbolic, legal, cultural, and physical force and violence can Jews maintain a state that gives open and legal privileges to one national group over another, and considers the homeland to be a homeland for Jews only while the indigenous Arab national group has grown to more than 1 million—over 16 percent of Israel's citizens.

The Zionist and later Israeli force was not met with submission and acquiescence. For Palestinians, resisting the takeover of their homeland was a *natural* human reaction to injustice. One does not have to rely on too much literature to explain this reaction. For example, Arendt argues that rage is a common reaction to the violation of a sense of justice. Furthermore, she maintains that "rage and violence that sometimes—not always—goes with it belong among the 'natural' *human* emotions, and to cure man of them would mean nothing less than to dehumanize or emasculate him. That such acts, in which men take the law into their own hands for justice's sake, are in conflict with the constitutions of civilized communities is undeniable; but their antipolitical character . . . does not mean that they are inhuman or 'merely' emotional."[34] The *form* of resistance may then be controversial but not the fact of the naturalness of resistance itself. Palestinians resisted and continue to resist, in various ways, the transformation of their homeland. Thus the encounter between Zionism and Palestinians is characterized by violence that is inherent in the Zionist project, and by resistance—often violent—that is the natural reaction to the injustice of the process of taking over the Palestinians' homeland. The dynamics of Zionist force and Palestinian resistance became a major source of fear for Israelis, precisely because of the context of the encounter of Zionism with Palestinians and the consequences of that encounter for Palestinians.

Palestinian Resistance and Israeli Fear

Various forms of resistance shaped the Palestinians' experience throughout their relationship with the Zionist movement and later Israel. "Resistance" was a constitutive element in their narrative but also a constitutive experience in their national history and identity, perhaps equaled only by exile and the dream of return. Unlike exile, resistance was a source of enormous pride for Palestinians because they stood up to injustice. Despite the inconsistencies of some acts of violent resistance with what is expected of "civilized communities," and regardless of the political and strategic wisdom of such acts, Palestinians felt that resistance was their human, natural, and political duty. Indeed, it is unimaginable, unnatural, and inhuman that Palestinians would have let this project continue without showing stiff resistance. Since violence is inherent in the Zionist idea itself, resistance to it by Palestinians is inherent in the human condition of reacting to injustice.

Resistance took different forms: violent resistance; endurance and remaining on the land while facing legal, political, and economic attempts at removal; and rejecting or "spoiling" settlement proposals which were viewed as unjust and as having been determined by the extreme power imbalance between Palestinians and Israelis. One of the most effective and least evident forms of resistance was the preservation of memories and the national narrative, at the core of which was a clinging to a right to the homeland—expressed now in the form of insisting on the principle of the right of return: Israel must be held responsible for the Palestinian exile, and the Jewish state in the Palestinian homeland must be denied legitimacy. This narrative is shared by all segments of Palestinian society, including Palestinians in Israel.[35]

At the national security level, the sense of threat that the Palestinian resistance has caused Israel has been minimal, although the suicide bombings during the second uprising (2000–2005) introduced a real security threat to individual Israeli citizens. Palestinian resistance over the years has never posed an existential threat to Israel. Israel's military power versus that of the Palestinians is almost absolute, because Israel has one of the strongest militaries in the world and the Palestinians are a militarily surrounded, strategically constrained, and economically underdeveloped (and more accurately de-developed) civilian population with land, sea, and air access to the outside world controlled by Israel.[36] There must be a serious reason why Israelis are so engulfed in fear, which many describe as an existential fear, when Israel can reach Palestinians in their bedrooms or offices by using airplanes, helicopters, or professional assassins. Israel can and did close every town and city and isolate Palestinians from the world, roll its tanks past their bedrooms, demolish thousands of their homes, and imprison them by the tens of thousands.

Nevertheless, despite Israelis' might, violence, and use of unmatched and often unrestrained force, their apprehension is genuine and should not be belittled or dismissed. On the contrary, the Israelis should face the root of their fear for many reasons, not the least of which is that fear, in combination with a culture of force, the availability of weapons of mass destruction, and dynamics of extremism is a lethal mixture. But for Israelis to confront their fear and its origins—which indeed is essential for both Israelis and Palestinians in dealing with the roots of their conflict—is not only a psychological matter. It requires that they confront the history and very essence of the Zionist project.

There is no question that, historically, Palestinians, and Arabs in general, failed to estimate the level and complex sources of Israeli fear. The many dialogues between Israelis and Palestinians over the years helped to inform Palestinians about some sources of that fear. Similarly, official encounters between elites during the period of the Oslo Accords must have contributed to a Palestinian understanding that Israeli society was engulfed by fear. I argue, however, that both Israelis and Palestinians have failed to address the real source of the Israelis' fear in relation to the Palestinians, a fear that I attribute mainly to the nature of the encounter between Zionism and the Palestinian national movement, and its consequences.[37]

Israeli scholars who studied this fear were right to point to its many causes: numerous wars with Arab states and the human loss that these wars entailed;

Palestinian resistance to occupation, particularly the recent use of suicide attacks; the border attacks by the Palestinian Liberation Organization (PLO) during the 1970s; the centuries of Jewish experience of persecution, pogroms, and anti-Semitism in Christian Europe; and the culmination of persecution in the Holocaust of European Jewry, an experience that will take generations of security, acceptance, acknowledgment, and apology by the perpetrators to heal. These powerful sources of fear cannot be overemphasized, particularly since the Zionist discourse often managed to mix them into one powerful blend.[38] Still, I contend that the most powerful source of fear in their relationship with the Palestinians emanates from experiences rooted in the nature of the Israeli encounter with them. Taking another nation's homeland and homes, dispersing the people of that land, and establishing a new homeland on its ruins must cause tremendous fear and anxiety in Israeli society. This fear is heightened by the fact that those who were usurped are a national community demanding to return to their homeland, at the same time reminding Israelis of their original crimes.

I put this argument in the form of a hypothesis. Although it is hard, it is not impossible to investigate this hypothesis empirically. I argue that, despite the elaborate Zionist narrative that discounts Palestinians and their fate, the mere existence of Palestinian refugees, and Palestinians in general, must raise serious, if silenced, questions about what really took place in the process of establishing Israel.[39] Under the surface, truths and realities that have been buried, literally and figuratively, still simmer, perhaps at a preconscious or even unconscious level.[40]

These circumstances explain why Israel has historically cared so much that Palestinians recognize it and more recently accept the legitimacy of the Jewish state. Israelis demanded recognition without articulating why such recognition was so essential for their security. My point is that recognition is so essential for the Israelis' sense of security because it legitimizes in the eyes of the victimizers and their victims what the Zionists did to Palestinians. Yet, ironically, the victimizers themselves are unable to explicate this point. Recently, this demand for recognition has been articulated as the recognition of the right of the Jewish people to have a Jewish state in Palestine.[41] Israelis insist on the issue of finality in negotiations with Palestinians, so that once the Palestinians accept a settlement they cannot later raise questions about rectifying the injustices that have been perpetrated. These circumstances also explain why demonstrations by Palestinian citizens in Israel, who are under the full domination and control of the state of Israel, raise such fear among the Jewish public. Such demonstrations, which are often held to protest Israeli policies toward Palestinian citizens or toward Palestinians in the Occupied Territories, are seen by the Jewish public as evidence that Palestinians do not accept the state's legitimacy and must be met with lethal police violence.[42]

Despite the strength of this source of fear, it is rarely discussed in Israel for good reason. By admitting to it, they would be agreeing that the implementation of Zionism was indeed a crime against Palestinians and that the Zionist project could not have been successful unless the Zionists had taken over the Palestinian homeland. Because this history is denied on the conscious level and in political discourse, and because a powerful alternative narrative was constructed based on the return of Jews to their own homeland, the source of fear cannot be openly faced. The anxiety festers at the subconscious level. This denial of history requires Zionists massively to distort the facts in order to deny that the Palestinians ever existed at all, or that they had a national identity and were a separate nation, or that they were expelled from their land.[43]

For obvious reasons, it is not easy to face this fear, as it would mean challenging the national narrative and national and personal identity.[44] The problem can only be resolved when it is faced in the context of genuine reconciliation between the parties. Reconciliation could provide Israelis with the security that they seek, and it would alleviate their dread *despite* what they have perpetrated against Palestinians. The paradox is, however, that the alleviation of fear that could be achieved by Palestinians acknowledging that Israel's existence is legitimate, although not that Zionism is legitimate or that Israel has the right to exist as an ethnic Jewish state, requires acknowledging the past injustices done to Palestinians. Genuine reconciliation requires facing historic truths, taking responsibility for past injustices, and framing future relations in terms of justice rather then power.[45] Reconciliation also would require a major political restructuring to enable full equality between individuals and national groups in Palestine, a change that would be incompatible with a Zionist framework or with Zionism. However, the more powerful party does not usually have sufficient incentives to engage in a genuine reconciliation process that would entail painful concessions and painful self-discovery.[46]

The existing power asymmetry between Israelis and Palestinians is exacerbated by an international climate conducive to the use of force, and by the culture of force governing Israeli relations with the Palestinians. It leads to a vicious cycle: it becomes possible and easier for many Israelis to resort to the force that they have always used against Palestinians in order to achieve the desired result, compelling the Palestinians to submit to the balance of power unwillingly and accept the legitimacy of the Zionist project. Left-leaning Israelis and Zionist groups seek official and unofficial diplomatic means to achieve the same result, while often paralleling the history of Zionism and the Palestinian national movement arguing that both sides have equally legitimate narratives as well as a history of violence, the need for recognition, and so on. This alternative approach seeks to achieve recognition of Zionism in return for a Palestinian state in the Occupied Territories.

In summary, the Israelis' fear of Palestinians is a tangible part of their national experience. Yet a main component of that fear emanates from the challenge to their own national narrative and from a refusal to confront historic truth and responsibility. Paradoxically, alleviating this fear requires facing it and admitting to the injustice that Israel inflicted by the very idea of Zionism and by the establishment of a Jewish state in Palestine. The anxiety permeating Israeli society is used to justify actions and policies motivated by ideological considerations. Thus it is not unrelated to the third component in the combustible mixture described above—the dynamics of political extremism.

Force, Resistance, and the Dynamics of Zionist Extremism

The combination of force, inherent in the Zionist project, together with the fear of the Jewish public emanating from taking over another nation's homeland, can bring about escalating extremism in Israeli society's interactions with the Palestinians. It is possible that extremism within Zionism becomes a logical, perhaps even inevitable, outgrowth of the dynamics of this encounter—as long as history is not confronted. I propose that the seeds of extreme views and behavior toward Palestinians are inherent in the dynamics that emerge in the process of *implementing* the Zionist ideology and Palestinian resistance.

For example, Zionist ideology makes enemies or potential enemies of Palestinians, those living in their homeland—both in Israel itself or in the West Bank and Gaza—or those who are refugees, if they resist the injustice inflicted upon them. One can even say that Palestinians in Palestine in the pre–Israeli state era were the enemies of the Zionist movement by their mere existence on the land that the Zionists claimed for themselves, even if the Palestinians did not show much resistance.[47] Similarly, in the post-state era, the mere existence of Palestinian citizens in the Jewish state and their natural growth threatens the character of Israel, as the state insists on Jewish ethnic identity.

If the mere existence of Palestinians threatens the Zionist idea, then Palestinians by definition are in a constant state of resistance. Thus Zionism placed

Israel (and before that, the *Yishuv*—in Zionist parlance, the Jewish political community in Palestine prior to 1948) in an inevitable position of feeling threatened by Palestinian resistance, and therefore of being in a state of constant readiness to use force. Resistance to the idea of the Jewish state leads to further threat and, accordingly, to the use of force to defend against the threat to the security of the nation and the state. Security and identity are defined mainly in ethnic terms: Jewish majority, dominance, and control. But Arab resistance was by no means limited just to passive resistance.

In the pre-state era, the indigenous people of Palestine resisted the waves of Jewish immigration that came to take their homeland. Resistance took the form of strikes, protests, revolts, conferences, sending delegations to the British and to Arab states, and armed resistance. Palestinians and their leadership resisted by rejecting the UN Partition plan for Palestine. In the war that ensued, they lost more areas of Palestine to the Zionist forces than were allocated to the Jewish state by Partition. Although Palestinian revisionist historians have examined the role played by the Palestinian leadership and the Arab states in "al Nakba," the catastrophe, which is the Palestinian term for the 1948 war, no questions have been raised about the morality of rejecting Partition.[48] Palestinians have always believed that establishing a nation for another group in their homeland was unjust and therefore could never be accepted. In the post-state era, resistance took different forms depending on where the Palestinian communities were located. In all cases, it meant conflict and confrontation with Israel as a state and Zionism as an ideology. For Palestinian citizens in Israel, the political program of equality for Arab and Jewish citizens led them to the very basic democratic principle that a state cannot be for one ethnic group only, and therefore Israel must be de-Zionized in order for Arabs and Jews to become genuinely equal. Palestinians in exile still hold the dream of returning to their homeland, which essentially means ending Zionism. Palestinians in the West Bank seek independence from Israeli occupation, but Israel has already physically and psychologically incorporated significant parts of the West Bank so that the feasibility of independence has become questionable, even though independence and statehood in the West Bank and Gaza would not necessarily mean the end of Zionism, and thus does not conflict with the essence of Zionism.[49]

The Zionist idea and its implementation inevitably placed Palestinians in a constant state of resistance, the form of which changed with place and time, while placing Jews IN ISRAEL in a permanent state of fear and threat that was used as justification for using force and violence in its various forms as described above. Thus the conflict and confrontation between Arabs and Jews in Palestine has continued for more than a century. The conflict, accompanied by a culture of force and the will and means to use it, as well as by a sense of threat (whose sources are left unexamined), created a new hegemony in Israel based on political and ethnocentric extremism. On the Zionist continuum, the movement toward the extreme Right has been a historical process that emerged in the context of the encounter with the Palestinians and their resistance. The socially and politically constructed threat (such as the "demographic danger") provided the easy justification for further use of force and greater control, the pillaging of land, discriminatory legislation, and changes in political attitudes and perceptions. Because Palestinian demands for equality, the right to return to their homeland, and liberation from occupation are irrepressible as basic human needs, and because Zionism is central to Israeli identity, Israel reacted with its readily available force. Through force, Israel encroached increasingly on Palestinian rights through expulsions, arbitrary military orders in the Occupied Territories, home demolitions, restrictive legislation, and land expropriation.[50] The cycle escalated with increased feelings of threat emanating from persistent and emboldened Palestinian demands, and Israel's use of force to try to eliminate that threat. The escalation inevitably led to extremism, which was accompanied by both social transformations and psychological changes compatible with and conducive to an escalation of extremism. Such societal and psychological transformations are predictable in the escalation stages of conflict.[51]

The Zionist political spectrum extends from the extreme Zionist Left, which subscribes to an independent Palestinian state in the Occupied Territories and supports granting many rights (though not completely equal rights) for Arab citizens within an ethnic Jewish state, to the extreme Zionist Right, which openly espouses expulsion and ethnic cleansing (actual or symbolic) of Palestinians from all of Palestine, including the Palestinian citizens of Israel. Both the Right and the Left oppose the right of return of Palestinian refugees, although they differ on the extent to which Israel should admit responsibility for the Palestinian Nakba. Both leftists and rightists oppose full equality for Palestinian citizens but differ on the extent of individual and collective equality that should be granted.[52] They agree that whatever rights are granted should be within the context of a Jewish (read Zionist) democratic state (an evident contradiction that most Israelis deny). Both share the view that Israel should remain an ethnic Jewish state.

Israeli extremism can be defined as attitudes lying more toward the right end of the continuum. Thus indications of Israeli extremism can be defined by attitudes and behavior toward, and conflicts with, the various Palestinian communities: the Palestinians who are Israeli citizens, the Palestinians in the West Bank and Gaza, and the Palestinians in exile. Although, unquestionably, there have been oscillations in the Israeli political spectrum over the years, the general trend of growing extremism is unmistakable. This extremism has recently evolved against the background of the latest Palestinian uprising. As a result, the Zionist consensus has moved closer to the Right, creating a new hegemony in Israel.[53]

Extremism is demonstrated by the composition of the government. Until 1977, all Israeli governments were led by Labor or its predecessors, but since 1977 only two Labor governments were formed in Israel: one from 1992 to 1996, when the prime minister was assassinated; and the other from 1999 to 2001, when the prime minister resigned and did not complete his term in office. While this change reflects as much social and economic change as political, one cannot ignore the significance of the contrast with earlier periods. The prime minister in office since 2001 is known as the most hawkish in Israel's history, and he was elected twice with persuasive majorities. In the last decades Israeli governments have included ministers who represented openly racist parties and parties whose political platforms specifically called for "transfer" (read ethnic cleansing) of Palestinians. Some ministers have blatantly described Palestinians as "strangers to this land" or openly view Palestinian citizens as enemies. The inclusion of these ministers in the Israeli government has legitimized their views and made such beliefs more plausible within the mainstream Zionist consensus.[54]

Israeli political thought and practice has witnessed a major shift starting in the late 1990s, and especially since the beginning of the second Palestinian *intifada*, or uprising, in 2000. The intifada was the impetus that exposed a trend which in fact had started years earlier. The dynamics that emerged after the failure of the Camp David summit and the start of the second intifada brought to the fore manifestations of extremism with ideological foundations that were within the range of Zionist thought but had not been fully invoked since the establishment of Israel.

The move to the Right is also demonstrated by the reversal of policies that culminated in the Oslo Accords—drastic changes in policies directed at Palestinian citizens in Israel and the reawakening of dormant antidemocratic political ideas. The result is that Israeli society is moving steadily and perceptibly toward unprecedented extremism. A few of the signs of this phase include the de-legitimization of the peace process and the Palestinian Authority (which changed somewhat since the death of Yasser Arafat); the open discussion of transfer; the wanton use of brutal force that often qualifies as war crimes; and the questioning of one's loyalty, even of Israeli Jewish citizens who pursue peaceful reconciliation with Palestinians.[55]

Extremism is also clearly reflected in policies toward the Arab population in Israel itself that has led to laws limiting the freedom of expression and organization of Arab Knesset members and Arab citizens; openly discriminatory government allocation of resources; a shift in Jewish public opinion against Arab citizens, including majority support for encouraging Arab citizens to leave; and the rise in the intensity and frequency of openly racist statements by opinion makers and politicians against Palestinian citizens—all of which have been documented.[56] For example, nearly two-thirds of Jewish citizens saw their Arab compatriots as a security threat in 2001, and more than 70 percent held this view in 2002.[57] The Jaffee Center survey of February 2002 showed that Jewish Israelis increasingly supported statements calling for the expulsion of Arab citizens. One-third of the Jewish Israeli population supported their transfer, and two-thirds encouraged their emigration from Israel. With regard to Palestinians in the Occupied Territories, support for their transfer or emigration reached 46 percent, up from 38 percent in 1991.[58] The move to the Right is even reflected in the self-definition of the Jewish public as right-wing or left-wing.[59] Perhaps the most blatant manifestations of growing extremism are public statements of animosity, racism, and frank hatred toward Palestinians, including Palestinian citizens of Israel. The statements permeate public discourse at all levels—the media, scholars, religious leaders, and government officials.[60] These views are unquestionably consistent with the force and violence that Israel has been unleashing daily in the last few years against Palestinians. The perceived threat that Zionism itself created allows many Israelis to apply unrestrained force, hold extreme views, and still feel righteous. Indeed, it is not unusual in Israel to hear citizens say that they feel Israel itself is under siege despite Israel having placed Palestinians under siege, literally, since late 2000.

Zionism's encounter with Palestinians has created the basis of an Israeli culture of force against Arabs that, together with continued Palestinian resistance, is capable of bringing Zionism to its utmost extreme—committing crimes against humanity that may either be a repetition of the 1948 expulsion of the Palestinians, whether gradually or partially, or the formalization of an apartheid-like system suitable to wield domination over the Palestinians. The psychological underpinnings for such actions are probably already present in large segments of the Jewish public, although I know of no research that has examined these issues directly. It is highly possible that under the appropriate regional and international circumstances, the Israeli public will sanction these actions or political plans against the Palestinians.

The Encounter with Palestinians and the Extreme Right End of the Zionist Spectrum

This chapter's analysis should not be viewed as a deterministic statement of the future of the Palestinian–Israeli encounter. The analysis does not necessarily lead us to conclude that Zionism must inevitably or in all cases move to the very Right end of the political spectrum. But it does argue that it is the most likely scenario. The analysis presents Zionism as a continuum, and contends that the culture of force and the intensely perceived threat—in part a social and political construct, such as the "demographic threat"—combined with Palestinian resistance, are conducive to dynamics of extremism. Yet, certain factors might reverse this trend and lead to the emergence of forces on the Zionist Left.

The prerequisites for reversing the dynamics of extremism involve convincing Israel and Israelis that at least some of the major assumptions of Zionism cannot be maintained if Israel wishes to reach a settlement, let alone a historical reconciliation with Palestinians. Israel will have to face at least part of the truth that the country that they settled belonged to another people, that their project was the direct cause of the displacement and dismantling of Palestinian society, and that it could not have been achieved without this displacement. Israel will also have to confront the realities of the occupation and the atrocities it is committing, and will have to accept that Palestinian citizens in Israel are indigenous to the land and entitled to seek the democratic transformation of the state so that they have equal access to power, resources, and decision making, and are entitled to rectification of past and present injustices.

These changes in Israel will not occur on their own, as the dynamics described above are not conducive to such transformation. A major factor that could encourage changes in this direction is pressure applied from the standpoint of a genuine concern of international powers about Israelis and Palestinians, and not only a strategic interest. Under appropriate international circumstances, sufficient pressure might be applied to reverse the trend of growing extremism. Palestinians themselves can also play a role in encouraging such changes, but the internal dynamics of their own encounter with Zionism decrease the likelihood of such a result. In the absence of such international pressure, and given the current circumstances in the region, the more likely direction of change is the one described in this chapter, which is for Zionism to swing to the utmost right.[61]

An example of the increased probability of this change is the open approval of extreme ideas in academic and political discourse in Israel. Morris, the Israeli historian who examined the emergence of the refugee problem, claimed that if all Palestinians had been expelled in 1948 to the lands east of the Jordan River, peace between Arabs and Jews could have been achieved by now.[62] Thus, instead of confronting the violence in this idea and in its implementation, this historian's assumption is that if more violence had been used (and more injustice inflicted) Zionism could have achieved a peaceful resolution. The mixture of force, fear, and the dynamics of extremism that evolved in the context of the encounter of Zionism with the Palestinians leads to a legitimization of this idea, and similar ones, without raising questions about its immorality. If mainstream Zionists (or even left-wing Zionists, as Morris is usually considered) openly regret the past because not enough Palestinians were expelled, one cannot avoid the conclusion that the more likely change on the Zionist continuum will be toward the extreme Right. If expulsion becomes impossible or unnecessary, other extreme measures—in all cases violent and forceful—such as apartheid, can be instituted in this climate of force, fear, and extremism. The combustible mixture created by the encounter between Zionism and the Palestinians can lead mainstream Zionism to similar ideas, and perhaps to acting on them under the appropriate international circumstances. Stopping or reversing these dynamics appears to go against history, but it is not an impossible outcome.

NOTES

1. I was originally asked, in preparation for the conference on which this volume is based, to address the issue of the national character in the conflict between Israelis and Palestinians, and how national character can contribute to understanding the collective behavior of both sides and the destructive dynamics of this protracted conflict. I am not comfortable, however, with the term "national character" to describe the collective behavior of a group. Although the term has been used beneficially and responsibly in some cases to describe the supposedly unique identity characteristics of a particular national group, it is a concept that can easily be misused and abused. The term carries the implications of essentialism in human values and social norms, discourages the historicization and contextualization of social and political cultures, and helps to provide popular—but simplistic and erroneous—explanations for a national group's

complex political and social attitudes, values, and behaviors. Instead, I chose to take the encounter between the Palestinian people and the Zionist movement—and later Israel—as the social and historical context within which the national experience has been evolving and the collective political behavior is being shaped.

2. For a discussion of Israel's war crimes in the Occupied Territories and continued violations of international law, see Nadim Rouhana and Nimer Sultany, "Redrawing the Boundaries of Citizenship: Israel's New Hegemony," *Journal of Palestine Studies,* XXXIII (2003), http://www.ciaonet.org/olj/jps/vol33-129/vol33-129ron01.html. See also Nimer Sultany, "Citizens without Citizenship—Mada's First Annual Political Monitoring Report: 2000–2002" (Haifa, 2003). For the entrenchment of Israel's official views on the right of return, see, for example, the Israeli Cabinet Statement on Road Map and the reservations on this plan sponsored by the U.S., Russia, the European Union, and the United Nations.

3. Anita Shapira, *Land and Power: The Zionist Resort to Force, 1881–1948* (Stanford, 1999), 16.

4. When Theodor Herzl himself wrote *The Jewish State,* he had not decided whether the homeland should be established in Palestine or in Argentina (Shapira, *Land and Power,* 16).

5. See, for example, David Ben-Gurion, *The Jews in Their Land* (Garden City, NY, 1974); Simha Flapan, *Zionism and the Palestinians* (New York, 1979); Arthur Hertzberg, *The Zionist Idea: A Historical Analysis and Reader* (Westport, 1970); Walid Khalidi, *From Haven to Conquest: Readings in Zionism and the Palestine Problem until 1948* (Beirut, 1971); Benny Morris, *The Birth of the Palestinian Refugee Problem* (Cambridge, 1987); Shabtai Teveth, *Ben-Gurion and the Palestinian Arabs* (New York, 1985); Nur Masalha, *Expulsion of the Palestinians* (Beirut, 1992), in Arabic.

6. For a review of debates within the Zionist movement on expulsion, transfer, or ethnic cleansing since Herzl envisioned "self-transfer," see Shabtai Teveth, *The Evolution of "Transfer" in Zionist Thinking* (Tel Aviv, 1989). Teveth mentions the following terms and ideas that were considered and suggested prior to 1937: expulsion by force (Israel Zangwill) or by paying the Palestinians money (Baron Edmund de Rothschild); "resettlement in Arab countries by agreement" (Leon Motzkin); "transfer by persuasion" (Aaron Aaronson); evacuation (Zeev Jabotinsky); and providing "sufficient inducement." For a detailed discussion of ideas and plans of transfer from 1882 to 1948, see Nur Masalha, *Expulsion of the Palestinians: The Concept of "Transfer" in Zionist Political Thought, 1882–1948* (Washington, DC, 1992).

7. Bi-nationalism was discussed and promoted as a political program by some pre-Israeli-state Zionist factions. But the more realistic the possibility of establishing a Jewish state in Palestine became, the less support the idea of bi-nationalism managed to garner. In addition, this option was never popular with the dominant Zionist factions. See Ian Lustick, *Arabs in the Jewish State: Israel's Control of a National Minority* (Austin, 1980).

8. I disagree that this is not a moral judgment and only reflects an ideological position. Even if those who claimed Palestine as their exclusive homeland had both an

objective and subjective historical and religious connection to the land, their claim to it is still immoral as it entails dispossessing another people (this is why the denial of Palestinians is ingrained in Zionist thinking, practice, and historiography). I do not argue the morality of this claim in this chapter, however, because it does not change the main point regarding the nature of the encounter between Zionism and the Palestinians. Suffice it to say that Palestinians view this claim of their homeland by others and its implementation as an enormous injustice. They also assume, and not without unreasonable foundations, that were it not for the Zionist project, Palestine under the British Mandate would have become an independent state of Palestine like neighboring Arab states.

9. For a discussion of these issues, see Rashid Khalidi, *Palestinian Identity* (New York, 1998); Muhammed Y. Muslih, *The Origins of Palestinian Nationalism* (Beirut, 1989).

10. The implementation of force against Arabs as instruments for achieving the goals of the Jewish state became imbued in the political and popular culture in Israel. Thus, one famous Israeli cultural maxim that reflects much of the relationship between the Israelis and the Palestinians is that Arabs—read Palestinians—understand only the language of force. This idiom has become so popular that it was even upgraded: "If they don't respond to force," the new maxim goes, "they will respond to more force." Another violent saying, less openly used, is that "a good Arab is a dead Arab."

11. One of Israel's unwavering security principles in dealing with Palestinians and Arabs in general is a policy of deterrence based on forceful punishment. While not unusual in conflict situations, Israel's active deterrence is founded on the belief that Israel cannot show any signs of weakness to Palestinians or other Arabs, precisely because the founders of the Israeli security doctrine, as argued by Bishara, were deeply aware of the extent of the crime committed against the Palestinians, did not expect Arab acceptance of Israel, and believed that nation building could only be achieved by force. See Azmi Bishara, *From the Jewish State to Sharon: A Study in the Contradictions of Israeli Democracy* (Ramallah, 2005), in Arabic.

12. Many Israeli historians—Zionist and non-Zionist alike—discuss the use of force that accompanied the Zionist project; however, most do not see the use of force as inherent in the idea of the Jewish state itself. The various justifications offered by Zionist historians and ideologues for the use of force and for taking over Palestine from its own people could provide for a fascinating study on psychological acrobatics. See, for example, Shapira, *Land and Power*.

13. The World Health Organization uses the following broader definition of violence: "The intentional use of physical force or power, threatened or actual, against oneself, another person, or against a group or community, that either results in or has a high likelihood of resulting in injury, death, psychological harm, maldevelopment or deprivation" (World Health Organization, *World Report on Violence and Health* [Geneva, 2002], http://www.who.int/violence_injury_prevention/violence/en/).

14. For a discussion of structural violence, see Johann Galtung, "Violence, Peace and Peace Research," *Journal of Peace Research*, VI (1969), 167–191.

15. See Hannah Arendt, *On Violence* (New York, 1970), 51. Although one might argue

that in some cases violence is the outcome of uncontrolled or uncontrollable popular emotions—as in mob violence—it is always true that the type of response legitimate authorities have to such violence carries the weight of a political instrumentality of the kind Arendt argues.

16. For an example of the instrumental nature of Zionist violence, see Saleh Abdel Jawad's chapter in this volume, chapter 4. The massacres conducted by the Zionist forces in the 1948 war were a successful instrument in achieving the goal of ethnically cleansing most of the Palestinian population. These massacres were not conducted merely out of hatred for Arabs, as were the massacres or pogroms against Jews in Europe.

17. Redeeming the land has strong religious connotations. On the religious connotation issue, see Nabih Bashir, *Judaizing the Place* (Haifa, 2004).

18. Theodor Herzl (ed. Jacob M. Alkow), *The Jewish State: An Attempt at a Modern Solution of the Jewish Question* (New York, 1946).

19. The land was purchased on behalf of the Jewish people and not just for the individual use of Jewish persons. Shapira mentions that Herzl, who was aware of the possible scrutiny of the "enlightened world" and that his "generosity" (in her words) toward the population, in terms of offering high prices for their land, stemmed from that possible scrutiny. Herzl does not seem to have had any concern about the moral issue of displacement (Shapira, *Land and Power*, 16–17).

20. Masalha, *Expulsion of the Palestinians*. Jawad, chapter 4 this volume; Ilan Pappe, *A History of Modern Palestine* (Cambridge, 2003).

21. The percentage of Arabs in the Jewish state, according to the UN Partition plan, was 42 percent (Masalha, *Expulsion of the Palestinians*). In the conditions of war that followed Israel's declaration of independence, Israel ethnically cleansed most of the Arabs in the areas that the UN Partition plan designated as the Jewish state. In the same war, it also occupied portions of the areas designated for the Palestinian state. If the Palestinians in these areas were not expelled, Arabs would have been a majority in Israel from its inception.

22. Morris puts the number at about 5,000. See Benny Morris, *Righteous Victims* (New York, 1999).

23. Israel's unwavering formal position, supported by the vast majority of Jewish citizens, is that it will never accept the return of Palestinian refugees to their homes in the context of a peace agreement with the Palestinians. Nor will it accept responsibility for making them refugees in the first place. See Nadim Rouhana, "Group Identity and Power Asymmetry in Reconciliation Processes: The Israeli-Palestinian Case," *Peace and Conflict*, X (2004), 33–52; and idem, "Truth and Reconciliation: The Right of Return in the Context of Past Injustice," in Ian Lustick and Ann Lesch (eds.), *Exile and Return: Predicaments of Palestinians and Jews* (Philadelphia, 2005).

24. For a discussion of the "emergency regulations" and their use in land confiscation, see Sabri Jiryis, *The Arabs in Israel* (New York, 1976); Lustick, *Arabs in the Jewish State*. For Israel's land policy, see Oren Yiftachel, *Planning a Mixed Region in Israel: The*

Political Geography of Arab-Jewish Relations in the Galilee (Brookfield, VT, 1992); idem, *Ethnic Frontiers and Peripheries: Landscapes of Development and Inequality in Israel* (Boulder, 1998).

25. Lustick, *Arabs in the Jewish State.*

26. David Kretzmer, *The Legal Status of the Arabs in Israel* (Boulder, 1990).

27. Meron Benvenisti, *Sacred Landscape: Buried History of the Holy Land since 1948* (Berkeley, 2001).

28. See Ann Kanaaneh, *Birthing the Nation: Strategies of Palestinian Women in Israel.* (Berkeley, 2002); Elia Zureik, "Demography and Transfer: Israel's Road to Nowhere," *Third World Quarterly,* XXIV (2003), 619–630; Masalha, *Expulsion of the Palestinians;* Rouhana and Sultany, "Redrawing the Boundaries of Citizenship."

29. Israel introduced a highly controversial law that limits the possibility of a spouse of an Israeli citizen to live in Israel if the spouse is a Palestinian from the Occupied Territories.

30. Several MKs (Members of the Knesset [Parliament]) in Israel called the law racist, and the Israeli Association for Civil Rights, and Adalah, the Legal Center for Arab Minority Rights in Israel, submitted a petition asking the Supreme Court to rule against the law based on the argument that it is discriminatory and racist. See http://www.adalah.org/eng/famunif.php.

31. For the UN Committee's report and further details about this law, see http://www.adalah.org/eng/famunif.php.

32. See Nadim Rouhana, *Palestinian Citizens in an Ethnic Jewish State: Identities in Conflict* (New Haven, 1997); Nadim Rouhana and Asad Ghanem, The Crisis of Minorities in Ethnic States: The Case of Palestinian Citizens in Israel, *International Journal of Middle East Studies,* XXX (1998), 321–346; Nadim Rouhana, "The Test of Equal Citizenship: Israel between Jewish Ethnocracy and Binational Democracy," *Harvard International Review,* XX (1998), 74–78; Rouhana and Sultany, "Redrawing the Boundaries of Citizenship."

33. See Meron Benvenisti, *Conflicts and Contradictions* (New York, 1987); Sara Roy, *The Gaza Strip: The Political Economy of De-Development* (Washington, DC, 1995); Raja Shehadeh, *Occupier's Law: Israel and the West Bank* (Washington, DC, 1988).

34. Arendt, *On Violence,* 64; emphasis in original.

35. Many Palestinians distinguish between at least two levels of legitimacy: the legitimacy of Israel to exist and the legitimacy of Israel to exist as a Jewish state. Although the first has been acknowledged by many Palestinians, the latter has not. If Palestinians were to recognize Israel as a Jewish state, they would be accepting the principle that Jews are superior to Arabs. They would also be acknowledging the right to establish a Jewish state in Palestine, which is tantamount to recognizing the legitimacy of the Zionist project.

36. For a discussion of Israel's de-development project in Gaza during the years of its direct occupation, see Roy, *The Gaza Strip.*

37. The Palestinian failure to estimate Israeli fear and to deal with it cannot be analyzed outside the context of the nature of this encounter, the power relations between Israel and Palestinians, the changing *perception* of these relations over the years, and the political culture in each community. Because the focus of this chapter is on the Israeli side, it is sufficient to say that the Palestinian failure fully to understand Israeli fear is at once surprising and paradoxical: as the weaker opponent, the Palestinians should have been more attentive to the Israelis' fear. But, the Palestinians did not necessarily perceive themselves as the weaker side strategically until the latter part of the last century. By then, many elites had developed a deep understanding of the Israeli fear, but the subjective and objective power asymmetry with the Israelis made it almost impossible politically to ask Israelis to confront their own history, the true source of their fear. It is not surprising, then, that the discourse on Zionism's responsibility and the fear of facing history takes place in intellectual rather than political circles.

38. See, for example, Daniel Bar-Tal and Yaacov Vertzberger, "Between Hope and Fear: A Dialogue on the Peace Process in the Middle East and the Polarized Israeli Society," *Political Psychology*, XVIII (1997), 707–740.

39. When I was offered a teaching position at Tel Aviv University, my hosts took me to lunch at the faculty club at what is known as the Green House, named for its outside color. I could not help but notice the Arabic architectural style of the place. Knowing that an Israeli institution would not choose Arabic architecture for one of its buildings, I asked about the colored floor tiles, an Arabic style of decoration. My hosts told me, with apparent embarrassment, that this was a house in the former Arab town of Al-Sheikh Mu'inis on the ruins of which Tel Aviv University is established. It must take enormous energy completely to suppress the moral questions that emerge from the reality that the former town's residents are scattered in various refugee camps in the region while a left-leaning academic institution enjoys their land. It must also take energy to suppress the fear that emanates from the demands of the rightful owners to return to their town.

40. Perhaps the appropriate areas for empirical study of this proposition are the fine arts, literature, and cinema, as they allow for unconscious and subconscious themes to be represented. Another possible avenue of study would be to conduct in-depth interviews about Palestinian refugees and the issue of the right of return. This author is currently conducting such a project.

41. See, for example, the Israeli government's reservations to the Road Map Peace Plan. Reservation 6 states: "In connection to both the introductory statements and the final settlement, declared references must be made to Israel's right to exist as a Jewish state and to the waiver of any right of return for Palestinian refugees to the State of Israel" (unofficial text of the reservations as published by *Ha'aretz*, http://www.haaretz.com/hasen/pages/ShArt.jhtml?itemNo=297230).

42. While Palestinians distinguish between two levels of legitimacy (see n. 35, above), the Jewish public does not accept this distinction. For Israelis, not recognizing Israel as a Jewish state is equivalent to not recognizing Israel at all (Sammy Smooha, *Arabs and Jews in Israel: Change and Continuity in Mutual Intolerance* [Boulder, 1992], II).
    In late 2000, Palestinian citizens in Israel held demonstrations to protest the kill-

ings of many Palestinians by Israeli forces in Jerusalem and other parts of the Occupied Territories after Sharon's uninvited visit to al-Aqsa mosque to demonstrate Jewish sovereignty over the site. During these demonstrations, Israeli police killed twelve Arab citizens, and wounded and arrested hundreds. The violence shocked the community and raised serious questions about the meaning of Israeli citizenship for an Arab in Israel. See Nadim Rouhana, "Shaking The Foundations of Citizenship," *Al-Ahram Weekly* (September 27–October 3, 2001).

43. See, for example, Stanley Cohen, *States of Denial: Knowing about Atrocities and Suffering* (Cambridge, 2001); Ilan Pappe, "Fear, Victimhood, Self and Other," *MIT Electronic Journal of Middle East Studies* I (2001), http://web.mit.edu/cis/www/mitejmes/.

44. See Rouhana, "Group Identity and Power Asymmetry"; idem, "Truth and Reconciliation."

45. See David Crocker, "Transitional Justice and International Civil Society: Toward a Normative Framework," *Constellations*, V (1998), 492–517; David Crocker, "Reckoning with Past Wrongs: A Normative Framework," *Ethics and International Affairs*, XIII (1999), 43–64; Louis Kreisberg, *Constructive Conflicts: From Escalation to Resolution and Their Transformation* (Lanham, MD, 1998); David Little, "A Different Kind of Justice: Dealing with Human Rights Violations in Transitional Societies," *Ethics & International Affairs*, XIII (1999), 65–80. For a discussion of justice in the context of the Israeli–Palestinian conflict, see Rashid Khalidi, "Attainable Justice: Elements of Solution to the Palestinian Refugee Issue," *International Journal*, LIII (1998), 233–252; Nadim Rouhana, "Reconciliation in Protracted National Conflict," in Alice Eagly, Reuben Baron, and V. Lee Hamilton, *The Social Psychology of Group Identity and Social Conflict: Theory, Application, and Practice* (Washington, DC, 2004). See also Yoav Peled and Nadim Rouhana, "Transitional Justice and the Right of Return of the Palestinian Refugees," in *Theoretical Inquiries in Law*, V (2004), http://www.bepress.com/til/default/vo15/iss2/art4/.

46. See Rouhana, "Group Identity and Power Asymmetry," for a discussion of historical circumstances that encourage and discourage reconciliation.

47. This is why Palestinians were expelled during the 1948 war even if they did not show any resistance to the Zionist forces. See Pappe, *A History of Modern Palestine*.

48. See Khalidi, "Attainable Justice."

49. Unlike the issues of full, equal citizenship and the return of refugees against which there is a solid Zionist consensus, no such consensus exists against a Palestinian state in the West Bank and Gaza. Zionist political parties differ on the extent and terms of supporting or opposing the establishment of such a state.

50. See, for example, Edward Azar, *The Management of Protracted Conflict* (Hampshire, 1990); John W. Burton, *Conflict: Resolution and Prevention* (New York, 1990).

51. See Louis Kriesberg, *Constructive Conflicts: From Escalation to Resolution* (New York, 2002, 2nd ed.).

52. See Rouhana, *Palestinian Citizens in an Ethnic Jewish State*, for an empirical

study of the various political factions regarding equality and full rights for the Palestinian citizens in Israel.

53. See Rouhana and Sultany's description of this hegemony as it applies to the Palestinian citizens in Israel, in "Redrawing the Boundaries of Citizenship."

54. The extent to which ideas once considered extreme have become acceptable in Israel is seen in the official legitimization of the ideas of Rehavam Ze'evi. Ze'evi is the founder of Moledet, a party whose core ideology is the ethnic cleansing of Palestinians from the Occupied Territories and the encouragement of Israel's Palestinian citizens to accept "voluntary" transfer. The Ministry of Education has instructed schools to include in their curricula Ze'evi's contributions to Zionism and to achieving its national goals.

55. See, for example, Office of the High Commissioner for Human Rights, "Question of the Violation of Human Rights in the Occupied Arab Territories, including Palestine," Commission on Human Rights resolution 2004/10, http://ap.ohchr.org/documents/E/CHR/resolutions/E-CN_4-RES-2004-10.doc.

56. Rouhana and Sultany, "Redrawing the Boundaries of Citizenship"; Nimer Sultany, "Israel and the Palestinian Minority, 2003," Mada's Second Annual Political Monitoring Report (Haifa, 2004).

57. See Asher Arian, "Israeli Public Opinion on National Security, 2000" (Tel Aviv, 2000); idem, "Israeli Public Opinion on National Security, 2001" (Tel Aviv, 2001); and idem, "Israeli Public Opinion on National Security, 2002" (Tel Aviv, 2002).

58. Rouhana and Sultany, "Redrawing the Boundaries of Citizenship."

59. Arian, "Israeli Public Opinion on National Security, 2002."

60. For a review of similar statements over the last few years, see Rouhana and Sultany, "Redrawing the Boundaries of Citizenship"; and Sultany, *Citizens without Citizenship.*

61. That Prime Minister Sharon is already considered a "moderate" within his own party and that his heirs apparent are considered more extreme is another sign that the trend continues to move toward further extremism.

62. Morris wrote in 2002 that David Ben-Gurion "probably could have engineered a comprehensive rather than a partial transfer in 1948," and then speculated that the Israeli leader would perhaps "now regret his restraint. Perhaps, had he gone the whole hog, today's Middle East would be a healthier, less violent place, with a Jewish state between Jordan and the Mediterranean and a Palestinian Arab state in Transjordan" (Benny Morris, "A New Exodus for the Middle East?" *The Guardian*, October 3, 2002).

6

CONFLICTING NARRATIVES OR NARRATIVES OF A CONFLICT

Can the Zionist and Palestinian Narratives of the 1948 War Be Bridged?

MORDECHAI BAR-ON

HUMAN HISTORY HAS amply proven that nations which experience prolonged wars may come to realize at a certain point that peace is preferable to continued war. Fatigue, rational calculations of cost, international intervention, and other motives may bring an end to strife. Peace is never an outcome of changes in the emotional sphere vis-à-vis the enemy. It may follow but not precede the end of the conflict. As the Franco-German case clearly shows, it took many years of peace, and often the arrival on the scene of a generation that did not experience the discord, before a change of heart occurred. Old opposing perceptions die hard even long after a hot conflict ends.

The requirement that a peace process should follow ideological and educational changes usually results in the prolongation of the conflict, not in its relaxation, since the inability of both sides to conform to the other's preconditions of ideological transformation is used as proof of dishonesty. The repeated demand of Israel's right-wing politicians that Palestinians should cleanse their school textbooks and official media transmissions of elements of incitement and hatred seems to be only an excuse to escape a need to make bold decisions despite mutual hatred, opposing narratives, and popular antagonistic perceptions. Similarly, Palestinian demands that Israel apologize for the evils perpetrated on them before peace can be achieved posits unnecessary stumbling blocks on the long road to peace.

As a veteran peace activist, I have been involved in many dialogues between Israelis and Palestinians. I believe that these efforts are necessary in order to prepare public opinion on both sides to support conciliatory political decisions. I have never indulged in the illusion that our activities in this arena will bring peace in and of themselves. Moreover, as so many peace activists have experienced time and again, some level of agreement may be reached by participants on the way the wrongs of the present situation must be perceived and on what the parameters of future solutions must include. They seldom reach agreement on the meaning of the past.[1]

Can or Should Conflicting Narratives Be Bridged?

Bridging conflicting narratives of past events and the meaning of past processes in our case seems to be impossible. Consider a simple example of conflicting terms: Can we really expect Israeli Jews to forsake their common designation of the 1948 war as their "War of Independence"? From their perspective it is not only an accurate designation but also constitutive of the way that they perceive their entire collective existence. Conversely, can we expect the Palestinians to relinquish their term for the war, "al Nakba" (the catastrophe)? This term is an accurate designation of what actually happened to them, as individuals and as a collective. It also became a constitutive term for their national self-perception as victims of the unjust Zionist project. These terms contradict each other in their implied meaning, since Israeli independence suggested, as it were, the demise of the Palestinian collectivity, or at least the loss of the greater part of the land which lent them their name; the term "al Nakba," on the other hand, is pregnant with moral indignation against the foundation of Jewish sovereignty and implies that the Jewish state was created in sin and represents a profound evil. These are certainly ideologically laden terms, but they are alive in the minds of millions and no sophisticated historiographical scholarship can eradicate these sentiments from their hearts.

Plurality of Narratives

As Akira Kurosawa's film, *Rashomon,* illustrates so well, even narratives of different participants in the same event are often dissimilar even when the individuals try to report honestly what they saw and believe actually happened. This conclusion is even more pertinent when people "remember" events that they did not participate in personally and know about only from secondary or tertiary sources. It is widely accepted today that much of the phenomenon that we commonly call "collective memory" is forged and constructed by competing interested elites. Intentional biases are therefore reflected in these so-called collective memories. These elementary characteristics of the ways that the past is "remembered" inevitably create a plurality of narratives. Even when the subject matter has lost much of its political acuteness, different groups continue to hold on to different narratives about their common past. One may assume that a loyal English Catholic will "remember" Queen Mary Tudor in different terms than will a devout Anglican. At least the former will probably find it awkward to add the adjective "bloody" to the queen's name.

This truism also applies to professional historiography. Even if we assume that historians are honestly committed to uncover the "truth," we shall discover that they always produce different narratives. I belong to the group who believes that many of the facts about events of the past can be ascertained objectively and agreed upon by historians, but that historiography always must and will go beyond bare facts. Selection of details to be told and personas to be characterized, interpretations about motives, establishing the meaning of events within the general context, and even the tone of a narration will always differ. Nor can historians escape their particular personal perspectives, and the perspectives of the readers for whom they write. The bare facts of the One Hundred Years War, for example, may have been agreed upon between French and British historians a long time ago. Still, a British historian will probably focus more on figures like the Black Prince and his bravery, and a French scholar will no doubt be more interested in the enigma of Jeanne d'Arc and her sad fate.

It is not a question of perspective that gives historiography its richness and fascination. Historians are required to be as accurate as possible, but they should equally recognize and legitimate the inherent plurality and variety of their trade. Historiographical revisionism is a universal, unavoidable, and normal phenomenon and should be welcomed, not shunned. Well-handled revisions of narratives tend to provide a higher accuracy and provide the reader with a more complex understanding of processes, even when we do not accept the details of a particular revisionist narrative. The recent debate about Zionism as a colonial movement, for example, when carried beyond the simplistic stage of defamation and name calling, may deepen our understanding of the Zionist project. Even those who feel obliged to defend the case of Zionism will have to explain in which ways Zionism was a unique kind of colonialism, and why, unlike other cases of colonialism, it has managed to withstand external pressures.

Exclusionary Narratives

Much of what has been stated thus far needs no further elaboration. The subject of this volume, however, offers a special case of differing narratives, specifically narratives that reflect an ongoing ideological and political conflict between two opposing national entities. We talk of narratives that are supposed to survey the history of a bitter conflict, evaluate its causal roots, and express views on its moral implications. In many respects these narratives are not only different but are diametrically opposed. Moreover, since these narratives constitute the central building blocks of the identities of the opposing collectivities, they tend to be exclusionary. Not only are they likely to deny the correctness of the opposing story, but they are also apt to negate the very existence of the foe as a collectivity. The opposing narratives, therefore, are conceived not only as untrue but also as insulting and morally corrupt.

By way of elucidation, in the common Israeli narrative there is a deep-seated conviction that the 1948 war was not only a decisive victory, but was also a case where the few Jews of Palestine overcame the overwhelming power of their enemies. The image of "little David vanquishing the giant Goliath" is deeply ingrained in the Israeli ethos. In fact, when modern Israeli historians try to explain to the public their recent discovery that in many phases of the war, especially in its later parts, the Israelis actually managed to deploy forces superior in numbers and equipment to the opposing Arab armies on the battlefield, they are often met with great anger and are shunned as "anti-Zionists."

Since only few Israelis think in terms of divine miracles, the implication of this popular perception is simple: The Jews who were few in number were morally, technologically, and spiritually superior to the Arabs and therefore were able to beat the "primitive" Arabs even though the latter were superior in numbers and equipment. Not surprisingly, this narrative offends and humiliates Arabs, who see it as just another proof of Israeli arrogance and try to refute the allegations and their moral implications.

During a series of lectures on the history of Zionism to a mixed group of Palestinian, Israeli, and Swedish students, I claimed that the Arab armies that entered Palestine in May 1948 were 40,000 strong. The Palestinian students challenged my numbers, stating that a Palestinian colleague had told them, only the previous day, that the number was only 25,000. The gap was not very wide and perhaps could have been bridged as far as the numbers were concerned, but that was not the real issue: more important was the sensitivity of the Palestinian students to my general assertion that, in 1948, the "invading" Arab armies were superior to the size of the Israeli army, not so much in the number of troops on the battlefield as in the quality of weapons that they had at that stage (which, by the way, explains many of their initial successes). Palestinians usually prefer to attribute the failure of the Arab armies to external factors, such as British perfidy and the corruption of the Arab regimes and their disunity, rather than to the general state of Arab civilization and culture at the time.

Zionist narratives are not only different but seem to subvert Arab and Palestinian self-esteem and self-identification. The same point applies to deep-seated Israeli fears of some of the basic images and narratives dear to the other side. As to the popular charge that Zionism is just one more example of colonialism, Israelis find it difficult to confront this basically correct assertion, since it is read to imply an innate evil ingrained in Zionism—a deterministic prediction that, like all other forms of colonialism, Zionism is doomed to perish.

The Case of Nadim Rouhana

Rouhana's chapter in this volume provides an excellent illustration of my proposition. The honesty of his presentation cannot be doubted. The grievances he lays out so eloquently are deeply felt and, from his perspective, reflect the truth. Yet a question arises: Can his narrative and accusations serve as a bridge on which Israelis and Palestinians can meet halfway and shake hands? Can even the most moderate and understanding Israeli agree to deny the legitimacy of the Jewish state? Can such an Israeli really be expected to embrace the original sin, or original crime, that Zionism inflicted upon the Palestinians?

One hundred years after the beginning of the Zionist immigration to Palestine, clearly no one can deny the basic argument that Jewish immigration to Palestine and the Zionist project in general are at the foundation of the conflict that developed two generations later. It is certainly true that if the Jews had not arrived in Palestine and created a sovereign state, there would be no Palestinian refugees and no conflict, but that claim adds little to our understanding of the tragedy. It does not consummate the story and surely is not the only causal explanation of what happened. Were the Zionists truly a band of criminals who frivolously dispossessed the Palestinians from their lands? Should the story not include an analysis of the motives and reasons that made Jews want to leave Europe at the end of the nineteenth century and during most of the twentieth century, and their resolve to demand for themselves the universal right of self-determination in Palestine and not elsewhere? This part of the narrative has little to do with the Palestinians but has much to do with the Jews who came to Palestine. The eventual plight of the Palestinians, therefore, cannot be understood without this second part of the tale. Rouhana overlooks it entirely, as he does the difficulties that the Zionists faced over the years. Neither party can be understood without a knowledge of the history of the indigenous people of that land, who, in the process, became "Palestinians."

There are many historiographical faults in the way Rouhana tells the story. The basic one is a common fallacy known as "post hoc—propter hoc." It is enough to read the daily newspapers to realize that violence and the use of force has indeed become the "central component" of the relations between Jews and Arabs in Palestine. It is also clear that force and violence are used by both sides. One may well ask whether the eruption of the last wave of violence perpetrated by Palestinians can be justified as a morally legitimate resistance. The popular word "resistance" that Rouhana uses to adorn the reaction of the Palestinians to Zionism cannot in itself legitimate every kind of violence or use of force in every situation.

The main problem with Rouhana's thesis, however, lies in his sweeping conclusion that "from the moment Zionism was conceived, force has been a central component of its relationship with Palestinians."[2] The Zionist endeavor was conceived and implemented during its first fifty years in a totally different world. Migration of Europeans to other countries was at its zenith and was not considered a sin. The Arabs who lived in Palestine did not yet appear in history as a unique nation with collective claims. That is why the League of Nations, in 1921, without moral hesitation, approved the right of the Jews to establish their homeland in Palestine despite the fact that other people had lived there for centuries. That is also why, during their first fifty years, Zionists were not obliged to think of the necessity of using force to realize their dreams.[3]

I recognize the validity and legitimacy of Arab resistance to the Zionist endeavor, but I also realize that when this resistance gained full momentum it was too late, since more than half a million Jews already lived in the country and had nowhere else to go. That is why the United Nations, in 1947, voted to partition the land as the only realistic solution. I fully understand the Palestinians' inability to accept that verdict, but weren't their resistance, and the violence and force they used, also components of the narrative, pieces in the chain of causation? Is it not possible for a Palestinian such as Rouhana to understand that, in 1948, the Jews of Palestine, to their chagrin, could not but use force to defend themselves and impose a solution that was legitimized by a majority of nations?

Although all of the above is true, the problem is that, in the context of this volume, "truth" can be contested. I have no doubt that my arguments have little chance of influencing Rouhana, as his oral arguments (at our meetings at Harvard University) not only failed to convince me but also made me angry. Such heated controversy does not feed on "truth." It gains its power and acrimony from the unavoidable gap in our perspectives and the distance between our conflicting identities. The intense emotions stirred up during our deliberations in the preparation of this volume testify to such a result. Indeed, there is no chance that I shall ever consider that my father and mother, who immigrated as Zionists to Palestine in 1924, were criminals. Nor do I consider my actions illegitimate when I gave the order "Fire!" and perhaps killed or wounded assailants in response to an ambush on the troop that I commanded on the way to Tel Aviv in December 1947.

The way that the majority of people on each side perceives the collective identities of both sides, Israeli and Palestinian, negates the very existence of the "opposing" entity. The foundation of Palestinian self-perception is inextricably connected to the land of Palestine, which obviously includes the entire area that today forms the territorial basis of Israeli existence. The first paragraph of the Palestinian Covenant reads: "Palestine is the homeland of the Palestinian Arab nation." The second paragraph specifies: "Palestine within the borders of the British Mandate is an indivisible territorial unit." This notion is naturally also based on "memories" of the time when the Arabs were the sole inhabitants, or at least composed an overwhelming majority of the people populating this land. Thus Palestinians have great difficulty in recognizing the Jews of Israel as a legitimate nation. It is odd, indeed, that the Covenant which defined the ideological basis of the Palestine Liberation Organization also introduced a special clause to un-define the Jews as a nation: "Judaism as a revealed religion does not constitute a nationality with an independent existence. The Jews are not one people with a personality of its own. Jews are rather citizens of the states to which they belong."[4]

For most Israelis, on the other hand, the prevailing perception is that Jews have a historic right to establish their state in the entire land of Israel, since the notion of a Jewish nationhood, fundamental to the Zionist ideology, is anchored in the memories of Jewish sovereignty during biblical times and during the era of the Second Temple. During the early parts of the twentieth century, the Zionist claim to a historic right to the land managed to gain international endorsement. This approval was the main justification given for the League of Nations' decision to give Great Britain a mandate over Palestine. Britain was expected to facilitate the creation of a national home for Jews in that land. However, international perceptions of legality and international morality have changed dramatically since World War II. Nevertheless, Israelis find it impossible to give up this archaic notion of a "historic right," which obviously excludes the rights of Palestinians and denies their existence as a separate national unit in the same land.

During one of the ideological debates that always takes place during World Zionist Organization conferences, I tried to argue that in today's world the notion of the "right of the Jews to the Land of Israel" has no legal or moral standing. Expectedly, colleagues from right-wing and centrist parties were enraged and heckled me. But even my own friends, ideologues of the Left, also preferred to uphold the notion and advocated a "two-state solution" as a pragmatic compromise. At best, they argued that the "right of the Jews" must be compromised by the simultaneous "rights of the Palestinians."

Many Palestinians realize, too, that at the end of the present conflict only very few of the remaining 1948 refugees will actually return to their homes inside the Green Line. They insist, nevertheless, that Israel must at least recognize, in principle, their "right of return," and publicly apologize for the evil done to them in 1948. These arguments are very much alive among Palestinians, but Israelis for their part see these demands as an existential threat and deny them. The diametrically opposed narratives of the way that the refugee problem was created do not so much touch on the way that the problem will be solved but rather on the way that each side perceives its collective identity and its moral foundation.

Some time ago Nabil Sha'at, the then Palestinian minister of foreign affairs, pronounced once more, in a speech to refugees in Lebanon, the solemn pledge of the Palestinian leadership to see to it that the refugees would all return to their homes, to Haifa and Jaffa. There was nothing new in his declaration, but Israelis were indignant.[5] Israel's public TV channel felt obliged that same evening to recycle an old story about a pamphlet allegedly found "recently" which showed that the Jewish Labor Union in Haifa, in April 1948, had pleaded with Palestinians to stay put and not leave the town. An old authority on these bigoted and tiresome arguments was called onscreen to regale viewers with a story that research has repeatedly proven to be false—that orders from Damascus encouraged the Arabs of Haifa to leave. Twelve years after the publication in Hebrew of Benny Morris's definitive and well-balanced analysis of the origins of the refugee problem, one might have hoped that such false arguments would have disappeared once and for all. But Israelis apparently find it vital for their well-being to stick to outdated narratives. The failure of academic research to change popular perceptions reveals that we do not deal with veracities but with the need, normal to all nations, to uphold the justice of their own creation.

Personal Memory—Transmitted Memory

The intensity, wide spatial expanse, and lengthy time span of the 1948 war allowed many Jews and Arabs living in Palestine to experience firsthand one or another of the many events, big or small, which occurred during that fatal year. Even those who may have personally escaped the horrors of the war feel intimately involved, as the events were transmitted in real time by relatives, friends, or the media. Every Jew or Palestinian over the age of sixty who grew up in Palestine and was at least five years old at the time of the war carries personal or transmitted memories. These "memories," fossilized over time through recurrent telling and the added impact of "collective memory" devices socially and administratively constructed over the years, ultimately become a dominant part of the culture and consciousness of the nation.

Most of my colleagues, especially the younger scholars, no doubt have encountered objections from an audience to the narrative they present, by the phrase: "Don't tell me, I was there!" I once encountered a Palestinian who listened to a lecture in which I tried to explain the rather complex circumstances that ended with the expulsion of the Palestinians from the town of Lydda in July 1948. It turned out that this man came from Lydda. He was seven years old at the time of the expulsion and remembered the two armed Israelis who entered his home and told his family to join their father, whom the Israelis had previously detained, and promptly to leave town. For this man, what occurred was obviously a straightforward case of eviction. But despite the fact that the Arabs of Lydda were clearly expelled, and that the collective experience of mass expulsion is certainly imprinted on this man, his personal experience is far from an explanation of the overall situation.

In one of the many battles that I personally experienced, the infantry platoon that I commanded came under heavy Egyptian machine gun fire, artillery shells, and mortar blasts. That night I lost seven of my men, and another dozen were wounded. The event exemplified for me and my men the great disparity in fire power between us and the enemy: we were equipped with much lighter arms, could not avail ourselves of artillery or air support, and were caught in the event by the enemy's overwhelming fire superiority. Can my memory serve as proof of the general imbalance of power at the time? It was mid-July, at a time when the edge began to tilt in favor of the Israeli forces. In other arenas of the war, even in other sections of my own brigade's activities, the Israeli Defense Forces (IDF) managed to concentrate troops far superior to those of the Arabs confronting them. Yet I am sure that, in the minds of my soldiers, their personal experience remained imprinted as a general truth about the war. Some may even respond to a learned analysis of the general power relations at that time by remarking, "Don't tell me, I was there!"

Personal memories inform the psychological basis of stubborn stereotypes that formulate the way an entire generation that lived through events later perceive them; such stereotypes constitute a barrier that hinders them from accepting other interpretations of what actually happened and blinds them to new insights. When the conflict persists, however, these personal memories become the bricks and mortar of national myths as they are transmitted to the next generation as trustworthy testimonies.

Other Barriers

Another obstacle that makes opposing narratives irreconcilable has to do with questions of periodization and conflicting perceptions of time. Most Israelis begin the story of the 1948 war with the attack on a Jewish bus near Lydda on November 30, 1947, the morning after the UN resolution for partition. Five Jews were killed. Israelis understand this event as the first violent signal that Arabs totally rejected the UN resolution, which Israelis had considered a fair compromise. Seen through this lens, the Palestinians appear to be the "aggressors" and the Jews the victims with no alternative but to defend themselves as best they could. On the other hand, the Palestinians' story begins with the unwarranted "invasion" of Palestine by European Jews in the late nineteenth century, which, from the outset, implied the eventual dispossession of the native people who had dwelled there for hundreds of years. To the Palestinians, the entire Zionist project was an act of aggression. But can a Jew, like myself, born in Palestine in 1928, believe that evil is inherent in his entire existence simply because he was born in Palestine, not Germany?

A further difficulty, in my opinion, is the recent intrusion of social and political scientists into provinces traditionally occupied by historians. These scholars use the tools and methods of their own disciplines to reanalyze and reformulate narratives of the past. Sociology, political science, anthropology, and psychology, for example, certainly play a major role in analyzing the present and paving the way for a better future. The use of paradigms, comparative studies, and the application of general rules are also obviously important in understanding complex situations. They place specific parameters of a conflict within a wider context, highlighting basic features of investigated phenomena and relativizing opposing positions. In so doing they extricate the protagonist from deeply rooted prejudices and antiquated conceptions.

Exploring the past, however, requires other methods and tools, and even a different state of mind. General paradigms such as "colonialism," "orientalism," or "ethnic cleansing" are reductionist and essentialist. They uncover factors common to a number of similar situations but lose the subtleties and complexities of specific historic developments. Historical events and processes are, by definition, unique and sui generis. In researching past events, generalizations and paradigms can serve only as a point of departure, at which time historians take over to explain how the case in question departed from the rule and evolved in its own special way. The historian's role is to discover and explain how events develop and ultimately become unique.

Zionism and the immigration of Jews to Palestine is one more example of the colonial phenomenon that, at the turn of the century, was still at its zenith. The Zionists themselves recognized this fact unashamedly when they used the word "colonial" in the title of many of their projects and institutions. Theodor Herzl did not hesitate to consult with the arch-imperialist Cecil Rhodes. At the time this took place, more than a hundred years ago, no one in Europe, the world to which both Rhodes and Herzl belonged, saw anything negative in their encounter. But having stated the basic attributes of Zionism, this paradigm loses much of its explanatory power. It contributes little to our understanding of the unique history of Zionism or the specifics of the Arab–Jewish conflict. The role of historians is to uncover not what made Zionism just another part of universal phenomena but what made it unique.

Historians' Responsibility

Bearing all these considerations in mind, I conclude that bridging the narrative gap, in the sense of reaching an agreement on a unified narrative, is futile. Such an effort, as the contributors to this volume all know from their experiences in putting together this book, often becomes an attempt to reassert the "truth" of one's own narrative against the "falsehood" of the other. Individuals who conceive the "bridge" in this way do not honestly believe that they can persuade the other in the truth of his/her own narrative. What they actually seek is the moral and intellectual support of a third party; their effort to bridge narratives is merely another ploy in the ongoing war of propaganda. Such an approach can only further mobilize historical research for continued strife. Rather than bringing the narratives closer, the gap between them deepens.

This is not to imply that nothing can be done to narrow the gap. I believe that historians are morally responsible to deconstruct perceptions and notions of the past that tend to encourage conflict and make reconciliation more difficult. Historians can and should minimize the exclusionist tendencies that often prevail in the process of constructing new national identities. Revisionists normally look inward, amending the narrative of their own side in the conflict. The demand that the opponent's narrative be revised adds to the strife, not to its resolution. Thus, scholarly confrontations between conflicting narratives can be fruitful only if each side concentrates on self-criticism, not on condemning the other. In national conflicts, the primary goal of historians must be courageously to revise the narratives of their own side instead of aggravating the discord by reinvigorating warlike myths and stereotypes, by repeatedly accusing the other of wrongdoing, or by self-righteously vindicating themselves. To the extent that historians are involved in the research of their opponent's stance, they must attempt to clarify the rationale behind the "enemy's" behavior and make room for greater compassion for those on the opposing side.

Self-critical revision involves three strategies:

1. To uncover and peel off the prevailing narrative's exclusionist nationalistic and self-congratulatory ideologies that tend to distort it.
2. To transcend simplistic generalizations and labeling, and discover the full complexity of the disputed events, both their motives and causations.
3. To try to understand the motives and rationale of the "enemy's" behavior, and to present the narrative with maximum sensitivity to the sensibilities of the opposite side, with human compassion and a deeper understanding of the tragic nature of the conflict.

Rarely in history are conflicts simple stories of a struggle between an evil aggressor and a righteous defender. More often, nations are prisoners of their own past and their own ideologies, and become entangled inextricably in a web of mutual acrimonies, suspicions, fears, and past mistakes. Historians are charged with untangling this web by exposing its genealogy. As members of one side, they are best equipped to know the details of their own side's record and should therefore be able to deconstruct the narrative of their side of the divide.

I revisit a central theme in the opposing narratives of the Arab–Israeli conflict: the question of who is responsible for the eruption and escalation of violence in the first phase of the 1948 war. There is hardly any question that, in December 1947, the fire that later spread throughout the country was ignited at that time by the Palestinians. Still, Israeli historians should be able to explain the rational and moral indignation that motivated the Palestinians to provoke violence, just as Palestinian historians should be able to explain why young Israelis could not but fight back at that stage. Indeed, the Haganah soon began to use retaliatory raids in response to Palestinian violence. These reprisals, which were partly motivated by a desire to take revenge but were also intended to deter Palestinians from further violence, achieved exactly the reverse. These retaliatory acts inevitably killed or injured many innocent people, pushing growing parts of the Palestinian population into a cycle of bloodshed. Thus the escalation of violence in January and February 1948 was not only a result of the Palestinian strategy but also of the Jewish response, truly a tragic vicious circle—tragic not only because of the pain that it caused but also, as in a good Greek tragedy, because of the fateful inevitability of the events that unfolded.

Israel's New Historians

Over the last two decades, the deconstruction of warlike narratives and attempts to close the narrative gap has ensued. The project taken up by Israel's "new historians" is indeed a worthy experiment in constructive self-criticism. Some of these new historians, however, overly eager in their cause, have been self-critical to an extreme, placing the entire blame on the Jewish side instead of offering an in-depth investigation of the inevitabilities inherent in the epidemiology of the conflict. Not surprisingly, most Israelis do not welcome this historiographical development, as they are usually unable to relinquish the deep-rooted prejudices of longstanding collective memories. The extreme nature of some of the new assertions may also explain why some of these revised narratives are rejected by a large segment of the Israeli public. Nevertheless, many of the new insights are productive and provocative in a positive way. The project reflects not only a normal progression in the pursuit of scholarship but also contributes significantly to a healthier self-perception among Israelis. Perhaps they will be encouraged to "think the unthinkable."

The historiography of Israel's foundation and early years was never uniform. From the very beginning a myriad of diverse and at times conflicting narratives appeared in print in an effort to create Israel's collective memory.[6] Yet most of these early publications stirred up limited controversy both in academic circles and among the general public. The debate over the so-called new historians began to rage only late in the 1980s and more acutely in the 1990s. Three young historians stood at the forefront of this new wave of historical revision: Morris, Ilan Pappe, and Avi Shlaim.[7] But more than their serious studies, which naturally attracted only a limited readership, an article by Morris in *Tikkun* at the end of 1988, and journalistic contributions by Shlaim, Pappe, and other historians and writers who joined the fray, sparked off a grand debate.[8] During the 1990s Israeli newspapers and academic journals published scores of angry articles about the controversy.[9]

The angry reaction of many Israeli intellectuals and the rejection of the new historians' narrative by wide sections of the Israeli public, especially among veterans of the 1948 war, indicated that these revisions had touched a raw nerve in the Israeli consciousness. In fact, the ongoing heated debate was not just an academic controversy. It was a cultural struggle over identities and self-perceptions, with deep political overtones. One keen observer noted that "the sharp opposition and the deep concerns these researches have aroused [...] resulted from a perception that they endanger the boundaries of the current [Israeli] identity and are seen as a threat to Israelis' self-image."[10]

Gutwein of Haifa University defined it well: "The innovation of the new historiography must be found not in the realm of research but in new public and political meanings which were attached to old data." He posits that the "New Historians do not assail previous research but extant memories." They try to suggest alternative memories and their "purpose is to impact the collective memory of Israel . . . focused on moral condemnation and attachment of guilt."[11] Shapira notes that "memory is the battleground of identity: whose share is larger in the struggle to achieve society's uppermost aspirations? Who was proven to be right? Who was the victim and who victimized?"[12] Thus the narratives and images against which the new historians direct their crusade are to be found in school textbooks, commemorative ceremonies, popular journalism, popular songs, and speeches of politicians rather than in serious historical research.[13]

Israeli revisionist historians are engaged in an ambitious project of reeducating Israelis. One may assume that what motivates them is the assumption that the Zionist common ethos and the popular Israeli perception of their past posits psychological obstacles to reconciliation with Arabs, and therefore their task as historians is to correct these deformations.[14] The goal of this project is nothing less than to change the parameters and reformulate Israel's perception of its own collective identity. In an introductory paper to a series of roundtable discussions between Israeli and Palestinian historians, "Collective Identities and the Middle East Peace Process," the initiators explicitly declared their aim: "How can we [as historians] make the identities [of Israelis and Palestinians] less absolute and less mutually exclusive."[15]

The Main Issues Revised

Academic revisions are generally limited to the period for which most of the relevant documents have already been declassified and made available to scholars. They deal mainly with the early years of the state of Israel, up to and including the 1956 Sinai campaign. More recently, research was completed on the 1960s and the Six Day War.[16] But the major offensive was launched on the narratives of the war of 1948 and its immediate aftermath. The new historiography focuses on six main tenets that Israeli popular opinion holds dear but that the new historians consider fallacious or—to use their favorite term—"false myths":

1. The 1948 war was initiated by the Arabs, who rejected the UN decision to partition Palestine and establish a Jewish state alongside an Arab state. The war was therefore, from this perspective, a desperate attempt by the Jews to defend themselves against the Arab onslaughts.
2. Israeli forces throughout the war were inferior in numbers and weapons to the Arab attackers. It was a struggle between "little but clever David" and "'giant but inefficient Goliath."
3. The British sided with the Arabs, increasing the heavy burden inflicted on the Jewish forces. The British, moreover, never actually intended to relinquish control of Palestine, but they now decided to do so via their Arab stooges.
4. The war ended in a stunning victory gained as a result of Jewish superiority in moral and combat capabilities. The Israelis put forth on the battlefield an animated force with distinguished commanders and fighters superior in their courage, endurance, and wisdom.

5. Full responsibility for the creation of the Palestinian refugee problem lies with the Arab leadership. It was a result of the flight of the
Palestinians who left their homes despite the pleading of Israeli
authorities, who asked them to stay.
6. The war ended only in fragile armistice agreements, not in full
peace, since the Arabs declined to accept the verdict of the war and
refused to recognize the very existence of the Jewish state in their
midst.[17]

The Various Revisions

The revisionists of Israel's political and military history can be divided into
three groups based on their motivations. The first group attempts to revive old
controversies that raged at the time of the events. Participants in these controversies, whose analysis and prognosis were defeated and the policies that they
advocated never tested, and their younger disciples try to vindicate those alternative policies, claiming that they not only were feasible but also preferable;
they could have avoided the escalation of the conflict or ended it peacefully
once it erupted. This approach views the "road taken" as a mistaken and la-
mentable policy and tries to convince the reader that the "road not taken"
would have been preferable for all parties involved. They rely in their reasoning
on the obvious fact that the road not taken will remain pristine, whereas the
road taken was marred by bloodshed and costly mistakes.

The main protagonist of this group is Simha Flapan, who, during the 1948
war, was a leader of the left-wing faction of Mapam. He believed at the time
that the creation of a bi-national state could be accomplished and was the preferred solution. Forty years later he blamed the Zionist leadership for not taking the road he and his colleagues had recommended and of violently extin-
guishing all prospects for its realization.[18] This group of historians believes that
the 1948 war was avoidable and became inevitable primarily because of the
non-compromising stance adopted by President David Ben-Gurion, and his
tendency to escalate violence and unnecessarily expand the territorial gains of
the Israeli forces as much as possible.[19]

Certainly many mistakes were committed over the years by both sides, and
the duty of historians is to expose them. But analyzing mistakes often leads
historians to deal with the ahistorical and unanswerable question: "What would
have happened if . . . ?" This historiographical technique is sometimes useful
to explain the nature and results of mistaken commissions or omissions, but it

may lead historians astray. Philosophically I am not a determinist, but as a historian I believe that the road taken has precedence over the road not taken not only because of the simple fact that there are reasons why things happen as they do but also because we can only know what actually happened and we must try to understand why. What may have happened had alternative decisions been made is something we will never know. Therefore, historians may use the "if" technique as a literary instrument for elucidation, but they must never overstate it as a certainty. Their energy must be dedicated to understanding why events transpired as they did.

The followers of Flapan gained very little attention in Israel. His scholarship did not even invite much anger. This failure may be explained by the fact that his thesis is incredible to most Israelis who are aware of the deep and lasting enmity and understandable hatred of the Arabs against the Zionist endeavor, which began long before the war of 1948. Although the war and the dispossession of Palestinians from their land surely contributed to this enmity, it did not initiate it. Therefore most Israelis do not believe that the Arabs would have accepted the founding of a Jewish state in their midst if only Israel had adopted a more appeasing strategy. There are many indications that, even at the time of the 1948 war, the vast majority of his own party did not accept the theories of Flapan and his friends. Their stance was too starkly contradictory to the realities people experienced. The repetitive violent attempts of the Palestinians to disrupt the Zionist project in 1920, 1921, 1929, and, especially during the great revolt of 1936–1939, became a central feature of the socialization of young Israelis and new immigrants alike. The personal experiences of many Israelis during the 1948 war reinforced the conviction that the overarching story could only be narrated as a Jewish defensive response to the total rejection by Arabs of Jewish political aspirations.

This self-positioning as victims also feeds on the traditional Jewish ethos that perceives gentiles as perennial enemies who are always harassing Jews and, if possible, exterminating them.[20] The experience of the Holocaust, only five years earlier, fortified this conviction.[21] Therefore it is not surprising that a thesis which tries to blame the conflict entirely or mostly on the Israeli side is doomed to be rejected or, at best, not be taken seriously.

Not So Heroic, Not So Few

The second group of revisionists wants primarily to refute the second and fourth "false myths" cited above. They attempt to prove that throughout the

1948 war the Jewish side was not only superior in organization and motivation but also in the number of fighting men and formations deployed on the battlefield. They also claim that in most phases of the war the Jews were also better equipped whereas the Arabs were not only ill-prepared and lacked unity of purpose and organization but also did not bring adequate forces to the field.[22] Some contend, moreover, that the Israeli army was not heroic, its commanders were mostly amateurs, and the number of their failures exceeded their victories.[23] This group may be described as "iconoclasts for iconoclasm's sake." Wistrich and Ohana explain the motivation of such iconoclasm with the assumption that "Israel has no further need for larger-than-life heroes, least of all role models of reckless bravery or military prowess."[24] Some of these iconoclasts are politically motivated, while others seem to believe that the time has come to educate the public not to yield to uncritical admiration of the Israeli army and its leadership, and to increase public understanding of the limitations imposed on the use of force in general.[25]

This tendency to look more critically at the performance of Israel's military may well have been motivated by the failures of Israeli forces in the War of Attrition during 1968–1970, and during the debacle of the 1973 war.[26] The massive protest movement which, in the winter of 1974, successfully brought into the streets tens of thousands of Israelis, mainly young demobilized reserve soldiers, determined primarily to depose General Moshe Dayan, an icon of Israeli bravery and prowess, from his position as Minister of Defense, helped to corrode the image of other Israeli generals and of the security establishment in general.[27] Doing so must be viewed as a revolutionary turn in the traditional Israeli self-perception and in the collective national identity, at the center of which was always the heroic and victorious Israeli army.[28]

Cultural Deconstruction

A special kind of historiographical and sociological critique has surfaced recently. This critique, which was inspired by recent Western cultural criticism, does not aim at the revision of a particular set of "distorted" narratives but instead at the Zionist ethos as a whole and offers a critique of dominant Israeli perceptions of identity. Its implicit ambition is to revise some of the basic traits of Israeli culture—viewed negatively by these authors—and to undermine the dominance of the Zionist ethos now prevailing in Israeli culture. Ophir defines well the ambition of this intellectual project as an attempt to "question both the Jewish–Israeli identity as well as the way by which this identity is acquired, since it subverts the capability of the Zionist ideology to continue to construct and spread this identity and deconstructs its last grain of efficacy."[29]

Although none of these authors admitted explicitly that his motivation was triggered by the contemporary Israeli grand debate on war and peace, one may guess that the new trend is a reflection of a deep sense of frustration stemming from an inability of the Israeli peace camp to transcend its marginal position in Israeli society. These authors seem to assume that the reason for that failure can be found neither on the level of political argumentation nor on the ideological level but rather in the very structure of the Israeli–Zionist culture as it evolved over the last century. This new version of revisionism must be seen as a total assault on the Zionist ethos and on Israelis' common identity.

Three scholars published books almost simultaneously in 2002, well into the second year of the second *intifada* (the *al-Aqsa intifada*). The hot political debate in Israel ever since the violence erupted in late 2000 has raged between the Israeli Right, which maintains that no political or diplomatic avenues can be followed until Palestinian violence is extinguished by the use of force, and the Israeli Left, which agrees that the suppression of Palestinian terror requires the use of force but demands a simultaneous political effort to ensure what is termed a "political horizon." The Right has gained the support of the majority of Jews in Israel, many of whom have lost faith in the ability or readiness of the Palestinians to come to an honest reconciliation, while only few have challenged the heavy hand exerted by the IDF on the Palestinians. The authors discussed in this section believe that this situation is anchored in deep cultural roots—the evil fruits of the Zionist endeavor itself. They challenge and reframe the endeavor itself.

Golani of Haifa University, so far a positivist historian, published an autobiographical and reflective essay, *Wars Don't Just Happen: About Memory, Power, and Choice.*[30] His motivation for writing this book is spelled out in the introduction, written by his friend and mentor Jacob Raz: "This book is published at the time in which power speaks and does not even need an apology. It is just there, acts and exists as if it was there from the time of creation, as one of the powers of nature, destructive but understandable. [. . .] Power is strong, fast, not too delicate; it acts with violence, kills, wounds, insults, corrupts. It has no mercy, certainly no compassion. It corrupted a long time ago the space left available for compassion."[31]

The main thesis of Golani's book is that from its earliest days the Zionist movement chose the use of power as the preferred way to fulfill its aspirations. This choice was transformed over the years into a comprehensive ethos into which young Israelis were nurtured. To be sure, this result is also true on the Arab side of the conflict, but "more than the two sides of the conflict react to what the other side does or abstains from doing, they react to their own conceptions and fears." Golani undertook to expose such corruption and to confront it.[32]

As he readily admits, Golani was not the first scholar to investigate the role of force, violence, and aggression in Zionism. Shapira analyzed the gradual transformation of the initial Zionist "defensive ethos" into an overwhelmingly "offensive ethos" which, according to her, came as a reaction to the Palestinians' growing violent opposition.[33] Her research ends with the 1948 war, whereas Golani decided to continue this line of argument and brought it up to date. In 1995, Ben-Eliezer published his study of the militarization of the Zionist movement. His main thesis was that the growing use of military power in the management of the conflict with the Arabs caused a thorough militarization of Israeli society.[34]

Golani takes this approach further. He suggests that "the use of violence was an integral part of the Zionist choice [. . .] this fact became clear already in the 1930s. The establishment of the state of Israel only intensified the use of violence." In his opinion, the Zionist movement used violence somewhat hesitatingly at the beginning, whereas today "Israel uses it with relish."[35] According to Golani, the use of force since 1948 has not necessarily been functional and rational. It has become a basic feature of the Israeli approach.

Hadari, in *Messiah Rides a Tank,* surveyed an immense volume of representations of what she terms "the public thought," that is, texts written by scholars, novelists, poets, journalists, and political personalities over a span of twenty years between 1955 and 1975, and discovered a clear pattern. During periods between the three major wars (1956, 1967, and 1973) Israeli society became saturated with a malaise that can be characterized as the loss of idealism, the lack of positive motivation, and general pessimism. The wars, on the other hand, brought about a wave of euphoria and messianic exhilaration. But an overarching process emerged that cut across these shifting moods: The public political culture of Israel replaced the initial "realist utopia" of the pioneering pre-state period with a militaristic values system in which the normative figure is a "messianic soldier" who represents a new "messianic, secular, but pious utopia." Moreover, Hadari detects a continuous process of "eroticization of war" in which the dominant figure is the "fighting soldier as the lover of the land." This "fighting masculine romanticism" connects the concept of "manhood" with "nationalism." "The masculine ideal becomes the symbol of a na-

_____

tional renaissance."[36] Hadari does not pretend to organize her work as explicit theory, but her entire style and use of terms turns her book into a strident and sweeping critique of Israeli identity in which war became a central theme of the Israeli unconscious.

The third assault on Israeli culture came from a declared "post-modernist," Zertal, who drew public attention by her blatant criticism of the way Israelis in general, and the Zionist leadership in particular, dealt with the horrors of the Holocaust. Her *Death and the Nation* continues to analyze the attitude of Israelis to the Holocaust but expands that discussion into a general investigation of the way that the Zionist movement—and later the state of Israel—made death and the fallen victims of the conflict into a central feature of its collective identity and self-perception.[37]

Drawing on Anderson, Zertal admits that the use of "holy victims" accompanies all nations in the process of "imagining themselves," but she points to the unique Israeli experience in which, "[f]rom the establishment of the State, the Holocaust and its dead are constantly present [. . .] in its laws, speeches, ceremonies, courts, newspapers, poetry, monuments, and memorial books."[38] She surveys the way that Israelis inextricably connected the Holocaust with the creation and justification of the Jewish state, but she also shows how the Holocaust discourse served to rationalize the building of its military power and the justification of its employment. "It gave birth to an old-new myth of an enormous scope that enjoined disaster and redemption, powerlessness and power, a myth which was extricated from history and its political dimensions."[39]

That Golani, Hadari, and Zertal chose to assail not just one particular facet or chapter of the collective memory, as did the original new historians, but the collective identity in its totality, seems to assure that their prospects of wielding a significant influence on the public is scant. Some narrow circles on the Left of the Israeli political spectrum may applaud their courage, but it is unlikely that a significant sector of the intellectual elite will negate perceptions which they helped to construct and have held dear for so long. All three, we must admit, expose facets of Israeli culture that exist and can be observed in real terms, but their reductionist approach turns their critique into a radical negation of basic features of the common Israeli collective identity. Their project is bound to fail.[40]

The End of Ideology?

The controversy over the new history soon became intertwined with another heated controversy between those who may be termed "loyal Zionists" and a group of writers who are often called "post-Zionists." This last term remains nebulous and conceals a great variety of ideological conceptions.[41] Essentially, the term indicates that "Zionism is a phenomenon which outlived its purpose, therefore the time had come to forge a new set of ideas and policies which have to be pursued from now on."[42] An analysis of post-Zionism will take us too far from the specific subject of this chapter. Instead, I highlight one issue on which both post-Zionists and new historians seem to agree fully: the declining need of Zionist ideology or even the negative role that ideology may play in the future.

The motivating force of Zionist ideology in shaping realities in Palestine over the last 100 years is well known. Every Israeli child is exposed at an early age to the famous Herzlian slogan: "If you wish it, it is no fairy tale."[43] The implication of this aphorism is that the Zionist dream is actually a fairy tale, but the power of will, the power of the idea, can turn it—and actually turned it—into reality. This indeed remained an important mental legacy and a main trait of the way Israelis perceive themselves vis-à-vis the realities that they have had to confront. Many Israelis still believe that Zionism can and should march on. A large banner was recently hung in the streets and the roads of the country by the Israeli Zionist Council: "We shall continue to dream the dream!"

Yet, on the Israeli Left, many believe that there are limits to the Zionist dream. That Zionism has already achieved its optimal aims is an idea that has begun to permeate growing sections of public opinion.[44] The conviction that, at least in its territorial dimension, Zionism may even have to retreat from some of its previous achievements is already widely accepted, according to public opinion polls. Moreover, according to this approach, Israel has reached a high level of normalcy, affluence, and stability. Zionist ideology is thus superfluous and redundant. According to this vision, Zionism should be replaced by modern, Western, and humanistic values.

Such an approach is unacceptable to the Israeli Right, especially to those who still dream of a "Greater Israel" and espouse the settling of the Occupied Territories. According to this school of thought, Zionism has not completed its mission and must march on; Zionist ideology must be upheld as the main motivating force behind Israel's policies. Right-wing propaganda often insinuates that the Left has betrayed the Zionist idea and deserted it. The settlers and their protagonists in the political establishment tend to utilize the very word "Zionism" to vindicate their expansionist policies. Often, after the murder of Jews in the occupied areas, settlers try to establish a new settlement on the spot of the incident and term it "an appropriate Zionist response."

This co-optation of the term "Zionism" by the Right has apparently motivated many intellectuals on the Left to claim that Zionism has outlived its purpose and now serves only conservative and reactionary ideals in Jewish society. Among the many schisms currently splitting Israeli society apart, this one seems the most bitter. The division between Right and Left is, above all, a crisis of identity: does Israel today embody Zionism on its march toward yet greater achievements or is it a ripe fruit of the Zionist project that no longer needs to continue its march, and instead should stabilize its achievements and adjust them to new realities?

The desire of new historians to liberate their work from the excesses of Zionist ideology is expressed in two ways: in their harsh criticism of the ideological bias that, in their view, tainted the writings of "old historians," and in the pedantic cleansing of their own writings of all vestiges of ideological prejudice. "Ideologically loaded" terms must be avoided: "immigrant" is preferred to "*olim*," "the war of 1948" rather than the "War of Independence," even "Palestine" instead of the "Land of Israel." Over many years, however, these old "loaded terms" encapsulated identity and now serve as hinges on which to hang Israel's collective memory. As Nora taught us, they become sanctioned "*lieux de memoire*."[45] Young historians' attempts to declare them invalid understandably arouse strong opposition. But if not taken to excess, this cleansing of the language may help historians write better histories.

Images of the "Other"

An important aspect of the work of many young Israeli historians that has a strong bearing on questions of identity is the attempt to reconsider the role that Palestinians played in the conflict. The Arabs in general, and the Palestinian Arabs in particular, were always the important "other" in Israeli society, especially since many Israelis originated in Arab countries, shared cultural traits with the indigenous societies, and wished to draw sharp lines of demarcation in order to establish clear boundaries for their national or religious Jewish self. The continuous, often violent, enmity of the Palestinian Arabs against Jews helped to demarcate those boundaries by sustaining images of the "other" as belligerent, evil, and uncivilized.

Until 1948, many Jews in Palestine maintained intensive, often friendly relations with Arabs, frequently striving to exonerate the "simple Palestinian people" from the guilt of violence and hatred. The popular explanation places blame on the Arab *effendi*, the rich landowners who exploited the Palestinian masses and incited them against the Jews, to divert attention away from their own plight. But the bloody and violent war of 1948 destroyed most of these rationalizations. The image of the naive but essentially well-intentioned Palestinian fellah could no longer be sustained.

That Jews had only limited contact between 1948 and 1967 with the few Palestinians who stayed behind and became Israeli citizens, and the total absence of ties with Arabs across the armistice lines, facilitated a new image of Arabs as unrelenting, cruel, and primitive enemies.[46] During this period of Israeli national solidarity, the phenomenon Erikson terms "affiliative loyalty" was in full sway among Israelis, who also developed "the passion of excluding others, that is, of knowing against what and whom one will stand and fall together." Israeli leaders, too, "found it necessary," as Erikson tells us, "to offer youth, as well as to the perennial adolescent in adults, some over-defined enemies against whom to maintain a sense of identity."[47]

In the aftermath of the 1967 war, Israelis once again came into contact with Palestinians in the Occupied Territories. By the end of the 1970s and during the 1980s, a growing number of Israeli Jews became involved in the peace movement and participated in many dialogues with Palestinians, including leaders of the Palestine Liberation Organization (PLO).[48] Many of these new associations received wide media coverage, and although negative images of the "Arab enemy" continued to prevail, a slow change of stereotypes could be observed in the circles from which most young historians come.[49] Many articles that portrayed Palestinians in human terms and brought their plight to the attention of the Israeli reader were regularly published in the press; Palestinian spokespersons were more often invited to take part in public events; and a number of documentary and feature films included "positive" Palestinian personas. Works of Palestinian writers, both novels and memoirs of political leaders, were translated into Hebrew and enjoyed a wide readership.[50] These changes could not fail to influence young historians who felt impelled to take another look at the Arab role in the conflict. Besides translations of works written by Arab historians, a few Israeli scholars started to publish more balanced descriptions and analyses of what transpired on "the other side of the hill."[51]

Why Now?

New history as well as the different trends of "post-Zionism" existed in the public sphere from the late 1950s, but only in the late 1980s did they gain dramatic momentum and become engulfed in a continuous and stormy public debate. The surfacing of these critical tendencies may be explained in a number of ways. Morris claims that the sheer passage of time induced the opening of the relevant archives where the "true narrative" could be found. Indeed, most new historians spend many weeks in the British Public Record Office, in the Israeli State Archives, and in many other places where the veracity of narratives can be checked through documents produced during the investigated period. Yet timing provides only a technical and partial explanation. The time factor is perhaps better attached to the fact that the new historians were born many years after wartime events and were therefore freed of the burden of Israel's dominant collective memory. Moreover, although they are devoid of personal memories of the early days of the Palestinian–Israeli conflict, they may have been witnesses to later phases of the conflict, namely, the 1973 war and the Israeli invasion of Lebanon in 1982.

These events stirred a growing wave of internal criticism and unleashed strong iconoclastic trends in Israeli society.[52] The diminishing respect for the old elites may also have inspired these young historians. They reflect a new ethos that has developed in Israel over the past two decades. There is a clear correlation between critical historiographical narration and sharply critical postures toward Israel's policies in the current conflict.[53]

One can also point to a more general trend in modern critical thought that certainly influenced most Israelis who studied and were constantly exposed to new trends in the current intellectual discourse in Western universities during the 1970s and 1980s. Israeli intellectuals were well acquainted with the post-structuralist theories of Foucault and the neo-Marxist thinking of Gramsci and Habermas, as well as the post-modern writings of Derrida and Baudriard and the post-colonial works of Said and Bhabha.[54] Despite the strident criticism of Said against Zionism and the State of Israel, his conceptual insights became popular among students and scholars in Israel and did not escape the attention of historians.[55] These influences introduced to the historical discourse a keener sensitivity and made historians more acutely aware of the subjectivity of the earlier prevailing perspectives.[56]

Theoria u Vikoret

Influenced by the recent critical theory and general expansion of cultural studies, a group of young historians, philosophers, sociologists, and students of cultural studies established a scholarly journal in 1991, under the auspices of the Van Leer Institute in Jerusalem, titled *Theoria u Vikoret* (Theory and Critique). Over the last ten years this journal has became the literary home of most postmodern, post-colonial, and post-Zionist scholars and critics of Israeli society. As the founders specified in the introduction to the first issue, they intended to concentrate on "the modes in which [Israeli] reality is represented in various cultural fields and . . . expose the ways in which cultural agencies, which deal with representation, work. We shall investigate the patterns of participation of those representational agencies in the construction of the social order and its replication or in the formation of power relations within society."[57]

Around this journal, an ideological and intellectual "Fabian Club" was informally established. It represents a wide spectrum of criticism of policies and revisions of old narratives concerning problems of gender, the Arab minority, nationalism, and ethnic rifts.[58] On the occasion of the jubilee of Israel (1998), Ophir, the founder of this group, edited a compendium of fifty articles, mostly written by post-Zionists. Each article focused on a theme that has preoccupied public attention in each of the past fifty years. Most of these articles were written in a way that can be subsumed under the term "new history" and thus became the best ideological concentration of the revisionist movement.[59] Some of the old "new historians" were also welcomed by this group, and its influence may be easily detected among many younger historians and the new generation of behavioral studies in Israel's universities.

Theoria u Vikoret, not surprisingly, has had only a limited influence on the general public, and its ideas have generated much opposition. It threatens to deconstruct important facets and features of Israeli identity. Nevertheless, the influence of this group has doubtlessly fortified skepticism and critical thinking among Israeli scholars, and has undermined their readiness openly to accept popular narratives and perceptions as well as the worth of authority in general. On the whole this new approach may yield better and more interesting historiography, for new methods that encourage young historians to problematize every event or social process are obviously an important starting point for deeper research.

Back to the Conflicting Narratives

Can these important trends in Israel's public discourse bridge the conflicting narratives of Jews and Arabs? If by "bridge" we mean develop greater mutual understanding and compassion, the answer is clearly "yes"; if the concept reflects a hope for a uniform narrative, the answer is clearly "no." Moreover, such pious hopes may hide a dangerous assumption. The joy with which Arab intellectuals embraced the new narratives betrays a misguided assumption that, at long last, Israelis see the "truth" and are ready to adopt the Arab narratives of the conflict. Indeed, Pappe, one of the original new historians, declared his intention to adopt the Palestinian narrative, but his isolation among Israeli intellectuals proves that this is not the road most Israelis will follow.[60]

The lesson Palestinians should learn from Israel's revisionist historiography is not how correct they are in their own narratives but rather how self-critical they, too, must become. I am not an expert on Arab historiography, but it seems that only a small bit of new history has appeared on the Palestinian side.[61] I say so with sadness, not self-righteousness, as I am fully aware that no symmetry can be drawn between the case of Israeli and Palestinian intellectuals. One should not forget that we, the Israelis, are still the occupiers, and they, the Palestinians, remain the occupied, uprooted, and dispersed people. The deep and in many ways justified sense of injustice and suffering that Palestinians must confront every day and everywhere in their land makes it very difficult for Palestinian historians to be more impassioned when they investigate the roots of their humiliations. The Jews of Palestine have already achieved and established their national sovereignty and collective identity. But the Arabs of Palestine are still in the middle of their uphill struggle to realize those goals. Nevertheless, writing in this context, I believe that my Palestinian colleagues will soon attain the self-confidence that will allow them to feel totally free to develop their work as historians.

Notes

1. On Israeli–Palestinian dialogues, see Mordechai Bar-On, *In Pursuit of Peace: A History of the Israeli Peace Movement* (Washington, DC, 1996) 199–218.

2. Nadim Rouhana, "Zionism's Encounter with the Palestinians: The Dynamics of Force, Fear, and Extremism," chapter 5 in this volume, 118.

3. The first to think in terms of force was Vladimir Jabotinsky, "The Iron War [1923]," in Zeev Jabotinsky, *Writings: On the Road to Statehood* (Jerusalem, 1959), 251–260, in Hebrew. But the majority of Zionists rejected the idea. Only after the massacres perpetrated by Palestinian Arabs in 1929, and more so in response to the Arab revolt of 1936, was the use of force legitimated by Zionist doctrine, and even then only defensively.

4. Yehoshafat Harkabi, *The Palestinian Covenant and Its Meaning* (Jerusalem, 1974), 25, in Hebrew.

5. Khaled Abu Toameh and Janine Zacharia, "Shaath: Refugees Have Right to Return to Israel," *Jerusalem Post* (August 17, 2003).

6. For a detailed analysis of these conflicting narratives, see Mordechai Bar-On, *Zikaron Ba Sefer: The Beginning of the Israeli Historiography of the 1948 War* (Tel Aviv, 2001), in Hebrew.

7. Benny Morris, *The Birth of the Palestinian Refugee Problem* (Cambridge, 1988); Ilan Pappe, *The Making of the Arab-Israeli Conflict, 1947–1951* (London, 1992); Avi Shlaim, *Collusion across the Jordan: King Abdullah, the Zionist Movement and the Partition of Palestine* (Oxford, 1988).

8. Benny Morris, "The New Historiography," *Tikkun,* III (1988), 3, reprinted in Benny Morris, *1948 and After* (Oxford, 1990), 1–34. Ten years later, both Morris and Shlaim published comprehensive textbooks on the history of the Zionist enterprise and the Arab-Jewish conflict: Benny Morris, *Righteous Victims: A History of the Zionist-Arab Conflict, 1881–1999* (New York, 2000); Avi Shlaim, *The Iron Wall: Israel and the Arab World since 1948* (New York, 1999). See also a sharp critique of both books by Anita Shapira, "The Past Is Not a Foreign Country: The Failure of Israel's 'New Historians' to Explain War and Peace," *New Republic* (November 29, 1999).

9. A comprehensive compilation of most of the articles published on the subject is Dan Michman (ed.), *Post-Zionism and the Holocaust: The Public Debate in Israel on "Post-Zionism" during the Years 1993–1996 and the Place of the Holocaust in It—A Reader* (Ramat-Gan, 1997), in Hebrew.

10. Amnon Raz-Krakotskin, "Historical Consciousness and Historical Responsibility," in Yehiam Weitz (ed.), *From Vision to Revision* (Jerusalem, 2000), 123, in Hebrew. These reactions validate David Lowenthal's advice to revisionist historians to prefer "a remote and malleable past to a recent one, perhaps too painful or too well known." See Lowenthal, "Past Time, Present Place: Landscape and Memory," *Geographical Review,* LXV (1975), 31.

11. Daniel Gutwein, "The 'New Historiography' and the Privatization of Memory," in Weitz, *From Vision and Revision,* 316, 324. Uri Ram, too, considers the historian's debate "a cultural-political event which has a meaning for the present." See Uri Ram (ed.), *The Israeli Society: Critical Aspects* (Tel Aviv, 1993), 64, in Hebrew.

12. Anita Shapira, *New Jew, Old Jews* (Tel Aviv, 1997), 16, in Hebrew.

13. On the narratives and images prevailing in Israeli school textbooks see Ruth Firer, *Agents of Zionist Education* (Tel Aviv, 1985), in Hebrew; Eli Podeh, *In Praise of Confusion and against Whitewashing: The Arab-Israeli Conflict in the Mirror of History Textbooks* (Jerusalem, 2000), in Hebrew. See also Eli Podeh, "History and Memory in the Israeli Educational System: The Portrayal of the Arab-Israeli Conflict in History Textbooks, 1948–2000," in *History and Memory,* XII (2000), 65–100. A good compilation of articles is Avner Ben-Amos (ed.), *History, Identity and Memory: Images of the Past in Israel's Education* (Tel Aviv, 2002), in Hebrew.

14. See Mordechai Bar-On, "Historiography as an Educational Project," in Ilan Peleg (ed.), *The Middle East Peace Process: Interdisciplinary Perspectives* (Albany, 1998), 21–40. Even Morris, an avowed positivist, admits that, "if in the process of advancing towards the 'truth' a few cows are slaughtered, what can we do?" See Benny Morris, "Between Theft and Conquest," *Ha'aretz* (August 30, 1995), in Hebrew.

15. See Israel/Palestine Center for Research and Information document signed by Peter Demant and Said Zeidani, June 13, 1995.

16. The more recent among them are Orna Almog, *Beyond Suez: Britain, Israel and the US, 1956–1958* (London, 2002); Michael Oren, *Six Days of War* (Oxford, 2002); Emanuel Gluska's unpublished Ph.D. thesis, "The Military Command and the Political Leadership of Israel in Front of the Security Problems of 1963–1967," Hebrew University, Jerusalem, 2000, in Hebrew.

17. Avi Shlaim added another fallacious assertion of the "old" Israeli historiography which claims that King Abdullah reneged on his previous understanding with the Jews, achieved during his meeting with Prime Minister Golda Meir in Naharaim at the end of November 1947. See Avi Shlaim, "The Debate about 1948," *International Journal of Middle East Studies*, XXVII (1995), 287–304. For a fuller treatment of these issues, see Mordechai Bar-On, *Zikaron Basefer* (Tel Aviv, 2001), 208–241, in Hebrew.

18. Simha Flapan, *The Birth of Israel: Myths and Realities* (New York, 1987).

19. The younger scholars who adhere to this approach are Yoram Nimrod, *War or Peace: Formation of Patterns in Israeli Arab Relations, 1947–1950* (Givat Haviva, 2000), in Hebrew; Pappe, *The Making of the Arab-Israeli Conflict*.

20. This perception is symbolized by the famous song every Jewish and Israeli family sing on Passover night: "Ve hi she'amda," whose refrain reads: "For not only hath one [enemy] arisen against us to destroy us, but in every generation many [nations] have arisen against us to destroy us."

21. For a recent treatment of the role that the Holocaust played in Israeli ethos and politics, see Tom Segev, *The Seventh Million: The Israelis and the Holocaust* (New York, 1993). See also Idit Zertal, *From Catastrophe to Power: Holocaust Survivors and the Emergence of Israel*, (Berkeley, 1998).

22. An exhaustive analysis of the balance of power during the war is Amitzur Ilan, *Embargo: Power and Decision in the 1948 War* (Tel Aviv, 1995), in Hebrew. For more on this question, see Benjamin Ze'ev Kedar and Alon Kadish (eds.), *Few against Many: Studies on the Balance of Power in Judas Maccabeus: Battles and the War of Independence* (Jerusalem, 2006).

23. The most pronounced protagonist of this approach, Uri Milstein, is not an academic historian, yet he wrote one of the most detailed analyses of the first phases of the war. See his *History of the War of Independence* (Tel Aviv, 1989–1991), in Hebrew.

24. Robert S. Wistrich and David Ohana (eds.), *The Shaping of Israeli Identity: Myth, Memory and Trauma*, a special issue of *Israel Affairs*, I (1995), vii.

25. Milstein published a special study in which he portrays Prime Minister Yitzhak Rabin as a commander who failed in battle and even showed cowardice and confusion. The book was published when Rabin became a contender for the office of prime minister; Milstein's attack was an attempt to discredit him. See Uri Milstein, *The Rabin File: How the Myths Swelled* (Tel Aviv, 1995), in Hebrew.

See also, for example, David Tal, "Did Israel Win the 1948 War and If Not Why Not?"

Zemanim, LXXX (2002), 42–54, in Hebrew. For a detailed analysis of the IDF's battles against the Egyptian army, see Tal, "Who Stopped the Egyptians in the 1948 War?" *Iyunim beTekumat Israel,* X (2000) 102–121. Tal has not yet volunteered his motivations beyond trying to write "good history." The imputation of his motivations are my own conjectures.

26. For a treatment of the War of Attrition, see Ya'akov Bar-Siman-Tov, *The Israeli-Egyptian War of Attrition, 1969–1970* (New York, 1980). Many books were published on the October war. I only mention Chaim Herzog, who at the time was the main radio commentator of the war and later served as Israel's president. See Herzog, *The War of Atonement* (London, 1977).

27. For a full treatment of the post–October War protest movement, see Moshe Livne, "Our Israel": The Rise and Fall of a Protest Movement," unpub. M.A. thesis, Tel Aviv University, June 1977, in Hebrew. For a brief treatment of this movement, see Bar-On, *In Pursuit of Peace,* 77–84.

28. In the Weberian tradition, Eric Cohen links this phenomenon to the "routinization" of past "charisma"; see Eric Cohen, "Israel as a Post-Zionist Society," in Wistrich and Ohana, *Shaping of Israeli Identity,* 203–214.

29. Adi Ophir, "Post-Zionism," in idem, *Working for the Present: Essays on Contemporary Israeli Culture* (Tel Aviv, 2001), 270. Ophir applies this effect to all modes of sociological and historiographical revisionism, but to my mind it is most suitably applied to the particular group described in this section.

30. Motti Golani, *Wars Don't Just Happen* (Tel Aviv, 2002), in Hebrew. His previous books include *Zion in Zionism: Zionist Policy on the Question of Jerusalem, 1937–1949* (Tel Aviv, 1992), in Hebrew; *Israel in Search of War: The Sinai Campaign, 1955–1956* (Brighton, 1998).

31. Golani, *Wars Don't Just Happen,* 11.

32. Ibid., 17.

33. Anita Shapira, *Land and Power: The Zionist Resort to Force, 1881–1948* (New York, 1992).

34. Uri Ben-Eliezer, *The Making of Israeli Militarism* (Bloomington, 1998). An earlier work on the growing involvement of the military in politics is Yoram Peri, *Between Battles and Ballots* (Cambridge, 1983).

35. Golani, *Wars Don't Just Happen,* 102.

36. Yona Hadari, *Messiah Rides a Tank: Public Thought between the Sinai Campaign and the Yom Kippur War, 1955–1975* (Jerusalem, 2002), in Hebrew. For her definition of terms, see the introduction, 17–42. The quotes are from 28 and 31, respectively. Hadari draws the connection between manhood and nationalism from George Mosse, *The Image of Man: The Creation of Modern Masculinity* (Oxford, 1996).

37. Idit Zertal, *Death and the Nation: History, Memory and Politics* (Tel Aviv, 2002), in Hebrew. The quote is from 13.

38. Zertal, quoted in Benedict Anderson, *Imagined Communities* (New York, 1991) 243; Zertal, *Death and the Nation,* 16.

39. Ibid., 229.

40. See also Yehuda Shenhav, *The Arab-Jews: Nationalism, Religion and Ethnicity* (Tel Aviv, 2003), in Hebrew. Shenhav's book deals with the suppression by Ashkenazi Zionist cultural dominance of the original "Arab" identity of Jews who immigrated from Arab countries—an essentially "orientalist" and "colonialist" ethos that relegated these immigrants, under the title "*Mizrahim,*" to the status of second-rate citizens in Israel.

41. For one attempt at clarification of the term, see Mordechai Bar-On, "Post-Zionism and Anti-Zionism: Differentiations, Definitions and Classification of the Issues and Some Personal Choices" in Pinhas Genosar and Avi Bar-Eli (eds.), *Zionism: A Contemporary Debate* (Sdeh Boker, 1996), 475–508, in Hebrew. Many chapters in this volume are also useful on the issue.

42. The quote is from ibid., 475. For a definition and analysis "from within," see Adi Ophir, "Post-Zionism," in idem, *Working for the Present* (Tel Aviv, 2000), 256–280, in Hebrew.

43. Theodor Herzl used this slogan as a motto for his utopian *Altneuland* (Vienna, 1902).

44. A general discussion of these issues can be found in Mordechai Bar-On, "Zionism into Its Second Century: A Stock-Taking," in Keith Kyle and John Peters (eds.), *Whither Israel? The Domestic Challenges* (London, 1993), 20–40.

45. Pierre Nora, *Les Lieux de Memoire* (Paris, 1984–92). See also idem, "Between Memory and History," *Representation,* XXVI (1989), 7–15.

46. For another analysis of the images of the Arabs in Hebrew children's literature, see Meir Hazan, "Fighting Journalism: The Reflection of the War of Independence in Children's Journals," *Kesher,* XXXII (2003), 114–125, in Hebrew.

47. Erik H. Erikson, *Dimensions of a New Identity* (New York, 1974), 95–96.

48. For a detailed treatment of this issue, see M. Bar-On, *In Pursuit of Peace,* 199–218.

49. The second intifada brought about a major setback in Israelis' readiness to view Palestinians in a positive light.

50. *Ha'aretz,* a daily read primarily by upper-middle-class, liberal, and better-educated readers, led this tendency, especially through articles by Gideon Levi, Amira Haas, and Dani Rubinstein. The novels of Emil Habibi and Anton Shamas, and the memoirs of Abu Yiad, the deputy head of the PLO, are notable examples. See Emil Habibi, *The Optimist: The Extraordinary Chronicle of the Disappearance of Said Abu el Nahas el Matash'al* (Jerusalem, 1984), in Hebrew; Soraya Hurafiya, *The Daughter of the Evil Devil* (Tel Aviv, 1993), in Hebrew; Anton Shammas, *Arabesque* (Tel Aviv, 1986), in Hebrew; Abu Iyad, *Abou Iyad, Palestinien sans Patrie: Entretiens avec Eric Rouleau* (Paris, 1978).

51. Among the books translated, see Rashid Khalidi, *Palestinian Identity: The Construction of Modern National Consciousness* (New York, 1997). On the beginnings of Palestinian nationalism, see also Baruch Kimmerling and Joel Migdal, *Palestinians: The Making of a People* (New York, 1993).

52. For a fuller discussion of the public reaction to the debacle of 1973, see Bar-On, *In Pursuit of Peace*, 69–92. For the wave of antiwar demonstrations during the Lebanese invasion, see ibid., 137–156. Chapters in this volume also include a more detailed bibliography on both subjects.

53. The new historians' feeling of betrayal when Morris published a strong critique of Palestinian policies during the second intifada points to this correlation.

54. See Michel Foucault, *The Archaeology of Knowledge and the Discourse on Language* (New York, 1982); Antonio Gramsci (ed. Frank Rosengarten), *Letters from Prison* (New York, 1994); David Forgacs (ed.), *An Antonio Gramsci Reader* (New York, 1988); Jacques Derrida, *Writing and Difference* (London, 2001); John D. Caputo (ed.), *Deconstruction in a Nutshell: A Conversation with Jacques Derrida* (New York, 1997); Edward W. Said, *Orientalism* (London, 1995); Homi Bhabha, *Location of Culture* (London, 1994); and Jürgen Habermas, *Theory and Practice* (London, 1974).

55. Beside scores of attacks in the media, the main anti-Israeli advocacies may be found in Edward W. Said, *The Question of Palestine* (New York, 1980); Said and Charles Hitchens (eds.), *Blaming the Victims* (New York, 1988).

56. On the influence of Said on Mizrachi young scholars, see Yaron Tzur, "Israeli Historiography and the Ethnic Problem," in Morris (ed.), *Making Israel* (London, 2003).

57. "Opening Remarks," *Theoria u Vikoret: An Israeli Forum* (the first issue was not numbered but the next one carried the number "2") (Jerusalem, 1991). The text was written by Adi Ophir, the first editor, and the influence of Foucault cannot be mistaken.

58. See, for example, the recent publication by the Van Leer Institute of Hannan Hever, Jehuda Shenhav, and Penina Musafi-Heler (eds.), *Mizrachi in Israel: Renewed Critical Investigations* (Jerusalem, 2002), in Hebrew. The editors are all active members of the *Theoria u Vikoret* group.

59. Adi Ophir (ed.), *50 to 48: Critical Moments in the History of the State of Israel, a Special Issue of Theoria u Vikoret* (Jerusalem, 1999), in Hebrew.

60. See Ilan Pappe, "The Bridging Narrative Concept," chapter 8 in this volume.

61. See, for example, Mustafa Kabha, "Arab Historiography of the 1948 War," an article to be included in a new volume of studies on the Israeli War of Independence (forthcoming). See also Saleh Abdel Jawad, "The Arab and Palestinian Narratives of the 1948 War," chapter 4 in this volume.

7

NARRATIVES AND MYTHS ABOUT
ARAB INTRANSIGENCE TOWARD ISRAEL

MARK TESSLER

NARRATIVES ARE REAL and deserve attention regardless of the degree to which they are historically accurate. Whether or not they *are* historically accurate is also important. But the fact is that Israelis and Palestinians have narratives that tell different stories about what has happened in Palestine since the beginning of the modern Zionist project. From one perspective, it does not matter whether the stories are accurate. That they are authentic is enough. The Palestinians' narrative is a product of their experience, just as the Zionists' is a product of theirs. It reflects how they perceived, interpreted, and evaluated the events and circumstances of their lives. Put differently, it is a community's own story—how the community understands and gives meaning to what it has endured. It is neither accurate nor inaccurate in a larger or more objective sense. It is simply one's story, subjective but real in the sense that it is the version of life and times that one not only tells but also believes. And to those who doubt this rendering of history, it may be said: if you had experienced what this community has experienced, it would be your narrative as well.

In a situation of conflict, acknowledging not only the authenticity but also the validity, and indeed the legitimacy, of the other side's narrative is important for at least two closely interrelated reasons. First, this acknowledgement humanizes the adversary. Such an acknowledgement is necessary for progress to be made toward resolving the conflict; it allows for the possibility, at least, of eventual reconciliation. Rather than demonizing one's historic adversaries, and thus believing that they are driven by irrational or immoral principles, accepting their narrative makes them human. Their story and sentiments are not the product of some primordial, intrinsic, and hence unchangeable impulse that makes them untrustworthy and undeserving of consideration. Rather, they constitute a logical, reasonable, and ultimately human response to the lives that they have lived. Acknowledging their narrative makes dialogue possible and accommodation imaginable.

Second, accepting the validity of the other's narrative has implications for the way a community understands its own narrative. More specifically, it leads to an appreciation of the fact that it *is* a narrative, authentic to be sure, and not necessarily inaccurate, but nonetheless a story rather than objective history. Recognizing the subjective character of the way people tell the story of their community's experience, including the story of its relationship with adversaries, brings an understanding that this narrative is not the only reasonable account of events and circumstances. This acceptance is also a necessary condition for dialogue, accommodation, and eventual reconciliation. A community is not required to disavow its own narrative. But it does need to be receptive to compromise, and that necessitates an appreciation not only of the humanity of the adversary but also of the fact that it does not have a monopoly on morality and truth.

As important as it is to view narratives from this perspective, questions about the degree to which a narrative is consistent with historical facts, to the extent these can be known, are certainly relevant and significant. One of the participants in the meetings on myth and narrative in Palestine/Israel sponsored by the Harvard University Program on Intrastate Conflict illustrated this question of reality by describing a man who told his psychiatrist that he was being chased by a woman with a knife. The sincerity of the man's belief was not at issue, nor was the fact that his belief might be the product of some real-life experience. But it was also important to know whether there really was a woman with a knife. This example may not be entirely apt; narratives, while authentic, need not be pathological. They are not necessarily about imagined rather than experienced history. But if the subjective character of narratives is recognized, it will be understood that the perception of events from which they are derived has the potential to give rise to myths and stereotypes.

Narratives are about explanation as well as description; they address questions not only about what happened but also about why it happened and who or what was responsible. Add the human and perhaps inevitable tendency to justify one's own actions and see others as largely responsible for one's problems, and it becomes clear that narratives are likely to have heroes and villains and may easily become one-sided. But are the heroes of the narrative really heroes, and are the villains actually villains? This question needs to be asked if a narrative is to be understood as a story and not objective history. No matter how sincere the conviction that one's story is true, sincerity and conviction cannot be the measures by which the accuracy of a narrative is judged.

Discussions a few years ago with several Israeli Jews of Moroccan origin helped me to appreciate the importance of inquiring into the accuracy of narratives. I asked these men and women why so many immigrants from Morocco were voting for the Likud party in Israel's parliamentary elections. "Because Likud will be strong with the Arabs," I was consistently told. "We came from Morocco and so we know what the Arabs are like. They don't like the Jews and so you have to be strong with them." This response was not unexpected. It appeared to be a widely held explanation for the partisan tendency of Israeli Jews of Afro-Asian origin. But I then told my interlocutors that I had lived for several years in North Africa, including Morocco, and had always thought that relations between Jews and Arabs in Morocco were largely harmonious. "Well, yes," they agreed. "But Moroccans are not like other Arabs."[1]

My book, A History of the Israeli-Palestinian Conflict (1994), presents the conclusions of several Israeli and other scholars who have conducted research on Jews of Afro-Asian origin. There is at least a possible disjuncture between the facts of Jewish life in Morocco and the story that is told by many Jews of Moroccan origin. Are questions about whether such a disjuncture actually exists of no importance, presumably because Jews of Moroccan origin are entitled to their narrative and it must therefore be accepted as valid and legitimate? The answer is no. I do not believe that recognition of a narrative's authenticity and validity makes a concern for the degree of its accuracy irrelevant.

The importance of determining the circumstances that brought approximately 200,000 Moroccan Jews to Israel in the 1950s and 1960s is illustrated by present-day debates about Israel's responsibility for the Palestinian refugee problem. Some supporters of Israel claim that there actually was an exchange of Arab and Jewish refugees, with Jews being forced to leave the Arab world and abandon their property to approximately the same extent as Palestinians who left the territory that became the state of Israel. Palestinians understandably respond that, even if true, it does not relieve Israel of its responsibility for their plight. If there is a debt to the Jews, it should be paid by the Arab states that are responsible, not by the Palestinians. But is there, in fact, such a debt, and, if so, to what extent? This is an important question, and one that cannot be answered adequately by referring only to the narrative of Jews of Afro-Asian origin. Based on my admittedly incomplete examination of the Moroccan case, I suspect that careful historical study will indeed reveal a gap between the facts of the Jewish exodus and the story told today by many Israeli Jews of Moroccan origin.[2]

It is against such a background that this chapter examines the Arabs' attitude toward peace with Israel. The story many Israelis tell, as do others who support Israel, is that Zionist leaders have consistently pursued peace, whereas Arabs have always been determined to destroy to the Jewish state. President Gamal Abdel Nasser of Egypt vowed to throw the Jews into the sea, we are told, and there is no more convincing illustration of Arab intransigence than the "Three No's" of the Khartoum Arab Summit that followed the June 1967 war: no to peace, no to recognition, no to negotiation. This story is a significant part of the Zionist narrative and is not necessarily inaccurate. On the other hand, it is not necessarily accurate. It is important to determine where, between these two poles, reality is situated. It is unreasonable to expect Israel to accept the principle of territorial compromise if the Arab world really is as intransigent as some Zionists insist. Alternatively, Israel should be condemned for rejecting compromise to the extent that this part of the Zionist narrative—Arab intransigence—is in substantial measure a myth.

The Decades following Israeli Independence

During the 1960s and 1970s, as well as earlier, many supporters of Israel insisted that the Arab world was determined to destroy the Jewish state. They pictured Israel as a small and beleaguered country, eager for peace with its Arab neighbors. The Arabs, by contrast, were portrayed as consumed with hate for the Zionist state and resolute in their opposition to Israel's existence. Although not all Israelis and supporters of Israel embraced this view, clearly it was the dominant Zionist narrative at the time. The following quotations are taken from works in which this narrative finds expression. In each quote, the emphasis is mine.

• "The record abounds with expressions of the Israelis' readiness to submit their differences with the Arabs to negotiation, and with affirmations of their hopes for the establishment of normal relationships which would promote the . . . development of their common area. That record is remarkable for the frequency of Israeli overtures, and for *the totality of Arab rejection*."[3]

• "*The annihilation of Israel and of its people* has . . . become a self-understood purpose demanded by the Arab future no less than by Arab history, by Arab honor and pride no less than by Arab pragmatic interest. It has become basic to all Arab thinking, and it is not kept secret. No Arab politician and—with the exception of one or two notable exiles—no Arab intellectual has expressed contradictory opinions."[4]

• "The essence of the conflict between Israel and the Arab states has been the *refusal of those states to acknowledge the existence and legitimacy of the State of Israel* and to accept it as a member of the family of nations in the Middle East. The major outstanding political problems of occupied territory and of displaced Arabs have resulted from that refusal."[5]

• "Extreme Arab opinion invariably begins that *Israel has no right to exist* as a sovereign Jewish state."[6]

Although not without merit, this version of the Arabs' position has for many years been incomplete and oversimplified; the closer one gets to the present, the more this account is false. With respect to early post-1948 history, there were possibilities for peace with Israel's most important neighbors, Jordan and Egypt. Jordan's early interest in an accommodation with Israel is fairly well known. Late in 1949, King Abdullah of what at the time was Transjordan participated in secret talks with Zionist leaders in order to explore the possibility of a separate peace between his country and Israel. Moreover, when it became clear that those talks would not produce a final settlement, he proposed a five-year nonaggression pact between the two states.[7]

The case of Egypt under Nasser is probably less familiar. Although documented in the scholarly literature, Nasser tends to be remembered among many supporters of Israel only for his bellicose speeches and policies leading up to and following the war of 1967. Forgotten is his regime's commitment to Egyptian development and his willingness to discuss peace with Israel in order that the energies and resources of the state might be devoted to domestic needs. In fact, however, there were secret negotiations between Israeli and Egyptian representatives in 1954, motivated primarily, in the judgment of a British politician with pro-Zionist tendencies, by Nasser's belief that "Israel ought not to distract him from the problems of Egypt, those of the social revolution."[8] Israeli analysts concur in this assessment, noting, in the words of one cautious observer, that it is "just possible that he [Nasser] was interested in reaching a more permanent peace with Israel."[9] Nasser's efforts did not produce any lasting results, and indeed Israel and Egypt went on to fight four wars. Israel is at least partly responsible for losing this opportunity, especially because of the provocative actions associated with what became known as the Lavon affair.[10]

Yet another important case, noted above, is the "Three No's" issued by Arab leaders in Khartoum in 1967. From the perspective of many Israelis and supporters of Israel, the Khartoum declaration is as compelling an indication of Arab intransigence as can be found. The actual story, however, although too complex to be readily summarized here, is, in fact, much less straightforward. The conference was dominated by more moderate Arab leaders and was boycotted by the more militant Arab states, including Syria and Algeria. The leader of the Palestinian Liberation Organization (PLO) did attend but boycotted the concluding session because of the conference participants' calls for a political rather than a military solution to the conflict, and also because of the proposal that Jordan and Saudi Arabia use their ties to the United States to pursue a diplomatic solution. The Arab assessment of Khartoum thus emphasizes not a militant rejection of Israel's right to exist but, rather, a desire to deny Israel a political victory and, therefore, the need for efforts at the international and diplomatic level to "ensure withdrawal from Arab lands which have been occupied *since the aggression of 5 June* [emphasis added]."[11]

This assessment is consistent with the response of most Arab states to UN Resolution 242, adopted by the Security Council in November 1967. Although disappointed that the resolution only called upon Israel to withdraw from "territory" captured in the June war, rather than "*all* territory" or at least "*the* territory," as they had sought, most Arab states, including the confrontational states, endorsed the land-for-peace formula set forth in the resolution. They insisted that Israel's withdrawal from Arab territory captured in the war be complete and that this withdrawal come before their recognition of Israel. Israel also accepted that formula, although it insisted that recognition and peace should come first, and also that its withdrawal, while significant, need not necessarily involve a complete return to the borders that existed before the war. Again, space does not permit a full account of the diplomatic negotiations that followed passage of UN 242. The point is, however, that accounts which stress abiding Arab intransigence and a militant commitment to the annihilation of the Jewish state are incomplete, simplistic, and in many ways false.

This is not to argue that there was no Arab rejectionism during this period or that Israel bears sole or even primary responsibility for the perpetuation and routinization of the conflict in the years after 1948. There is no shortage of provocative statements and actions by both Arabs and Israelis during this period. Each sees the other as the root cause of the problem, and some on both sides see a false and unjustified symmetry in judgments, such as the preceding, that Israelis and Arabs both are both responsible for the failure of early diplomatic efforts to make progress toward peace. Apportioning responsibility is not the purpose of this chapter, and readers wishing a fuller treatment can consult my *History of the Israeli-Palestinian Conflict.*[12] The purpose of the present discussion is simply to show that there is as much myth as reality, and probably even more myth than reality, in a Zionist narrative that emphasizes "the totality of Arab rejection" and an unshakeable Arab commitment to "the annihilation of Israel and of its people."[13]

The Present Situation

Anti-Israeli sentiment has been strong and widespread in the Arab world during the last few years. It has been fueled most recently by the U.S.-led war against the Saddam Hussein regime in Iraq and the subsequent American occupation of that country. Moreover, there has been much debate about the motives of the American administration's project in Iraq, especially as its claims that Saddam had weapons of mass destruction and was connected to al Qaeda have become less and less credible; critics have alleged that the *real* objective of the American invasion was the desire to remove an Arab regime willing and perhaps able to challenge Israel.[14] Partly for this reason, Israeli as well as American flags were burned when 200,000 Moroccans demonstrated in Rabat, in 2003, against the "imperialist aggression" of the American-led coalition.[15]

More generally, anti-Israeli sentiment has been growing among Arabs since the outbreak of the *al-Aqsa intifada* in 2000. For example, a survey carried out in seven Arab countries by Zogby International in late 2002, by which time the number of fatalities among both Palestinians and Israelis had risen dramatically, found that the vast majority of respondents in every country had a "very unfavorable" impression of Israel.[16] In Saudi Arabia, the Zogby data indicate that the percentage was about 95 percent. It was roughly the same in the United Arab Emirates and Kuwait, and the figures were only slightly lower in Jordan and Egypt, two countries that have peace treaties with Israel. In Jordan, 85 percent of those interviewed had a "very unfavorable" impression of Israel, and another 6 percent had a "somewhat unfavorable" view. In Egypt, 80 percent had a "very unfavorable" view, and another 4 percent reported a "somewhat unfavorable" impression of Israel.[17]

It is essential to put these observations into perspective, however. To do so it is necessary to ask two interrelated questions: Are Arab attitudes toward Israel enduring, or do they vary according to circumstances and events? Do these attitudes reflect opposition to Israel's right to exist or to the actions and policies of the Israeli government? Addressing the first of these questions, it is instructive to examine the reception that Israel received in many Arab states following the Israel–PLO accord of 1993. The second question, and to some extent the first as well, may be explored with public opinion data from the Arab world. These data may be examined to learn not only about the nature and distribution of relevant Arab attitudes but also about the factors that shape these views.

The previous observations about Jordan, Nasser's Egypt, the Khartoum conference, and UN 242 suggest that Arab attitudes during the two decades following Israeli independence were not invariably and uncompromisingly opposed to an accommodation with the Jewish state. There were also expressions of a willingness to make peace, or at least to explore the possibilities for peace, from a number of other important Arab states, including Lebanon, Morocco, and Tunisia. Finally, moving into the 1970s and 1980s, there was the 1977 peace initiative of President Anwar Sadat of Egypt. It resulted in a peace treaty between Israel and Egypt which many believe would have led to an accommodation with other Arab countries had Israel's Likud-led government not refused to negotiate a withdrawal from the West Bank and Gaza. There also was the 1981 peace initiative of Saudi Arabia. The Saudi plan, supported by many, though not all, Arab states, called for the creation of a Palestinian state on the West Bank and in Gaza, with its capital in East Jerusalem, and for that state and other Arab states to live in peace with Israel.

These initiatives lead to the conclusion that Arab hostility toward Israel in the post-1967 period was perpetuated in very large measure by continuing Palestinian statelessness, and that if the Palestinians had been given a state alongside Israel in a portion of historic Palestine there would no longer have been any basis for opposing peace with the Jewish state. This was not the position of all Arab states, of course. Moreover, some supporters of Israel argue that Arab initiatives and peace proposals were neither serious nor sincere, apart from that of Sadat. Yet developments associated with and following the 1993 Israel–PLO accord make it impossible for all but the most ideologically oriented of Israel's supporters to speak about an unshakable Arab insistence on the destruction of the state of Israel.

In signing the Oslo Declaration of Principles and agreeing to participate in a peace process that presumably would involve withdrawal from the West Bank and Gaza, Israelis expected, and had the right to expect, that Israel would be accepted by the Arab world and have normal relations with Arab states. Despite continuing rejectionism in some quarters, normal concourse did occur to a degree that was revolutionary. This development demonstrated, as noted, that once there was an agreement endorsed by the PLO, with provisions for Palestinian statehood, leaders and elites in a growing number of Arab countries concluded that there was no longer any reason to oppose peace with Israel. The Arab case against Israel, in other words, was based on the dispossession and statelessness of the Palestinians. With the establishment of a Palestinian state, under terms agreed to by the PLO, many and very probably most were ready—and in some cases even eager—to make peace with Israel and establish normal relations with the Jewish state.

Unprecedented Arab–Israeli contact and cooperation blossomed on an individual, bilateral, and multilateral basis in the wake of the 1993 accord. In Jerusalem and Tel Aviv, in Arab capitals, and in Europe, Arab and Israeli businessmen and others met to discuss a wide range of joint ventures and other collaborations. A sense of the new momentum and its revolutionary character is given in the following excerpt from an *International Herald Tribune* article, written only eight months after the Israel–PLO accord was signed. The article is entitled "When Former Enemies Turn Business Partners."

> Israel's transition from pariah to potential partner is most evident in the overtures to Israel by Arab governments and businessmen seeking potentially lucrative deals. Since September, Israeli officials have received VIP treatment in Qatar, Oman, Tunisia, and Morocco. Qatar is studying how to supply Israel with natural gas. Egypt has launched discussions on a joint oil refinery, and officials talk of eventually linking Arab and Israeli electricity grids. . . . Millionaire businessmen from Saudi Arabia, Kuwait, Qatar and Bahrain [are] jetting off to London, Paris, and Cairo to meet Israelis, while Jordanians, Egyptians and Lebanese are rushing to Jerusalem for similar contacts.[18]

This account notes the expanding network of Arab–Israeli contacts and relationships after September 1993. Other examples include Israeli assistance to Oman on drip irrigation and desalination, the signing of an Israeli–Jordanian peace treaty, the opening of an Israeli "Bureau de Liaison" in Morocco, Israeli-Tunisian cooperation on tourism, and an Egyptian–Jordanian–Israeli plan, with Saudi support, to deal with pollution in the Gulf of Aqaba. Saudi Arabia and other Gulf Cooperation Council countries ended their secondary and tertiary boycott of Israel at this time, and Arab states ceased their practice of challenging Israeli credentials at the United Nations. It is also noteworthy that Sheikh Abdel-Aziz ibn Baaz, Saudi Arabia's highest theological authority, issued a *fatwa* in late 1994 affirming the right of Saudi rulers to pursue normal relations with Israel. He cited a verse from the Qur'an: "If thy enemy moves toward peace, you shall too, placing your dependence on God."[19]

Still another tangible expression of the new era in Arab–Israeli relations was the convening of a series of international conferences to promote development in the context of peace. In 1994 King Hassan II of Morocco hosted the first of these conferences in Casablanca, with the goal of further normalizing Arab–Israeli relations clearly understood by all. The conference was attended by representatives of 61 countries and 1,114 business leaders. Its leaders issued a declaration stating that they were "united behind the vision . . . of a comprehensive peace and a new partnership of business and government dedicated to furthering peace between Arabs and Israelis."[20] Follow-up conferences were held in Jordan and Cairo in 1995 and 1996, respectively.

Not all Arab states followed suit, and the heady optimism of this period may seem naïve when viewed from the vantage point of 2005, after four years of fighting between Israelis and Palestinians in the West Bank and Gaza and the Israeli flag being burned in several Arab capitals. The Israeli withdrawal from Gaza in the summer of 2005 should set in motion a new dynamic—or perhaps it will not. But the point that Arab attitudes toward Israel are contextual, with a strong instrumental dimension, should nonetheless be clear. During a period when it seemed that Israelis and Palestinians had agreed on a two-state solution and were prepared to end their century-old conflict, large and growing numbers of Arab leaders and elites concluded that they no longer had any reason to oppose peace and normal relations with Israel. On the contrary, many rushed to take advantage of what they regarded as an important opportunity to obtain benefits for themselves and their countries.

The eventual failure of the Oslo peace process has spawned competing narratives about responsibility for the breakdown of negotiations and the violence associated with the al-Aqsa intifada. Each side sees the other as bearing primary responsibility, even though the reality is much more complex and provides ample basis for criticism of both Palestinian and Israeli actions.[21] The problem, however, is that many Israelis and Palestinians mistake their narratives for fact; they find in the failed peace process a confirmation of their own inaccurate views of the other side's character and motivation. Israelis and Palestinians each began the Oslo process with doubts about the other's intentions, and each went forward, often reluctantly, with the idea that doing so would test whether the other side was *really* prepared for significant and perhaps painful compromise. After 2000 the general view on each side was that the other side had failed the test and thereby revealed its true purpose. This fact was demonstrated, in Palestinian eyes, by the continued growth of Jewish settlements in the West Bank and Gaza. In Israeli eyes, it was demonstrated by continuing Palestinian violence against Israelis, including civilians inside the Green Line.

A recent analysis by an Israeli scholar summarizes the official narrative of his government regarding Palestinian responsibility for the failure of the peace process. It emphasizes the alleged rejectionism of Yasser Arafat and, more generally, "the ultimate violation and failure of the agreements by turning to violence and terrorism." He adds that, "as we move along the [Israeli political] continuum from left to right, these explanations become more emphatic and paramount as the official Israeli narrative."[22] The point here is not that Israel has an official narrative or that it is one-sided. That is to be expected and applies equally to the Palestinians. Rather, at issue is that this narrative does not present itself and gain credibility as a narrative, as a legitimate and understandable story regarding a series of events. Instead, to the extent that it appears to confirm myths and stereotypes about the Palestinians and other Arabs, it is taken as history and its accuracy is seen as self-evident.

Against this background, this chapter has posed two questions: First, are Arab attitudes toward Israel enduring, or do they vary in accordance with events? And, second, do anti-Israeli sentiments express opposition to the existence of a Jewish state in the Middle East or, rather, to the actions and policies of Israeli governments? Developments in the years following the Oslo Accords strongly suggest that Arab attitudes are indeed contextual and that for the most part Arabs seek territorial compromise and not the liquidation of the Jewish state. This observation has been reaffirmed even after the breakdown of the peace process, such as in the call by Saudi Arabia in 2002 not only for peace but also for normal relations between Israel and the Arab world. The conditions posed in the Saudi statement were that Israel should withdraw from all Arab territory captured in June 1967, including the Golan Heights, and that a Palestinian state should be established in the West Bank and Gaza, with its capital in East Jerusalem. The Saudis introduced a proposal to this effect at the 2002 Arab League Summit meeting in Beirut, and their call for peace and normalization in return for territorial compromise was endorsed unanimously by those at the summit.

With the death of Arafat, Israel's withdrawal from Gaza, and Palestinian parliamentary elections, there was talk in 2005 about a revival of the peace process. This talk continued as the Gaza pull-out was completed on schedule in late summer. Optimism, even cautious optimism, was probably premature. But if there is eventually to be renewed progress toward peace, it will be important for Israel and its supporters to have an accurate and balanced view of

Palestinians and other Arabs, and toward this end to eschew one-dimensional characterizations that see only enduring and unshakeable opposition to Israel's existence.

The Attitudes of Ordinary Citizens

The preceding assessment is based on the actions of Arab states and their leaders, leaving open the question of whether very different views might be held by ordinary men and women. Perhaps, despite the apparent "moderation" of many Arab leaders, most ordinary citizens in the Arab world *are* implacably opposed to Israel's existence. This argument will certainly be made, especially since opinion polls carried out in a number of Arab countries in 2002 and 2003 revealed that negative attitudes about Israel were widespread. Even in the country with the least unfavorable attitudes, Morocco, 66 percent had a "very unfavorable" impression of Israel, and another 24 percent had a "somewhat unfavorable" impression.

The data needed to probe deeper are limited, making it hard to advance conclusions that will be accepted by all, regardless of their political tendencies. Nevertheless, the available data strongly suggest that the attitudes of ordinary Arab citizens, like those of Arab leaders, are highly sensitive to context, meaning that they are not primordial, and reflect judgments about Israeli policy rather than an enduring opposition to Israel's existence.

The bulk of the most reliable information about ordinary Palestinians' attitudes toward Israel comes from polls conducted by Palestinian research centers in the West Bank and Gaza. The Palestine Center for Research and Studies, reorganized as the Palestinian Center for Policy and Survey Research, and the Jerusalem Media and Communications Centre are among the most important, although not the only, Palestinian institutions carrying out systematic public opinion research. Between them, they have conducted hundreds of polls since 1993. With excellent sampling procedures and a corps of trained interviewers, both centers, and to a lesser extent others as well, provide a wealth of data to gauge the attitudes of ordinary Palestinians in the West Bank and Gaza, and to assess the factors shaping those attitudes.

Data from the West Bank and Gaza are clear and consistent: despite some minor fluctuation in response to particular events, roughly two-thirds to three-quarters of the respondents in representative national surveys supported peace with Israel. The questions asked about peace in general, sometimes the peace process and reconciliation in particular, but the findings are strikingly consistent

Table 7.1. Attitudes toward Peace with Israel among Palestinians
in the West Bank and Gaza Surveyed in 1995, 1998, 2001, and
2002 (in percents)

	1995	1998	2001	2002
very or somewhat favorable	81	70	73	74
very or somewhat unfavorable	19	30	27	26

both over time and across surveys conducted by different research centers, which contributes to one's confidence in the results. A selection of these findings is shown in table 7.1, which presents the results of surveys conducted in 1995, 1998, 2001, and 2002.[23]

It should be added that support for the *principle* of peace and reconciliation does not mean that Palestinians necessarily have confidence in Israel or the peace process. From their perspective, the period following the 1993 Israel–PLO accord did not see a reduction or even a freezing of Israel's presence in the Occupied Territories. On the contrary, it appeared to many Palestinians that Israel was using the peace process to buy time to expand the number of Jewish settlers in the West Bank and Gaza (and East Jerusalem) and thus make it increasingly unlikely that the question of borders and other final status issues would be resolved in a way that gave Palestinians meaningful statehood. But while this disappointment and distrust are also reflected in survey findings, it was all the more significant that support for peace and reconciliation remained high.

All of the studies reflected in table 7.1 performed bivariate and multivariate statistical analyses of the data in order to determine the effects of different variables, or factors, on attitudes. Thus, although the table presents only univariate frequency distributions that indicate general tendencies, the scholarly publications that reported on these surveys also examined the various factors that may be correlated with, and account for variance on, Palestinian attitudes toward peace with Israel.[24] Two general conclusions emerged from these more sophisticated analyses, both of which support this chapter's thesis that context and instrumental calculations significantly affect attitudes.

First, orientations and attachments associated with Islam have at most only limited explanatory power; there is no empirical support for the proposition that Muslim Palestinians with a stronger attachment to or involvement in their religion are less likely than other Palestinians to have a favorable attitude toward Israeli–Palestinian peace and reconciliation. That truth is illus-

Table 7.2. Attitudes toward Peace with Israel among West Bank and Gaza Palestinians Surveyed in 2001 and Grouped by Degree of Religiosity (in percents)

	supports or strongly supports	opposes or strongly opposes
very religious	72.5	27.5
religious	72.7	27.3
somewhat religious	73.8	26.2
not religious	74.5	25.5

trated by the bivariate pattern shown in table 7.2, which compares the attitudes of more and less religious West Bank and Gaza Palestinians interviewed in 2001. The published analyses of the Palestinian data employed various survey questions and standard scaling techniques to measure religious orientation. They also employed multivariate statistical techniques in order to examine the relationship between attitudes toward peace and religious orientations with other factors held constant. In all cases, the findings are consistent with the pattern illustrated in table 7.2. Contrary to what is suggested by the "clash of civilizations" thesis and other assertions that Islam promotes hostility toward non-Muslims, the data clearly show, at least at the individual level of analysis, that Islam does not encourage opposition to peace with Israel.[25]

Relevant public opinion data from other Arab societies are rare. Systematic and rigorous research of political attitudes has been scarce in the Arab world, and this is particularly the case concerning research that investigates attitudes toward Israel. But two older studies, from 1988 and 1994, provide usable data; findings from four Arab nations—Lebanon, Jordan, Egypt, and Kuwait—are presented in table 7.3. The data show that support for peace ranges from 85 percent among Egyptians surveyed in 1988 to about 55 percent among Jordanians and Kuwaitis interviewed in 1994 and 1988, respectively. Just slightly more than 60 percent of Lebanese respondents interviewed in 1994 also expressed support for peace. A more recent study carried out in Jordan in 2002 asked respondents whether they favored strengthening Jordanian–Israeli relations. The study found that 27 percent favored it, another 26 percent preferred to keep relations at their present level, based on the 1994 Israel–Jordan peace treaty, and 47 percent wanted relations with Israel to be weakened.

These findings not only show that there is considerable variation with respect to attitudes about Israel, they also lend additional support to the view

Table 7.3. Attitudes toward Peace with Israel among Lebanese and Jordanians Surveyed in 1994 and Egyptians and Kuwaitis Surveyed in 1988 (in percents)

	very or somewhat favorable	very or somewhat unfavorable
Lebanon	61	39
Jordan	56	44
Egypt	86	14
Kuwait	55	45

that opposition to peace is neither universal nor enduring. Moreover, and of particular relevance for the present discussion, in none of the surveys is attitude affected by religious orientation. As with the Palestinian data, individuals who are more religious or otherwise have strong Islamic attachments are no less likely than others to be among those who favor peace with Israel.[26] Thus, again, it would be incorrect, at least at the individual level of analysis, to assume that the practice of Islam is an obstacle to Arab–Israeli peace.

The second general conclusion to emerge from a more sophisticated analysis of the survey data is that considerations of political economy, in contrast to considerations of religion and culture, do play an important role in shaping Arab attitudes toward Israel. This factor has been explored in detail in a number of different Palestinian data sets; the results consistently show that attitudes toward economic well-being and toward political leadership are important influences on relevant political attitudes.[27]

To illustrate, table 7.4 shows that West Bank and Gaza Palestinians who believe that peace with Israel will bring economic benefits are more likely than others to favor reconciliation after a Palestinian state has been established. Table 7.4 uses responses to a question about economic benefits for the respondent and his or her family, but the pattern is the same when using an item that asks about benefits for the Palestinian people in general. Judgments about the performance of the Palestinian Authority are similarly related to attitudes about reconciliation with Israel, and all of those political and economic assessments are also related in the same way to survey questions that ask about personal interaction with Israelis under conditions of peace. Each of these relationships is strong and statistically significant, and each remains so when examined with other factors held constant. Thus, again, it is clear that Palestinian and Arab attitudes toward Israel are neither unvarying nor uniformly hostile but, rather, are shaped in significant measure by contextual factors and instrumental considerations.

Table 7.4. Attitudes toward Reconciliation with Israel among West Bank
and Gaza Palestinians Surveyed in 2001 and Grouped by Views about the
Economic Consequences of Peace (in percents)

	supports or strongly supports	opposes or strongly opposes
peace will be economically beneficial	79	21
peace will have no economic impact	64	36
peace will be economically harmful	55	45

Recent data from a coordinated study by Khalil Shikaki, a Palestinian scholar, and Yaacov Shamir, an Israeli scholar, provide additional support for this chapter's thesis.[28] These data, from parallel opinion surveys carried out in the West Bank and Gaza and in Israel in December 2004 and January 2005, illustrate particularly well the centrality of myths and misperceptions in the Israeli–Palestinian conflict, among Palestinians as well as among Israelis and their supporters. Data from the Palestinian territories show that most Palestinians continue to support peace and, more specifically, that they accept Israel's existence as a Jewish state. The survey in Israel showed, however, that most Israelis believe that Palestinians think otherwise—that most Palestinians do *not* support peace or recognize Israel's existence as a Jewish state. Interestingly, this misconception is also common among Palestinians; many respondents told the interviewers, in contrast to what the surveys show to be the case, that they believe that their own acceptance of Israel is the position of only a minority of Palestinians. In commenting on the obstacles to peace posed by such misconceptions, Shikaki and Shamir conclude their analysis by emphasizing the need to translate the individual attitudes elicited by polls into genuine *public* opinion, into a clear and recognized collective consensus based on fact rather than myth.

Conclusion

Arab states and ordinary citizens in the Arab world have often challenged Israel's right to exist. This was a prominent theme in Arab political discourse in the years following Israel's independence, and, even today anti-Israeli sentiment in the Arab world is sometimes expressed in ways that suggest opposition to more than Israeli policy. This hostility is only part of the story, however, and frequently, and more recently, it is not the most important part. A unidimensional narrative with Zionist peace seekers as heroes and Arab rejectionists as villains is just that, a narrative. Unending Arab intransigence is, therefore, as much myth as reality.

This narrative nonetheless remains current among at least some Israelis and supporters of Israel. Here, for example, are excerpts from several books and articles published in 2002, 2003, and 2004. This is just a sample. Those seeking more need only search the Internet for such topics as "Arab intransigence" and "destruction of Israel."

• "Arab leaders have repeatedly made ample use of the lowest common denominator among the region's masses: hatred toward the 'taboo' that the Jews and Israel are."[29]

• "The attempt to destroy the Jewish state has gone on since it came into existence in 1948. For over a half century, the majority of Arabs have persisted in seeing the state of Israel as a temporary condition, an enemy they eventually expect to dispense with."[30]

• "Arafat is less interested in the liberation of the West Bank and Gaza, or even the establishment of a Palestinian state, than in the PLO's historic goal of Israel's destruction."[31]

• "The war against the Jews goes on. Jewish children are shot in their beds, and the shooters are celebrated as heroes . . . And across the Arab world, from Pakistan to Morocco, hundreds of millions have nothing better to do than to chant for death to the Jews."[32]

• "The attempted de-legitimization of Israel is the ideological expression of Palestinian and Arab refusal to accept the Jewish state in the Middle East . . . In the Arab Muslim world, the culture of hatred of Jews permeates all forms of public communications . . . The intensity of the anti-Jewish invective surpasses that of Nazi Germany in its heyday."[33]

• "The racism and denial of legitimacy characteristic of apartheid are actually applicable to Arab and Islamic rejection of Jewish rights. In the Middle East, Jews are a tiny and oppressed minority, struggling to maintain cultural identity and survive in a hostile and violent environment."[34]

It is difficult to know for sure how seriously these works are taken—or should be taken. Some who tell these stories may be aware that they are unfairly one-sided and do not do justice to a much more complex reality. In this case, presumably, these individuals have concluded that a measure of distortion is in Israel's strategic interest and hence justifiable. Alternatively, and perhaps more likely, many believe the narrative that they are putting forward. After all, sincerity and conviction are an essential part of what defines a narrative. Belief and conviction are not the measure of a narrative's accuracy, however. Events and circumstances can give rise to more than one story. A narrative is not objective history. Indeed, the distance between narrative and myth can be short. In the case considered here, narratives that assign a central role in the Israeli–Palestinian conflict to relentless, unchanging, and unconditional Arab opposition to Israel's existence, whether self-serving or sincere, travel a considerable portion of that distance.

NOTES

1. These quotations are paraphrased summaries of personal conversations between the author and various Israelis of Afro-Asian origin.

2. See Mark Tessler, "The Political Culture of Jews in Tunisia and Morocco," *International Journal of Middle East Studies*, XI (1980), 59–86. For a fuller discussion and additional references, see idem, *A History of the Israeli-Palestinian Conflict* (Bloomington, 1994), 308–311.

3. Frank Gervasi, *The Case for Israel* (New York, 1967), 170–171.

4. Samuel Katz, *Battleground: Fact and Fantasy in Palestine* (New York, 1973), 182.

5. Michael Curtis et al., *The Palestinians: People, History, Politics,* (New Brunswick, NJ, 1975), 1.

6. Wolf Blitzer (ed.), *Myths and Facts: A Concise Record of the Arab-Israeli Conflict* (Washington, DC, 1976), 1.

7. Avi Shlaim, *Collusion Across the Jordan: King Abdullah, the Zionist Movement, and the Partition of Palestine* (Oxford, 1988), 537–538.

8. Quoted in Raymond Baker, *Egypt's Uncertain Revolution under Nasser and Sadat* (Cambridge, MA, 1978), 37. See also Tessler, *History of the Israeli-Palestinian Conflict*, 339–340.

9. Yair Evron, *The Middle East: Nations, Superpowers, and Wars* (New York, 1973), 34. See also Itamar Rabinovitch, *The Road Not Taken: Early Arab-Israeli Negotiations* (New York, 1991), 199–200.

10. The Lavon affair involved a secret Israeli plot to blow up the U.S. Information Agency Library and other public buildings in Cairo and Alexandria in an attempt to foster anti-Egyptian sentiment in the United States at a time when Egypt was seeking American assistance and negotiating with the British over their bases in the Suez Canal Zone. The plot was uncovered, and most of its participants were captured and

tried. For additional information, see Tessler, *History of the Israeli-Palestinian Conflict,* 341–342.

11. See Mahmound Riad, *The Struggle for Peace in the Middle East* (London, 1981), 54–57. See also Fred Khouri, *The Arab-Israeli Dilemma* (Syracuse, 1985), 312–313.

12. Tessler, *History of the Israeli-Palestinian Conflict.*

13. See notes 3–6, above.

14. For a broader assessment of the impact on popular attitudes of America's strong and frequently uncritical support for Israel, see "The Pew Global Attitudes Project," The Pew Research Center for the People and the Press, December 19, 2001. The Pew report states, "Not surprisingly, public dissatisfaction with America's Middle East policy is perceived to be highest in largely Islamic countries. In particular, citizens of those countries . . . have a strongly unfavorable view of U.S. policy toward Israel."

15. Associated Press, March 30, 2003.

16. Fatality and casualty figures for this period are provided by Btselem. See http://www.btselem.org/English/statistics/.

17. Zogby International, "Arab Nations' 'Impressions of America' Poll," (Utica, NY, 2002). See also Tessler, "The Nature and Determinants of Arab Attitudes toward Israel," in Derek Penslar and Janice Stein (eds.), *Contemporary Antisemitism: Canada and the World* (Toronto, 2004), 96–120.

18. Caryle Murphy and Nora Boustany, "When Former Enemies Turn Business Partners," *International Herald Tribune,* May 24, 1994. See also Peter Waldman, "Guns and Butter: Khashoggi is Back, Angling for a Profit from Middle East Peace," *Wall Street Journal,* February 4, 1994. For a fuller discussion, see Tessler, "Israel at Peace with the Arab World," *Occasional Papers of the Emirates Center for Strategic Studies and Research* (Abu Dhabi, 1995), 7–37.

19. Youssef Ibrahim, "Muslims Argue Theology of Peace with Israel," *New York Times,* January 31, 1995.

20. "Middle East/North Africa Economic Summit: Casablanca Declaration," distributed by the Israeli Consulate Information Department, November 2, 1994.

21. Arie Kacowicz, "Rashomon in Jerusalem: Mapping the Israeli Negotiators' Positions on the Israeli-Palestinian Peace Process, 1993–2002," *International Studies Perspectives,* VI (2005), 252–273. See also Hussein Agha and Robert Malley, "Camp David: The Tragedy of Errors," *New York Review of Books,* XLVIII (August 9, 2001).

22. Kacowicz, "Rashomon," 260.

23. Details about the studies on which table 7.1 is based, including sampling methods, the interview schedule, and evidence of measurement reliability and validity, can be found in the following publications: Tessler and Jodi Nachtwey, "Islam and Attitudes Toward International Conflict: Evidence from Survey Research in the Arab World," *Journal of Conflict Resolution,* XLII (1998), 619–636; Tessler and Nachtwey, "Palestinian Political Attitudes: An Analysis of Survey Data from the West Bank and Gaza," *Israel*

Studies, IV (1999), 22–43; Nachtwey and Tessler, "The Political Economy of Attitudes Toward Peace among Palestinians and Israelis," *Journal of Conflict Resolution,* XLVI (2002), 260–285; Jacob Shamir and Khalil Shikaki, "Determinants of Reconciliation and Compromise among Israelis and Palestinians," *Journal of Peace Research,* XXXIX (2002), 185–202; Shikaki, "The Transition to Democracy in Palestine," *Journal of Palestine Studies,* XCVIII (1996), 2–14.

24. See publications cited in note 23 for methodological information. See also Tessler, "Arab and Muslim Political Attitudes: Stereotypes and Evidence from Survey Research," *International Studies Perspectives,* IV (2003), 175–180.

25. Samuel P. Huntington, *The Clash of Civilizations and the Remaking of World Order* (New York, 1996).

26. Tessler and Nachtwey, "Islam and Attitudes Toward International Conflict." See also Tessler and Jamal Sanad, "Will the Arab Public Accept Peace with Israel: Evidence from Surveys in Three Arab Societies," in Gregory Mahler and Efraim Karsh (eds.), *Israel at the Crossroads* (London, 1994).

27. Nachtwey and Tessler, "Political Economy of Attitudes Toward Peace among Palestinians and Israelis."

28. Khalil Shikaki and Yaacov Shamir, presentations at the University of Michigan, January 31–February 2, 2005.

29. Yossef Bodansky, *The High Cost of Peace: How Washington's Middle East Policy Left American Vulnerable to Terrorism* (Roseville, CA, 2002), 2.

30. Daniel Pipes, "Arabs Still Want to Destroy Israel," *Wall Street Journal* (January 18, 2002).

31. Efraim Karsh, *Arafat's War: The Man and His Battle for Israeli Conquest* (New York, 2003), from the book jacket.

32. Yaacov Lozowick, *The Right to Exist: A Moral Defense of Israel's Wars* (New York, 2003), 1.

33. Mortimer B. Zuckerman, "The New Anti-Semitism: Graffiti on the Walls of History," *UN Chronicle,* XLI (2004), http://www.un.org/Pubs/chronicle/2004/issue4/0404p34.html.

34. Gerald M. Steinberg, "Abusing 'Apartheid' for the Palestinian Cause," article in the *Jerusalem Post,* distributed by the Conference of Presidents of Major American Jewish Organizations from the *Daily Alert* (August 25, 2004), of Jerusalem Center for Public Affairs.

8

THE BRIDGING NARRATIVE CONCEPT

ILAN PAPPE

BRIDGING NARRATIVES APPEAR mainly in the deconstruction of fictional plots where they are usually intercalated chapters, short pieces connecting the so-called plot chapters. In classical Greek plays they are the pieces that the omniscient narrator introduces to form bridges between acts in the drama, thus leading the audience through the dialogues and events onstage. Some historians also assume this role of providing bridging narratives; for example, in Castel's book, *Tom Taylor's Civil War,* the historian produces his own dramatic bridging narrative, providing an overview of the fighting that gives readers invaluable context for Taylor's eyewitness reports.[1] Insights of this type are relevant for the work of historical construction.

The concept of the bridging narrative suggested here is expanded beyond its literary or dramatic applications and refers not only to the historian's presence in the emplotment of the historical narrative but also calls for a more blunt intrusion into the orientation of the reconstruction.[2] The historian's navigations through the plots of the past are motivated by the wish to change the events of the present. Besides requiring the historian's "presence," it calls for a relativist perspective on historiography, a critical approach to hegemonic ideologies, and a good sense of historiographical contexualism.

The absence of clear conceptualization requires a working definition for the bridging narrative concept, a definition that can serve not only for the case study of the Palestine question but also for historiographical efforts within nations at war or societies torn by historical conflicts in the contemporary world. A bridging narrative can be defined as a conscious historiographical effort that is undertaken by historians in societies wrought with long internal and external conflicts in order to connect conflicting narratives and historiographies. A bridging narrative is a historiographical enterprise that is intrinsic to the more general reconciliation effort.

If we limit this definition to intra-national conflicts, the bridge is built by historians on each side of the divide. It is initiated by historians who belong to the stronger party and are willing to recognize the other side's narrative and at the same time adopt a more critical approach toward their own.

I offer several imperatives or preconditions that should underlie the project of developing a bridging narrative. The first and obvious precondition for such a historiographical approach is a political atmosphere conducive to and open for any act of reconciliation. As noted, the process is initiated by the stronger party in a given balance of power, and the process becomes fruitful if it is reciprocated by the other, weaker side.

This process began in Israel with the emergence of what became known as the "new history," professional historiography written by a group of several Israeli historians in the late 1980s whose portrayal of the 1948 war challenged the official Zionist version.[3] The gist of this effort—the willingness to assess their country's past with a critical eye—led to a rejection of the principal claims of mainstream Israeli historians and a legitimization of the past claims of Palestinian historians. This new orientation narrowed the gap between the opposing national narratives of the conflict's history.

The self-criticism was not limited to the 1948 war but was also used in new research into both earlier and later periods. The new history expanded into an intellectual movement that I termed the "post-Zionist" scholarship of Israel, a trend that developed in Israel in the 1990s but was driven by a generation of academics who had spent long periods as advanced students outside Israel.[4] Most of these academics were social scientists who became interested in their local history, having experienced traumatic events such as the 1973 war, the political earthquake of 1977, the peace with Egypt, and the controversial Lebanon war.

The new historians at first denied that they were affected by these or other political events. They adamantly contended that only new evidence had led them to develop their views, and they refused to recognize any impact of politics or ideology on their works. The more convinced among them attributed their views almost entirely to the declassification of Israeli archives. The documents made available to them were presented as the only true narrative of past events. This true narrative legitimized some claims made by Palestinian historiography and rejected others.

The new history on a certain level was received coldly and unenthusiastically by Palestinian historians. The presentation of Israeli historiography and archives as the sole gate to the past was seen as insulting, lofty, and akin to neo-colonialism. Palestinian historians writing on that period looked for a more constructive dialectal dialogue with their Israeli counterparts.[5]

Only a handful of Israeli historians learned to accept Palestinian demands for a more productive exchange through a long process of intimacy, learning, and respect for the individual and collective Palestinian experience. Documents or evidence supplemented existing local knowledge, in the same way that white South Africans did not need to wait for the secret archives of the Bureau of State Security (BOSS) to be opened to know how black Africans had been treated during apartheid. For the positivists among the revisionists, the discourse of proof was needed in order to construct a bridge. For the more relativist ones, the discourse of trust was employed for the same purpose. The empiricist pretensions led to an inevitable clash between new historians and the Palestinian historians who were invited, in 1998, to begin such a dialogue by *Le Monde Diplomatique*.

In the face of a positivist approach to their history, the Palestinian participants requested, but did not receive, an explanation of why "objective" Israeli historians had chosen the Palestinians' own cultural holocaust as a subject matter. The Israeli answer was inadequate, to say the least, as it doubted the Palestinians' ability to attain the expertise or the historical materials necessary to write their own history. After the Palestinians' land had been taken away and their past history in it denied, they were given a small portion of land back, but their history was still appropriated by archival positivists in Israel.[6]

From a positivist point of view, no clear evidence existed for some of the major claims in the Palestinian narrative, such as a mass expulsion of Palestinians in 1948, including the massacre of thousands of Palestinians and the destruction of almost 400 villages.

But a dialectical process of historiographical work was on its way that did not rely solely on documents lying in the Israeli state archives. The Paris meeting for signing the economic agreement coincided with the end of the first chapter in the Oslo peace process. The signing of the Oslo Accords in 1993 began a five-year phase in which the Israeli occupation in the West Bank and the Gaza Strip was rearranged in return for mutual recognition between the Palestinian Liberation Organization (PLO) and Israel. In the second phase, meant to begin in 1998 but delayed until the summer of 2000, an attempt was made to resolve all of the outstanding problems blocking the way to a comprehensive peace.

One of the problems was the future of Palestinian refugees, the solution to which was closely associated with the issue of responsibility; more precisely, Palestinians demanded the right of return based on a certain interpretation of the past. Their insistence that the Palestinian narrative be associated with the then current peace process rippled throughout the Palestinian world—in the diaspora, the refugee camps, the Occupied Territories, and, finally, among the Palestinian minority in Israel. The last group began to link its own struggle for citizenship in Israel with the Palestinian narrative of 1948, a process that matured in 1988 when the Palestinian minority in Israel, more than one million people, refused to celebrate Israel's independence day and opted, instead, to observe the *Nakba,* meaning "catastrophe," the Palestinian term for the 1948 war.

The second precondition for a historiographical approach to bridging narratives is the adaptation of a soft, relativist method for writing history within a context of national conflicts. I mean that a sea of facts is exposed to view in as wide a spectrum as possible. Thus, empirical evidence is gathered, examined, and accumulated as in any positivist historical enterprise, but then the emplotment of that mass evidence is not neutral, or objective, particularly when it deals with the history of a conflict still active while partisan historians are writing its historiography.

Apart from certain ideological variations, bridging narrative projects mounted elsewhere were hindered by the pure positivist nature of professional historiography. As historiographical debates progressed, the writing of history became less elitist, more interdisciplinary, and sensitive to a dialectical relationship between power and knowledge. Allowing contemporary agendas to be part and parcel of the historical enterprise is no longer a heresy. Historical reconstruction, therefore, becomes a joint historiographical undertaking by individuals who remove themselves from their national and positional identities (invaders versus invaded, occupiers versus occupied, and colonizers versus colonized).

Bridging history implies a fresh understanding of how context affects the perceptions of historical events, and how the power structure of a state determines the nature of dialogues between present and past. It is the process by which a shift in power relationships outside the scholarly world affects movements within research paradigms. It can be termed "positionality," that is, the conscious effect of one's own politics of identity on historical research.

Some post-Zionist scholars were not satisfied with merely researching history but wanted to explore more general historiographical questions of power and knowledge. They were in the vanguard of constructing a bridge to the other side. They made a conscious effort to learn the Palestinian narrative, examine it academically, and, after accepting certain chapters in it, were willing to work with Palestinians in historical research. Their efforts were reciprocated by a small, but significant, group of Palestinian historians.[7]

A third precondition is a change within the power structure of the cultural field that determines historiographical perspective. As with deprived groups such as ex-colonies, ethnic minorities, and women, a favorable shift in the production of knowledge does not necessarily reflect any significant improvement in the fields of politics or economy. However, the political protest of those deprived groups must have been successful enough to generate a change in the production of knowledge or powerful enough to persuade the global academic and cultural systems of knowledge production that its version was no less valid than that of the hegemonic party, and perhaps in the process that it erodes the international and even local status of the stronger party's knowledge producers. In the Palestinian case, the intifada of 1987 was strong enough to persuade the international scholarly community of the legitimacy of the Palestinian historical version, and to de-legitimize, to a degree, the Israeli-Zionist version. That change was part of a more comprehensive shift in attitudes toward non-Western historical perspectives, a shift to which the Palestinian intellectual Said contributed more than anyone else. The legitimization process meant that the Palestinian narrative, or part of it, was accepted as professionally valid, while at the same time parts of Israeli historiography were exposed as merely ideological and polemicist.

The positionality and contexuality of the new enterprise ensure a multi-perspective approach that is important in tracing the areas of agreement and coping with points of disagreement along the joint journey into the past. The new approach provides the most important rubric of all—relevance. Irrelevant or unimportant issues and facts are either erased or marginalized according to historians' contemporary agendas so as to realize the destructive or constructive power of the narrative (and not just to use the power of history to promote historians in universities). In the process, the hegemonic party relinquishes its dominance over knowledge while the weaker party lessens its commitment to its ideological, historical narrative.

A bridging narrative in the Israel–Palestine conflict was possible only at the end of a stage where Israel was defeated in the field of knowledge in its struggle against the weaker party. During an earlier stage, Israelis determined the agenda and resolved the orientation of the historiographical enterprise, thereby colonizing not only the land but also its history. This earlier takeover had conveyed the message that, by and large, the Israelis were the victims of the conflict and the rational party in the struggle over Palestine, whereas the Palestinians were irrational, if not fanatic, intransigent, and immoral.

The fourth precondition for a historiographical approach to a bridging narrative is methodological. Because a bridging narrative cannot be based on elitist and nationalist history, it is likely to take the form of cultural and social history rather than politics. The story of the dominant and powerful is often the story of a political elite. Highlighting the victim's side of the story can only be done with the help of social and cultural history when the political game has marginalized the victim.

This conscientious divorce from elitist and political history requires expertise in interdisciplinary approaches, so that historians seek ordinary human subjects such as women, workers, and peasants, rather than generals, politicians, or statesmen for a given context of a conflict history. This research orientation may reveal that the lives of people do not always revolve around the grand and dramatic events that one reconstructs based on diplomatic and political archives. Social history, not to mention the cultural history of national conflicts in the Middle East, is still a barren land awaiting future scholars. But this new history is beginning to be produced in the wake of critiques of national historiographies.

The motivation of our particular case was what Doumani called the drive to bring Palestinians back into the history of Palestine.[8] This reintroduction of the Palestinians into the country's history was part of a Palestinian response to one of Zionism's major claims that, in pre-Zionist Palestine, Palestinians had no meaningful existence, a claim that was contradicted by reconstructing "from below" the life of a Palestinian community in the pre-Zionist era. The seeds for a bridging narrative are sown into the soil of this initially national response to the hegemony of Zionist historiography. It was only by including the lives of non-elite Palestinians in the pre-1882 land—peasants, women, and traders, who were the majority—that the black hole drawn by Israeli historiography was filled with a picture of a vibrant and organic human society.

The search for non-elite history became the main basis for a joined narrative, anti-elitist in principle. This approach was also attempted from other angles, by historians abroad, such as Lockman, who adopted a relational paradigm to the writing of Palestine's history.[9] Such works reconstructed the economic reality in Palestine under the British Mandate as a unitary integrated system and did not interpret it as a segregated reality, as national historians from both sides have done.

❖ Ilan Pappe ❖

Developing a history of non-elites requires not only a relational approach but also a deep understanding of concepts such as the "third space" that was offered by Bhabha, West, and others.[10] The third space seeks to reconstruct an individual story within the collective story produced by the national narratives of the occupier and the occupied. The reconstruction, or narrative, should re-veal the fluidity of the structures that compose the communities of individu-als. This new narrative of Palestinian history demonstrates that the colonizer was not always powerful nor was the colonized always powerless, just as the occupier was not always in control nor the occupied just a pawn. It emphasizes, instead, that external factors were always active and internal factors always passive.

The interdisciplinary, relational, social history built up from below signifi-cantly challenges the military history of the conflict. The political elites enticed their national historiographies, whether they were victorious or defeated ac-tors, to treat war as a heroic and dramatic event. But the new history takes historians away from military history per se and directs them toward a social history of the military operation.[11] In the particular case of the 1948 war in Palestine, for instance, social and cultural history may raise intriguing ques-tions about how much the war was not really a war but in some parts of the country was nothing less than ethnic cleansing.

This question can be answered once we begin a morphological analysis of the war in its various civil localities—villages, neighborhoods, and road junc-tures. These events have to be reconstructed not only with the help of military archives but also using oral history and adding the civilian point of view. Such an analysis can also involve rereading military documents as texts that conceal more than they reveal, and as documents that can be deconstructed in order to salvage new information. The little research that we already have indicates clearly that, contrary to the description that emerges from the Israeli mili-tary archives, in many parts of Palestine, in 1948, there was no actual war but rather widespread operations of ethnic cleansing. Civilians, not soldiers, are the subject matter, and therefore historical research should be focused on eth-nic cleansing rather than military maneuvers. Without the other preconditions mentioned above, this kind of research would not have been possible.

This has been a methodological revolution with two key features: The first is the salvaging of fresh meanings from known texts, as offered by postmod-ernist hermeneutics and literary criticism.[12] This salvaging calls for reinter-preting written documentation with more empathy for victimized, occupied, and deprived people. An example is feminist historiography, which chronicled women of the past with the help of male texts that were reread with an open mind. The second feature is a more intensive, more proper use of oral history as a valid historiographical resource. Oral history can lead us, as it did in the case of the history of the African slaves in America, to evidence not found in the political archives.[13] The elevation of oral testimonies to the level of military documents has only recently been employed in the study of Palestine's history, as a part of a purposeful attempt to lend equal legitimacy to Israeli and Palestinian sources. In the past, Israeli historians legitimized oral history only when reconstructing the history of the Holocaust but dismissed categorically the use of Arab or Palestinian oral sources for the history of the conflict in general and of al Nakba in particular.

The Bridging Narrative Effort

Nationalism in Palestine on the eve of the first wave of immigration in 1882 gives us our first example of a bridging narrative. The use of critical approaches to the phenomenon of nationalism could allow a bridging narrative to remove nationalism from the imagination, sphere of identities, and conduct of the Muslims, Christians, and Jews who lived in the various Ottoman provinces of what is now Palestine. This removal would provide a refreshing departure from the tendency of Israeli historiography to "Zionize" the old Jewish settlements in Palestine, and from the Palestinian historiographers' inclination (including that of some pro-Palestinian historians) to nationalize rebellions in the Ottoman period, such as the 1834 revolt, which had little to do with modern notions of nationalism.[14]

As for the early years of Zionism, there seems to be a consensus about the land issue in Palestine. There is no factual argument about the purchase of land by the Zionist movement between 1882 and 1936; the land system, the social hierarchy, and Zionist ideology enabled the expansion of Jewish settlements in Palestine. The conflicting narratives hitherto either regarded the purchase of land as a redemption of an ancient homeland—as the Israeli–Zionist professional historiography would have it—or as an imperialist invasion, as the professional Palestinian historiography would claim. A resolution of this issue is crucial to understanding how the Jewish–Palestinian conflict developed, and it is possible to extract that resolution from the controlling hands of historians loyal to a particular national narrative. A non-national bridged perspective could form the basis for historians' identification with the farmers and peasants who lived on the land until they were evicted—victimized both by absentee landlords who sold the land cultivated by the *fellahin* (peasants) as well as by Zionist territorial ambitions.[15]

Another relevant topic is the social cohabitation and wider areas of economic interaction between Jews and Arabs during the period of the British Mandate. Occupational and class energies united Jews and Arabs and, had it not been for a very aggressive policy by the political elites, particularly the Jewish Histradrut (General Trade Union), these interactions could have been an even more widespread phenomenon. Had the national elites not intervened on both sides, workers, teachers, clerks, and businessmen would have come together by virtue of common occupations or even because of class solidarity, which would have outweighed segregation based on national identification. As I have shown in *The Israel/Palestine Question,* the history of Mandatory Palestine is dotted with such attempts to break away from segregationist spheres of identity, all of which were aborted by the national leaderships on both sides.[16]

The study of history at the primary level of peasants, workers, clerks, and women has already begun and has revealed a pantheon of historical heroes from all national, ethnic, and religious groups, as well as a purgatory full of politicians. The history of strikes, for instance, next to the history of joint economic ventures exemplifies such a bridged narrative.[17]

The study of religion during the Mandate also opens new vistas for a bridging narrative. Popular religion, a concept so well articulated by Geertz, was sanctioned in Palestine as holy and sacred, with sanctuaries for all three monotheistic religions.[18] The lack of possessiveness and the ambivalent identity of many of these sanctuaries were typical of the late Ottoman period and early Mandatory period. In the 1930s, and more so after 1948, religion was nationalized and politicized, and became a segregating and racist force, whereas in the past (and possibly in the future) religion brought people together in times of grief and celebration.

The introduction of an orientalist paradigm to the study of the Jewish position highlighted the existence in Israel, since 1948, of Sephardic Jews who were ethnically and culturally Arab.[19] These immigrants were forced to lose their Arabic customs on arrival in order to fit the Zionist dream of an ethnic Jewish state, but at the same time they were pushed to the social and geographical margins of society. This phenomenon explains the great paradox that has accompanied the lives of these people ever since. Although most of the right-wing electorate comes from these communities—and with it a very racist and hostile attitude toward everything Arab—they still preserve their traditional Arab and Sephardic roots as the best form of protest against the Ashkenazi establishment that has perpetuated their deprivation and frustration. The deconstruction of their socialization in the early years of statehood can provide a joint research project, based on Said's orientalism, into the victimization of everything that was and is Arab within the Jewish state.

The next step toward building a bridging narrative will be to encourage joint work by social and cultural historians who are interested in history from below, who wish to reconstruct the lives of non-elite groups, and who are brave enough to challenge their own national narratives. Above all, they want to install in their pantheon of heroes and heroines men and women of peace and reconciliation rather than generals and politicians of war and destruction.

Notes

1. Albert Castel, *Tom Taylor's Civil War* (Lawrence, KS, 2000).

2. "Emplotment" is Hayden White's term for the fictional narratives that he claims historians use no less than authors. See his *Metahistory: The Historical Imagination in 19th Century Europe* (Baltimore, 1975).

3. Avi Shlaim, "The Debate about 1948," in Ilan Pappe (ed.), *The Israel/Palestine Question (Rewriting Histories)* (London, 1999), 171–192.

4. Ilan Pappe, "Critique and Agenda: The Post-Zionist Scholars in Israel," *History and Memory*, VII (1995), 66–91.

5. Nur Masalha, "A Critique of Benny Morris" in Pappe, *Israel/Palestine Question*, 211–220.

6. For a report on this debate, see Edward Said, "New History, Old Ideas," *Al-Ahram Weekly* (May 21–27, 1998).

7. See Ilan Pappe, "Post-Zionist Critique on Israel and the Palestinians," parts 1–3, *Journal of Palestine Studies*, XXVI (winter 1997), 29–41; (spring 1997), 37–43; (summer 1997), 60–69.

8. Beshara Doumani "Rediscovering Ottoman Palestine: Writing Palestinians into History," in Pappe, *Israel/Palestine Question*, 11–40.

9. Zachary Lockman, *Comrades and Enemies: Arab and Jewish Workers in Palestine, 1906–1948* (Berkeley, 1996).

10. See the introduction to Homi Bhabha (ed.), *The Nation and Narration* (London, 1990).

11. Omer Bartov, *The Eastern Front, 1941–45: German Troops and the Barabarisation of Warfare* (Hampshire, UK, 1985).

12. Hans George Gadamer, *Truth and Method* (London, 1975).

13. Philip D. Curtin, *The African Slave Trade: A Census* (Madison, 1969).

14. For example, see Baruch Kimmerling and Joel Migdal, *Palestinians: The Making of a People* (New York, 1993), 3–35.

15. For a similar approach, see Kenneth Stein, *The Land Question in Palestine, 1917–1939* (Atlanta, 1984).

16. Ilan Pappe, *A History of Modern Palestine: One Land, Two Peoples* (Cambridge, 2003), 109–115.

17. Ibid., 72–107.

18. Clifford Geertz, *Islam Observed: Religious Development in Morocco and Indonesia* (Chicago, 1986).

19. Ella Shohat, "Sepharadim in Israel: Zionism from the Standpoint of Its Jewish Victims," *Social Text,* XIX (1988), 1–20; Yehuda Shenhav, *The Arab Jews* (Tel-Aviv, 2004), in Hebrew.

9

THE PSYCHOLOGY OF BETTER DIALOGUE BETWEEN TWO SEPARATE BUT INTERDEPENDENT NARRATIVES

DAN BAR-ON AND SAMI ADWAN

> The basic working assumption is that there is a dialectical relationship between schooling and violent conflict and that this relationship needs to be explicitly recognized and explored as part of the process of educational change in the wake of civil strife in order to make a meaningful contribution to post-conflict reconciliation and peace building. It is a major concern in post-conflict situations to avoid replication of educational structures that may have contributed to the conflict.
>
> Sobhi Tawil, Alexandra Harley, and Lucy Porteous,
> "Curriculum Change and Social Cohesion in
> Conflict-Affected Societies" (Geneva, 2003)

Discourse over the Israeli–Palestinian conflict rotates around the struggle over whose narrative describing the history of the conflict—the Israeli or the Palestinian—is the true or the morally superior one. In the years since the Oslo Accords, many efforts have been invested to create a bridging narrative between the two conflicting stories.[1] The authors of this chapter assume that it is not possible to develop such a bridging narrative in the near future, except among a few exclusive and elite groups. However, the Israeli and Palestinian narratives are intertwined like a double helix, but they are still separate and should be acknowledged as such. For example, the Balfour declaration will always be a positive event for Israeli Jews, who see it as the international community's first acknowledgment of the need for a national homeland for the Jewish people, even before the Holocaust. For the Palestinians, the same declaration will always have negative connotations—the first of many events whereby the international community ignored their need for a national home on the same piece of land (for details, see the appendix to this chapter).

Levinas suggested that the totality of the self cannot contain the infinity of the otherness of the other.[2] He claimed that we will never be able to represent that infinity within our own totality. It is therefore a constant struggle to determine how much and what qualities of the otherness of the other we can represent in our totality. In periods of war and conflict, this general tendency becomes even more worrisome as societies and nations tend to develop their exclusive narratives that, from their individual perspectives, become the only true and morally superior narrative. These narratives morally exclude each other and devalue and dehumanize their enemy's narrative.[3] If the opponent's narrative is described at all, it is presented as morally inferior and irrational. The enemy is depicted as faceless, as well as immoral, espousing manipulative arguments. In conflict situations, the experience of identity invariably evokes codes of exclusion, difference, and distinction. Belonging to a collectivity always concerns the delegitimization of that collectivity and the application of the "logic of conflict and contention."[4] These narratives become embedded in everyday culture, national and religious festivals, the media, and children's school textbooks.

Textbooks are one of the formal representations of the society's ideology and its ethos. They impart the values, goals, and myths that the society wants to instill into the new generation.[5] Children growing up during war and conflict know only the narrative of their own people, a narrative that is supposed to convince them, overtly and covertly, of the need to dehumanize the enemy. It usually indoctrinates children with a rationale that justifies the use of power to subjugate the enemy. This process not only causes the development of narrow and biased understandings among children but also leads to negative attitudes toward the other.[6]

Since the early 1950s Palestinians have been using Jordanian and Egyptian school books in their schools in the West Bank and Gaza, respectively. These school books were still used after Israel occupied the West Bank and Gaza during the 1967 war, but the books were censored. Palestinians started preparing their own school books after the Palestinian National Authority (PNA) was established in 1994. The first Palestinian-produced textbooks were introduced for grades 1 and 6 in the school year 2000–2001. Each year, the Palestinian Curriculum Center, under the supervision of the Palestinian Ministry of Education, has produced textbooks for two additional grades only. These books gradually replace the Jordanian and Egyptian texts. The Palestinian educational system is centralized, which means that the Ministry of Education is the sole producer of textbooks and all schools use the same ones.[7]

Israelis have a longer history of producing textbooks, having begun before the state of Israel was established. The Israeli educational system is more de-centralized than the Palestinian one. Schools and teachers have some freedom to choose the textbooks they want to use from a list of approved textbooks issued by the Ministry of Education. To a limited extent, teachers may also choose texts from the open market, but a closer examination shows that all Israeli textbooks use similar strategies of manipulation and exclusion regarding Palestinians.[8]

A comprehensive analysis of the terminology in the narratives about Palestinian and Israeli history and civic education also shows that both texts reflect a culture of enmity. The same terminology in the texts on each side has different meanings for each side; what is positive for one is negative for the other.[9] In Israeli texts, for example, the war of 1948 is called the "War of Independence," whereas Palestinian texts refer to it as "al Nakba" (the catastrophe). Israeli texts refer to the first Jewish immigrants to Palestine as "pioneers," but Palestinian texts refer to them as "gangs" and "terrorists." The heroes of one side are the monsters of the other. Most of the maps in the texts eliminate the cities and towns of the other side, and the texts deny the legitimacy of each other's rights, history, and culture. Neither side recognizes the other's sufferings. The Holocaust is barely mentioned in Palestinian texts, and the trauma of Palestinians is ignored in Israeli texts.[10] Some texts even fail to agree on facts, such as the number of Palestinian refugees in 1948. Israelis write that there were between 600,000 and 700,000 Palestinians who became refugees as a result of the 1948 war, whereas Palestinians observe that more than 1 million Palestinians were *expelled* as a result of the 1948 fighting.

Based on these realities, in 2002 we chose to develop an experimental, innovative school booklet that contained two narratives—one Jewish Israeli narrative and the other Palestinian—organized around certain dates or milestones in the history of the conflict. Students on both sides learned in their mother tongue the narrative of the other, in addition to their own familiar story. We hoped that this method would promote attitudes of acknowledgment and respect for the other side. We assumed that a bridging narrative, if it materialized at all, would emerge only after many years of clear change in which the two societies moved away from a culture of war toward a culture of peace. This change requires time and the ability to mourn and work through the painful results of the long and intractable violent conflict. We certainly cannot expect the desired bridging narrative to develop while the conflict continues. Still, we did expect that through the process of developing narratives with teachers, the two narratives could become less hostile and humiliating and more sensitive of the other side, and thus more acceptable to students.

An important consideration was the role of teachers, who are the real agents of change. They have to internalize the paradigm shift from a single, hateful narrative supporting the conflict to two narratives that are somewhat neutral regarding each other. Studies have shown that teachers have more power than mere written texts in forming children's understandings and value systems.[11] As a result, we created a project that focused on the central role of teachers in the process of using shared history texts in the classroom. After the booklet was translated into Arabic and Hebrew, the teachers were to develop narratives and use them in their ninth- and tenth-grade classrooms. Through the students' mutual interaction, they were supposed to become more sensitive to each other's painful issues and thereby develop more interdependent narratives.

The Participants

A team that would work on this narratives project was chosen by the co-founders of Peace Research in the Middle East (PRIME), Sami Adwan and Dan Bar-On, and two history professors, Adnan Musallam (Bethlehem University) and Eyal Naveh (Tel Aviv University and the Kibbutz Teachers Seminar in Tel Aviv). The team included an equal number of men and women teachers: six Palestinian history and geography teachers (ages twenty-eight to sixty-seven), six Jewish Israeli history teachers (ages thirty-four to sixty-five) and five international delegates (four women and one man, ages twenty-four to thirty-seven), as well as one female Jewish Israeli observer. The teaching experience of the teachers ranged between seven and thirty-five years. Most of the Palestinian teachers were from Hebron, Bethlehem, and East Jerusalem, and had never before participated in dialogue encounters with Israelis. Several of the Israelis teach in high schools in the center and north of Israel, and had participated in previous encounters with Palestinians.

Peace-building under Fire

All the participants convened six times for three-day workshops at the New Imperial Hotel in the Old City of Jerusalem in March, June, and August 2002; in January and April 2003; and in Anatalya, Turkey, in August 2003. Because of the fragile political and military situations at the time, it was uncertain until the last minute whether the Palestinian teachers could obtain permits to enter

Jerusalem or be able to reach the places where the permits were issued. The workshops were called off several times, but each time we found ways to organize them again. All took place as planned, except for the March 2003 seminar, which was delayed until April as a result of war in Iraq.

As the project operated within the context of the Palestinian–Israeli conflict, it is critical to note the reality of everyday life for the participants. First, although both sides were in a bleak situation, there were differences and asymmetry regarding the intensity of the general realities each experienced.[12] For Palestinians, that reality had an unrelenting effect on daily life under occupation, always under the thumb of the Israeli army. Their freedom of movement was restricted; they were subjected to curfews and border checkpoints; and they feared shootings, killings, and house demolitions. Many Palestinians had suffered serious losses and had their own homes or those of relatives damaged. For Israelis, meanwhile, Palestinian suicide attacks caused daily anxiety about riding buses, going downtown, or going anywhere, for that matter, where there were crowds. Many on both sides feared sending their children to school.

The Israeli participants had to become even more attentive to the Palestinian limitations, their restricted movement, and the threats against them from fellow Palestinians for their participating in our joint project. Israelis had more freedom to move, and so they had to obtain the Palestinian travel permits and bring the papers to the Palestinians. This was actually detrimental to the project, as it gave the representatives of the stronger, Israeli side more power. Travel assistance, therefore, had to be provided tactfully, matter-of-factly, and without too much discussion. Moreover, the public on the oppressed side usually reacts more aggressively toward those who are seen as betraying the common cause or who favor normalization with the perceived enemy, as these have been defined in the Palestinian public discourse. So it was important for the Palestinian teachers to maintain a low profile and not draw too much attention to themselves within their own communities.

Moving between the Emotive and
the Task-oriented Approaches

The daily activities of the project revealed the advantages and disadvantages of attempts to construct a single, or bridging, narrative. At the first workshop in March 2002, teachers became acquainted with one another by sharing personal details of their lives and listening to the Palestinians' stories, all filled with painful moments related to Israeli violence or oppression. This was a difficult but necessary process as it later enabled the teachers to work together more openly on their joint tasks.[13] Sharing personal stories was an essential aspect of this project under the extreme conditions of the ongoing conflict. The asymmetry of power relations and violence outside the project had to be represented in the room through personal experiences of storytelling before a pragmatic, task-oriented approach could be introduced to bring about more symmetrical relationships.[14] One had to envision a future, different, post-conflict state in order to accomplish this task. This envisioning could occur only after people were able to share their pain, fear, and mistrust. Such a process had to be undertaken anew in each seminar, as the Israeli–Palestinian confrontations between the seminars eroded some of the closeness that had been gained during the seminars themselves.

We formed three mixed, Israeli–Palestinian task groups. Each group created a list of events relevant to the Palestinian–Israeli conflict and then chose one event on which to concentrate. In the plenary session the teachers discussed their lists and preferences, and together chose three events. One group focused on the Balfour Declaration of 1917, another on the 1948 war, and the third on the first *intifada* (uprising) of 1987. A method was devised to allow groups to communicate and coordinate their relevant narrative, which was later reviewed at the second workshop. Naveh and Musallam provided their professional views of how such narratives should be developed and what should be included. The international participants did some of the translations when necessary, summarized the work of the task groups, and wrote an evaluation at the end of each seminar.

In the second workshop in June 2002, teachers developed their parallel narratives partially by working in the original task groups and partially by working in national groups. The workshops were conducted in English. Between the second and third workshops, the respective narratives were translated into Hebrew and Arabic.

During the third seminar in August 2002, the teachers had their first opportunity to read both narratives in their respective languages. They were to present these new narratives to their pupils the following year. This time, most of the work was done in the plenary session. We expected the encounter to be difficult, requiring a balance between loyalty to one's own society, in which it was customary to be hostile toward the other side, versus sensitivity to the narrative and feelings of the other side. It was gratifying to find that *all of* the teachers accepted the narratives as valid, and, surprisingly, most of the questions posed during these sessions were informative: Was the translation precise? Who was the person you mentioned in 1908? Why did you try to describe this event so briefly, whereas the others are described at length? At that stage there were almost no attempts to deny the legitimacy of the other's narrative.

We interpreted the success of this part of the project to the fact that participants on each side felt familiar and therefore safe with and in their own narrative and could therefore more easily accept and relate to the other's narrative. More difficult issues were bound to arise when both narratives were presented to pupils in regular classrooms and when the teachers came together again to discuss their reactions.

The first school booklet with narratives covering the events of 1917, 1948, and the first intifada was expected to be ready in November 2002. However, the continued and renewed curfews on the Palestinian towns, and the additional necessary proofreading of the texts and their translations, did not allow us to produce them in Hebrew and Arabic until February 2003; the English version did not come out until June 2003.[15] Teachers began testing the booklet in their classrooms, exposing it to hundreds of Israeli and Palestinian students in this experimental phase. The January and April 2003 teachers' workshops focused on sharing the students' first responses, making corrections, supporting the teachers in their work, and developing three additional narratives around newly chosen events. The three periods to be added included the 1920s, 1930 to 1948, and the 1967 war. The teachers' decision to add these three periods gave the booklet historical continuity, filling in the gaps between the booklet's initial time frames of 1917 and 1948. The teachers divided the historical periods between them and committed themselves to prepare a draft for the August 2003 workshop.

"Our narrative tells the facts, their narrative is propaganda": The Pupils React

It is customary to give seminars to teachers to accommodate new learning materials and then let them introduce the new materials in their own way in classrooms, without following up on what actually happened in encounters with students. We knew, however, that under the harsh conditions of the conflict we would have to follow up, as the encounter with the pupils could be problematic and discourage the teachers in their efforts to develop this new approach. Thus, the fifth workshop in April 2003 focused on the teachers' initial impressions of their students' reactions after presenting the two narratives in their classrooms for at least one of the three historical periods (usually the one that they helped to develop) to at least one class for one to three sessions.

The teachers generally reported that the students were surprised, interested, and curious when presented with the two narratives, but they also observed some resentment. The Palestinian students' responses were affected by the difficult situation of their everyday lives at the time, with the curfew and the occupation, and many of them perceived the two narratives through that lens. It was much harder for them than for the Israeli pupils to listen to the other side's narrative. For example, some of the Palestinian students were antagonistic to the Israeli narrative of the Balfour Declaration, which was consistent with the ways they had been brought up to disbelieve the Israeli narrative:

• "Our narrative tells the facts, their narrative is propaganda."

• "They have no place in our land."

• "If they suffered from persecution, why do they do it to us?"

• "This is our natural right; this is the land of our fathers. Who gave them the right to settle in our land?"

• "There is a commitment of the British to bring the Jews to the land. They should not have done it."

• "They do not have a historical right in Palestine. We have a right since ancient times."

• "They see us as aggressors, but we are the original inhabitants of this land. They came from far away, and they are aggressors."

The teachers struggled with these reactions, and some found creative ways to handle them. For example, in reacting to a student's argument about facts and propaganda, the teacher said: "Think about the pupils of the other side who say exactly the same thing about our narrative," thereby making the student aware of the problem of the single narrative approach. Other teachers were confronted by students who wondered why the teachers taught a text that they did not believe in, one that represented the "other side's point of view"? Why did the teachers not just denounce it? The teachers' experiences showed us that the move from a single narrative to the two-narrative approach was a paradigmatic shift for which the teachers had to be thoroughly prepared.[16]

In another exchange, an Israeli teacher tried to differentiate between the narrative and the reality, but the distinction was not valid for the Palestinian teachers and pupils at a difficult time in the Israeli occupation. The reactions of the Palestinian students showed that they could not accept the Israeli narrative in a positive or understanding way when the harsh reality of the occupation so colored their reactions.

Some Israeli teachers also had to struggle with the negative arguments of students. Other students expressed interest and curiosity about the Palestinian narrative, saying that they had learned new things about the other side's position. In a questionnaire that one Israeli teacher gave to his students after introducing the two narratives, many said that teaching both narratives was a good idea. But some pupils were concerned that by acknowledging the narrative of the Palestinians they could be denying the truth of their own narrative, an argument that clearly required the teachers to intervene: Why does accepting the other side's story necessarily threaten the justification of one's own story?

The teachers from both sides were confronted with the issue of students questioning their credibility: If these texts were "the enemy's propaganda," why teach them in class, especially at this time of violent conflict? At that point the teachers themselves looked anew at the narratives that they had created and agreed upon earlier. The students' arguments had created a crisis among the teachers concerning the purpose of the project. If the narratives simply replicated the conflict's legitimacy and the illegitimacy of the other side's narrative, what was the sense of teaching the two narratives in the classroom? The teachers needed to debate these questions with one another and to find satisfying answers within the context of the workshop.

Moving out of Deadlocks

The teachers could easily have been stymied at this point and, following the reactions of their pupils, might have justified their own narrative and delegitimized the other side's. But that would have undermined all that they had invested and developed. Should they move forward, clarifying anew the goals of the project in order to be better prepared for their future classes, or should they retreat into the ethnocentric narratives that support each side's view of the conflict?[17] The pupils' reactions helped the teachers to elicit their own negative emotional reactions, especially under the dreadful conditions of their daily lives that they tried to repress or could not express. But the teachers did not regress to the ethnocentric discourse that dominated the societies in which they lived. The conflict had created a new opportunity for self-examination that was essential for the process to move forward.

Some teachers now observed that while the booklet that they had created was good, it could be improved. One teacher offered the image of "two blind people shouting their story without listening to the other." Teachers responded by observing that their own dialogue around the development of the narratives had not entered the booklet and should be represented in the texts or in the teacher's guide. The term "propaganda," used earlier, was replaced by the term "partial picture." The discourse among the teachers took a turn, and they made several new observations: the narratives that they created represented more extreme views than those that they had expressed in their earlier encounters, so it was necessary to create a dialogue between the narratives. Instead of mutual exclusion, they would have to introduce some level of mutual inclusiveness. The teachers were motivated to try to work out a way to introduce changes into their original texts. They also reacted to specific sensitivities expressed by their pupils. For example, some of the Palestinian pupils did not want the Israeli flag on the top of each page, marking the Israeli narrative, and they were willing to give up the Palestinian flag in their section. Both flags were removed from the booklet.

One could still sense that it was hard for some of the teachers to accept that "what is an accident for one side is a deliberate act of violence for the other," as in the instigating event of the 1987 intifada, in which an Israeli driver hit and killed five Palestinian workers, on December 9, 1987. But a different discourse developed, in which teachers from both sides expressed their feelings and thoughts more openly, trying to redefine what the project actually was about. Now they no longer wanted to create a bridging narrative but instead a better dialogue between the two narratives, maintaining some interdependence between them as well as differences. They tried to resolve this conflict by developing a pragmatic approach to the narratives themselves. The two narratives could be rewritten repeatedly, according to the teachers' revised thinking, and in response to changes occurring outside the workshop.

Some teachers wondered if the creation of the narratives would ultimately increase hatred between the two peoples, and they sought to find ways to avoid reinforcing the self-centered attitudes of each side. The teachers also had a role in helping students learn to deconstruct texts, for when students deconstructed only the text of the other side, teachers had to demonstrate that their own text could also be deconstructed by the other side. The validation of the other side's narrative was a very important component of this process, as it was important for the students to become more critical about texts presented by the media.

It soon became obvious that the narratives should have some interdependence. Before this stage, it seemed that each side wanted to tell its own story, including only what that side saw as important. After accommodating the re-actions of their students, however, the teachers showed greater readiness to confront each other's narratives and to cooperate, negotiate, and reach agree-ments about the events or issues that each side wanted to emphasize, taking into consideration the feelings and attitudes of the other side.

For the teachers, the idea of the two narratives survived, even if there were problems with implementing that idea. The teachers felt a sense of ownership, despite the difficulties that they had faced in their classrooms amid the dete-riorating external situation. They believed that they had achieved a higher level of communication, and after six workshops both sides acknowledged that they had learned a lot from the other side that they had not known before. For example, Israelis, who knew about the massacre of Jews in Hebron in 1929, learned that Arab families had also been massacred. A Palestinian teacher who thought that the British had exiled only Arabs during the Mandate admitted that he was surprised to learn that extremists from both sides had been ex-pelled.

The organizers of the seminar encouraged the teachers and praised their achievements in trying to teach their pupils to appreciate the legitimacy of the other side's narrative, even though this mood of cooperation was not matched in the world outside, particularly for the Palestinians still living under the oc-cupation and its accompanying humiliations. But the organizers also stressed that political conditions were not yet ripe to achieve the ultimate goals of the project, and that the aim was not necessarily to create a bridging narrative. They pointed out that it was normal and expected for at least some students to have negative reactions initially to the other side's narrative, but just making students aware of the other side's point of view was important, given the in-tractable conflict. One also observed different abilities among the teachers to withstand classroom pressure and to try to make students view the other's nar-rative differently.

Transforming Hateful Single Narratives into Two Mutually Sensitive Ones

This chapter describes a project in which Palestinian and Israeli teachers de-veloped a joint school booklet of two narratives that they taught in their class-rooms. Some of the teachers' and pupils' reactions were summarized and formed a basis for developing additional narratives. All of these activities took place under extremely severe conditions, during the Israeli occupation and attacks against Israelis by Palestinian suicide bombers. After the group met several more times in 2005, the entire process culminated in the publication of a book, *Palestinians and Israelis Learn the Narrative of the "Other,"* which embodied the double narratives of nine events or historical periods along with a teacher's guide.

This project was a grass-roots attempt to build peace under conditions which seemed hopeless at the time.[18] The teachers' strong motivation to continue, even in light of the difficult political situation and some of their students' harsh reactions, indicated how important this process was and what it achieved, especially as our group of teachers generally represented the average Israeli and Palestinian teacher.

The idea of developing two separate narratives is linked to the proposed, political two-state solution to the Israeli–Palestinian conflict. In other post-conflict contexts (such as South Africa), where a single-state political solution emerged, one could think in terms of developing a bridging narrative; but when there are two societies that want to live separately, side by side, a two-narrative solution seems more suitable.

The appendix to this chapter shows that the two narratives are asymmetrical: although the Israeli narrative is more reflective and self-critical, the Palestinian narrative is less so. This difference probably arose because the Israelis had an established state for fifty-five years, whereas the Palestinians were still struggling to establish their state. In some measure, participants in the project observed, the Palestinian narrative was similar to Israeli texts produced in about 1948.

When the Israeli and Palestinian teachers read their own narrative, they seemed to feel secure enough and open to accept the validity of another narrative. Perhaps this openness indicated that both societies were insecure regarding their national identity. Mutual insecurity is one of the basic social-psychological characteristics of this conflict and could partially account for the need to have two separate narratives during intense discord. In that sense, the idea of the intertwined narratives can be interpreted differently. People on each side must feel secure with their own narrative, which needs to be acknowledged by the other, before they can relate positively to a different account of the same events. The process of both sides developing mutual sensitivity to the narrative is critical for success.

Still, when the teachers were confronted with their pupils' reactions, they found that their separate narratives were still embedded in the conflict and created negative reactions among students of the opposite side. When this negation occurred, a possible response that had gone unheeded earlier, when developing the narratives, changes were required in some of the expressions and content of the booklet to make the narrative more inclusive, more interdependent, and more sensitive to the needs and sensibilities of each side.

The bursts of violence that occurred beyond our workshop often affected our interactions. Yet, we were rewarded with glimmers of hope and enthusiasm for the implementation of our project in the schools. The success of this project, in contrast to similar, earlier ventures with Israeli and Palestinian teachers, was the result of four important factors:

1. The timing of the project introduced a sense of urgency that created a positive counterweight to the violence outside our workshops. That we always explored these external conditions through storytelling enabled the teachers to become deeply involved in their mutual tasks.

2. The authors' leadership of the project offered a role model of a serious endeavor that combined academics, professionalism, and financial and managerial skills.[19] The authors improved their own understanding of the conflict thanks to their long-term commitment to each other and to the project.[20]

3. The creation of real texts, a concrete product that could be distributed to students and discussed, was very important for students and teachers who had difficulty with abstract discussions and evaluations.

4. The presentation of their students' responses allowed teachers to express their own feelings toward the opposite side's narrative in ways that they dared not express openly before. Citing the most extreme student reactions led to an open discussion about the two narratives, about Palestinian–Israeli relations both in the past and the present, and about the project's goals and realistic expectations.

The authors acknowledged to each other that peace could come only if both sides won; a peace with only one winner would have no value. Adwan added: "The disarmament of history can happen only after the disarmament of weapons. But one can prepare it now." The events of the last years have highlighted the fact that we have been slow to approach a formal peace agreement. Still, a grass-roots peace-building process involving face-to-face encounters between Jewish-Israeli and Palestinian peoples will be necessary in order to achieve sustainable peace. Furthermore, the booklet that these teachers created and its implementation in their classrooms provides a concrete way to spread the effects of this face-to-face encounter between a small group of teachers. As Mead once said, "Never doubt that a small group of thoughtful committed citizens can change the world."[21] In this case, never doubt that a small group of committed, Palestinian and Israeli Jewish teachers can change the world when the time is ripe.

Appendix: A Sample of the Two Narratives of the Balfour Declaration

(in the original there are empty lines between the two narratives for the students to write in their own reactions)

The Israeli Narrative
From the Balfour Declaration to the first White Paper

Introduction

The birth of the Zionist movement Zionism, the Jewish national movement, was born in the nineteenth century when the ideology embodied in the Enlightenment was disseminated in the European Jewish community. These new ideas planted the first seeds of Jewish nationalism; the subsequent birth of Zionism was the result of several factors:

1) The rise of modern anti-Semitism —a deeply-rooted and complicated mixture of traditional religious hatred augmented by "scientific" racism which categorized Jews as a depraved and pernicious race.

2) The disappointment of Western European Jews with the emancipation which pledged that the position of Jews in society would equal that of the Christians. The Jews were discouraged

The Palestinian Narrative
The Balfour Declaration

Historical background

In April 1799 Napoleon Bonaparte put forth a plan for a Jewish state in Palestine. During the siege of Acre, he sought to enlist Jewish support in return for which he promised to build the Temple. The project failed after the defeat of Napoleon in the battles of Acre and Abu-Qir. It represents the first post-Renaissance expression of cooperation between a colonialist power and the Jewish people.

However, it was the events of 1831–1840 that paved the way for the establishment of a Jewish state in Palestine. Lord Palmerston, the British Foreign Secretary in 1840–1841, proposed establishing a British protectorate in the Ottoman Empire to be settled by Jews as a buffer area—an obstacle to Mohammed Ali of Egypt and to political unity in the Arab regions.

when it became clear that in many instances there was equality in name only. Discrimination continued.

3) New European nationalist movements such as those appearing in Italy and Germany inspired similar aspirations among the Jews.

4) An important element was the longing for Zion, an integral aspect of Jewish religious and national identity throughout history. This longing stemmed from the biblical promise that the land of Israel was given to the people of Israel by the God of Israel, and on memories of those historical eras when the people of Israel lived independently in their land. This concept inspired the national anthem, written at that time:

Hatikvah: The Hope

As long as in our heart of hearts
the Jewish spirit remains strong,
And we faithfully look toward
the east,
Our eyes will turn to Zion.
We have not yet lost our hope,
The hope of two thousand years,
To be a free people in our land—
The land of Zion and Jerusalem.

The Zionist movement was born in the major centers of Jewish population in Europe, and its purpose was to return the Jewish people to its land and put an end to its abnormal situation among the nations of the world. At first there was a spontaneous emergence of local associations ("Lovers of Zion") out of which an organized

Britain launched a new policy supporting Jewish settlement in Palestine after Eastern European Jews, particularly those in Czarist Russia, whose living conditions were poor in any case, suffered cruel persecution. Consequently, with the rise of nationalism, Zionism appeared as a drastic international solution to the Jewish problem, transforming the Jewish religion into a nationalist attachment to a special Jewish homeland and a special Jewish state. Other factors influencing the birth and development of the Zionist movement were the increasingly competitive interests shared by European colonialists in Africa and Asia, and the Zionist colonialist movement for control of Palestine.

British imperialism found in Zionism a perfect tool for attaining its own interests in the Arab East, which was strategically and economically important for the Empire. Likewise, Zionism used British colonialist aspirations to gain international backing and economic resources for its project of establishing a Jewish national home in Palestine.

This alliance of British imperialism and Zionism resulted in the birth of what is known in history books as the Balfour Declaration (November 2, 1917). It is a conspicuous example of the British policy of seizing another nation's land and resources and effacing its identity. It is a policy based on political movement was established, thanks to the activities of "The Father of Zionism," Theodore Herzl [whose Hebrew name is Benjamin Ze'ev Herzl].

In 1882 there was a small wave of immigration [aliya/aliyot] to "the land" [i.e., the land of Israel], the first of several. The purpose of these aliyot was not just to fulfill the religious obligations connected to the land, as had been the case in the past, but rather to create a "new" kind of Jew, a productive laborer for whom Zionism is to create a refuge for the Jewish people in the land of Israel, guaranteed by an open and official legal acknowledgment.

There were two basic approaches to Zionism:
1) Practical Zionism focused on increasing immigration, purchasing land, and settling Jews on the land. By 1914, in the first two waves of immigration, nearly 100,000 people immigrated (although most of them later left the country). Dozens of agricultural settlements were established and there was a significant increase in the urban Jewish population.
2) Political Zionism focused on diplomatic efforts to get support for Zionism from the great empires in order to obtain a legal and official charter for wide-scale settlement in the land.
Chaim Weizmann, who became Zionism's leader after Herzl's death, integrated both aspects of the movement

aggression, expansion and repression of a native people's aspirations for national liberation.

For the Palestinians, the year 1917 was the first of many—1920, 1921, 1929, 1936, 1948, 1967, 1987, 2002—marked by tragedy, war, disaster, killing, destruction, homelessness and catastrophe.

Dividing the Arab East

Imperialist Britain called for forming a higher committee of seven European countries. The report submitted in 1907 to British Prime Minister Sir Henry Campbell-Bannerman emphasized that the Arab countries and the Muslim-Arab people living in the Ottoman Empire presented a very real threat to European countries, and it recommended the following actions:
1) To promote disintegration, division and separation in the region.
2) To establish artificial political entities that would be under the authority of the imperialist countries.
3) To fight any kind of unity—whether intellectual, religious or historical— and taking practical measures to divide the region's inhabitants.
4) To achieve this, it was proposed that a "buffer state" be established in Palestine, populated by a strong, foreign presence which would be hostile to its neighbors and friendly to European countries and their interests.
Doubtless the recommendations of Campbell—Bannerman's higher com-

[In the original there is a picture here of the moshav Nahalal, a semi-cooperative agricultural settlement that was established in 1921 in the Jezreel Valley.]

The Balfour Declaration

The first time any country expressed support for Zionism was in a letter sent by Lord Balfour, to help establish a Jewish political entity in the land of Israel.

Letter from Arthur James Balfour, Minister of Foreign Affairs, to Lord Rothschild, a leader of the Jewish community in Great Britain. It came to be known as the Balfour Declaration. The letter was dated November 2, 1917, shortly before the end of World War I. It expressed the support of the British Government for establishing a national home for the Jewish people in the land of Israel:

> *Foreign Office*
> *November 2nd, 1917*
> *Dear Lord Rothschild,*
>
> *I have much pleasure in conveying to you, on behalf of His Majesty's Government, the following declaration of sympathy with Jewish Zionist aspirations which has been submitted to, and approved by, the Cabinet.*
> *"His Majesty's Government view with favor the establishment in Palestine of a national home for the Jewish people, and will use*

mittee paved the way for the Jews to Palestine. It gave British approval to the Zionist movement's policy of separating Palestine from the Arab lands in order to establish an imperialist core that would insure foreign influence in the region.

Jewish imperialist projects in Palestine followed in quick succession. World War I, 1914–1918, was a critically important period for Zionist and British imperialist policies for Palestine. Included in an exchange of letters between Sharif Hussein of Mecca and Sir Henry McMahon was the Damascus Protocol (July 14, 1915). Sharif Hussein indicated to McMahon the boundaries of the Arab countries in Asia to which Britain would grant independence—the Arabian Peninsula, Iraq/Mesopotamia, Syria and southern parts of present-day Turkey. He excluded Aden because it was a British military base. McMahon's response in a letter dated October 24, 1915, designated areas to be excluded from the Independent Arab States—the Syrian coastal areas west of Damascus; Homs, Hama, and Aleppo provinces; and the two regions of Alexandretta and Marsin. The exclusions did not include Palestine. The second letter is known as the Hussein-McMahon Agreement.

In May 1916 Britain and France signed a secret document—the Sykes-Picot Agreement—to divide the Arab East *their best endeavors to facilitate the achievement of this object, it being clearly understood that nothing shall be done which may prejudice the civil and religious rights of existing non-Jewish communities in Palestine, or the rights and political status enjoyed by Jews in any other country."*

I should be grateful if you would bring this declaration to the knowledge of the Zionist Federation.

Yours sincerely,
Arthur James Balfour

at a time when Britain was exchanging letters with Sharif Hussein about recognizing the independence of the region. In the agreement Britain and France pledged to divide the Ottoman Empire as follows

[A map of the Ottoman Empire is here in the original.]

1) The Lebanese and Syrian coasts were given to France.

2) South and middle Iraq were given to Britain.

3) An international administration in Palestine excluding the two ports of Haifa and Acre.

4) A French zone of influence, including eastern Syria and the Mosul province.

5) Transjordan and the northern part of Baghdad province would be a British zone of influence.

NOTES

UNESCO held a conference in Geneva (April 3–4, 2003), entitled "Curriculum Change and Social Cohesion in Conflict-Affected Societies." Seven such societies were discussed. The epigraph to this chapter is taken from the report of that conference (Sobhi Tawil, Alexandra Harley, and Lucy Porteous, "Curriculum Change and Social Cohesion in Conflict-Affected Societies" [Geneva, 2003]).

1. See Ilan Pappe, "The Bridging Narrative Concept," chapter 8 in this volume.

2. Emanuel Levinas, *Totality and Infinity* (Pittsburgh, 1969).

3. Susan Opotow, "Reconciliation in Times of Impunity: Challenges for Social Justice," *Social Justice Research*, XIV (2001), 149–170.

4. Tawil, Harley, and Porteous, "Curriculum Change and Social Cohesion in Conflict-Affected Societies."

5. Michael W. Apple, *Ideology and Curriculum* (London, 1979); Pierre Bourdieu, "Cultural Reproduction and Social Reproduction," in Richard Brown (ed.), *Knowledge, Education and Cultural Change* (London, 1973), 71–112; Alan Luke, *Literacy, Booklet, and Ideology* (London, 1988).

6. Dan Bar-On, *The Others within Us: Changes in the Israeli Collective Identity from a Social Psychological Perspective* (Beer Sheva, 1999), in Hebrew.

7. Israel-Palestine Center for Research and Information (IPCRI), "Analysis and Evaluation of the New Palestinian Curriculum," submitted to the Public Affairs Office, U.S. Consulate General, Jerusalem, March, 2003; Sami Adwan and Ruth Firer, *The Narrative of the 1967 War in the Israeli and Palestinian History and Civics Textbooks and Curricula Statement* (Braunschwieg, 1999). See also Nathan J. Brown, "Contesting National Identity in Palestinian Education," chapter 10 in this volume.

8. Eyal Naveh and Eyal Yogev (ed. Dafna Danon), *Histories: Towards a Dialogue with Yesterday* (Tel Aviv, 2002), in Hebrew; Magne Angvis and Bodo von Borries (eds.), *Youth and History: A Comparative European Survey on Historical Consciousness and Political Attitudes among Adolescents* (Hamburg, 1997); Dan Bar-Tal, *The Rocky Road Toward Peace: Societal Beliefs in Times of Intractable Conflict: The Israeli Case* (Jerusalem, 1995), in Hebrew. See also Eyal Naveh, "The Dynamics of Identity Construction in Israel through Education in History," chapter 11 in this volume.

9. Sami Adwan and Ruth Firer, *The Narrative of Palestinian Refugees during the War of 1948 in Israeli and Palestinian History and Civic Education Textbooks* (Paris, 1997); Adwan and Firer, *The Narrative of the 1967 War.*

10. In 2004, a group of Israeli Palestinians, headed by Emil Shufani, a Greek Orthodox priest from Nazareth, traveled to Poland to visit Auschwitz as part of their wish to learn about Jewish suffering there and its impact on contemporary Jewish Israeli society (Hava Shechter, personal communication, 2004). Earlier chapters in this book make the same points as made in this paragraph.

11. Naveh and Yogev, *Histories;* Angvis and von Borris, *Youth and History.*

12. Ifat Maoz, "An Experiment in Peace: Reconciliation-aimed Dialogues of Israeli and Palestinian Youth," *Journal of Peace Research,* XXXVII (2000), 721–736.

13. Joe H. Albeck, Sami Adwan, and Dan Bar-On, "Dialogue Groups: TRT's Guidelines for Working through Intractable Conflicts by Personal Storytelling in Encounter Groups," *Journal of Peace Psychology,* VIII (2002), 301–322.

14. Dan Bar-On and Fatma Kassem, "Storytelling as a Way to Work through Intractable Conflicts: The TRT German-Jewish Experience and Its Relevance to the Palestinian-Israeli Context," *Journal of Social Issues,* LX (2004), 289–306.

15. An example of the first part of the Israeli and Palestinian narratives, accounting for the Balfour Declaration in 1917, appears in the appendix to this chapter.

16. Thomas S. Kuhn, *The Structure of Scientific Revolutions* (Chicago, 1962).

17. Shoshana Steinberg and Dan Bar-On, "An Analysis of the Group Process in Encounters between Jews and Palestinians Using a Typology for Discourse Classification," *International Journal of Intercultural Relations*, XXVI (2002), 199–214.

18. Ifat Maoz, "Peace Building in Violent Conflict: Israeli-Palestinian Post–Oslo People to People Activities, *International Journal of Politics, Culture and Society*, XVII (2004), 563–574.

19. Ifat Maoz, "Power Relations in Inter-group Encounters: A Case Study of Jewish-Arab Encounters in Israel," *International Journal of Intercultural Relations*, XXIV (2000), 259–277; idem., "Multiple Conflicts and Competing Agendas: A Framework for Conceptualizing Structured Encounters between Groups in Conflict: The Case of a Coexistence Project between Jews and Palestinians in Israel," *Journal of Peace Psychology*, VI (2000), 135–156.

20. During a conference in May 2003 in Würzburg, Germany, on family constellations, the authors led a workshop in which German therapists were asked to role play the Israeli and Palestinian teachers developing their texts around the events of 1948 and the 1987 intifada. The participants agreed, at the end of this powerful exercise, that they had learned a good deal about the conflict and about the difficulties each side had in reconciling with the other. Another, similar workshop was organized in Rejika, Croatia, in June 2003, for a group of practitioners from fourteen countries, who also said that the exercise had helped them to reflect on their own experiences.

21. Margaret Mead, *New Lives for Old: Cultural Transformation—Manau, 1928–1953* (New York, 1975).

10

CONTESTING NATIONAL IDENTITY
IN PALESTINIAN EDUCATION

NATHAN J. BROWN

PALESTINIAN IDENTITY, like Palestinian soil, is sharply contested terrain. This is most obviously—and noisily—true internationally. But it is hardly unusual for questions of national identity to involve complex and controversial international questions. The Palestinian case is unusually, though not uniquely, complicated in that here national identity does not merely concern historical and territorial issues but also existential matters. Palestinians considering their identity immediately confront three existential questions: What is Palestine? Who are the Palestinians? What political values should Palestinians embrace? Complicating matters still further, the very legitimacy of these questions is debated: Is there even such a place as Palestine, and is there a specific people that can be called Palestinian?

The debate is not simply international. Palestinians have argued among themselves over their national identity and the precise geographical demarcation of Palestine. What is the relationship between Palestine and neighboring Arab states, or between being Palestinian and being Arab or Muslim? Also questioned are the historical roots of Palestinian national identity.

Palestinians have been unusual, though, again, not unique, in facing these issues in the absence of any state apparatus for developing and inculcating authoritative versions of national identity. The Palestine Liberation Organization (PLO), founded in 1964, gradually gained legitimacy over the next two decades and posited itself as the "sole, legitimate representative of the Palestinian people." But its ideological apparatus never had authority over any Palestinian population. Not until 1993 and 1994 did a quasi-state entity arise, the Palestinian National Authority (PNA), which forced to undertake defining the Palestinian nation at a time when fundamental political and identity issues had yet to be resolved domestically or internationally. It did so with only some of the tools available to a sovereign actor.

The contested nature of national identity led most social scientists more than a generation ago to abandon the concept of national character. Only in the past decade have identity issues again become central concerns for many social science disciplines. Most Palestinians, however, do not seem to feel that they have the luxury of discarding the focus on national identity merely because the concept is difficult to define. Indeed, the most impressive, and perhaps the only achievement of the Palestinian national movement is the creation of a powerful national identity. Khalidi noted the contrast in this regard between Palestinian nationalism and Zionism:

> For Palestinians the contrast could not be greater: they have yet to achieve self-determination, independence, or statehood; they are only now painfully integrating their feeble parastate, which grew up in exile, into an administration with the limited powers the Israelis allow them; they have an economy in shambles after three decades of occupation and several years of *intifada* (which probably had as devastating an impact on the Palestinian economy as did the 1936–39 revolt); they control virtually no resources and have no real allies in the world. The Palestinians, of course, do have one asset in spite of everything: a powerful sense of national identity, which we have seen they were able to develop and maintain in spite of extraordinary vicissitudes.[1]

Indeed, while the construction of the PNA was hampered for a host of international and domestic reasons, it did allow for a fuller and more authoritative expression of national identity than was possible previously—always under watchful and sometimes unfriendly international eyes, but far more autonomously than had ever been the case in the past. One of the first areas transferred from Israeli control to the new PNA was education, not simply for Palestinians living under PNA security control but for the entire Palestinian population of the West Bank (including Jerusalem) and Gaza. Thus one of the first important projects of the PNA was to develop a Palestinian national curriculum, which turned out to be the only project that the PNA undertook that ran on schedule.

The great interest in developing a Palestinian curriculum is unsurprising given decades of contests for control over schooling. During the British Mandate, Palestinians criticized the educational system for skirting all issues connected with nationalism and identity. After 1948, schools educating Palestinians in the former territory of the British Mandate followed three different curricula: schools in Gaza adopted the Egyptian, the West Bank followed the

Jordanian, and Israel developed its own curriculum for the Palestinian population that remained in its territory. In 1967, when Israel gained control of the West Bank and Gaza, the system changed only slightly. Use of the Egyptian curriculum continued in Gaza, while the West Bank maintained its connection to Jordan. Israel did attempt to convert East Jerusalem schools to its own Arabic curriculum but abandoned the effort when parents deserted the system in protest. Israel also reviewed the Egyptian and Jordanian books and removed material it deemed offensive or undesirable.

Palestinian educators were anxious to assert control over their curriculum. Indeed, an effort to write a Palestinian curriculum actually began even before the creation of the PNA: UNESCO recommended the establishment of a Palestinian curriculum center in 1990, and that proposal slowly progressed until 1993, when a conference to begin the project was held in Jerusalem. The PNA assumed oversight in 1994 and signed an agreement with UNESCO to establish its own Curriculum Development Center to develop a proposal. That body began work in 1995 through a committee that was headed by a Palestinian political scientist, Ibrahim Abu Lughod, and set itself the demanding task of completing its work within a year.[2]

After reviewing existing curricula in use, consulting with educators, and holding town meetings, the Abu Lughod committee issued a 600-page report that recommended a comprehensive rethinking of existing educational practices, pedagogy, and curricula, all of which it denounced as outmoded, stale, authoritarian, destructive of the individual, and based on rote learning.[3] After submitting its report, the Abu Lughod committee dissolved, and implementation fell to the Ministry of Education. In developing its own proposal, the education ministry retreated from some of the more radical ideas, and much of the critical language, in the Abu Lughod reports, and presented its proposal to the Cabinet and the Palestinian Legislative Council.[4] Both bodies approved the proposal with very minor modifications, and the education ministry then constructed an entirely new Curriculum Development Center to write new textbooks. In the meantime, Palestinian schools used the Jordanian and Egyptian curriculum, although the PNA did rush out a supplementary series of textbooks, entitled *National Education,* for grades 1 through 6 as an interim measure to give the curriculum at least a minimal Palestinian content.

The Center began by writing books for grades 1 and 6 in 2000, grades 2 and 7 in 2001, grades 3 and 8 in 2002, grades 4 and 9 in 2003, and grades 5 and 10 in 2004. The high school curriculum was slated to begin in 2005 and 2006. All Palestinian schools in the West Bank and Gaza, including East Jerusalem, use the new completed books. The curricular uniformity is remarkable given the diverse administrative authorities over Palestinian schools, with systems administered by the PNA for public schools in the West Bank and Gaza; the United Nations Relief Works Agency (UNRWA) for schools in refugee camps; Israel for East Jerusalem schools; Jordan for some Jerusalem schools; as well as churches and private organizations. The new curriculum is comprehensive, covering history, geography, Arabic, mathematics, English, science, national education, civic education, religion (with separate books for Islamic and Christian education), art, and calligraphy. Schools are required to adhere to the curriculum and textbooks authorized by the PNA; private schools may introduce supplementary materials, but use of such materials is limited as there is so much to cover in the official curriculum.

The composition of the new curriculum occasioned both international and domestic debate. International controversy centered on charges that the Palestinian curriculum incited students to hate Israel and Jews. The charges stemmed largely from an attempt to hold Palestinians responsible for the content of Egyptian and Jordanian books that were used while the PNA authored its own.[5] More germane to this inquiry is the domestic debate concerning the content of the new curriculum and textbooks. When the PNA began writing a national curriculum and set of texts for the first time, it found itself forced to develop authoritative, though often ambiguous, answers to three fundamental questions of identity: What is Palestine geographically? What is a Palestinian? What is a Palestinian citizen? The following sections review the approaches to these questions that the PNA embarked upon during the three phases of the curriculum project: the original Abu Lughod committee proposals, the plan developed by the Ministry of Education, and the final version of the textbooks.

What Is Palestine?

From the beginning of their efforts to write a new curriculum, Palestinian educators and leaders faced a series of difficult questions on the nature of Palestine, especially concerning geography. How should Palestine be represented? Was it to be the patchwork created by the explicitly interim Oslo Accords? Did Palestine consist of the West Bank and Gaza alone, the vision Palestinian leaders insisted on for their state but which remained unrecognized internationally? What about the areas in pre-1967 Israel? Were those who fled those areas in 1948 not Palestinian? But if they were, did their hometowns become non-Palestinian at some point? And was the Arab population that remained Pales-

tinian or Israeli or perhaps a combination of the two? These issues were difficult for adults to resolve, but now the authors of the textbooks were supposed
to delineate answers for children.

The Abu Lughod committee deliberately avoided answering, or even posing,
such questions, fearing that they were a distraction at that time. Instead, the
committee simply called for the new curriculum to teach the "facts," a vague
solution, especially since the committee did not specify what the facts were and
had actually criticized existing educational practices for focusing on the numb-
ing inculcation of facts. The committee seemed to believe that an emphasis on
relative truth and critical thought would allow students to confront those questions on their own, at least over the long run. 'Ali Jarbawi, a committee member, recalls:

> We were asked, how do you define Palestine? What are the boundaries? We
> were asked this over and over. Is Haifa a Palestinian city? This was on the sur-
> face, but the more sophisticated question was: What are you going to do about
> history? We accept peace. But are you going to say Haifa was not Arab? We said
> we did not want to falsify history. . . . But we were introducing a method that
> would allow people to think about these issues. We couldn't put much in the
> report because people would take the few sentences and then say, "That's
> why you're doing the whole report." You can't impose normalization by a com-
> mittee that looks for offending sentences. You need a new way of looking at
> things.[6]

Jarbawi's suggested approach neither guided textbook writers nor resolved
internal debates on the definition of Palestine. Few Palestinian adults wanted
students to decide for themselves what a map of Palestine looks like.

When the curriculum was developed by the Ministry of Education and debated in the Palestinian Legislative Council, members argued over the geography that should be taught and the cities that should be considered Palestinian.
But despite their sense that the Palestinian curriculum should address such
matters, Council members were no more able than the Abu Lughod committee
to give concrete and coherent guidance.[7] Thus it fell to the Curriculum Development Center to work out an approach. This placed the Center in a difficult
position, as its tendency in controversial matters was to fall silent or rely on
clear guidance from the PNA leadership.

Remaining silent over the course of the entire curriculum seemed impossible. In 1994, when the series of textbooks, *National Education,* was hastily
issued by the education ministry to supplement the Egyptian and Jordanian
books, it managed to cover six grades without a clear map of Palestine. One

discussion of the Palestinian economy in this earlier set of books included the following passage on fishing: "Palestine looks out over the coast of the Mediterranean Sea. Among its coastal cities are: the city of Gaza, Dayr Balah, Khan Yunis, and Rafah" (all are in the Gaza Strip).[8] Sixth graders were presented with a blank box, with the instructions: "In the neighboring rectangle, sketch a map of Palestine" and its administrative divisions.[9] These sorts of solutions earned Palestine no international credit and provoked only domestic derision as overly timid. Clearly blank spaces and awkward silences could not be sustained across an entire curriculum.[10]

Nor could textbook writers take refuge in authoritative statements from the PNA leadership. There were none to draw on. Books for grades 1 and 6 were written at the same time as the final-status talks between Israel and the PLO; subsequent books were written during the second intifada. In that context, no clear geographical definition of Palestine was possible.

The portrait of Palestine that finally emerged in Palestinian textbooks displays, not surprisingly, all the marks of unresolved domestic and international conflicts. At first glance, Palestine appears to be a timeless historical entity. Textbooks for seventh graders tell of a Canaanite myth of a bird who flew away looking for food, but so missed its homeland that it endeavors to return. Lest the symbolism be too subtle for the students, the book asks whether the story can be applied to those in the Palestinian diaspora.[11] Neither Palestine as a political and social entity, nor Palestinians as a people, emerge at any point; they appear to have existed since the beginning of time.

A time line in the books displays the history of Palestine through its various stages, beginning with the Canaanites, whose Arab nature is affirmed throughout, followed by the Pharaonic, Philistine, and Davidic eras. After that, Palestine splits into Judea, Israel, and Phoenicia, with the latter two held by Assyrians later on, but all are eventually reunited in the Babylonian, Persian, Greek, Roman, and Byzantine periods. Perhaps only the omission of the Hasmonean kingdom makes the time line differ from the chronology that might be presented in an Israeli school. Continuing into more modern times, Palestine becomes Muslim under the Rightly Guided Caliphs, the Umayyads, 'Abassids, Franks (i.e., Crusaders), Ayyubids, Mamluks, and Ottomans. Next it falls under the British Mandate, following which it is distributed among Jordan, Egypt, and the state of Israel. The Jordanian and Egyptian zones fall under Israeli occupation after 1967, but Palestine emerges in 1994 with no partner or division indicated—as if it were a political entity and suggesting that at that point

Palestine was suddenly limited to only those limited areas administered by the PNA.

The time line suggests some of the official awkwardness in the geographical conception of Palestine. On deeper examination of the texts, Palestine's time-lessness and current geographical nature become far murkier. If there is any issue that has attracted more international attention, it is the maps in Palestinian textbooks that do not clearly label Israel but mention cities within Israel's pre-1967 borders. The maps omit much more than the borders of Israel, however; they also assume the existence of a Palestinian state often without any borders. The books include many maps, and all present the ambiguous borders of Palestine without addressing the subject directly in the text. Maps of the entire area of Mandatory Palestine, including what is now Israel, are sometimes historical or topographical in order to avoid drawing political boundaries. Israel is not indicated, but often neither are Jordan, Syria, Lebanon, and Egypt. Other maps clearly mark the area of Palestine but also demarcate the West Bank and Gaza with different colors or dotted lines, without explaining what these lines signify. The 1967 lines are sometimes referred to as the "Green Line," which is the Israeli terminology. Sometimes Palestine's provinces are drawn and include only the West Bank and Gaza. One map indicates that Palestinian telephone area codes cover only the West Bank and Gaza. That these area codes straddle the 1967 borders and are shared with Israel goes unmentioned.

Maps indicate cities within the 1967 borders of Israel that have had significant Palestinian populations before and after 1948 (Jaffa, Nazareth, Beersheva, Akka, and Haifa), but the significance is not explained. Are they included because they are the birthplace of many schoolchildren's grandparents or because they still house Palestinians? The accompanying text does not help. When the cities are explicitly mentioned, it is often in connection with the past. In one case, a large picture of Jaffa accompanies a unit devoted to an author from that city who writes of his leaving the city in 1948; in the background of the picture, most of Tel Aviv looms unexplained. In a second-grade text, a family takes a trip to Jaffa, smelling lemons and oranges along the way.[12] This is the Jaffa of the past; current Palestinian drivers entering the city will pass through densely populated suburbs and traffic, and are more likely to smell diesel fumes than citrus odors.

The textbook authors simply fail to explain the Oslo Accords, Palestinian borders, checkpoints, or many other sensitive issues. Perhaps the most puzzling map is of the province of Jenin.[13] It would be difficult to find an area more devoid of Israeli settlements, but there is one and it is omitted from the map. The province is largely surrounded by the 1967 Israeli border, but neither a border nor anything on the far side of the border is indicated. Pre-1967 Israel is terra incognita.

The books bear the marks of unresolved controversies both among Palestinians and with the neighbors of the emerging Palestinian state. The geographical vision of the books implicitly follows commonly used Palestinian political terminology in distinguishing between "historical" Palestine, "natural" Palestine, marked by the borders of the British Mandate era, and "political" Palestine, which has no recognized borders but encompasses all of the territories occupied by Israel in 1967, including East Jerusalem. Although this vision explains much of the geography of the books, it is never made explicit.

Who Are Palestinians?

If the definition of "Palestine" is oblique because of international ambiguities, the definition of "Palestinian" is indirect because of domestic uncertainties. The definition of Palestinian national identity must take into account both internal disagreements and external pressures. The external disputes have proved far easier to resolve than the internal ones.

In grappling with the issue, the Abu Lughod committee settled on a definition of Palestinian identity that included three dimensions.[14] The first related to the homeland, the *watani* dimension; in this aspect, Palestine was defined in both historical and cosmopolitan terms as the land where the three heavenly religions originated, three continents meet, and the Palestinian people built their civilization and cultures, old and new. Casting Palestine in this way was designed to foster appreciation of pluralism and variety while simultaneously developing a spirit of mutual accommodation and belonging. The second dimension was the national, or *qawmi,* facet in which Palestinian identity was given Arab and Islamic aspects, which were credited with historically helping to deepen and preserve Palestinian identity. The third dimension was the international, or *duwali,* aspect, which stressed both Palestine's contributions to the world as well as the world's influence on Palestine. This last dimension was particularly complex, as it included immigration over the ages; the Palestinian discovery of the Western world; Palestinian migration, both voluntary and forced through *al Nakba,* or "the catastrophe," the Palestinian term for the 1948 war; and the existence of a large and far-flung diaspora.

The committee's approach was notable for its decision not to emphasize two aspects of Palestinian identity. First, religion was merely a part of the qawmi dimension, a secular approach to religious identity. Indeed, the committee even considered some radical reform of religious education such as greatly reducing it or switching to an emphasis on comparative religion or ethics rather than religious knowledge. Ultimately religion proved to be too controversial a subject even for the daring Abu Lughod committee to resolve within its year of operation; the committee reported the various ideas but did not propose its own. Second, the committee seemed to take pains to avoid defining Palestinian national identity in terms that would alienate non-Palestinians. Although the report referred to the difficulties Palestinians had experienced, noting in passing that the international setting had both positive and negative impact, the committee stressed connections and linkages, and avoided concentrating on the distinctiveness of Palestinian identity or enmity against other nationalities.

This approach proved too radical for the Ministry of Education, however, which reworked the proposed concept of identity, emphasizing religion in particular. The officially sanctioned plan rejected the options for reforming religious education that were reviewed, but not endorsed, by the Abu Lughod committee and advanced, instead, an explicitly religious approach; the intellectual basis of the entire curriculum was now said to be faith in God.[15] Authoritative structures, such as family, were treated with far greater respect. And while the Abu Lughod committee presented Palestinian identity as consisting of Palestinian, Arab, and international dimensions, the plan devised by the education ministry paid far less attention to the international dimension and designated the Islamic dimension as distinct rather than combined with the Arab dimension.[16]

The books that were finally produced reflect the Ministry of Education's emphasis on religion, family, and national identity. Indeed, most striking about the new books is how the various authoritative components are interlinked: God, nation, homeland, and family all deserve loyalty and obedience. Sixth graders are taught that a "society free from crime" depends on family, school, and other institutions.[17] Lessons concerning proper social behavior intrude on virtually every subject, sometimes supported by Qur'anic verse. First graders studying the Arabic language are taught a story of an honest boy who returns money dropped by a vendor at school; the story is followed with a Qur'anic verse to memorize and additional lessons on the value of cleanliness.[18] Sixth-grade Arabic education begins by warning students that the best gift bestowed by God is the mind but that those who do not use it will turn toward evil and destruction.[19] A sixth-grade science book uses verses from the Qur'an to buttress its teachings on human races and natural forces, such as wind; it adduces a scientific justification for neat and proper behavior, such as sitting up straight.[20] Religion, school, science, and parents all stand in positions of overlapping authority. Even hygiene is linked to religious and family duties.

The Palestinian nation often stands at the center of the structures of authority. Given the opportunity to write a comprehensive curriculum for the first time, the Palestinian educators inserted nationalist symbols in every conceivable location and illustration in the new books. Every school flies a Palestinian flag, homes have pictures of the Dome of the Rock, classrooms exhibit nationalist slogans on blackboards, computers display Palestinian flags, and a school bus carries the name "Palestine School." Jerusalem is mentioned in every possible context, and even children playing soccer wear the jerseys of the Palestinian national team. In language class, a grammatical point is illustrated with a quotation from the 1988 Declaration of Independence. The texts do not merely deliver the message subliminally; they ask children to color the flag, describe their duties toward Jerusalem, and repeat "I am from Palestine" and "my nationality is Palestinian." In learning calligraphy, second-grade students copy the phrase "Jerusalem is in the heart of every Arab."[21] Seventh graders graduate to the rather leading question "Beloved Palestine, How Can I Live Far from your Peaks and Valleys?"[22] The students read nationalist writings when studying Arabic and count Palestinian flags while learning arithmetic. Students do not merely study English; they learn it from books entitled *English for Palestine.*

The textbooks propound a seamless sense of national identity. Religious, territorial, family, and Arab identities are not only complementary but are often coterminous to the point that they might be confused with one another. And they are timeless. According to a second-grade text, Palestine is the "land of fathers and grandfathers." Its first inhabitants were the "Arab Canaanites" who "built a number of cities, including the city of Jerusalem, which they named Yabus."[23]

The implicit sliding among national, state, and religious identity is sometimes made explicit through direct instruction: sixth graders are taught that Islam makes defense of the homeland a religious duty. They are introduced to a series of concentric circles: family, town, province, state, the Islamic world. The same lesson explicitly inculcates that Palestinian, Arab, and Muslim identities are simultaneous and reinforce one another. "Arab and Islamic history" form a single topic.[24] The introduction to the sixth grade text reads: "If the Arabs before Islam were dispersed groups that were not disciplined by any system, they were able to arise by way of the Islamic order, and the Muslim Arabs became leaders in science, culture, and morals."[25] As part of their national education, sixth graders are taught that Islam and the Arabic language unify the Arab homeland, even including Christians who live together with Muslims under the banner of Islam.[26] The textbooks insist on national unity, especially among Muslims and Christians. The importance of tolerance and unity are stressed so insistently that one might suspect that sectarian tensions run quite strong. Tolerance is described not simply as necessary for national unity but also as a religious injunction for both Muslims and Christians.[27] It is not simply sectarian divisions that seem to worry the authors: for all the emphasis on family, students are also instructed that tribalism and familism are undesirable and un-Islamic.[28] But passed over silently are other areas that divide Palestinians— divisions between residents of camps and those in towns, and between those in the West Bank and in Gaza, as well as differences among various political ideologies, and between those in historic Palestine and those in the diaspora.

The Ministry of Education and the textbooks that it produced shy away from a relatively complex and cosmopolitan approach to national identity. In the process, the ministry resolved all domestic fissures by ignoring them or insisting they did not exist.

The international aspects of Palestinian identity proved more difficult for all concerned, and only partially because of Israel. The Abu Lughod committee's approach of emphasizing connections between Palestinians and the rest of the world was rejected, probably because it was too ambiguous to educators writing a curriculum that stressed national identity so strongly. As a result, the texts that emerged tended to pass over Palestine's place in the broader world. Exploring the relationship between Palestinians, on the one hand, and Israel, Zionism, and Jews, on the other, might logically be seen as central to any attempt to educate Palestinians about their past and present. But such topics are treated only at the margin.

Where non-Palestinians (Israelis or otherwise) appear in the text, they do so in ways that sharply distinguish them from Palestinians. Sometimes the contrast is antagonistic: Israelis appear in the book—generally unlabeled but clearly identifiable as Israelis—almost exclusively as soldiers. Non-Israelis are also portrayed in a vague but negative manner. Sixth graders are taught as part of their "national education" that imitating a teacher is good but imitating youth in ways "not appropriate for our genuine Arab culture and our traditions and customs" can be bad—and they are treated to an illustration of two delinquents.[29]

All of these images draw sharp distinctions between Palestinians on the one hand and Israelis and Westerners on the other, but not all non-Palestinians are portrayed negatively. In one book an Israeli settlement, easily identifiable with its red roofs, fence, and Israeli flag, is perched on a hilltop overlooking a Palestinian village: no conflict is implied nor explanation given.[30] Westerners are not always drawn as offensive but also appear as tourists who should be treated warmly and given assistance. With their loud shirts and their cameras dangling from their shoulders, they appear not at all hostile but merely incongruous.

What Is a Palestinian Citizen?

The most subtle and least noticed question the PNA was forced to face in writing the new curriculum was the sort of Palestinian citizenship that should be fostered. Here the Abu Lughod committee developed its most far-reaching proposals, going so far as to call for the abolition of the current curriculum to allow for a new one that served the broader needs of Palestinian individuals and the society as a whole.[31] So rather than ask, "What body of knowledge should students be taught?" the committee essentially posed the question, "What kind of citizen do we want?" Two elements of this new approach appear consistently throughout the Abu Lughod report: first, education must be democratic, although the word "democracy" itself was not always used; and, second, it must foster independent, critical thought. The largely unspoken purpose of this revolution in pedagogy went beyond the needs of individual students to the perceived exigencies of a thoroughly democratic society.

The first innovation was a democratic classroom, which did not mean that students could elect their teachers or textbooks but that they should learn in an atmosphere of freedom, mutual respect, and an acceptance of the relative nature of truth. Teachers should transform themselves from classroom authorities to guides who help students teach themselves and one another. The second pedagogical innovation, an emphasis on critical thought, also grew out of a harsh view of the existing instructional approach in which "the teacher views the learning student as a 'container to be filled.'"[32] The existing curriculum places teachers at the center of the educational process, and its philosophy "relies on the storage of information." This fails to lead to the development of "creative, critical thought"; indeed, the goal of the current curriculum is "not to change but to imitate."[33] In opposition to this traditional curriculum, the report focused its proposed methods "on considering the student the center of the instructional process and on creating students who are lifelong learners."[34] The new curriculum was to

> make manifest **that truth is not absolute or final and that definitive canons do not exist.** Learning cannot take place by giving the students **information** as if it is a collection of **facts** that must be memorized. The curriculum must develop the critical, analytical sense among the students by concentrating on following the scientific method, which focuses fundamentally on **the importance of verification by the accuracy of information and the credibility of sources.** Free, open, unshackled inquiry must take the place of receipt of what the curriculum sets out and arranges. The curriculum must therefore encourage the process of understanding instead of **the development of the ability to memorize . . .** What is important is not obtaining information but how to use it.

> The curriculum must focus as well **on developing independence of thought among the students.** This is what makes the individual able to interact with his environment and surroundings. The individual is the basis of society, and the independence of the individual is the basis of the existence of a vital, active society.[35]

This statement presents what was to be the essence of the new curriculum— the shift from teacher's authority to student's individuality, from absolute to relative truth, from receiving knowledge to discovering it, from uniformity to pluralism, from constituting a dutiful member of society to fostering an active and freethinking citizen.

This image of citizenship proved far too radical for the Ministry of Education. Its curriculum plan abandoned much of the reforming language, rejected the talk of "relative" over "absolute" truth, and scaled back the commitment to individualism, creativity, and critical thought. Its treatment of tradition and the family stated:

> The Palestinian cultural heritage has played a vital role in preserving the Palestinian identity. Bringing tradition into life does not mean using it as seclusion or a shelter; on the contrary, it means providing the young people with principles of understanding their own limits and to what extent they can participate in international culture. The role of the curriculum is deepened to include full and better understanding of tradition and produce a creative thinking ability to preserve and develop it, too.

> The Palestinian family is best known for its unity and perfect welfare of its members. It is very probable that family relationship is the strongest bond that marked the preservation of the unity of the Palestinian society despite the geographical dispersion the Palestinians are subject to. The Palestinian cur-

riculum has taken into consideration the importance of keeping the solidarity and unity of the family and methods of developing the internal relationships that strengthen it.[36]

More directly, "Education is basically built on the principles of breeding the individual on the basis of serving the society as a whole. The ultimate goal of education is to enable the individual to perform his duties successfully."[37] Critical thought and individuality have their place, but the underlying purpose of the curriculum is to transmit and preserve values rather than evaluate or change them.

The members of the Abu Lughod committee were boldly entering a debate that was then gathering momentum among educators in the Arab world regarding the purposes of education. In 2002 the new approach advocated by reformers gained international attention when it was included in the United Nations Development Program's *Arab Human Development Report*. That report called for "a new education structure that puts humanity at the centre of the cultural process." It identified a series of principles that would have been familiar to any reader of the earlier Abu Lughod committee report: "The individual should be central to the learning process"; "Without denigrating higher values and established creeds, intellectual and cultural heritage should not be immune to criticism and change in the face of scientific evidence. Dialogue should be valued as an indispensable process, one that is as likely to end in agreement as in creative disagreement. Creative human effort lies at the heart of progress. Arab education systems should be restructured to give precedence to creativity and the dignity of productive work"; "Education should help the young to cope with a future of uncertainty, acquire flexibility in the face of uncertainty and contribute to shaping the future."[38] In 2003 the second Arab Human Development Report went into further detail:

> Some researchers argue that the curricula taught in Arab countries seem to encourage submission, obedience, subordination and compliance, rather than free critical thinking. In many cases, the contents of these curricula do not stimulate students to criticise political or social axioms. Instead, they smother their independent tendencies and creativity.[39]

The Abu Lughod committee released its report before the topic had generated such international concern. There was little interest in the project, except in Palestine. More important, there were few specific models on which to draw. The emphasis on individuality and a critical approach to tradition proved too daring for many of those actually involved in writing the books. Thus, when some of the textbooks were finally issued, beginning in 2000, they reflected the older insistence on transmission of authority while acknowledging the newer stress on independent thinking. Most texts generally emphasize authority, while the pedagogy encouraged by the new books makes notable forays in cultivating individualism and critical thought. Although the approach of the Abu Lughod committee is subordinated, it has not been abandoned totally.

Regarding content, the books reiterate the message of obedience to parents and connect it to national and political loyalties. First graders are taught in Islamic Education:

> I love my mother who bore me, and I obey her / I love my mother who nursed me, and I obey her / I love my mother who teaches me, and I obey her.
>
> I love my father who provides for me, and I obey him, / I love my father who teaches me, and I obey him, / I love my mother and my father, and I obey them.[40]

Even so, the texts often make concessions to a far more active pedagogy that moderates much of the stress on authority. Most often, the new attitude is expressed indirectly; the texts make a tremendous effort to engage students actively and consider practical applications and further thought. The books pepper their lessons with outside activities, essays, questions for reflection and study, and encouragement of critical thinking. Seventh graders, for instance, are asked to bring in a newspaper story that has a point of view different from their own, and it is suggested that they collect two articles on the same subject from different newspapers to compare them.[41] Seventh graders also study civil society by examining local organizations. They begin studying democracy in a family setting, in which women have a voice and differences are settled through dialogue. Students are even told of human rights organizations but without mentioning the PNA's strained relations with them.[42]

Far more daringly, the books occasionally push students to engage in critical thought when dealing with difficult and sensitive topics. Sixth graders are asked to evaluate the policies used by Mu'awiyya, the fifth caliph and founder of the Umayyad dynasty, in solidifying his authority and building his state. They are then asked to consider the hereditary method for selecting rulers, an assignment that is likely to lead some students to question early Muslim and current Arab political practice in certain countries.[43] Sixth graders are also asked to confront the situation in which parents instruct their children to do something wrong. The problem is addressed in a book by Salih, a righteous Muslim who instructs his family on religious matters each day after evening prayers. He explains that children are required to obey their parents except in such circumstances. This lesson is followed by a discussion of the rights of children in Islam and an invitation for students to give their opinions on some difficult situations, in which, for example, a father forbids his son from continuing his studies or his daughter from playing sports because she is a girl.[44] More broadly, the books impart varied messages on gender, many clearly inspired by the progressive desire to question traditional roles. Eighth graders being instructed in civic education are told to "choose a case of family violence from a story we heard, read about, or lived," and then "select a judge, a prosecuting attorney, a defense attorney, and a jury" in order to hold a fair trial.[45] They are to consider whether a woman prevented from working outside the house by her husband is a victim of violence.[46] Students are also told to write three clauses for a draft Palestinian family law.[47]

The process of writing the curriculum involved assigning different subjects to discrete teams. Thus some of the differing approaches were debated among different subject teams. Civic education books are the most daring and provocative in adopting critical pedagogy. Religion is generally the last frontier for the newer approaches—those responsible for teaching students Islam show little enthusiasm for individuality and creativity among elementary- and intermediate-school students, although they are not entirely free from the influence of the newer approaches.

Occasionally the advocates of different approaches to the curriculum debated one another.[48] Yet in an odd way, the conditions of the second intifada encouraged experimentation and diversity, as it was difficult for the various teams to meet, much less communicate with other teams. Education ministry officials overseeing the process allowed the teams free rein in that period.

Conclusion

Much of the writing on textbooks—especially, but not exclusively, that which is aimed at non-scholarly audiences—posits them as authoritative voices, produced by states working to inculcate a specific image of national identity. Yet the importance attached to textbooks, although probably exaggerated, ensures that they will not only be instruments of instruction but also objects of controversy. That has certainly been the dual position of Palestinian education, as both international and domestic actors have hotly debated what the textbooks should say and how they should say it.

On the issue that has drawn the most international attention, namely, the treatment of Israel and Jews, the PNA textbooks are more remarkable for their omissions than for their content. Palestinian schools do not teach hate through their books, but they cannot teach children how to accomplish what has eluded adults, which is to resolve the issues that have bedeviled Palestinians since before 1948.

Still remaining, as well, are the contentious issues that arose in the attempt to write the first Palestinian curriculum: exactly how Palestine, Palestinians, and Palestinian citizenship are to be defined. An attempt to use the educational system to develop a cosmopolitan and complex sense of national identity has been deflected, at least for now, by those who feel that national identity is far too essential to Palestinian survival to subject it to experimentation. The textbooks that the PNA finally produced show dedication to the principle that national identity depends on loyalty to authority and that different sources of authority—family, locality, nation, religion, and humanity—are not merely harmonious but almost identical.

NOTES

1. Rashid Khalidi, *Palestinian Identity: The Construction of Modern National Consciousness* (New York, 1997), 205.

2. I refer to the body as the "Abu Lughod committee" to distinguish it from the "Curriculum Development Center" later established by the Palestinian Ministry of Education to write the new textbooks. The late Abu Lughod himself objected to my terminology in a personal communication, but I have persisted in using it to avoid confusion between the two very different but identically named bodies.

3. The bulk of this information comes from the Abu Lughod committee report, "A Comprehensive Plan for the Development of the First Palestinian Curriculum for General Education" (Ramallah, 1997). I also conducted interviews with Ibrahim Abu Lughod in October 1999 and 'Ali Jarbawi, a member of the committee, in January 2000.

4. General Administration of Curricula (Palestinian Curriculum Development Center), *First Palestinian Curriculum Plan* (Jerusalem, 1998).

5. I have written elsewhere of this controversy. See Nathan Brown, *Palestinian Politics since the Oslo Accords: Resuming Arab Palestine* (Berkeley, 2003).

6. 'Ali Jarbawi, personal interview, January 2000.

7. Dalal Salama, Palestinian Legislative Council (PLC) deputy, personal interview, February 2000.

8. *National Education* (1995), Grade 3, 31.

9. *National Education* (1995) Grade 6, 20.

10. In a PLC session that I attended in 1999, a deputy sarcastically quoted the sentence about the Palestinian coast.

11. *National Education* (2001), Grade 7, 7.

12. *Our Beautiful Language,* Grade 2, 60–61.

13. *Principles of Human Geography,* Grade 6, 48.

14. *Comprehensive Plan,* especially the section entitled "The Basic Elements, Philosophy, and General Educational Goals of the Palestinian Curriculum," 61–67.

15. *First Palestinian Curriculum Plan,* 7.

16. Ibid., 26.

17. *Civic Education,* Grade 6, Unit IV.

18. *Our Beautiful Language,* Grade 1, part 2, unit 6.

19. *Our Beautiful Language,* Grade 6, part 1, 4.

20. *General Science,* Grade 6, part 1, 10–11.

21. *Arabic Writing,* Grade 2, 22.

22. *Arabic Writing,* Grade 7, 4.

23. *National Education* (2001), Grade 2, part 1, 4–5.

24. *Islamic Education,* Grade 6, part 1, 66–69.

25. *Arab and Islamic History,* Grade 6, introduction.

26. *National Education* (2000), Grade 6, unit I, part 1.

27. Ibid., Grade 6, Unit III, "Tolerance" section.

28. Ibid., "Values" section.

29. Ibid., "Imitation and Creativity" section.

30. The illustration is in *Our Beautiful Language,* Grade 1, part 2.

31. See, for instance, *Comprehensive Plan,* 59–60.

32. Ibid., 35.

33. Ibid., 53–54.

34. Ibid., 104.

35. Ibid., 455–456 (emphasis in original).

36. *First Palestinian Curriculum Plan,* 8.

37. Ibid., 9–10.

38. United Nations Development Program (UNDP), "Arab Human Development Report 2002," chapter 4 (2002), http://www.undorg/rbas/ahdr/Chapter4.pdf.

39. UNDP, "Arab Human Development Report 2003" (2003), 53, http://www.miftah .org/Display.cfm?DocId=2603&CategoryId=8.

40. *Islamic Education,* Grade 1, part 1, 39.

41. See the unit on the media, in *Civic Education,* Grade 7.

42. *Civic Education,* Grade 7, 46, mentions al-Haqq and the Palestinian Independent Commission for Citizens' Rights.

43. *Arab and Islamic History,* Grade 6, unit on "The Umayyad Caliphate."

44. *Islamic Education,* Grade 6, 45–61.

45. *Civic Education,* Grade 8, 58.

46. Ibid., 46.

47. Ibid., 59.

48. See, for instance, Al-Buraq Center for Research and Culture, "Proceedings of a Workshop Concerning the Curriculum for Civic Education for the Eight Elementary Grade in Palestinian Schools," unpub. (Ramallah, May 24, 2003).

11

THE DYNAMICS OF IDENTITY CONSTRUCTION IN ISRAEL THROUGH EDUCATION IN HISTORY

EYAL NAVEH

History Education and Public Discontent: The Uproar over Schools' Textbooks

In late 2003 Israeli Prime Minister Ariel Sharon was deeply troubled. His bodyguards—young Israelis who graduated from the Israeli public school system—demonstrated complete ignorance of their national heritage. They did not know basic facts about the history of their society, could not recognize the major historical figures or events in Israel's history, and were oblivious to the heroic and tragic past of the Jewish nation. Sharon expressed his dismay to the minister of education, who passed the message on to the history inspector. As far as this author knows, no real measures have been taken to improve the historical literacy of young Israelis. Yet the reaction of the prime minister, the minister of education, and many other concerned public figures is typical and has been repeated regularly in the last decade. "Soldiers don't know who David Ben-Gurion was," exclaimed a headline in *Ma'ariv* in 2000, in the wake of a survey carried out in dozens of units of the Israel Defense Forces (IDF). "They don't know the words to the national anthem, 'Hatikvah,' they don't know when the Lebanon War began."[1]

Ignorance and apathy indicate a weakening of Zionist consciousness among the younger generation, graduates of the secular public school system. This trend bothers many Israeli officials, who defined this phenomenon as an identity crisis and envision the future in apocalyptic terms. They see the young generation as deracinated—drifting away from its rightful place, cutting itself off from its national identity and its historic and cultural roots. After all, beyond achieving political sovereignty, the aim of Zionism has always been to foster a

responsible citizenry with a sense of collective identity, committed to building
an outstanding model society, modern and just. Yet, barely fifty years later, sovereignty is taken for granted, but the unique and idiosyncratic Zionist identity
is rejected as pertaining to an earlier age.

Israeli youth are indeed showing a tendency to adopt alternative identities.
Many of them are captivated by an individualistic, post-nationalist, and global
identity that may express itself in journeys of self-discovery to India and South
America or in a yearning to join the Western "global village" in London, New
York, or Silicon Valley. This identity worships at the shrine of self-fulfillment,
personal comfort, and material success, and scorns the values of social solidarity and the sense of mission and collective achievement that characterized
previous generations. Other young people, in contrast, long for an essentially
Jewish tribal identity rooted in the holy land, the tombs of the righteous, and
the yeshivas. This identity reveres the Torah, the Messianic vision, and the ut-
terances of venerated rabbis, and scoffs at the values of Western enlightenment
and the modern achievements that were a beacon for practical Zionism. Some
of these young people combine religious Messianic faith with radical nationalism, appropriating for themselves the flag of Zionist fulfillment—to the great
annoyance of veteran Zionists, humanists, and secularists, who protest this
trend as a distortion of Zionism's original goals. The future identity of Israeli
society worries many people, who, lacking any other clear redress, charge the
educational system with both the responsibility for the younger generation's
decline and the duty to remedy it.

Accordingly, in 2001, Minister of Education Limor Livnat announced that,
beginning with the 2001–2002 school year, the curriculum for all mainstream
public high schools would include a new subject, "Heritage." Concurrently the
education minister took an unprecedented step and ordered the withdrawal of
a ninth-grade history textbook, *A World of Changes,* published by the education ministry.[2] This extreme move, in fact, represented the adoption of the
recommendations made by a committee of experts that had been appointed
by the Knesset Education Committee, which had unanimously decided that
the textbook should not be introduced until numerous distortions in the text
were corrected.[3] The Knesset Education Committee met to discuss the book in
late 2000, in response to efforts spearheaded by Yoram Hazony, then the director of Shalem Center, a neo-conservative think tank. Shalem Center researchers demonstrated for the benefit of public figures, academics, professors, and
teachers, that this textbook on twentieth-century history was rife with errors, devalued the national heritage, and presented a distorted picture of Jewish

and Zionist history that included a negative, unbalanced perspective on the achievements and struggles of the state of Israel.[4] The book was sparsely distributed throughout the educational system, since a majority of history teachers had decided to give preference to two other books, *Journey to the Past* and *The Twentieth Century.*[5]

Just a year earlier, however, *The Twentieth Century* had appeared on the agenda of the Knesset Education Committee, placed there at the initiative of a right-wing group who wanted the book's distribution postponed until certain corrections were made. The attempt to enlist the support of the Knesset Education Committee came after the failure of an advertising campaign intended to persuade parents and teachers not to buy the book or use it to teach.[6] But when the committee members met in late 1999, their opinions were divided.[7] Moreover, Yossi Sarid, the education minister at the time (from the liberal, left-of-center Meretz party), expressed his total support for the book and warned that he would reject any demand to re-examine and revise its contents.

These incidents exemplify the stormy conflict that has raged for at least the last decade over the place of history in Israel's education curriculum. Short-term political motives, understandably, have played a significant role in the course and immediate results of the public debate; from a longer-term perspective, however, the controversy reflects a genuine effort by Israeli society to accept the changes it is undergoing and to resolve questions about its future identity.

Israel's population is a constellation of ever changing nationalities, ethnicities, and communities, and is, in fact, multicultural. Recounting the history of this dynamic nation of immigrants requires communication between individuals and groups with different stories of their past and present, different dreams and hopes for the future. A plurality of views and a multitude of identities and group memories are characteristic of human experience in general and of a changing society in particular. But many people see this vast array of stories, which reinforces the trend of multiple identities, as a factor accelerating the disintegration and fragmentation of society. It undermines the unique common historical narrative that was designed to create a collective national identity.

The argument that a collective identity is needed to unify the nation in the face of domestic and especially external threats has characterized Israeli society throughout its entire existence. The memory of a mythic past encompassing not only courage and heroism but also harsher themes of destruction and disaster has also left its imprint on the way Israelis engage with history. Although the debate about history naturally concerns past events, it also focuses on the relevance of those events to what is happening today, and on the consequences of those events for the future. The controversy over how history is to be taught in the schools regularly spurs wrestling matches between conflicting political identities. But it also exposes a rich repertoire of varying opinions on historical knowledge, the means of disseminating it, its value, and its educational and ideological roles.

The debate over teaching history in the Israeli educational system reflects the various approaches toward the discipline of history in general and toward history education in particular that are being discussed throughout the Western world. Should Israel's schools focus on inculcating heritage and collective memory? Should they take an academic approach in an effort to uncover historical truths through critical investigation? Should they incorporate postmodern arguments that challenge the very pretension of historical objectivity, substituting narratives, discourses, and representations of the past for real events and facts?[8]

These questions have generated public debates over the teaching of history in countries around the world, particularly in societies that are breaking away from a collective, monolithic heritage and adopting patterns of identity associated with multiple and occasionally conflicting stories of the past. The authority of the national heritage is also typically challenged by groups and sectors that question the very necessity of enlisting the past for purposes of legitimacy. Thus debates over the teaching of history are especially common in Western democracies where these arguments are encouraged as an expression of freedom of speech, and where changing perspectives and proliferating narratives are welcome.

In contrast to Western democracies that enjoy stability and security on their own soil, Israeli society continues to be embroiled in a regional conflict that, according to many official spokespersons, threatens its very existence. Its continuing struggle against this external threat, accompanied by profound internal dissension, considerably influences the ways that Israelis deal with societal rifts and is a notable factor in the controversy surrounding the teaching of history. Thus, the debate goes far beyond professional disagreements between teachers, educators, and others in the field. It reflects differing views on the state's role as educator and the extent to which it has a duty to construct a national identity.

This public dispute also reflects the transitional character of Israeli society over the last years. Many signs indicate that Israeli society is breaking away from the monolithic memory instilled by the canonical Jewish-Zionist narrative, yet no other narrative has been created to replace it nor is likely to be. To many, a transitional stage of this nature is a crisis that casts serious doubt on Israel's future as a democratic Jewish state. Many are convinced that the inculcation of a collective, unifying historical heritage remains an essential weapon against enemies of the state and an important source of relief and healing for internal schisms. The present is seen as a dangerous crossroads, a confusing time that easily engenders despair; it represents a dissipation of illusions, a kind of intermission between the disappointed hopes of the past and a future shrouded in obscurity. This existential situation carries with it much uncertainty and unease, deep anxiety, and mental fatigue, all of which infuse passion and anger into the debates over history in Israeli schools.

The Effort to Create a Monolithic National Identity in Israel

The current malaise contradicts the Zionist project of national Jewish renewal through the creation of a new Israeli identity. The reconstruction of collective memory through teaching history was indeed a conscious attempt practiced by the Zionist leadership prior to the formal creation of the state. Nation building constituted a major educational and cultural activity during the 1920s, 1930s, and 1940s. It created a unique paradigm of education, directed to the youth of the Yishuv (Jewish society in Palestine prior to the creation of the state). On the eve of independence, about 600,000 Jews constituted the population of Israel. Most of them were immigrants from east and central Europe, as well as descendants of European Jews. During the first decade of Israel's existence the population tripled, absorbing Jews from the Arab world as well as Holocaust survivors. Within one decade, Israeli society was transformed into a multiethnic conglomeration, with enormous diversity in its culture, heritage, values, beliefs, and behavior.

Faced with this diversity, the state of Israel championed the principle of the "melting pot" for the first two decades of its existence, an idea validated by a monolithic ideological vision that demanded unity and uniformity. The melting pot ideology was in fact a one-way street. New immigrants had to blend into the existing Israeli identity. At the heart of this ethos was the image of the "new Jew"—the trailblazer of the Zionist movement. The Israeli archetype, the sabra, was idolized as a new person, brave and proud, muscular and tanned, handsome and authentic, close to the land, hardworking, modern, and efficient, willing to sacrifice for his country, without the fears that supposedly characterized the Jewish identity in exile.

As Oz wrote:

> The Zionist revolution aspired not only to obtain a bit of land and tools of statehood for the Jews, but also—perhaps mainly—to upend the spiritual pyramid as well as the economic one. To change the norms, create a new ideal, new focuses of solidarity and a new scale of desires. . . . Pioneering involved sacrifice and repression. People were forced to choke back "forbidden" nostalgia for the landscapes of their childhood, for the cultures in which they had lived, for longed-for realms, for a softer climate, for good manners, for big cities. . . . Everyone agreed to undergo metamorphosis and be a new person, no longer a Jew but a Hebrew, tanned, strong, and brave, free of complexes and Jewish neuroses, a person who loved to labor and loved the soil.[9]

The denigration of the diaspora was the leading ethos of the new Israeli identity, counterbalancing the revived "new Israeli sabra" against the "diasporic other."[10] This identity transformation actually contradicted the social reality of the Israeli population in the 1950s and 1960s, which in fact comprised a mosaic of many "others," yet lacked the cultural legitimacy of such diversity. To implement the revolutionary act that Zionism implied, it was apparently impossible to define the Zionist identity of the "new Jew" without rejecting the "old Jew" of the diaspora. Indeed, this rejection gradually became entrenched as a pattern of identity construction.

In fact, the survivors of the European Holocaust were received with mixed emotions; traditional diasporic rejection was tempered with feelings of guilt and attributions of blame. At the same time, some of the impulse to reject the diaspora was carried by the Jewish immigrants from Arab countries whose traditional customs, clan or ethnic identities, and cultural affinities to Islam were alien to the Zionist ethos of the "new Jew." Thus, the shaping of the new collective identity of the new Israeli in its sovereign state was automatically linked to the definition of three distinct types of the "other": the familiar diaspora "other"—an image inspired, paradoxically, by anti-Semitic stereotypes, and perceived as a significant old-fashioned contrast from which the new Jew had to be emancipated; the unknown oriental Jewish "other," who had to be educated and integrated; and the Arab "other," who was seen as both inferior and hostile.[11] These three "others" manifested by their very existence the still unfinished Zionist project of building and shaping a new Israeli character. They served to strengthen the stereotype that eventually had to disappear by the time identity construction was deemed to be complete.

The denigration of the diaspora was folded into the historical meta-narrative of the Zionist movement—the story of returning from exile to sovereignty. Prime Minister David Ben-Gurion, the unchallenged Zionist leader, expressed this narrative in his public speeches and writing. According to that narrative, the creation of the state of Israel was both a renewal of the glorious past and the necessary stage toward a messianic vision. The new Israeli society was linked by a sort of eschatological jump from the prophets and warriors of ancient times, particularly the second temple period, to the redemption of the future. As such, the founders internalized that they were the collective inheritance of ancient Hebrews, who, after almost 2,000 years of exile, had returned to "history" to take full responsibility for their destiny within a redemptive nation.

In order to cope with the paradox of a new beginning that is the natural outcome of an ancient past, aimed at a redemptive future, Israeli culture had to re-create a particular imagined community. Young Israelis were to view themselves as the offspring of biblical and ancient figures, such as Jehoshua conquering the land from the Canaanites, David triumphing over Goliath, the Jewish Maccabees rebelling against the Greek-Syrians, the Zealots on the walls of Jerusalem, the martyrs of Masada, and the warriors of Bar-Kochba fighting the Roman Empire. The struggle against the British Empire, the uprising of Jews in Warsaw against the Nazis, and, above all, the fight with the Arabs in 1948 were perceived as other struggles, meaningful and inspirational within this historical meta-narrative.[12]

This narrative was nourished by a model of Jewish identity, familiar both in ancient history and in the diaspora period. The Jew was the weak and righteous victim pitted against the big, strong, evil-intentioned *goy*. That plot was always based on binary contrasts—a war of the "sons of light" against the "sons of darkness." The specific enemy is conditional—Egyptians, Babylonians, Persians, Greek-Syrians, and Romans in ancient times; pagan, Christian, and Muslim anti-Semites during the diaspora; British Mandate leaders, Nazis, Arabs, and Soviets in modern times—but the enemy's potential existence is permanent. Only a war for national sovereign existence could solve the existential problem of the Jewish people; even after the establishment of the state, the mythological battle continued against another strong evil, the hostile Arab world that encircled the little state of Israel with murderous intent.

The power of the paradigm of returning from exile to sovereignty lay in the idea that history could be manipulated and changed. This demanded the formation of an active, task-oriented Israeli reality, the opposite of diasporic existence, which was supposedly driven by *force majeure*, giving Jews no control over their fate. The new Israeli identity demanded that citizens be alert, results-oriented, and fully aware of their historical burdens and current responsibilities. Indeed, after the establishment of the state, Ben-Gurion jettisoned the history of the diaspora and ignored the fact that Zionism had developed in Europe as a modern secular movement. His messianic vision focused on the formation of a consciousness of place, a yearning for a long-familiar place to which return was the beginning of redemption; hence the shortcut linking the distant past with the present, and emphasizing Zionism's direct connection with the holy territory of Eretz Israel (the Land of Israel). Through the dream of redemption, Ben-Gurion thought he could more easily bring the masses of traditional Jewish immigrants from oriental countries into the Israeli reality of the 1950s. In the eyes of these immigrants, they arrived in Israel not because of modern Zionist or socialist views but to fulfill a centuries-old messianic vision.[13]

Many Faces, Common Fate, One Soul:
The Creation of an Ethnocentric History Curriculum

These ideas were transferred in various ways into the educational system and the history curriculum. The choice of study topics, the organization of eras in the historical account, the emphasis on certain periods and events, the building of a distinct historical process, and even the tone of the discourse constructed the paradigm of returning from exile to sovereignty. The same theme was served at the experiential and emotional levels by the development of school ceremonies, participation in state functions, pilgrimages to monuments and memorials, and the choreography of holidays. These practices linked education to the task of identity construction.

The "returning from exile to sovereignty" meta-narrative had been incorporated in the first history core curriculum of 1954 and was perceived as a unifying, systematic, and formal body of knowledge that young people should know. But this unifying national system excluded the ultra-Orthodox Jews, who refused to accept state authority, and also overlooked the Arab population. When translated from a vague historical sentiment into a formal national history curriculum, it was applied primarily to the secular and religious Zionist section of the Jewish population.

Ben-Zion Dinur, a prominent historian and the second minister of education, provided guidelines for the national curriculum. His spirit loomed over the program and determined its content. He considered himself, and was perceived by others, as the national historian of the new state and, like Ben-Gurion, he enforced the ethnocentric paradigm. Indeed, the first goal of the core curriculum was to strengthen the national identity of Israeli children. The elementary school curriculum published in 1954 stated that the teaching of history had to "instill in children love for the state of Israel and a desire to act for its benefit and to safeguard its existence." Its main objective was "to impart to pupils knowledge of the great past of the Jewish people—its spiritual heritage, its deeds and its vision, as well as knowledge about the peoples who have come into contact with the Jewish people, and their mutual influence."[14] The same spirit was expressed in the goal of the supplementary program for secondary school: "To implant national awareness in the hearts of young people, to strengthen in them the sense of sharing the Jewish destiny, to instill in them a love for the Jewish people."[15]

The development of world history and human civilization were marginalized in the history program; instead, curriculum designers filled the syllabus with important and unique events in the history of regimes and economies under which Jews had lived and worked for generations. As a result, entire geographical regions, societies, and peoples disappeared from the historical stage altogether. The curriculum and textbooks stressed the Zionist narrative, which became the core of the historical account of the Jewish nation. According to this narrative, the Jewish nation had begun its journey in the ancient land of Israel, where it had first become a people and an independent political entity, and to which it returned after many, many years of exile to take up where it had left off. It was the return to the land of Israel—the Jewish people's sole, eternal heart's desire—that invested this historical narrative with significance and determined its emphases.

Meanwhile, the primary purpose of world history courses was to explain the context of the yearning for Zionist renewal, and a considerable portion of the syllabus was devoted to the European Jewish community—the cradle of the Zionist movement. In selecting Jewish history topics, curriculum designers focused on increasing pupils' knowledge of the culture of European Jews and the peoples among whom they lived. The 1954 curriculum included lessons on fifty-three subtopics concerning the period preceding the establishment of the state, fourteen of them pertaining to world history (about 26 percent). The remaining thirty-nine topics were devoted to Jewish history (approximately 74 percent) and mostly involved descriptions of diasporic life and its negative aspects, so that Zionism would be seen as a unique historical imperative. Oriental Jews barely appeared in the curriculum, as their communities had not had much to do with the Zionist movement and their culture was perceived by European Jews as vulgar, religious, and inferior, unsuited to a school curriculum with a modern secular orientation.[16]

The first history core curriculum of 1954 was trapped in ethnocentricity. Nevertheless, because those who wrote the curriculum were broad-minded historians, they sought to integrate Zionism and Jewish nationalism into universal values and existentialist views. Thus, both the core curriculum and textbooks presented the establishment of the Jewish state as a fulfillment of the Western vision of enlightenment. The alleged duality of the national-Jewish element and the universal element was portrayed as a problem linked to the anomaly of the diaspora, a problem that was eliminated by the establishment of the nation-state and the disposition of the Jewish people within the family of nations. In this view, even describing the model high school graduate as an active young fighter and settler did not conflict with teaching personal autonomy, as the creation of the individual in the service of the nation was perceived as the highest form of individual fulfillment.

Although the history curriculum was designed primarily to create a new cognitive and rational identity, a patriotic calendar of ceremonies, remembrance days, and holidays was incorporated in the daily school routine to foster emotional identity. Many scholars argue that the pedagogical effectiveness of the festive and memorial events was immeasurably greater than anything achieved in history classes. The school ceremonies supported the unification of the historical narrative, and emphasized the establishment of the state of Israel as a necessary step for survival as well as redemption. The content of national holidays focused on the theme of prolonged struggle in the familiar pattern of the virtuous few outnumbered by powerful villains: at Hannukah, Greeks against Maccabees; at Purim, the evil Haman against Mordechai and Esther; at Passover, Pharaoh against Moses and the children of Israel who fled slavery for freedom; on Holocaust Remembrance Day, the Nazis against the ghetto rebels; on Memorial Day and Independence Day, the multitudinous Arab armies against the 1948 fighters. All of these associations created an artificial narrative consisting primarily of the creation of an "alternative messianic time."[17] Thus the War of Independence was perceived as settling an old score, and the fighters of the 1948 generation were seen as the scions of the Maccabees.

The institution of the patriotic calendar and schoolchildren's visits to monuments and memorials to heroism were an integral part of the educational activity, designed to establish the desired cultural code. The places to which schools and Zionist youth movements made pilgrimages—for example, the wrecks of armored cars at Sha'ar Hagai (on the road to Jerusalem), a Syrian tank at Degania, a roaring lion at Tel-Hai (upper Galilee), the bullet-riddled water towers in Negba and Yad Mordechai (in the Negev)—were all encircled with a symbolic aura in the public consciousness and became icons of both the myth of the place and the myth of the heroic deed. Trips to monuments throughout the country reinforced an awareness of the connection between the national territory and the mythical past as well as the recent Zionist era.[18] These ritual trips, in conjunction with the history curriculum, gradually unified the historical narrative as a founding myth of the new state of Israel and a necessary source of constructing its national identity.

In this tight cognitive-emotional structure, Holocaust remembrance obviously assumed a unique but problematic place. The ambivalent attitude of Israeli society to the survivors of the Holocaust affected the way Holocaust remembrance was incorporated in the educational system. The Holocaust was not studied at all in secondary schools as a history subject until the end of the 1960s, and, in elementary schools, only a few classroom lessons were devoted to the subject in the framework of Holocaust Remembrance Day events. Yet the Holocaust was present in daily life, political rhetoric, and state ceremonies, and the use of Holocaust remembrance symbols became a major component in the construction of Israeli collective memory. The Holocaust had become a prime justification for the state both domestically and in the eyes of the international community. The lesson that Zionism drew from the Holocaust demanded that Israeli youth take an active part in the redemption of their people, thereby avenging, remembering, memorializing, and providing consolation for a people that had arisen anew from the ruins of its life.[19]

These ideas, forged in the spirit of the times, were at the center of the school ceremonies that instilled Holocaust memory through sacred ritual. But, lacking the distance in time needed for analytical examination, the only possible way to cope with that era was at the emotional level, and even that was partial and problematic. Israelis' response to the Holocaust was a mixture of deep shock at the dimensions of the catastrophe, self-reproach over the paucity of international aid extended to the Jews of Europe, and anger rooted in rejection by the diaspora. This anger increased with the experience of crisis and loss, and was expressed in feelings of superiority toward the refugee Holocaust survivors as well as toward those who ignored the call to emigrate to Palestine and went, supposedly, "like sheep to the slaughter."[20]

In describing the way that the state of Israel dealt with the Holocaust, Shapira defined the 1950s as years of silencing personal memory. The Holocaust was tolerable as a public memory but difficult to bear as a private memory.[21] This remote silence was further amplified by the Holocaust survivors themselves, who, in their tortured yearning to fit into and belong to Israeli society, imposed upon themselves a mute restraint: "Everything that happened to us in the long war years," testified Appelfeld,

> was curled within us silent and blind: a mysterious oppressive lump that had no connection with consciousness. . . . The questions that came from outside did not help. They were questions reflecting an abysmal lack of understanding, questions from that world that had nothing to do with the world from which we had come. . . . And so we learned to be quiet. . . . [I]n that quiet there was, of course, not only the impossibility of translating the traumatic sights into everyday language. There was a desire here to forget, to bury the bitter memories deep in the bottom of the soul. A place where no alien eye, not even your own, will be able to reach them. The horrors of war did not bring us to ourselves, nor to the tradition of our forefathers. If ever a desire arose within us, it was a desire to run away from ourselves, from everything that sounded Jewish . . . We wanted to be different, not ourselves, not our recent past.[22]

The familiar contrast between the passive Jews of the diaspora and the active Zionist pioneers led Israeli society to commemorate the individuals with whom it could readily relate: the partisans who fought against the Nazis, and especially the fighters of the Warsaw ghetto uprising. The leaders of the uprising, identified with the fighters of Masada, the defenders of Tel Hai, and the soldiers of the War of Independence—the main heroes of school memorial ceremonies. In this way, even the memory of the Holocaust was melted and molded in the crucible of the concepts and symbols that governed the lives of Israeli children during the 1950s and 1960s.

Seeds of Change: From Uniformity to the Necessity of Pluralism, the 1970s and 1980s

Although it is difficult to plot dynamic processes with any accuracy, it is probably correct to say that the period from the war of 1967 (the Six Day War) to the war of 1973 (the Yom Kippur War) was a watershed between the era of the 1950s and 1960s and the following decades. The main change was a gradual disengagement from unification under the authority of the state as educator and a growing awareness of pluralism not yet as an alternative value but as a fact of life stronger than any ideology. As decades proceeded, more and more voices claimed that the idea of unification had taken the form of a hegemonic discourse creating the illusion of a monolithic society. Under the smooth surface of that society, however, disparate voices whispered, neither speaking with one another nor finding expression or legimation in the main discourse. The apparent image of a uniform Israeli society hid an unstable pluralism, creating temporary solutions for the coexistence of internal contrasts and unresolved contradictions. Thus the new processes shaped a climate that blew away the cover of uniformity, liberating the muffled voices of pluralism and, ultimately, penetrating the educational system as well.

The ability of the large, complex edifice of the educational system to internalize and react to new trends was expected to be limited and slow, especially in the hyper-dynamic reality of Israeli society, but by the early 1960s, the uniform curriculum instituted by Dinur came under criticism. Lamm, one of the prominent opponents of the state ideology, argued that the unified state educational system was unable to respond to the needs of a heterogeneous population. He warned against allowing the process of unification in the educational system to become oppressive and prevent alternative voices from being heard.[23] Support for cultural pluralism grew stronger along with such warnings, as Aharon Yadlin, later appointed education minister, remarked: "Fostering ways of thinking does not have to be at the expense of a sudden abandonment of the values of cultural and community heritage."[24]

Increasing calls for a reassessment of the educational system were linked to the advent of systematic thinking about the field of education and derived from the initiatives of university education departments involved in independent research. In 1966 a curriculum center was set up in the education ministry, inspired and directed by Benjamin S. Bloom of the University of Chicago. Underlying the new approach was the recognition that, because society and its needs were constantly changing, the educational system required a wide margin of flexibility and as many procedures for updating as possible. Curriculum development was defined as an act of design, experimentation, and follow-up, based on the structure of the discipline being learned and on the students' psychological and mental needs. Putting theory into practice, the new curricula reflected a clear trend toward raising achievement levels, as it abandoned the old focus on mission and ideology.[25]

In 1975 the curriculum division in the education ministry published a new core curriculum for history that differed pedagogically from the existing one in a number of essential ways. The focus of instruction was no longer teachers inculcating the state's positions as dictated to them but rather the concept of history as "the whole of human experience . . . being inherently a selective examination."[26] The methodological assumptions of the core curriculum concerning the problems of historical study and the relative truth that it represented also guided the writing of new textbooks, which tended to encourage independent study by developing varied sources.

The 1975 history curriculum played down the old ethnocentric emphasis and expanded the number of chapters devoted to world history. The curriculum, and the textbooks written for it, lessened the overtones of the triumphant Zionist narrative and decreased its ideological bias. However, the traditional idea of returning from exile to sovereignty was preserved. The weakening of the ideological and mission-oriented focus, together with a new emphasis on subject matter and new insights into the methods of teaching as well as the nature of the discipline of history, indicated that the designers of the 1975 curriculum were responding to the changes that had occurred in Israeli society. Yet the monolithic worldview relaxed its grip mainly on the level of intentions and declarations. The actual content of the 1975 curriculum preserved the Zionist ethos of the "new Israeli Jew" despite its recognition that a more pluralistic approach was required; the difficulty of including "others" in the hegemonic historic narrative was still evident.

In 1976, about a year after the implementation of the core curriculum in history, the Ministry of Education established the Oriental Jewish Heritage Center to offer Sephardic children cultural and historical models with which they could identify and to give Israeli society a window onto the rich Sephardic heritage.[27] In its efforts to foster a concept of cultural pluralism, the center managed to effect some changes, mainly in the literature and citizenship curricula; but the history curriculum remained virtually untouched.

The core curriculum, argued Ben-Amos, did not offer any scope for real pluralism, as it chose to describe Sephardic communities in the folkloristic terminology of the Zionist ethos instead of in the autonomous terms of the communities themselves. The latter might have revealed the spiritual richness and unique culture of those communities. The failure of the efforts to "cleanse" the historical narrative of its divisive preconceptions was reflected in the 1981 controversy over the television series *Pillar of Fire*, which focused on Zionist achievements. Prominent representatives of the Sephardic community petitioned the Supreme Court to forbid the broadcasts, claiming that the series distorted history by ignoring the contribution of the oriental Jewish communities to the Zionist movement.[28]

Oddly enough, on the seemingly more complex subject of the Israeli–Arab conflict the 1975 curriculum did represent change and innovation. The inclusion of the conflict in the compulsory history program was the outcome of a process in which Israeli society, including its educational system, had gradually become more open to examining its life and conflicts in the Middle East from new perspectives. The publication of new academic studies on the Palestine Liberation Organization (PLO) and the Arab world, especially those by Harkavi and Porat, brought these matters into public consciousness. Central to the debate was the extent to which the Arab position should be presented in the words of its spokespersons and whether Israeli youth should be confronted with their "truth"? Some claimed that even if young people were to react with confusion, that such a response was only natural and human, that it would be conducive to openness, and that understanding the enemy would not weaken the Israeli youth. Knowledge of Arab language, culture, and history, moreover, would help bridge the chasm between the two sides. Their opponents, in contrast, argued that a picture of the Arabs' side of the argument might promote feelings of guilt toward Arabs, especially Israeli Arabs, and create among pupils "a constant schizophrenia, self-flagellation, and unnecessary agonizing."[29]

Although these debates were confined to the academic world, they reflected a sense of existential security that constituted a crucial foundation for coping with painful questions and controversial subjects. Moreover, they contributed to the creation of an atmosphere that would eventually permit the integration of the Israeli–Arab conflict into high school history programs in the mid-1970s. Nevertheless, the issue of attitudes toward Arab citizens of Israel remained obscure in the 1975 curriculum, and their narrative was completely ignored.

The 1975 curriculum was also called upon to deal with the subject of the Holocaust, yet the essential changes in the teaching of the Holocaust only were made four years after the curriculum was implemented. The revolution in the way that Israeli public institutions dealt with the Holocaust began with the Eichmann trial in 1961, when Holocaust survivors, called to testify in court, told their stories for the first time. The trial was much more than a legal proceeding and was conducted as a national educational event. For weeks the trial was the center of public attention, and, after it ended, the Holocaust could no longer be dismissed as a private memory. Subsequent events that further cracked the wall of silence and repression around the Holocaust, and increased the public's willingness to listen to the personal memories of survivors, included the widespread existential anxiety in the waiting period preceding the Six Day War, the shattering of the Israeli "superman" image by the Yom Kippur War, and increased Arab terrorist attacks, including the murder of Israeli athletes at the Munich Olympics and the killing of the Ma'alot children in 1974 by Palestinian terrorists.

In 1979, the State Law of Education was amended to add Holocaust remembrance and heroism to the list of educational objectives. Thirty lessons, one-third of a yearly academic unit, were allocated to this purpose, claiming that "the Holocaust must be felt first of all as an experience . . . not from a broader historical context and not in the framework of scientific research."[30] Although the educational system had supposedly placed the Holocaust in the context of systematic history instruction, the Holocaust was still presented primarily as an emotional story isolated from the overall picture of this complex period in twentieth-century history. The didactic dilemma—whether to teach the Holocaust as a memory (the emotional level) or in the context of historical discussion (the cognitive level)—thus remained unresolved.

In the mid-1980s educators began to develop an integrative approach to teaching the Holocaust that dealt with the inherent contradiction between emotion and cognition. The existentialist approach, as Schatzker defined it, emphasized the Jews' struggle to survive in an inhuman situation. Understanding such a struggle requires that one directly identifies with it, which can be achieved by using methods such as film, theater, and oral testimony that address the pupil's emotional experience. The late 1980s saw the beginning of such practices as sending groups of students to visit the death camps in Poland, reenact the death marches, and so on. These informal tools proved to be much more effective than conventional teaching both in guaranteeing the Holocaust a place in the collective memory and in reinforcing the Zionist lesson.

This effectiveness approach proved to be a double-edged sword, however, when many of these tools were mobilized to serve manipulative political purposes.[31] The debates over teaching the Holocaust in the educational system were always overshadowed by the division of Holocaust remembrance into Right and Left, with each side using the catastrophe differently for its own needs. The right wing saw in the Holocaust the tragic essence of the Jewish fate, and slotted it in the familiar mold of a war of "sons of light" against "sons of darkness," a war in which "we" are the victims and "they" are the attackers. The use of the Holocaust narrative as an inexhaustible source of existential anxiety also gave rise to a narrative of "involuntary victors"; whether the enemy was Nazi or Arab, he had to be exterminated.[32] The anxiety of the Left, in contrast, was caused specifically by the experience of ruling over a large Arab population and the fear that Israeli soldiers would come to resemble brutal Nazis. The liberal Left sought to emphasize the rational–universal–democratic dimension in teaching the Holocaust in order to prevent the emergence of racism and fanaticism in Israeli society. Thus the assimilation of the Holocaust in the polarized Israeli experience, no longer as a founding trauma alone but increasingly as a memory subject to conflicting interpretations and manipulative political uses, has made the teaching of it a problematic, unresolved issue even today.

Contemporary Identity:
Mosaic of Subcultures and the Post-Zionist Challenge

The process of identity transformation has intensified in Israeli society from the 1980s to the present. This tendency toward change, seemingly the beginning of a conscious pluralism, accelerated and radicalized the movement toward abandoning collectivist values, and brought Israeli society to a point of real identity crisis. The political map and the public discourse were taken over by virtually impenetrable cultural and ethnic blocs that waged a political and ideological struggle in an atmosphere of mutual antagonism. The growing radicalization and factionalism were fueled in part by the increased strength of three new power centers: the Shas movement representing traditional Jews from an oriental background, the parties of immigrants from the former Soviet Union, and the parties representing Israeli Arabs.

Kimmerling noted six subcultures in Israeli society: (1) a secular civil subculture, based on a "yuppie," mainly Ashkenazi, upper and middle class; (2) a national-religious subculture, the hard core of which is found in the settlements in the Occupied Territories and supported primarily by the traditional religious Ashkenazi middle class; (3) an ultra-Orthodox subculture that is anti-Zionist in origin and has become Judeo-centric, tribal, and nationalistic; (4) a traditional oriental subculture, including the children of immigrants from Asia and Africa; (5) a Russian immigrant subculture that keeps within a cultural bubble of its own; (6) an Arab subculture, very heterogeneous in terms of class, education, and habitation, but homogeneous in its identity as a national minority that is entitled to equal civil rights and has suffered the trauma of expulsion and dispossession. Each of these groups adheres to a different mode of collective identity, which makes the Israeli population a heterogeneous sociocultural mosaic. According to Kimmerling, the existence of these subcultures is not recognized by the state educational system, which still reflects an anomalous situation, namely, an obsolete Zionist hegemony with no relevance for any of the subcultures comprising Israeli society.[33]

The murder of Prime Minister Yitzhak Rabin in 1995 revealed the depth of the rifts in Israeli society and the profound separation between different circles of cultural affinity. The murder also sharpened the dichotomy between the collective-political sphere and the personal-private sphere. At one end of the spectrum it laid bare deep ideological disparities and radicalized positions, and at the other end it called attention to Israelis' anxiety and despair at the magnitude of the rifts, and the almost nihilistic feeling of those living affluent lives segregated from politics and indifferent to the realities around them.[34] The withdrawal of the affluent, who reject involvement in all sociopolitical matters, receives support from academic intellectuals—the representatives of postmodernist relativism—who champion a social leveling process that regards all views as legitimate since nothing is absolutely true or valid.

Israel is, in fact, undergoing a process of fragmentation, with a crumbling social solidarity. The question as to whether that process should be defined as dangerous regression or welcome progress is one of the disputes dividing Israeli society. The participants in the dispute do not generally question the need to recognize multiculturalism but focus on the issue of timing. Can a society that still fights for its legitimacy amid a hostile environment allow free rein to multiculturalism even before it has solved its existential social and political problems?[35] The arguments as to whether multiculturalism is a destructive or constructive value gradually filtered into the educational system. They were also reflected in the discussions of the new curriculum committee that was established in 1991 to review history in the schools.

The new committee also had to deal with the research and academic activities of the new historians and critical sociologists, characterized since the mid-1980s as post-Zionists. It is hard to define "post-Zionism"—a sort of catchall term for multifaceted, even conflicting, criticisms of the Zionist narrative. In the view of the philosopher Dan,

> Post-Zionism means Israeli nationalism based on territorial minimalism, without any specific social or moral aspirations, without any significant religious dimension, without the adoption of a traditional culture, without eschatological foundations, without a deep-rooted Hebrew language that draws upon its origins, and based on the desire to achieve both a fuller normalization of Is-

rael's status among the nations and spiritual integration, from a position of equality with other cultures.[36]

In spite of this vague definition, many intellectuals are labeled as post-Zionist. Some welcome the label, others accept it reluctantly and with qualification, still others ignore it completely, and some reject it. But post-Zionism has undoubtedly extended beyond the university and influenced other cultural realms such as theater, filmmaking, journalism, art, literature, and law.

Given the great academic, intellectual, artistic, and linguistic wealth of the post-Zionist message, the paucity of social movements and political bodies committed to the post-Zionist agenda is conspicuous. The post-Zionist outlook, which seeks to foster a democratic civil consciousness unencumbered by the shackles of nationality and myth, has an extremely marginal impact on establishment politics. In the Knesset, only the Arab parties and perhaps a few members of extreme leftist factions pay any attention at all to post-Zionism. The most prominent extra-parliamentary political bodies that translate post-Zionist claims into a clear political position are a small movement calling on soldiers to refuse to serve in the territories beyond the Green Line (the borders of Israel which were determined in 1949 after the war of independence, and held until 1967, excluding the Occupied Territories of the 1967 war), and members of civic organizations demanding the establishment of two states for two peoples based on the 1967 borders.

To politicians and other representatives of the establishment, post-Zionism is loathsome. They portray it as a movement that advocates dismantling the Zionist ethos, abolishing the Law of Return, and undermining the foundations of the Jewish state in order to replace those icons with a state for all its citizens.

According to Ram, "post-Zionist ideology talks about what comes or might come after Zionism in the historical sense. Post-Zionist ideology is unique in its twofold acknowledgment of, first, the reality that the Zionist movement created in Israel/Palestine, and, second, the wrong that was done to the Palestinians —dispossession and oppression." Ram argues that this acknowledgment does not negate the state of Israel, but rather represents an effort to reform it, in the direction of de-Zionization. "Post-Zionism of this kind involves . . . an ideological and political struggle to change the Israeli collective identity . . . and an aspiration to begin distinguishing between nation and state in Israel—in other words, to create a universal democratic framework in which no particular national tradition or ethnic group is given special status."[37]

The struggle over the desired image of society inevitably focuses on the state of education and teaching in the schools. Indeed, since the post-Zionists' main interest is replacing the national paradigm with a paradigm of civil identity, they attack the state educational system for creating a nationalized education and inventing a national tradition. Ram mentioned the works of the new historians as reflecting the creation of an alternative historical consciousness in Israel, yet he was dubious as to whether it had any resonance in the educational system:

> I doubt whether within the educational system there is really a post-Zionist debate, for reasons connected to the nature of the educational discipline— which always endorses the consensus, following it rather than preceding it. However, I know of all sorts of think tanks focusing on alternative education, democratic education, and so on. All these things that are emerging are signs of the breakdown of national homogeneity, but I doubt they can be seen in the classroom yet.[38]

Similar views have been expressed by other post-Zionists. Morris, for example, contended that the "old historiography" was most clearly reflected in the textbooks for elementary and secondary schools and in Ben-Gurion's writings.[39] Pappe noted that, although new and provocative directions have been evident in the field of history for some time, none of these changes has apparently reached school curriculum developers.[40]

The post-Zionist critique has not, in fact, infiltrated the formal educational system to the same degree that it has other fields. Moreover, it seems that post-Zionists, focusing on their battle against nationalism, on the one hand, and their struggle to advance a universal, democratic society, on the other, avoid the no-man's land in between. The critical debate does not engage directly with the educational system but goes "over its head," at times showing a considerable measure of dismissive contempt. The staff of teachers' colleges, as well as teachers, student teachers, principals, supervisors, school counselors, curriculum writers, pedagogical advisers, and educational ministry employees have remained outside the post-Zionist debate; only lately have a small proportion of them begun to participate in it. Many of those in the educational field are completely unaware of the existence of post-Zionist criticism concerning the various aspects of Israeli identity formation; for many others, the very concept of post-Zionism is a kind of red flag denoting a danger against which defenses must be erected.

The minority of teachers who have responded to post-Zionist criticism did not address its substance but rather expressed anger that such heresies were voiced. For example, Knoller, former vice principal of the prestigious Reali School in Haifa, called the arguments of the post-Zionists "ex cathedra poison," and expressed concern that they would influence hundreds of pupils who would enter school and learn the "distortions of Zionism."[41] Amnon Rubinstein, a former education minister, also reacted angrily and anxiously to the post-Zionist critique, worrying that the heretical views would percolate down from the university and influence elementary- and secondary-school pupils.[42] Livnat, the present minister of education, in mounting a crusade against the influence of post-Zionism in the schools, declared that such arguments might be heard in the academic world but to infiltrate these ideas into the public school system was inconceivable.[43] Although right-wing politicians lead the crusade against post-Zionism, members of the political center and the political Left do not reject this crusade. While officially committed to freedom of expression, many liberal politicians seem reluctant to defend the legitimacy of the post-Zionist voice in a democratic society.

Despite the rejection of post-Zionism as an alternative ideology, post-Zionism is present as a situation—a state of mind among many Israeli youngsters, a sort of existential reality without any ideological components—in the secular public school system. Ironically post-Zionism seems already to have won the battle for the soul of the average pupil, who has been in a "post-Zionist state" with respect to national heritage. Many students demonstrate ignorance, hate history lessons, lack identification with their heritage and tradition, utter poor Hebrew, do not recognize the geography of their country, and avoid any commitment to the society at large. Indeed, the educational system is a subject of pessimism and concern to the public, as well as to office holders and policy makers. They perceive clear signs of crisis.

Supervisors, principals, and teachers, who are trapped in flowery rhetoric, decide the educational agenda. Overwhelmed by impossible demands, overcrowded classes, and low salaries, many of them remain cut off from innovations in all fields of knowledge. They are faced with apathetic, materialistic, and ignorant young people who lack the ability to address the issue of their identity—an alienated generation that has no values or yearnings and rejects teachers' efforts with arrogant contempt, sometimes even violence. Such alienation is ominous and extremely dangerous; it gives rise to a kind of materialistic nihilism or, alternatively, to a chauvinistic right-wing nationalism—two possibilities that characterize the decline of a national ethos in a society and that completely block the horizon of the ethos of civil society that is sought as its replacement.

The New History Curriculum and
the Issue of Multi-Narratives

The new history curriculum had to address these crises of identity transformation, but it is doubtful whether it has really met the challenge. The introduction to the new core curriculum of 1995 acknowledged that "twenty years is long enough for a curriculum to become outdated, even a history curriculum. Within such a span of time the trend of research, professional knowledge, nature of society, and accumulating experience in schools are likely to change the curriculum and the way a subject such as history is taught in school."[44] Yet, from the outset, the new history curriculum committee focused on designing a history curriculum solely for the state secular schools. This decision established an absolute distinction between the two different educational-ideological trends: state secular and state religious.

The introduction to the new curriculum stated that its purpose was to expose the student to new historical research and to develop critical reading skills. It also emphasized the ability to glean information from literature, films, and computerized databases, and to interpret a written text with the help of analytical questions. These additions to the 1995 curriculum reflected the increase in information sources accessible through the media, as well as the opening of the schools to academic research and to critical discourse about Israel's past. The curriculum's goals in the area of values applied mainly to teaching history as a bulwark against closed minds: "To foster a thinking person and to deter dogmatism; to develop mechanisms of defense against brainwashing or manipulative information; to foster an awareness of the need to examine all information critically; and to foster the student's ability to understand the positions of those different from him or her."[45]

The new curriculum sought to overcome the old division between world history and Jewish history:

History is one, and this oneness is expressed, among other ways, in the use of identical basic concepts. Since we are dealing with the history intended for the Jewish population in the State of Israel, it is twined around the central thread of Jewish history; but that history is always studied within its general context.[46]

The inclusion of Jewish history as a component of world history rather than as a separate, self-sufficient subject was a trend that distinguished the 1995 curriculum from those preceding it and indicated how far the teaching of history had come in Israel. At the same time, the new curriculum retained elements of the national-ethnocentric orientation. Teaching the historical narrative of the state of Israel while ignoring the Arab population as part of Israeli society was the most glaring example. In addition, the focus on Western cultural influence reduced considerably the light shed on the history of the Arab states that surround Israel and on the Arab culture that constituted the background of oriental Jews. The new curriculum paid only marginal attention to those groups. Even the history of the Russian world, from which roughly 1 million immigrants arrived in the 1990s, received only minimal treatment.

In contrast to past emphases on ideological and political history, the 1995 curriculum gave more space to social and cultural history, responding to the perceived needs of pupils at the end of the twentieth century and current trends in historical research. A significantly larger number of study topics was devoted to contemporary history, meaning up to the mid-1990s and including the cold war and the policy of détente, the oil crises, the development of the welfare state, postmodernism, the computer revolution, mass communication, international companies, a missile defense system, globalization, and the rise of fundamentalism. The curriculum included cross-disciplinary sections that deviated from the chronological framework in order to present subjects of special interest. These subjects, as stated in the introduction to the curriculum, served the view of the longue durée in history and offered a framework for dealing with, for example, intercultural encounters, technological and demographic developments, science and daily life, and ceremonies and rituals.

Although this curriculum was adopted by the school system only a few years ago and its impact is still difficult to assess, it is impossible to ignore the dispute growing around it and the protests that have dogged it since the beginning. The curriculum and the textbooks that it inspired exposed the existential tension between liberal democracy and nationalism, between the legitimacy of different perspectives and the tradition of national history education as a means of constructing collective identity and solidarity. Academic and public discourse in Israel has been open for some time to new historical narratives and a critical view of the traditional national realms of memory. Yet the effort to give school history classes opportunities to grapple with complex questions that have equivocal answers has aroused a fierce controversy that may tilt the balance back in the direction of reconstructing a univocal historical narrative.

Toward the end of Israel's sixth decade as a state, it faces the complex challenges of a society with many voices that has not yet managed to reconcile its cultural and ethnic diversity. Nor has it developed a defense against the emergence of marginal groups that spread fanaticism, incitement, and violence. The shattering tensions and divisions in Israeli society are demonstrated daily by arguments over the Jewish–Arab conflict, minorities waking up to demand a redefinition of their status and their share of the political pie, and the alienation and separatism of social groups that emphasize their uniqueness in terms of religion, ethnicity, culture, and interests. Every attempt to achieve a dialogue between the two extremes threatens the divisive movements that feed on open social wounds. Such attempts also run into an opposition that retroactively wins academic support based on the relativistic ideology of political correctness and the new spirit of enlightenment. Thus, in place of demands to remedy wrongs in the name of justice and social equality, public discourse in Israel in recent years has been about discrimination, attribution of blame, and self-segregation. This trend, which fosters what Hughes defined in another social context as "a culture of complaint," once again keeps Israeli society from coming to grips, as it must, with the complex and highly charged issues of a divided society.[47]

In every democratic educational system, struggles take place over the design of a society's cultural image, objectives, and identity. Such battles are often channeled into history education, which is perceived as one of the central disciplines in the curriculum because of its potential influence in shaping future citizens. Yet, as this chapter has attempted to show, dealing with the jumble of ideas and opinions associated with the discipline of history penetrates to the heart of Israeli identity since such ideas both derive from it and seek to define it. In a strife-ridden society, however, controversies that weaken the basis of values for a democratic pluralistic life make pluralism and difference appear as chaotic forces threatening every effort to identify the foundations of a shared story that can express all of the different narratives. At the same time it is possible, perhaps imperative, to see in the varied cultural fabric of Israeli society a great source of blessings, as Oz claims:

> People whose social ideal is one way and people whose social ideal is the opposite from it can all potentially fertilize each other. That is how a culture's soil is—it is apt to bloom just where there is a meeting of opposites, of tensions, of differences. . . . But someone who tries to fulfill his dreams should know that the price of fulfillment is compromise . . . compromise with reality, with constraints, compromise with others at home and abroad.[48]

Compromise here means the building of a bridge between different experiences of participation and the recognition that Israel's historic narrative can no longer be taught as one story and one memory but only as a mosaic of intercommunicating stories and memories. However, preliminary efforts to promote this compromise, as expressed in the new textbooks introduced at the end of the 1990s, aroused great anger in various circles along the length of Israel's political and social spectrum.

NOTES

1. *Ha'aretz* (December 31, 2003); *Ma'ariv* (September 24, 2000).

2. Dani Ya'akobi (ed.), *A World of Changes* (Jerusalem, 1999), in Hebrew.

3. "Report of the Committee to Examine the History Textbook *A World of Changes*" (March 4, 2001), 2–35, in Hebrew.

4. Yoram Hazony, Daniel Polisar, and Michael Oren, "The Quiet Revolution in Teaching Zionist History: A Comparative Study of Education Ministry Textbooks on the Subject of the Twentieth Century (Ninth Grade)" (Jerusalem, 2000), in Hebrew.

5. Eyal Naveh, *The Twentieth Century: On the Threshold of Tomorrow* (Tel Aviv, 1999), in Hebrew; Ktziah Tabibian (ed.), *A Journey to the Past: In the Right of Liberty* (Tel Aviv, 1999), in Hebrew.

6. "Oppose, Don't Buy, Study, or Teach It," *Ha'aretz* (September 10, 1999), A-6, in Hebrew.

7. Minute #25, Meeting of Knesset Education Committee, November 9, 1999.

8. For a detailed analysis of this dilemma of modern history education, see Peter Seixas, "Schweigen! Die Kinder! Or, Does Postmodern History Have a Place in the Schools?" in Peter N. Stearns, Peter Seixas, and Sam Wineburg, *Knowing Teaching and Learning History* (New York, 2000), 19–37.

9. Amos Oz, *Under This Blazing Light: Essays* (Tel Aviv, 1979), 127, in Hebrew. An abridged, English-language edition of this book is available as Amos Oz (trans. Nicolas de Lange), *Under This Blazing Light: Essays* (Cambridge, 1995).

10. See Dina Porat, "Forging Zionist Identity prior to 1948—Against Which Counter-Identity?" chapter 3 in this volume.

11. Dan Bar-On, *The "Others" within Us: Changes in the Israeli Identity from a Psychosocial Perspective* (Beersheva, 1999), 1–14, in Hebrew.

12. See Mordechai Bar-On, "Conflicting Narratives or Narratives of a Conflict: Can the Zionist and Palestinian Narratives of the 1948 War Be Bridged?" chapter 6 in this volume.

13. Anita Shapira, "Ben Gurion and the Bible: The Forging of an Historical Narrative?" *Middle Eastern Studies*, XXXIII (1997), 654, 662, 668.

14. *Curriculum for State and State-Religious Elementary Schools, History* (Jerusalem, 1954), in Hebrew.

15. *Supplement to the Secondary School Curriculum* (Jerusalem, 1955/1956), in Hebrew.

16. Arik Carmon, "Education in Israel: Issues and Problems" in Walter Ackerman, Arik Carmon, and David Zucker (eds.), *Education in an Evolving Society: Schooling in Israel* (Tel Aviv, 1985), 154–157, in Hebrew; Ruth Firer, "The Image of Edot Hamizrach: Jewish-History Textbooks, 1948–1967," *Iyunim Behinuch* (Studies in Education), XLV (1986), 23–33, in Hebrew; Ruth Firer, *Agents of Zionist Education* (Tel Aviv, 1985), 186, in Hebrew.

17. Avner Ben-Amos and Ilana Bet-El, "Holocaust Day and Memorial Day in Israeli Schools: Ceremonies, Education and History" in Rivka Feldhay and Immanuel Etkes (eds.), *Education and History: Political and Cultural Contexts* (Jerusalem, 1999), 457–479, in Hebrew.

18. Maoz Azaryahu, *State Cults: Celebrating Independence and Commemorating the Fallen in Israel, 1948–1956* (Sde Boker, 1995), 62–64, 116–118, in Hebrew.

19. Firer, *Agents of Zionist Education*, 32; Anita Shapira, *New Jews, Old Jews* (Tel Aviv, 1997), 94, in Hebrew.

20. Bar-On, *The "Others" within Us*, 12–14.

21. Shapira, *New Jews, Old Jews*, 99. See also Porat, "Forging Zionist Identity."

22. Aron Appelfeld, *First-Person Essays* (Jerusalem, 1979), 35–40, in Hebrew.

23. Zvi Lamm, "Educational Pressure and Opposition to Education" and "Dialogue: Certificates of Social Inequality," in Lamm, *Pressure and Opposition in Education* (Tel Aviv, 2000), 9–22, 212–213, in Hebrew.

24. Aharon Yadlin, "The Turning Point in Curriculum Development" in Shevach Eden (ed.), *On the New Curricula* (Tel Aviv, 1971), 13–16.

25. Carmon, "Education in Israel," 150–151.

26. Ibid.

27. Not until the 1980s did all of the director-general's circulars begin to contain training programs involving the Center for the Integration of Oriental Jewish Heritage. For further discussion on this subject, see Avner Ben Amos, "Pluralism Impossible? Ashkenazi and Sephardic Jews in Israel's History Curriculum," in David Chen (ed.), *Education Toward the 21st Century* (Tel Aviv, 1995), 267–276, in Hebrew. See also Orit Ichilov, *Citizenship Education in an Emerging Society* (Tel Aviv, 1993), 88–90, 92–94, in Hebrew.

28. Ben-Amos, "Pluralism Impossible?" 274.

29. Elie Podeh, *The Portrayal of the Arab-Israeli Conflict in Israeli History and Civics*

Textbooks, 1953–1995 (Jerusalem, 1997), 22, in Hebrew. The quotation is from *The Israeli-Arab Conflict and Its Significance in Education,* Booklet 6 (Tel Aviv, 1969), 95, in Hebrew.

30. Nili Keren, "Preserving Memory within Oblivion: The Struggle over Teaching the Holocaust in Israel," *Zmanim,* LXIV (1998), 59, in Hebrew.

31. Chaim Schatzker, "Problems in Teaching the Holocaust Today," in Feldhay and Etkes, *Education and History,* 442–447.

32. Nurith Gertz, *Myths in Israeli Culture: Captives of a Dream* (London, 2000), 67–83.

33. Baruch Kimmerling, "Culture War," *Ha'aretz* (June 7, 1996), in Hebrew.

34. Gadi Taub, *A Dispirited Rebellion: Essays on Contemporary Israeli Culture* (Tel Aviv, 1997), 13–21, in Hebrew.

35. Bar-On, *The "Others" within Us,* 47.

36. Yosef Dan, "On Post-Zionism and on False Messianism," *Ha'aretz* (March 25, 1994), in Hebrew

37. Uri Ram, "Post-Zionist Ideology," *Ha'aretz* (April 8, 1994), in Hebrew.

38. Ibid.

39. Benny Morris, *1948 and After* (Oxford, 1990), 5.

40. Ilan Pappe, "The Influence of Zionist Ideology on Israeli Historiography," *Davar* (May 15, 1994), in Hebrew.

41. Gabriel Knoller, "Ex-Cathedra Poison," Letters to the Editor, *Mosaf Ha'aretz* (June 17, 1994), in Hebrew.

42. Amnon Rubinstein, *From Herzl to Rabin and Beyond: 100 Years of Zionism* (Jerusalem, 1997), in Hebrew.

43. *Yediot Aharonot* (May 14, 2001).

44. Ministry of Education and Culture, *History Curriculum for State Schools, Grades 6–9* (Jerusalem, 1992), 2.

45. Ibid., 11.

46. Ibid., 3.

47. Robert Hughes, *Culture of Complaint* (New York, 1994).

48. Amos Oz, *All the Hopes: Thoughts on Israeli Identity* (Jerusalem, 1998), 15, in Hebrew.

CONTRIBUTORS

Sami Adwan is co-Director of the Peace Research Institute in the Middle East (PRIME) and Professor of Education at Bethlehem University, Palestine. He is author of *The Status of Religious Education in Palestinian Schools* (2001) and co-author (with Ruth Firer) of *The Israeli–Palestinian Conflict in History and Civics Textbooks of Both Nations* (2004); *The Palestinian and Israeli Environmental NGOs in Peace Building* (with Dan Bar-On) (2004); *Victimhood and Beyond* (2001); and *The Role of Palestinian and Israeli NGOs in Peace Building* (2000).

Dan Bar-On is Chair and Professor of Psychology in the Department of Behavioral Sciences, Ben-Gurion University, and co-director (with Sami Adwan) of PRIME. He is author of *Legacy of Silence: Encounters with Children of the Third Reich* (1989); *The Indescribable and the Undiscussable* (1999); and *Fear and Hope: Three Generations of Holocaust Survivors' Families* (1998).

Mordechai Bar-On is a historian and research fellow at the Yad Ben-Zvi Institute in Jerusalem. He served for twenty-two years in the Israel Defense Forces (IDF) as a career soldier, and as Chief Education Officer, retiring with the rank of colonel. He is author of *The Beginning of the Israeli Historiography of the 1948 War* (2001); *Smoldering Borders: Studies in the History of the State of Israel, 1948–1967* (2001); *In Pursuit of Peace: A History of Israel's Peace Movements* (1996); *The Gates of Gaza: Israel's Defence and Foreign Policy, 1955–1957* (1994); *Etgar ve Tigra: Israel's Road to Suez* (1991); and *Peace Now: A Profile of a Protest Movement* (1985).

Daniel Bar-Tal is Professor of Psychology at the School of Education and Director of the Walter Lebach Institute for Jewish–Arab Coexistence through

Education, Tel Aviv University. He is co-editor of the *Palestine-Israel Journal* and author of *Stereotypes and Prejudice in Conflict: Arab Representation in the Israeli Jewish Society* (with Yona Teichman) (2004); *Shared Beliefs in a Society* (2000); and *Group Beliefs* (1990).

Nathan J. Brown is Professor of Political Science and International Affairs at George Washington University. He is author of *Palestinian Politics since the Oslo Accords* (2003); *Constitutions in a Nonconstitutional World* (2001); *The Rule of Law in the Arab World* (1997); and *Peasant Politics in Modern Egypt* (1990).

Saleh Abdel Jawad is Associate Professor of History and Political Science at Birzeit University. He is author of *The Israeli Assassination Policy in the Al-Aqsa Intifada* (2001); *Toward a Palestinian Strategy on Jerusalem* (1998); and *The Israeli-Palestinian Declaration of Principles: Present and Future Perspectives* (1994).

Eyal Naveh is Professor of History and Chair of the General and Interdisciplinary Studies Program at Tel Aviv University and Professor of History at the Kibbutzim College of Education. He is author of *Crown of Thorns: Political Martyrdom in America, Reinhold Niebuhr and Non-Utopian Liberalism* (2002); and *Histories: Toward a Dialogue with the Israeli Past* (2002); and four history textbooks written for the Israeli educational system.

Ilan Pappe is Senior Lecturer in the Department of Political Science at Haifa University and the head of the Emil Touma Institute for Palestinian Studies. His books include *A History of Modern Palestine: One Land, Two Peoples* (2003); *The Making of the Arab-Israeli Conflict, 1947–1951* (1992); *Britain and the Arab-Israeli Conflict* (1988); and *The Israel/Palestine Question* (edited) (1999).

Dina Porat is head of the Chaim Rosenberg School for Jewish Studies, Alfred P. Slaner Chair for the Study of Racism and Anti-Semitism, Department of Jewish History, Tel Aviv University, and Director of the Stephen Roth Institute for the Study of Contemporary Anti-Semitism and Racism. Her publications include *Beyond the Corporeal; The Life and Times of Abba Kovner; Am Oved and Yad-Vashem* (2000), which received the Zandman Award and the Buchman Award; and *The Blue and the Yellow Stars of David, The Zionist Leadership* *in Palestine and the Holocaust, 1939–1945* (1990), which won the Yad Ben-Zvi Award and the Kubowitzki Award.

Robert I. Rotberg is Director of the Belfer Center's Program on Intrastate Conflict and Conflict Resolution at Harvard University's Kennedy School of Government. He is also President of the World Peace Foundation. His many authored and edited books include *Battling Terrorism in the Horn of Africa* (2005); *Crafting the New Nigeria: Confronting the Challenges* (2004); *When States Fail: Causes and Consequences* (2004); *State Failure and State Weakness in a Time of Terror* (2003); and *Ending Autocracy, Enabling Democracy: The Tribulations of Southern Africa, 1960–2000* (2002).

Nadim N. Rouhana is Professor in the Institute for Conflict Management and Resolution, George Mason University. He is the author of numerous articles and *Palestinian Citizens in an Ethnic Jewish State: Identities in Conflict* (1997).

Gavriel Salomon is Director of the Center for Research and Peace Education at the University of Haifa, where he is Professor of Educational Psychology. He is the author of *Technology and Education in the Information Age* (2001); *Communication* (1981); *Communication and Education* (1981); and *Interaction of Media, Cognition and Learning* (1979); and is the editor of *Peace Education* (2002) and *Distributed Cognitions* (1993).

Mark Tessler is Samuel J. Eldersveld Collegiate Professor of Political Science and Vice-Provost for International Affairs at the University of Michigan. He is author or co-author of *Islam, Democracy and the State in Algeria: Lessons for the Western Mediterranean and Beyond* (2004); *Area Studies and Social Science: Strategies for Understanding Middle East Politics* (1999); *Democracy and Its Limits: Lessons from Latin America, the Middle East and Asia* (1999); *Democracy, War and Peace in the Middle East* (1995); and *A History of the Israeli-Palestinian Conflict* (1994).

INDEX